A to Z

of international trade

by Frank Reynolds

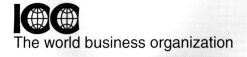

ICC
The world business organization

Published in March 2002 by

ICC PUBLISHING S.A.
International Chamber of Commerce
The world business organization
38 Cours Albert 1er
75008 Paris, France

Reprinted in September 2002

ICC publication 623
ISBN 92 842 1277 4

Preface

The more business goes global, the more businessmen and traders need to understand the language of international trade. This means, first, knowing what the definitions of the key trade terms mean, and second, knowing how they work in practice.

A to Z of International Trade succeeds on both counts. Not only does it provide lively definitions of carefully selected terms and phrases used in international trade, it places these in context by linking them to well-researched and focused summaries of the disciplines they represent.

There is a special quality of vision involved in creating such a useful book. Its author, Frank Reynolds, a respected business journalist and trade consultant, is to be commended for the broad knowledge he brings to the subject matter and for the lucidity with which he explores it. There are other trade dictionaries on the market, but none, I venture, offers the multi-dimensional approach of *A to Z of International Trade*. This is a dictionary with a difference.

ICC was created in 1919 largely to facilitate the flow of international trade. Publications like *A to Z of International Trade* fall within that tradition and speak directly to those who require a deeper understanding of how trade works and how to derive the maximum benefits from it.

Maria Livanos Cattaui

Secretary General
International Chamber of Commerce
Paris, France
February 2002

Table of contents

Acknowledgements

The author would like to thank the following for their invaluable editing assistance:

Robert Abrahams
Roy Becker
Catherine Callahan
William Maron
James McCarthy Jr.
Robert Phaneuf
David Walker

The following ICC titles have been quoted from:

Incoterms 2000™®*
ICC publication No. 560 – ISBN 92.842.1199.9 Published in its official English and French versions by the International Chamber of Commerce, Paris.Copyright © 1999 – International Chamber of Commerce (ICC)
*Incoterms is a trademark of ICC, registered in the European Union and elsewhere.

ICC Guide to Export-Import Basics
ICC publication No. 543 – ISBN 92.842.1194.8
Published by the International Chamber of Commerce, Paris.
Copyright © 1997 – International Chamber of Commerce (ICC)

A User's Handbook to the ICC Uniform Rules for Demand Guarantees
ICC publication No. 631 – ISBN 92.842.1294.4
Published by the International Chamber of Commerce, Paris.
Copyright © 2001 – International Chamber of Commerce (ICC)

Each is available from **www.iccbooks.com** or

ICC Publishing, 38 cours Albert 1er, 75008 Paris, France,
fax: +33 1 49 53 29 02.

ICC Publishing, Inc., 156 Fifth Avenue, Suite 417, NY 10010, USA
Fax: +1 212 633 6025

Introduction

International trade involves vocabularies and procedures that differ from domestic commerce in many respects. The reason is obvious. By definition, the parties are in different countries, and this brings obstacles not normally found in domestic business. Law, commercial practice, language, currency and culture differ among nations. Distances in both place and time are often greater, and information can be more difficult to obtain. Goods are frequently handed off from one carrier to another, increasing transportation risk.

Over millennia, traders have devised ingenious ways of overcoming these obstacles. More recently, the internet revolution has taken the breakthroughs made over time in the procedures and documentation to an amazingly high level.

Despite faster and better ways of doing nearly everything, the vocabularies and procedures unique to international trade are still very much alive. They present barriers for novices and even for experienced practitioners outside their own disciplines.

This book was designed to help overcome these barriers, starting with a good user-friendly dictionary. It is not the world's largest, as it was designed to include only those terms and organizations that people involved in trade are likely to encounter. Taking this a step further, we have provided translations of the most commonly used terms in French, German, Italian and Spanish.

Eight appendices cover the trade-specific disciplines, and we have added another for e-commerce which is becoming the most important of all. Each is co-authored by an industry expert, and contains information useful for anyone outside the discipline it covers. An experienced foreign trade banker would learn little new in the two banking appendices, but quite a lot from those covering shipping, sales contracts, Incoterms and insurance.

Sellers and buyers will also benefit, since all service providers ultimately work for them. We provide these principals with a bird'seye view of all trade-related disciplines, so they can choose the best service providers for their needs.

Seven industry experts both assisted me with content and helped edit this book. If we have done our job, our readers will find the jargon of international trade less esoteric and its procedures more transparent.

Frank Reynolds

An explanation for the user

This dictionary is designed to be clear and easy to use, but a couple of pointers will make for plain sailing from the start.

■ Symbols at the beginning of certain definitions show that a fuller explanation can be found in one of the *Focus on* sections at the end of the book. Simply use the thumb tag to get there. Here is a summary of the symbols:

✈	**Focus on Air transport**
🏛	**Focus on Bank collections**
@	**Focus on e-commerce**
⊞	**Focus on Incoterms**
🦮	**Focus on Insurance**
LC	**Focus on Letters of credit**
⚓	**Focus on Liner vessel shipping**
✍	**Focus on Sales contracts**
⊟	**Focus on Vessel chartering**

The above list is repeated at the bottom of each page of the Key definitions AZ section.

■ Another useful reference tag is the ‹brackets› placed around any word used within the text of a definition that can be found fully defined in its own right. Simply look it up alphabetically in Key definitions with the help of the alphabetical thumb tags.

■ The Key words in five languages have ✅ on the thumb tag.

■ Notes and website addresses stand out in shaded boxes and the use of a second colour makes for clearer reading throughout.

Truly a dictionary with a difference.

A to Z
of international trade

Key definitions AZ

Air transport ✈

Bank collections 🏛

e-commerce @

Incoterms 🏁

Insurance ⛱

Letters of credit LC

Liner vessel shipping ⚓

Sales contracts ✍

Vessel chartering ⛴

A

A/S ⟨limited liability⟩

AAA ⟨American Arbitration Association⟩

AAR Against all risks. See ⟨all risks⟩

AB ⟨limited liability⟩

abandonment The refusal of merchandise by the designated consignee.

ABEDA ⟨Arab Bank for Economic Development in Africa⟩

about [LC] A L/C term meaning plus or minus 10% of whatever immediately follows. The terms approximately and circa are synonymous.

absolute quota ⟨import quota⟩

acceptance [m] The act of formally acknowledging a debt by signing a financial instrument called a ⟨draft⟩. When done by a non-bank party, a trade acceptance is created. When done by a bank, a banker's acceptance is created. See ⟨banker's acceptance⟩.

acceptance date [m] The date on which a ⟨draft⟩ was signed. For drafts drawn at "X days from sight," the acceptance date begins the time period toward maturity.

accepting bank [LC] A financial institution that executes a banker's acceptance.

accession The process of a country's adhering to a legal instrument, such as a bilateral or multilateral treaty.

accessorial charge ⟨surcharge⟩

accomplished bill of lading A ⟨bill of lading⟩ that has been surrendered to the ⟨carrier⟩ in return for the shipped goods.

account party ⟨applicant⟩

ACCT ⟨Agence de Coopération Culturelle et Technique⟩

ACH ⟨automated clearing house⟩

acknowledgment ① Confirmation of receipt of a ⟨purchase order⟩, usually indicating the approximate shipping date. ② Confirmation sent by a bank confirming receipt of a ⟨collection⟩.

ACP ⟨African, Caribbean and Pacific Countries⟩

Acrobat Reader A program created by Adobe which allows users to display and read Portable Data Format (PDF) files (⟨Portable Data Format⟩). May be downloaded for free at www.adobe.com.

⟨see entry in dictionary⟩   ✈ Air transport   🏛 Bank collections   @ e-commerce   🏁 Incoterms

across the board tariff reduction ⟨linear tariff reduction⟩

act of God The operation of uncontrollable natural forces.

actual carrier ⟨undercarrier⟩

actual total loss A marine insurance term for situations where nothing salvageable remains of the insured goods.

Acuerdo de Cartagena ⟨Andean Group⟩

AD ⟨antidumping⟩

ad valorem According to value. Import duty or tax expressed as a percentage of value. For example, the import duty for a product classified under ⟨Harmonized System⟩ 381120 is 2.5 per cent of the dutiable value.

ad valorem equivalent The amount collected under a ⟨specific duty⟩ or ⟨compound duty⟩, expressed as a percentage of the value of the imported item.

ADB See either ⟨African Development Bank⟩ or ⟨Asian Development Bank⟩.

admission temporaire ⟨carnet⟩

ADR ⟨alternative dispute resolution⟩

advance freight Freight charges paid in advance and non-refundable, even if the cargo is not delivered, provided that failure to deliver resulted from causes beyond the ⟨carrier⟩'s control.

advance payment guarantee (= advance payment bond) A guarantee that advance payments will be returned if the party having received such payment does not perform its part of the contract.

   ⟨Standby letters of credit⟩ **are often used for this purpose.**

adventure 🗗 A marine insurance term for voyage.

advice of payment/non-payment or **acceptance/non-acceptance** 🏛 Reports sent by ⟨presenting banks⟩ to inform ⟨drawer⟩s or their banks about the status of pending ⟨collections⟩.

advised L/C ⟨unconfirmed L/C⟩

advising bank 🆊 A bank that passes a ⟨letter of credit⟩ on to the ⟨beneficiary⟩ or another designated third party without adding its confirmation.

advisory capacity A term indicating that an agent or representative is not empowered to make definitive decisions or adjustments

---

🗗 Insurance   🆊 Letters of credit   🗘 Liner vessel shipping   🖾 Sales contracts   🗗 Vessel chartering

A

without approval of the 〈principal〉 represented. This is the opposite of 〈without reserve〉.

AEF 〈Africa Enterprise Fund〉

aerotropolis A cluster of logistics-related facilities located around an air-cargo hub, used by shippers for just-in-time response.

affidavit A statement sworn under oath before an authorized official.

affreightment ① A contract between a shipper and a 〈carrier〉, setting forth their respective transportation obligations. ② A synonym for 〈charter〉.

AFREXIMBANK 〈African Export Import Bank〉

Africa Enterprise Fund (AEF) The AEF, operating under the 〈International Finance Corporation〉, assists small- and medium-sized enterprises in sub-Saharan Africa.

> For more information, visit the AEF website at
> www.ifc.org/abn/aef/aefhtm.

African, Caribbean and Pacific Countries (ACP) Developing countries that are designated beneficiaries under the 〈Lome Convention〉.

African Development Bank (ADB) Provides financing through direct loans to Africa member states to cover the foreign exchange costs of Bank-approved development projects in those countries. Over 50 African countries are members and ordinarily receive loans.

> For more information, visit the ADB website at www.afdb.org

African Export Import Bank (AFREXIMBANK) Founded in 1993 and headquartered in Cairo, Egypt, AFREXIMBANK offers short-term export trade financing to African exporters to enhance intra-African trade and African exports.

> For more information, visit the AFREXIMBANK website at
> www.afreximbank.com.

African Management Services Company (AMSCO) Established in 1989 by the International Finance Corporation, AMSCO provides temporary managers and management training to support the development of African companies.

> For more information, visit the International Finance Corporation
> website at www.ifc.org.

African Project Development Facility (APDF) The APDF was established in 1986 as a UN Development Programme project with the International Finance Corporation as executing agency and the African Development Bank as regional sponsor. It seeks to

---

accelerate development of productive enterprises sponsored by private African entrepreneurs as a means of generating self-sustained economic growth and productive employment in Sub-Saharan Africa.

African Regional Organization for Standardization (ARSO) Established in 1977 and headquartered in Nairobi, Kenya, ARSO promotes and coordinates standardization, quality control, certification and metrology practices in Africa through African Regional Standards (ARS).

> For more information, visit the ARSO website at www.arso-oran.org.

after sight ⟨at X days date⟩ or ⟨at X days sight⟩

after-sale Service A collective term for attention to a transaction that normally takes place after the sale (and often after delivery) is accomplished. Typical after-sale service functions include installation, training, warranty-related repair and replacement part support.

> After-sale service is an extremely important consideration because of the normally greater distances between sellers and buyers in international trade.

AG ⟨Australia Group⟩

AG (Aktiengesellschaft) ⟨limited liability⟩

against all risks ⟨all risks⟩

AGB ⟨Alliance for Global Business⟩

Agence de Coopération Culturelle et Technique (ACCT) Created in 1970 and headquartered in Paris, France, ACCT promotes cultural and technical cooperation among French-speaking countries.

Agence Française de Développement (AFD) Headquartered in Paris, France, the AFD is the lead agency in the French Ministry of Cooperation and Development in providing funds for aid and cooperation.

> For more information, visit the AFD website at www.afd.fr.

Agency for International Development (USAID) Founded in 1961, AID administers US Government foreign economic assistance.

> For more information, visit the USAID website at www.usaid.gov.

agent An independent person or legal entity, which acts on behalf of another (the "⟨principal⟩"). In international transactions, this term normally refers to a sales representative who prospects on behalf of a foreign principal, earning a commission on sales eventually

---

A

concluded between the principal and the ultimate client. This is distinguished from sales through employees and subsidiaries – that are not independent – or through distributorship relations, which involve the distributor's buying and reselling in his or her own name. Sales agents should also be distinguished from buying or purchasing agents, as their respective rights and obligations are quite different.

1. As the term "agent" connotes a certain level of implied authority, many principals designate such trading partners as "representatives" to avoid this implication.

2. When appointing agents, prudent principals clearly specify within the agency agreement the level of authority they wish to delegate. See 〈advisory capacity〉 and 〈without reserve〉.

3. Prudent principals acquaint themselves with the law of their trading partner's country before executing agency, representation or distributorship agreements. In some jurisdictions, terminating a relationship with even a non-performing trading partner can be difficult and expensive.

Agreement on the Importation of Educational, Scientific and Cultural Materials 〈Florence Agreement〉

Agricultural Goods, WTO Agreement A World Trade Organization agreement establishing rules and commitments to ensure a fair market-oriented system for trade in agricultural goods and products.

AIB Depending on the content, see either 〈Arab International Bank〉 or 〈Association for International Business〉

AID 〈Agency for International Development〉

air freight consolidator ✈ A company that obtains a low freight-of-all-kinds freight rate from an air carrier in return for volume, and consolidates small shipments, often to fill air freight containers. Such enterprises often perform forwarding tasks and issue their own "house" 〈air waybills〉 to each shipper, backed up by "master" air waybills issued by the 〈undercarrier〉 for the consolidated shipment. See also 〈consolidation〉.

air freight forwarder ✈ In many respects, air freight forwarders perform the same functions as 〈air freight consolidator〉s, except that smaller forwarders may co-load with others rather than actually perform their own consolidations.

air waybill (AWB) ✈ Transport document issued by a 〈carrier〉 for air transportation. If issued by the actual carrier, it is a master air waybill. If issued by an air freight 〈consolidator〉 or 〈forwarder〉, it is a house air waybill. Air waybills are never negotiable.

aircraft agreement The GATT Agreement on Trade in Civil Aircraft

---

came into force in 1980. It eliminated tariffs on civil aircraft, engines, most components and ground flight simulators. It also addressed government procurement, supports and standards on these items. Twenty-two countries have subscribed to this plurilateral agreement.

> The ⟨WTO⟩ General Agreement on Trade Services implemented rules and obligations to liberalize trade in services, including air transport services. See ⟨General Agreement on Trade Services⟩.

airport-to-airport ⊠ The main carriage transportation movement from the departure airport on the seller's side to the arrival airport on the buyer's side.

Aktiebolag ⟨limited liability⟩

Aktiengessellschaft (AG) ⟨limited liability⟩

ALIDE ⟨Latin American Association of Development Financing Institutions⟩

all risks (AR) ⟲ The broadest type of standard marine insurance coverage generally available in the US market. ⟨London Institute of Underwriters "A" Clauses⟩ offer virtually the same coverage to other markets.

> 1. The name is misleading, as "all risks" does not include coverage for the perils of ⟨war risk⟩, ⟨strike, riot and civil commotion⟩. These additional coverages are available for most markets, usually at modest additional premiums.
> 2. Since there is no worldwide standard nomenclature for all risk coverage, traders should determine exactly what is/is not covered, and arrange for any additional coverage they deem necessary.

Alliance for Global Business (AGB) A coordinating mechanism of leading international trade associations created to provide business leadership on information society issues and electronic commerce. Its Global Action Plan for Electronic Commerce calls for minimal government regulation and emphasizes business self-regulation as the most effective way of building confidence in transactions over open networks.

> For more information, visit the AGB website at www.intug.net/agb/

alongside This vessel shipping term means that cargo is to be placed on the ⟨wharf⟩ or on a lighter within reach of the vessel's crane so that it can be loaded aboard. See ⟨Free Alongside Ship⟩.

> The concept of alongside does not compute well with liner shipping at modern ports, where outgoing cargo is delivered to a port gateway or ship line terminal that could be located some distance from the wharf.

alternative dispute resolution (ADR) A general term for a variety of

---

⟲ Insurance   LC Letters of credit   ⬇ Liner vessel shipping   ⬧ Sales contracts   ⊡ Vessel chartering

A

dispute resolution mechanisms that may be used as alternatives to traditional litigation before governmental courts or tribunals. This term includes such techniques as conciliation, mediation, re-negotiation and mini-trial. Some experts also consider arbitration as an alternative dispute resolution mechanism.

amendment 🄻🄲 An advice by the issuing bank of any proposed change to L/C terms and conditions.

American Arbitration Association (AAA) Perhaps the world's largest arbitration forum; the great bulk of cases handled under its rules and procedures are domestic US cases, although it does have specific rules for international cases.

American Foreign Trade Definitions (= Revised American Foreign Trade Definitions). A set of sales terms published in 1941 that have become obsolete in favour of the current version of ⟨ICC⟩ ⟨Incoterms⟩.

> As some abbreviations appear with different meanings in both the American Foreign Trade Definitions and Incoterms with confusing results, buyers and sellers should use the current Incoterms version and clearly indicate this.

American terms ① 🛫 An insurance term used to distinguish conditions of American policies from those of other countries. ② An exchange rate showing the number of currency units per US dollar.

AMF ⟨Arab Monetary Fund⟩

AMSCO ⟨African Management Services Company⟩

AN ⟨arrival notice⟩

analysis certificate ⟨certificate of analysis⟩

Andean Group (= Grupo Andino = Andean Pact = Acuerdo de Cartagena). An association of five Latin American countries that promotes regional economic integration and political cooperation. Members include Bolivia, Colombia, Ecuador, Peru and Venezuela.

> For more information, visit the Andean Group website at www.comunidadandina.org.

anti-boycott regulations Some countries (such as the United States) prohibit their nationals from participating in or assisting with secondary boycotts targeted against friendly countries or particular ethnic or religious groups.

antidumping Laws enacted to remedy ⟨dumping⟩, which is defined as the sale of goods to a foreign market at less than fair value.

⟨see entry in dictionary⟩ 🛫 Air transport 🏛 Bank collections @ e-commerce ▦ Incoterms

A

> **Antidumping duty is an additional tax to normal import duty that is assessed on an imported good to raise its cost price to fair value.**

Antidumping, WTO Agreement A ⟨World Trade Organization⟩ agreement that gives member countries the right to defend themselves against dumped imports while preserving proportionality and avoiding abuse.

antitrust A collective term for government regulations designed to prevent one or a limited number of parties acting in collusion to restrain trade in a manner detrimental to the public interest.

antonim airket (AP) ⟨limited liability⟩

AP (antonim pirket) ⟨limited liability⟩

APDF ⟨African Project Development Facility⟩

APEC ⟨Asia-Pacific Economic Cooperation⟩

apparent damage 🗊 🗊 🗊 This is the opposite of ⟨apparent good order and condition⟩.

apparent good order and condition 🗊 🗊 🗊 A stated or implied agreement from a ⟨carrier⟩, a carrier's agent, or other ⟨bailee⟩ that the referenced goods were free of obvious damage or shortage at the time they were handed over for transportation. The resulting transport document or warehouse receipt will be "clean," that is, not bearing a "foul" notation.

> **This statement is seldom expressed, as it applies by implication. All transport documents without expressed foul notations are considered to be clean.**

applicant 🄻🄲 The party applying for the issuance of a ⟨letter of credit⟩ (also called the account party).

application (for a letter of credit) 🄻🄲 Instructions from the ⟨applicant⟩ to the ⟨issuing bank⟩ to open a ⟨letter of credit⟩.

application service provider (ASP) ① An entity which licenses, maintains and leases software programs to business clients. ② Software programs accessed and used by business clients on their computers, from service providers' computers, over the internet.

appraisal The process of determining the value of a given item. Customs services use appraisal formulas for determining the value of goods on which ⟨ad valorem⟩ duty is payable.

approximately ⟨about⟩

AR ⟨all risks⟩

🗊 Insurance   🄻🄲 Letters of credit   🗊 Liner vessel shipping   🗊 Sales contracts   🗊 Vessel chartering

A

Arab Bank for Economic Development in Africa (ABEDA) Founded in 1973 and headquartered in Khartoum, Sudan, ABEDA promotes economic and technical cooperation among Arab and African States. **For more information, visit the ABEDA website at www.badea.org.**

Arab International Bank (AIB) Founded in 1971 and headquartered in Cairo, Egypt, the AIB provides financing to support development of foreign trade among Arab states.

Arab League ⟨League of Arab States⟩

Arab Maghreb Union ⟨Maghreb States⟩

Arab Monetary Fund (AMF) Founded in 1976 and headquartered in Abu Dhabi, United Arab Emirates, the AMF promotes Arab integration in monetary and economic affairs.

arbitrage The simultaneous buying and selling of the same commodity or foreign exchange in two or more markets in order to take advantage of price differentials.

arbitrary ⚓ An additional ⟨freight⟩ charge that ship lines assess for serving markets outside the hinterlands of their normal base ports of call. For instance, an Irish arbitrary is often applied to shipments made through container hub ports in the United Kingdom.

arbitration A process of dispute resolution in which a neutral third party (arbitrator) renders a decision after a hearing at which both parties have an opportunity to be heard. Arbitration may be voluntary or contractually required. The advantages of arbitration – as opposed to litigation – are neutrality, confidentiality, reduced costs, faster procedures and the arbitrator's expertise. Internationally, the main arbitration body is the ⟨ICC International Chamber of Commerce ⟩ Other arbitration institutions include the London Court of International Arbitration, the Stockholm Court of Arbitration and the ⟨American Arbitration Association⟩.

arrest The restraint of a vessel by a government authority pending resolution of a legal proceeding.

arrival notice (AN) ✈ ⚓ Advice from a ⟨carrier⟩ to a ⟨notify party⟩ that a shipment is or will soon be available at its destination.

arrived ship ⧄ A term used in vessel chartering to indicate that the vessel is ready to load or unload, and that laytime allowed under the ⟨charterparty⟩ begins. To qualify, the vessel must have reached the contractual loading/unloading place, must be ready in all respects for loading/unloading, and ⟨notice of readiness⟩ must have been given in accordance with the charterparty.

⟨see entry in dictionary⟩   ✈ Air transport   🏛 Bank collections   @ e-commerce   ⊞ Incoterms

ARSO ⟨African Regional Organization for Standardization⟩

AS Depending on the context, see either ⟨at sight⟩ or ⟨limited liability⟩.

A

as fast as the vessel can (FAC) 🄰 A vessel chartering term meaning the maximum rate at which a vessel can load or unload.

as freighted 🄻 An explanatory note to a freight surcharge explaining that it is to be calculated in the same manner as the freight charge itself.

> ⟨**Bunker adjustment factors**⟩ **are usually calculated on an "as freighted" basis. By contrast, currency adjustment factors are based on the total amount of freight payable, rather than on the number of revenue tons.**

ASEAN Free Trade Area ⟨Association of Southeast Asian Nations⟩

Asia-Pacific Economic Cooperation (APEC) An informal group of Asia Pacific countries that provides a forum for ministerial level discussion of a broad range of economic issues. Within the APEC, the Sub-Committee on Customs Procedures (SCCP) manages customs co-operation, and has issued a "Best Practices Handbook" for use by its member countries.

> **For more information, visit the APEC website at www.sccp.org or www.apecsec.org.sg.**

Asian Development Bank (ADB) The ADB helps finance economic development in developing countries in the Asian and Pacific area through the provision of loans on near-market terms with its Ordinary Capital Resources (OCR), and on concessional terms through the Asian Development Fund (ADF).

> **For more information, visit the ADB website at www.adb.org.**

ASP ⟨application software provider⟩

assignee 🄻 A party to whom all or part of the proceeds of a ⟨letter of credit⟩ have been formally pledged, usually through a bank.

assignment of L/C proceeds 🄻 Instructions to a bank to pay a third party directly from payments made against a ⟨letter of credit⟩.

assignor 🄻 A ⟨letter of credit⟩ beneficiary who formally pledges all or part of the L/C proceeds to one or more third parties, usually by executing an assignment of proceeds document at a bank.

assist A customs term for types of help rendered to a seller by a buyer, such as production tooling, design work, etc. Under certain circumstances in some countries, the dutiable value of imported goods must be increased by the value of assists.

🄰 Insurance   🄻 Letters of credit   🄻 Liner vessel shipping   🄰 Sales contracts   🄰 Vessel chartering

A

Association for International Business (AIB) @ An open membership world trade resource featuring an e-mail discussion group with over 11,000 members in more than 200 countries. Membership comes from business, education, government and non-government organizations. Basic membership is available at no charge.

> **For more information, visit the AIB website at www.AIBCenter.com.**

Association of Southeast Asian Nations (ASEAN) ASEAN promotes political, economic and social cooperation among its member countries. It has established a Common Effective Preferential Tariff (CEPT), and is in the process of establishing the ASEAN Free Trade Area (AFTA).

> **For more information, visit the ASEAN website at www.asean.or.id.**

assured 🔻 The party covered under an insurance policy.

assured payment system An arrangement in an exchange-for-value system under which completion of timely settlement of a payment instruction is supported by an irrevocable and unconditional guarantee from a third party (typically a bank or syndicate of banks or clearing house).

at sight (AS) 🏛 Term indicating that whatever action it pertains to must be undertaken immediately. This term is commonly used on ⟨drafts⟩ accompanying bank ⟨collections⟩ to indicate that they are immediately payable (literally as soon as the ⟨drawees⟩ see them). However, in practice, payments are often deferred until the arrival of the goods covered by such collections, since the buyers have no need for the accompanying documents until then. Drafts drawn at sight are also frequently required by ⟨letters of credit⟩.

at X days date or **at X days sight** 🏛 Terms used on ⟨drafts⟩ to indicate that they are payable at some future time after they are presented.

ATA ⟨carnet⟩

ATC ⟨Textiles and Clothing, WTO Agreement⟩

Australia–New Zealand Closer Economic Relations Agreement (CER) An agreement, implemented in 1983 and aimed at increasing trade links by liberalizing trade, thereby allowing for more efficient use of each country's resources.

Australia Group (AG) The AG is an informal forum through which industrialized member nations cooperate to curb proliferation of chemical and biological weapons.

⟨see entry in dictionary⟩   ✈ Air transport   🏛 Bank collections   @ e-commerce   ▦ Incoterms

authentication (as used in open network communications). A term describing the process of identification of individuals and businesses through the use of digital certificates. See also ⟨digital signature⟩.

authentication (as used in payment systems). The process of confirming that a payment instruction is genuine, that it arrived exactly as it was sent, and that it came from the stated source.

authority to pay An advice addressed from a buyer through its bank to a seller through a correspondent bank in the seller's country, authorizing the correspondent to pay a named seller's ⟨draft⟩(s) up to a specified amount against drafts drawn on the correspondent. The authority to pay normally specifies documents that must accompany the draft(s). It can be cancelled or changed at any time until the drafts are presented and paid by the correspondent bank, at which time it becomes irrevocable.

> **This L/C-substitute works approximately in the same way as a ⟨revocable letter of credit⟩. Since revocable L/Cs do not provide real payment, the value of authorities to pay is questionable.**

authority to purchase This L/C-substitute is similar to an ⟨authority to pay⟩, except that the ⟨draft⟩s are drawn on the buyer rather than on the correspondent bank.

> **This L/C-substitute works approximately the same as a ⟨revocable letter of credit⟩. Since revocable L/Cs do not provide real payment, the value of authorities to pay is questionable.**

automated clearing house (ACH) An electronic clearing system in which payment orders are exchanged among financial institutions, primarily by magnetic media or telecommunication networks, and handled by a data-processing centre.

aval 🏛 A guarantee notice that a third party (other than the ⟨drawee⟩) places on a ⟨draft⟩. This is used when a buyer's credit is in itself not sufficient to justify a sale, and a more creditworthy party is willing to guarantee the deal. It is also used in ⟨forfaiting⟩, where a government agency or bank avals drafts, thereby enhancing their appeal in rediscount markets.

> **Some national laws require that avaled drafts be protested if unpaid when due, in order to give guarantors notice that their contingent liabilities may be called.**

average 🗗 For purposes of this book, an insurance term for a loss or damage incident that is less than total.

average adjuster 🗗 A person specializing in settling ⟨marine cargo insurance⟩ claims.

🗗 Insurance 🔲 Letters of credit ⬇ Liner vessel shipping ◿ Sales contracts 🄿 Vessel chartering

AB

AWB ⟨air waybill⟩

B2B ⟨business to business⟩

B2C ⟨business to consumer⟩

B2G ⟨business to government⟩

B/L ⟨bill of lading⟩

back letter ⬇ ① A complement to a contract laying down rights and/or obligations that for whatever reasons the contracting parties cannot state in the original contract. ② A letter of indemnity provided by a shipper to a ⟨carrier⟩, inducing the carrier to provide a ⟨clean transport document⟩ under circumstances where this would not otherwise be done.

back order A portion of an order that is to be shipped at a later time. See also ⟨partial shipment⟩.

back to back L/C 🄻🄲 A second and separate ⟨letter of credit⟩ that has been collateralized by another (first) L/C.

BAF ⟨bunker adjustment factor⟩

bag A receptacle of flexible material with an opening at the top.

bailee A party having temporary custody of the property of another, such as a ⟨carrier⟩ or a warehouse.

bailment A contract under which a party has temporary custody of the property of another, as in ⟨contracts of carriage⟩ or warehousing.

balance of payments (BoP) A statistical summary of international transactions. These transactions are defined as the transfer of ownership of something that has economic value in monetary terms from residents of one country to residents of another. The transfer may include goods (tangibles), services (intangibles), income on investments and financial claims on, and liability to, the rest of the world, including changes in a country's reserve assets held by the central monetary authorities. Many governments break down the BoP to its component subtotals, such as balance of trade, balance on services trade, balance on investment income, and balance on unilateral transfers.

balance of trade (BoT) The difference between a country's total merchandise ⟨import⟩s and ⟨export⟩s for a specific time period. If exports exceed imports, a country is said to enjoy a favourable balance of trade; if not, the trade balance is unfavourable.

This concept is perhaps more meaningful when applied to trade between two countries, rather than one country and the rest of

---

⟨see entry in dictionary⟩ ✈ Air transport 🏛 Bank collections @ e-commerce ⊞ Incoterms

the world.

bale A shaped packing unit tied or bound under tension.

B

Banco Latinamericano de Exportaciones (BLADEX) Founded in
1979 and headquartered in Panama City, Panama, BLADEX is a
multinational bank providing short-term (95 per cent) and medium-
term (5 per cent) financing. Borrowers are primarily Latin American
commercial banks of member countries, which finance specific
trade transactions for their customers.

For more information, visit the BLADEX website at www.blx.com.

bank draft A payment order from a bank, similar to a cashier's
⟨cheque⟩.

Bank for International Settlements (BIS) Founded in 1930 and
headquartered in Basle, Switzerland, the BIS promotes cooperation
among central banks in international financial settlements.

For more information, visit the BIS website at www.bis.org.

bank guarantee A contract between a bank (as guarantor) and a
beneficiary, in which a bank commits itself to pay a certain sum
under certain specified conditions. A demand bank guarantee is one
in which the bank agrees to pay against the simple written demand
of the beneficiary.

**Some countries do not permit their domiciled banks to issue bank
guarantees, but the same purpose can be achieved with ⟨letters
of credit⟩, particularly ⟨standby L/Cs⟩.**

Bank of Central African States (BEAC) Established in 1973 and headquartered in Yaounde, Cameroon, BEAC issues a common currency
unit, the Central African franc, which is guaranteed by France.

banker's acceptance 🄻🄲 A ⟨draft⟩ accepted by a bank for maturity
at a future time.

bankers' bank A bank that is established by the mutual consent of
independent and unaffiliated banks to act as a clearinghouse for
financial transactions.

banner advertisement An electronic image, with or without text,
appearing on a web page, which, when mouse-clicked, links the
user to another web page or website. These are generally used to
promote a product, a service, or another e-commerce portal.

Banque Française du Commerce Extérieur (BFCE) is a French
Government-owned agency, which lends officially supported
credits at preferential interest rates.

bar coding A computer-readable numbering system commonly used for

B

product identification or shipment routing. The two most commonly used systems are the European Article Numbering System (EAN) and the Universal Product Code (UPC) used in the United States.

bareboat charter (= demise charter) ⊟ A vessel chartering arrangement whereby the owner leases the vessel to a ⟨charterer⟩ for an agreed period of time. Although actual vessel ownership remains with the owner, the charterer operates the vessel as though it were his or her own, appointing the master, hiring the crew, and maintaining complete control for the duration of the agreement.

barratry Willful wrongdoing on the part of a ship's master and/or crew contrary to the interest of the shipowner or ⟨charterer⟩.

barrel (Bbl.) A unit of liquid measure consisting of 158.937 litres, 42 US gallons, or 34.97261 imperial gallons. This is usually used for oil.

barrier material A packing substance designed to withstand the penetration of moisture, gas, oils, etc.

barter A form of ⟨countertrade⟩ involving the direct exchange of goods and/or services for other goods and/or services, without the use of money and without the involvement of a third party. Barter is an important means of trade with countries using unconvertible currencies.

base port ⬇ Major ports which ship lines call on with their large (usually transoceanic) vessels. Cargo bound for ports within the base port hinterland is transshipped on feeder vessels. See also ⟨feeder vessel⟩ and ⟨hub and spoke⟩.

base rate (= basic transportation rate) ⬇ The "pure" cost of transportation, to which surcharges and other accessorial charges are added.

basis point 1/100 of 1%, i.e., 100 basis points equals one per cent, often used in interest calculations.

basis weight The weight in grammes of one square metre of paper, used in calculating the strength of packing materials.

batten A reinforcing member attached at right angles to a wood box, barrel, or crate.

> **To prevent introduction of non-native pests, some jurisdictions prohibit the importation of non-treated coniferous wood packing materials from certain originating countries.**

Bbl ⟨barrel⟩

BBS ⟨bulletin board system⟩

⟨see entry in dictionary⟩   ✈ Air transport   🏛 Bank collections   © e-commerce   ⊞ Incoterms

B

BCEAO ⟨Central Bank of West African States⟩

BDEAC ⟨Central African States Development Bank⟩

BEAC ⟨Bank of Central African States⟩

beam The extreme width of a vessel.

bearer document A ⟨negotiable instrument⟩ such as a pawn ticket, a duly-endorsed ⟨cheque⟩ or one payable to the order of cash, or a negotiable ⟨warehouse receipt⟩, whereby the holder is considered to be the owner of the goods that the bearer document represents.

> The most commonly used bearer document in foreign trade is a duly endorsed negotiable ⟨marine (ocean) bill of lading⟩. Ownership to the shipped goods is conveyed from one party to another by endorsing and passing on the B/L, and this document must be surrendered to the ⟨carrier⟩ by the final owner in exchange for the goods.

belly cargo Freight accommodation under the main deck of a vessel or airplane.

beneficiary ① 🆗 The party to whom a ⟨letter of credit⟩ is opened, generally the exporter-seller. ② The recipient of any benefit, such as the party to be paid under a contract of insurance. ③ In payment systems, a party to whom funds are allocated through the crediting of an account.

Bern Convention A major multinational treaty concerning the scope of copyright protection to be accorded works prepared by foreign persons whose countries are signatories. It provides copyright protection in the form of national treatment and also requires member countries to provide certain minimum protections for specified types of works.

berth The place at a wharf where vessels can be loaded and/or unloaded.

berth terms ⟨liner terms⟩

Besloten Vennooschap (BV) ⟨limited liability⟩

BEUC (Bureau Européen des Unions de Consommateurs) ⟨European Consumers' Organization⟩

beyond point The final inland point in through transport.

BFCE ⟨Banque Française de Commerce Extérieur⟩

BIAC (Business and Industry Advisory Committee to the OECD) ⟨Organization for Economic Cooperation and Development⟩

🛆 Insurance 🆗 Letters of credit ⬇ Liner vessel shipping 🖺 Sales contracts 🅿 Vessel chartering

B

BIC ⟨International Container Bureau⟩

bid bond A ⟨bond⟩ or guarantee, which has been issued as security for one party's bid. If that party, known as the ⟨principal⟩, wins the bidding process and then fails to take up the resulting contract, the beneficiary may obtain payment under the bond guarantee. Bid bonds are usually worded to cancel automatically if the principal is not the successful bidder, or if successful, takes up the contract. See also ⟨surety⟩.

BIE ⟨Bureau International des Expositions⟩

bilateral An agreement or arrangement involving two parties.

bilateral clearing agreement A government-to-government reciprocal trade arrangement whereby two nations agree to a trade turnover of specified value over one or more years. The value of the products traded under the agreement is denominated in accounting units expressed in major currencies – such as "clearing US dollars", "clearing Swiss francs", etc. Exporters in each country are paid by designated local banks in domestic currencies.

bilateral investment treaty (BIT) An agreement establishing the terms and conditions for private investment by parties of one country in the country of the other.

bilateral trade agreement A formal or informal agreement involving commerce between two countries.

bill A document giving evidence of indebtedness of one party to another.

bill of exchange A ⟨draft⟩. An unconditional order addressed by a creditor (⟨drawer⟩) to a debtor for the payment of a specific sum.

bill of lading (B/L) ▣ ⬇ A transport document issued or signed by a ⟨carrier⟩ evidencing a contract of carriage and acknowledging receipt of cargo. This term is normally reserved for carriage by truck (truck B/L), vessel (marine or ocean B/L), or ⟨multimodal transport⟩. All B/Ls must indicate the date of issue, name of shipper and place of shipment, place of delivery, description of goods, whether the freight charges are prepaid or collect and the ⟨carrier⟩'s signature.

- **truck bills of lading** are really waybills, and are never negotiable.

- **negotiable marine B/Ls** show the word "order" in the consignee field, and become either bearer instruments when endorsed in blank or restricted bearer endorsements when endorsed to a particular party.

- **non-negotiable marine** B/Ls (also called straight B/Ls) do not show the word "order" in the consignee field; therefore only the party shown in the consignee field has the right to take delivery. Some countries (such as the UK) do not recognize non-negotiable B/Ls as B/Ls at all, but classify them as "⟨sea waybill⟩s". It is therefore important that sellers and buyers of goods to be shipped by vessel agree whether the B/L is to be issued in negotiable form.

binding A provision in a trade agreement that no tariff rate higher than the one specified in the agreement will be imposed during the life of the agreement.

BIS ⟨Bank for International Settlements⟩

BIT ⟨bilateral investment treaty⟩

BLADEX ⟨Banco Latinamericano de Exportaciones⟩

blanket policy ⟨open marine cargo insurance policy⟩

BOAD ⟨West African Development Bank⟩

Bolero @ A private-sector organization dedicated to automating international trade transactions. Bolero is a joint venture of ⟨SWIFT⟩ and the London-based insurer TT Club, and has the backing of several major international banks.
> **For more information, visit the bolero website at www.bolero.net.**

bona fide True, genuine.

bond ⟨surety⟩, ⟨surety-ship bond⟩ or ⟨guarantee⟩

bonded warehouse A facility designated by a country's customs service where goods may be temporarily stored without the payment of duty, until such time as they are withdrawn into that country's customs territory. Goods subsequently shipped to foreign points are not subject to duty in the country where the facility is located.
> **Some countries do not permit manufacturing operations within bonded warehouses.**

booking ⚓ A reservation made with a ⟨carrier⟩ for a particular shipment on a particular voyage or flight. Unless the carrier is also arranging for pickup, it will provide delivery instructions to the party making the booking.

booking number ⚓ A unique number assigned to a ⟨booking⟩.

booking rollover the simultaneous cancellation of a ⟨booking⟩ on a particular vessel and rebooking of the same cargo on a subsequent vessel.

B

BoP ⟨balance of payments⟩

BoT ⟨balance of trade⟩

bound rates Duty rates resulting from GATT negotiations that are incorporated in a country's schedule of concessions and are thus enforceable as an integral part of the ⟨WTO⟩ regime. If a WTO member country raises a tariff to a higher level than its bound rate, the major beneficiaries of the earlier binding have a right to receive compensation, usually in the form of lower duties on other products they export to that country.

bounty ⟨subsidy⟩ and ⟨countervailing duty⟩

box A rigid container, generally rectangular, with closed faces.

> To prevent introduction of non-native pests, some jurisdictions prohibit the importation of non-treated coniferous wood packing materials from certain originating countries.

boxboard Paperboard used in cartons.

boycott Refusal to do business with a party or class of parties. The best-known example in foreign trade is the Arab League boycott of Israel. Some countries have regulations prohibiting their nationals from participating in boycotts against friendly countries (⟨anti-boycott regulations⟩), although they require their nationals to participate in their own boycotts.

breakbulk cargo ⊟ ⬇ Non-containerized cargo that may be grouped or consolidated for shipment, and then is later broken down, sub-divided or distributed at a further destination point. It may also be cargo that is too large to fit into containers. Breakbulk cargo is often unitized on pallets or packed in boxes.

bribery Giving or promising money or other valuable consideration toward the end of corrupting a person's behaviour.

bridging credit Borrowing ahead of receiving payment for a sale, or short-term credit to a borrower pending receipt of funds from another source.

brokerage ① In shipping, a commission paid to a freight ⟨forwarder⟩ by a ⟨carrier⟩ for placing cargo, or a commission or fee paid to a shipbroker for arranging a vessel charter. ② In insurance, a commission paid by an insurer to the agent placing coverage with it.

broker's cover note ⟨cover note⟩

browser ⟨web browser⟩

bruce box A wire-bound container.

B

To prevent introduction of non-native pests, some jurisdictions prohibit the importation of non-treated coniferous wood packing materials from certain originating countries.

Brussels tariff nomenclature (BTN) A classification system used for customs purposes. The BTN was incorporated into and forms the core of the ⟨Harmonized System⟩ (HS).

BS ⟨bunker adjustment factor⟩

BT ⟨limited liability⟩

BTN ⟨Brussels tariff nomenclature⟩

buffer stocks Commodity stockpiles managed in such a way as to moderate price fluctuations. Goods may be sold from a stockpile when prices reach or approach predetermined ceiling prices, and they may be purchased for the stockpile when prices reach or approach a predetermined floor level.

bulk cargo ⊟ Cargo that is loaded and carried aboard ship in a loose form, without mark or count, and has homogeneous characteristics. Coal is a typical bulk cargo.

bulk carrier A transporter (usually an ocean-going vessel) of large heavy cargoes. "Dry" cargoes are usually mineral ores (such as phosphates or manganese) as opposed to "liquid hydrocarbons," a phrase that usually refers to petroleum.

bulletin board system (BBS) An electronic message system that allows users to post messages for other users to read. Accessed over the internet and hosted by websites, bulletin boards are a popular method to share information and to post trade opportunities. Posted messages are retained for a period of time, and these messages are linked (or, "threaded") to one another, allowing a user to follow the history of a linked message.

bunker adjustment factor (BAF = bunker surcharge = BS) ⬇ An additional charge added to the base rate ocean freight cost reflecting the cost of fuel (called bunkers) to be used for the voyage. This charge is separate from the base rate freight cost because fuel costs are more frequently subject to fluctuations.

bunkering Fueling a vessel.

Bureau Européen des Unions de Consommateurs (BEUC) ⟨European Consumers' Organization⟩

Bureau International des Expositions (BIE) (= International Exhibitions Bureau). Established by the Paris Convention of 1928, BIE is an international organization that regulates the conduct and

---

⟲ Insurance   LC Letters of credit   ⬇ Liner vessel shipping   ◿ Sales contracts   ⊟ Vessel chartering

BC

scheduling of international expositions of a non-commercial nature in which foreign nations are officially invited to participate.

For more information, visit the BIE website at www.bie-paris.org.

business to business (B2B) @ Electronic communication over the internet between two businesses.

Business and Industry Advisory Committee to the OECD (BIAC) ⟨Organization for Economic Cooperation and Development⟩

business to consumer (B2C) @ Electronic communication over the internet between a business and a consumer.

business to government (B2G) @ Electronic commerce and communication conducted over the internet between a business and a government agency.

buy-back (compensation). A form of ⟨countertrade⟩ whereby exporters of heavy equipment, technology or even entire manufacturing facilities agree to purchase a certain percentage of the output of the new facility once it is in production.

BV (Besloten Vennooschap) ⟨limited liability⟩

C&F ⟨Cost and Freight (CFR)⟩

C&I ⟨Cost and Insurance⟩

CA ⟨certificate of authority⟩

CABE ⟨Central American Bank for Economic Integration⟩

cabotage Government restrictions reserving domestic transportation (between points within the country) to domestically registered ⟨carrier⟩s.

CAC Depending on the context, see either ⟨currency adjustment charge⟩ or ⟨Codex Alimentary Commission⟩.

CACM ⟨Central American Common Market⟩

CAD Depending on the context, see either ⟨cash against documents⟩ or ⟨Corporación Andina de Formento⟩.

CAF ⟨currency adjustment charge⟩

Cairns Group Established in 1986 and headquartered in Cairns, Australia, the Cairns Group is an informal association of agricultural exporting countries including Argentina, Australia, Bolivia, Brazil, Canada, Chile, Colombia, Costa Rica, Fiji, Guatemala, Hungary, Indonesia, Malaysia, New Zealand, Philippines, South Africa, Thailand and Uruguay.

C

Caisse Centrale de Coopération Economique (CCCE) ⟨Agence Française de Développement⟩

Calvo doctrine A legal principle that jurisdiction in international investment disputes lies with the country in which the investment is located; thus, a foreign investor has no recourse beyond the host country's local courts.

Canadian Commercial Corporation (CCC) By serving as the prime contractor in government-to-government sales transactions, the CCC facilitates ⟨export⟩s of a wide range of Canadian goods and services by matching buyer needs with Canadian firms capable of meeting them.

Canadian International Development Agency (CIDA) Founded in 1968 and headquartered in Hull, Quebec, Canada, CIDA is Canada's official agency tasked with supporting sustainable development in developing countries.

> For more information, visit the CIDA website at www.acdi-cida.gc.ca/index.htm.

cancel To revoke or make void.

capital Property or wealth that yields income expressed in terms of money.

capital goods Industrial products or other goods that are used in the creation of additional wealth, such as machine tools.

captain's protest An ⟨affidavit⟩ prepared by a ship's master on arrival at port, showing conditions encountered during the voyage. Normally, this is done to mitigate the shipowner's liability for cargo.

cargo Goods being transported.

cargo insurance 🛆 Insurance placed on goods during transportation.

cargo sharing The reservation and division of maritime traffic between designated trading partner countries, which agree that vessels owned or controlled by either will carry a specified percentage of the ⟨cargo⟩ moving between them.

Caribbean Common Market (CARICOM) Established in 1973 and headquartered in Georgetown, Guyana, CARICOM is in the process of developing a single market for free movement of ⟨goods⟩, ⟨services⟩, persons and capital, as well as a common external tariff.

> For more information, visit the CARICOM website at www.caricom.org.

Caribbean Development Bank (CDB) Established in 1969 and

🛆 Insurance 🆛 Letters of credit 🛈 Liner vessel shipping 🛆 Sales contracts 🅿 Vessel chartering

c

headquartered in St Michael, Barbados, the CDB promotes economic development and cooperation by providing long-term financing for productive projects in Caribbean Common Market member countries and UK-dependent territories in the Caribbean.
For more information, visit the CDB website at www.caribank.org.

CARICOM ⟨Caribbean Common Market⟩

carload rate The freight charge for the exclusive use of a rail car.

carloader A consolidator of cargo for shipment by rail, either by rail car or by trailer on flat car. See also ⟨trailer on flat car⟩.

carnet (ATA = admission temporaire/temporary admission). An international customs document for the temporary duty-free admission of goods into a country for display, demonstration or similar business purposes. ATA Carnets are issued by national chambers of commerce or other similar organizations afilliated to the ATA internatinal guarantee chain. The chain is administered by the World ATA Carnet Council (WATAC) of the ⟨World Chambers Federation (WCF)⟩, which is a specialized division of the ⟨International Chamber of Commerce (ICC)⟩. The national organizations affiliated to the ATA chain guarantee the payment of duties to local customs authorities, should the goods not ultimately be re-exported.
As some countries do not participate in the ATA carnet system, be sure to check on all proposed destination countries with your local carnet-issuing organization.

carnet (TIR = transport international routier). A document issued pursuant to the 1949 TIR Convention permitting sealed road transport shipments to traverse other European TIR-member countries without undergoing customs inspection until reaching the destination country.

carriage Transportation.

Carriage and Insurance Paid to (CIP)... named place of destination (Incoterms 2000) 🔠 An Incoterm designed for omnimodal use, where the seller arranges and pays for main carriage to the agreed place on the buyer's side and provides at least minimum insurance cover, but ceases to be responsible for the condition of the goods once they are handed over to the first ⟨carrier⟩.

carriage contract ✈ ⧄ ⚓ An agreement between a ⟨carrier⟩ and another party for transportation. The other party will normally be the seller (or seller's agent) with freight prepaid shipments, or the buyer (or buyer's agent) for freight collect shipments. Contracts of

C

carriage are normally expressed by the transportation document that the carrier signs or issues (<air waybill>, truck bill of lading, marine bill of lading, <sea waybill>, <multimodal transport document>, etc.). Since carriers will normally take instructions from the party with which they contract carriage, carrier selection can be an important consideration for sellers and buyers alike.

Carriage of Goods by Sea Act (UK COGSA) There are actually two "Carriage of Goods by Sea Acts" in force in the United Kingdom, and each deals with a different facet of marine carriage. The first, the Carriage of Goods by Sea Act of 1971, deals with <contracts of carriage> along the lines of the Hague-Visby Rules of 1968, and applies to vessel shipments made to or from UK ports. It is to some extent similar to US COGSA, except that it is a more modern piece of legislation. The second, the Carriage of Goods by Sea Act of 1992, deals with the situation of buyers who themselves did not enter into contracts of carriage but find themselves with such contracts as holders in due course. For instance, in the <CFR> and <CIF> Incoterms, the seller enters into a contract of carriage with a <carrier>, and then sells the freight prepaid contract along with the goods to the buyer. COGSA 1992 paints the buyer into the contract picture.

Carriage of Goods by Sea Act of the United States (US COGSA) The United States Carriage of Goods by Sea Act of 1936 is based on the Hague Rules of 1924, and US COGSA prevails in situations where they differ. US COGSA applies to vessel shipments in foreign trade made to or from the United States ports.

1. Under US COGSA, carriers can limit their liability to USD 500.00 per "package" or "customary freight unit" for unpackaged shipments. Such customary units could be short, long or metric tons, or their volumetric equivalents, or units such as a pleasure boat.
2. Other US legislation covering marine transport includes the Harter Act of 1893 covering domestic waterborne transport (lacking a clause paramount invoking US COGSA), and the Pomerene Act of 1916 covering all <bills of lading> issued in the US for domestic carriage and outbound international shipments.
3. There is considerable interest in creating new legislation to bring US COGSA up to date.
4. Despite US COGSA, some carriers are willing to negotiate increased liability for favoured customers. This is particularly true after the Ocean Shipping Reform Act of 1998 was implemented in 1999.
5. Do not confuse US COGSA with other bodies of law, such as the <Carriage of Goods by Sea Act of the United Kingdom> (UK COGSA).

Carriage Paid to (CPT)... named place of destination (Incoterms 2000) ⊞ An <Incoterm> designed for omnimodal use where the

C

seller arranges and pays for main carriage to the agreed place on the buyer's side, but ceases to be responsible for the condition of the goods once they are handed over to the first ⟨carrier⟩.

carrier ✈ ⚓ A party taking on transportation responsibility. This party may be an actual carrier (called an "⟨undercarrier⟩") or a "non-equipment-operating" carrier such as a ⟨non-vessel-operating common carrier⟩ or an ⟨air freight consolidator⟩.

carrier liability limit The maximum amount of money for which a ⟨carrier⟩ is legally liable for loss or damage to cargo.

> **This can be surprisingly low. For example, under the US ⟨Carriage of Goods by Sea Act⟩ of 1936, maximum carrier liability is set at USD 500.00 per package or shipping unit (which could be an entire shipper-packed container). Under the ⟨Warsaw Convention⟩ as amended, it is 17 ⟨Special Drawing Rights⟩ (approximately USD 20.00) per kilo for airfreight shipments.**

cartage ① Transport of goods by truck to or from a main ⟨carrier⟩ (i.e., vessel or aircraft) or ⟨bonded warehouse⟩ or ⟨free trade zone⟩ within the local port or airport commercial zone, usually under the supervision of customs authorities. ② The charge for such services.

cartel An organization of independent producers formed to regulate the production, pricing or marketing practices of its members in order to limit competition and maximize its market power.

carton A rectangular folding boxboard container.

case of need 🏛 A local party that a presenting bank may contact for assistance in obtaining compliance with a ⟨collection⟩ The case of need's name and address along with its scope of authority is normally detailed in the collection letter.

cash 🏛 against documents (CAD) Payment terms used in bank ⟨collections⟩ that require the ⟨drawee⟩ to pay before receiving certain documents. Typically, the ⟨drawer⟩ will send these documents to the drawee's bank with instructions that it secure payment before releasing them. This is very similar to ⟨sight draft documents against payment (SD/DP)⟩ terms, except that with CAD no draft is drawn.

cash on delivery (COD) A payment term under which payment for the shipped goods is to be made to the ⟨carrier⟩ at time of delivery. This practice is not recommended in foreign trade because of differing methods of operation employed by carriers in different countries and because neither the carrier nor the consignee may have access to foreign exchange. ⟨Sight draft documents against payment⟩ or ⟨cash against documents⟩ are often preferred alternatives as they use the banking system, which is better equipped to process payments and

---

convert currencies.

> **Do not confuse this term with "⟨freight collect⟩," which simply means that the freight charge is to be paid by the consignee.**

cash with order (CWO) A payment term whereby the buyer remits at the time the order is placed.

> **Under cash with order the buyer is actually extending credit to the seller rather than vice versa.**

casualty An adverse chance event, such as the disappearance of or damage to goods in transit.

catalog (online) A software package that runs as part of the website, holding a listing of items, item descriptions, item specifications, and images of the items. Online catalogs are a chief feature of virtual trade shows, and are often found within an e-store (⟨electronic store⟩).

CBL Combined transport bill of lading. See ⟨combined transport document⟩.

CBM Cubic metre.

CCAO ⟨West African Clearing House⟩

CCC ⟨Canadian Commercial Corporation⟩

CCC Customs Cooperation Council. See ⟨World Customs Organization⟩.

CCCE ⟨Caisse Centrale de Coopération Economique⟩

CCEWeb @ An organization dedicated to automating international trade transactions, with the backing of several major international banks.

> **For more information, visit the CCEWeb website at www.cceweb.com.**

CCFF ⟨Compensatory and Contingency Financing Facility⟩

CDB ⟨Caribbean Development Bank⟩

CE Mark ⟨Conformité Européene⟩

CEAO ⟨West Africa Economic Community⟩

CEEAC ⟨Economic Community of Central African States⟩

CEN ⟨Comité Européen de Normalisation⟩

CENELEC ⟨Comité Européen de Normalisation Electrotechnique⟩

Central African Common Market Established in 1998 to replace the old regional customs union, the Market groups Cameroon, Central African Republic, Chad, Congo Brazzaville, Gabon and Equitorial Guinea.

🅣 Insurance 🅛🅒 Letters of credit 🅛 Liner vessel shipping 🅢 Sales contracts 🅟 Vessel chartering

C

Central African Customs and Economic Union (UDEAC) ⟨Economic Community of Central African States⟩

Central African States Development Bank (BDEAC) Founded in 1977 and headquartered in Brazzaville, Congo, BDEAC was created to provide loans for economic development and to support integration projects.

Central American Bank for Economic Integration (CABEI) CABEI was established in 1961 to promote economic integration and development. It is associated with the Central American Common Market and headquartered in Tegucigalpa, Honduras.

> For more information, visit the CABEI website at www.bcie.org

Central American Common Market (CACM) CACM was established in 1960 and restructured in 1973 to cover all products traded within the region and establish a common external tariff – headquartered in Guatemala City, Guatemala.

central bank A government agency that controls a nation's monetary policy; i.e., holds banking reserves and controls the issuance of currency and the flow of credit. Central banks can also influence the exchange value of their currencies; either directly by implementing exchange control policies and intervention in currency markets, or indirectly by adjusting local interest rates.

Central Bank of West African States (BCEAO) Under the authority of the West African Monetary Union, BCEAO operates as a central bank and issues a common currency for its member states.

> For more information, visit the BCEAO website at www.bceao.int.

CEPGL ⟨Economic Community of the Great Lakes Countries⟩

CER ⟨Australia–New Zealand Closer Economic Relations Agreement⟩

certificate of analysis A document attesting that specified goods have undergone specified testing with specified results. In trade, this is usually the result of an agreement between the seller and the buyer, or of a requirement of one of their governments.

> When used as a required document under ⟨letter of credit⟩ terms, the details and identity of the party providing the analysis should be mentioned. If this is not done, banks will accept any document appearing on its face to be a certificate of analysis issued by any party other than the ⟨beneficiary⟩.

certificate of authority (CA – as used in the public key infrastructure) ©️ Certification from an institution (called a certification authority) trusted to provide certification for parties (called certification service providers) who record the identities of public key holders. See also

⟨certification service providers⟩, ⟨open network systems⟩, and ⟨public key infrastructure⟩.

C

> **For more information, visit the GUIDEC website at www.iccwbo.org/home/guidec/guidec.asp.**

certificate of free sale Government certification that products such as food, drugs, medicine or cosmetics are approved for unrestricted sale in the country in which they originate, or from which they are exported.

certificate of inspection A document certifying that the specified goods were in good condition immediately prior to shipment.

> **1. Some countries require inspection prior to shipment for price, quantity and quality verification and identification of the contract goods. For details on this practice, ⟨pre-shipment inspection⟩ and its resulting document, ⟨clean report of findings⟩.**
> **2. When used as a required document under letter of credit terms, the details and identity of the party providing the inspection should be mentioned. If this is not done, banks will accept any document appearing on its face to be an inspection certificate issued by any party other than the beneficiary.**

certificate of insurance ⟨insurance certificate⟩

certificate of manufacture A document in which a producer certifies that the manufacturing has been completed and that the referenced goods are now at the disposal of the buyer.

certificate of origin Certain nations require a signed statement as to the origin of imported items. Such certificates are usually attested by semi-official organizations such as local chambers of commerce.

> **Although the ⟨World Customs Organization⟩ and ⟨World Trade Organization⟩ are working on a single set of origin criteria in worldwide use, none exists at this time. Some countries and free-trade arrangements (such as the ⟨NAFTA⟩) require that origin be certified in terms of special criteria such as tariff shift or percentage of value. Traders are well advised to assure that any applicable origin rules are understood and any required documentation is obtainable before concluding sales contracts.**

certificate of weight A document attesting that a particular shipment is of a certain weight.

certification service provider (CSP) @ A party who records the identities of public key holders to ensure communications integrity of digitally signed communications in an open network. CSPs must
a. use only technologically reliable information systems and trustworthy personnel;
b. have no conflict of interest;
c. refrain from contributing to a breach of duty by a subscriber;

🛧 Insurance   🇱🇨 Letters of credit   ⬇ Liner vessel shipping   ◿ Sales contracts   🄿 Vessel chartering

C

d. refrain from acts or omissions that significantly impair reasonable and foreseeable reliance on a valid certificate;

e. act in a trustworthy manner toward a subscriber and persons who rely on a valid certificate.

See also ⟨digital signature⟩, ⟨open network systems⟩, and ⟨public key infrastructure⟩.

For more information, visit the GUIDEC website at www.iccwbo.org/home/guidec/guidec.asp.

CET ⟨common external tariff⟩

CEXT ⟨common external tariff⟩

CFR ⟨Cost and Freight⟩

CFS ⟨container freight station⟩

chaebols Korean conglomerates, characterized by strong family control, authoritarian management and centralized decision-making.

charter ⊠ ⊟ The hiring or leasing of an aircraft or a vessel. See also ⟨bareboat charter⟩, ⟨dry charter⟩, ⟨time charter⟩, ⟨voyage charter⟩, and ⟨wet charter⟩.

charter party ⟨charterparty⟩

charterer ⊠ ⊟ The party hiring or leasing an aircraft or vessel.

charterparty (charter party) ⊟ A contract under which a ⟨charterer⟩ agrees to rent/hire the use of a ship or part of a ship from a shipowner. The charterer in some cases will be empowered to issue his or her own ⟨bills of lading⟩, known as charterparty bills of lading, subject to the conditions of the original charterparty contract.

1. The charterparty itself is not a bill of lading, but a contract between the shipowner and the charterer.
2. Do not confuse charterparty with "parties to the charter," who are the shipowner and the charterer.

chassis An undercarriage on which containers are transported over the road.

chat room ⟨discussion room⟩

check ⟨cheque⟩

checker ⊥ A carrier-designated person who is responsible for examining cargo being handed over for shipment, for signs of damage or loss. See also ⟨apparent good order and condition⟩ and ⟨apparent damage⟩.

cheque (check). A written order from one party (the ⟨drawer⟩) to another (the ⟨drawee⟩, normally a bank) requiring the drawee to

C

pay a specified sum on demand to the drawer or to a third party specified by the drawer. This instrument is widely used for settling debts and withdrawing money from banks.

chime A protective rim around the ends of a drum or cask.

CIDA ⟨Canadian International Development Agency⟩

CIF ⟨Cost, Insurance and Freight⟩

CIF&C ⟨Cost, Insurance, Freight and Commission⟩

CIP ⟨Carriage and Insurance Paid⟩

circa ⟨about⟩

CIS ⟨Commonwealth of Independent States⟩

CISG ⟨United Nations Convention on Contracts for the International Sale of Goods⟩

CITEL ⟨Inter-American Telecommunication Commission⟩

claim A demand, as one's due, or for compensation, such as against a ⟨carrier⟩ or ⟨insurer⟩.

claimant A party presenting a demand for compensation, as in freight or insurance claims.

clause paramount ⟨paramount clause⟩

claused B/L ⟨foul transport document⟩

clean collection 🏦 ① A letter of instructions to a presenting bank accompanied by a ⟨draft⟩ and often invoices, but not accompanied by any document restricting possession or ownership of the relevant goods. This is the opposite of a ⟨documentary collection⟩ ② A letter of instructions accompanied by a ⟨cheque⟩ drawn on a bank located outside the clearing range of the payee's country's banking system.

clean draft A ⟨draft⟩ to which no documentation has been attached. See also ⟨clean collection⟩.

clean float A system in which exchange rates are determined by market forces rather than by government intervention or restrictions.

clean receipt A ⟨receipt⟩ containing no damage or shortage notations.

clean report of findings A document issued by a pre-shipment inspection agency engaged by the importer's country, indicating that the relative shipment conforms to the criteria established by that government. Typically, pre-shipment inspections cover price

c

verification and physical inspection of the goods to determine that they conform in quantity, quality and kind to the importation approval. See also ⟨pre-shipment inspection⟩.

clean transport document ✗ 🏦 ⚓ A ⟨receipt⟩ for goods without any adverse notation indicating damage or shortage, issued by a ⟨carrier⟩. Goods covered by clean transport documents are said to be received in "apparent good order and condition." Transport documents bearing adverse notations are called variously "claused," "unclean" or "foul," and are the opposite of clean transport documents.

> There is no reason to show the word "clean" on the face of a transport document, as all transport documents without adverse notations are considered clean.

closed conference ⟨conference (liner)⟩

closed network communications (= intranets) @ A system of business communications where access is limited to pre-approved participants who conduct communications according to written and approved procedures, and maintain record systems designed to facilitate quality assurance, in compliance with legal obligations between the users and the organization responsible for operating the system. Closed network technologies such as EDI combine the functional capabilities of computers and telecommunications, permitting the computer-to-computer transmission of commercial information. See also ⟨electronic data interchange⟩.

> For more information, visit the GUIDEC website at www.iccwbo.org/home/guidec/guidec.asp.

closing date (closeout date) ⚓ ✗ The latest date that goods can arrive at a carrier terminal for transportation on a given voyage or flight.

CMR ⟨International Road Transportation Convention⟩

co-loading An indirect carrier (air or NVOCC) or consolidator's accepting cargo from another indirect ⟨carrier⟩ or ⟨consolidator⟩ in order to completely fill containers.

COD ⟨cash on delivery⟩

code of conduct In general use in trade law, any international agreement that prescribes or recommends standards of behaviour by nations or multinational corporations deemed desirable by the international community.

Codex Alimentarius Commission (CAC = CODEX) A subsidiary of the United Nations Food and Agricultural Organization and the ⟨World Health Organization⟩, CODEX develops food standards and

Recommended International Codes of Hygienic and/or Technological Practices. Commission standards are voluntary, becoming enforceable only if accepted as national standards. It was founded in 1962 and is headquartered in Rome, Italy.

For more information, visit the CODEX website at www.codexalimentarius.net.

COFACE ❮Compagnie Française d'Assurance pour le Commerce Extérieur❯

COGSA UK/US ❮Carriage of Goods by Sea Act❯

collateral An interest in property given by a debtor to a creditor in order for the creditor to secure payment of the debt. For example, an applicant for a ❮letter of credit❯ might pledge the goods for which the credit is opened as security to the ❮issuing bank❯.

collect freight ❮freight collect❯

collecting bank 🏛 Any bank, other than the ❮remitting bank❯, that is involved in processing a collection. (In collection parlance the remitting bank is the bank to which the ❮drawer❯ has entrusted the handling of a collection, usually the drawer's bank of account.)

collection 🏛 A set of documents including a letter or completed form indicating the ❮drawer❯'s instructions (called a collection letter), and often accompanied by a ❮draft❯ or drafts, invoices, packing lists and other documents as agreed by the drawer and ❮drawee❯. Collections accompanied by documents restricting possession or ownership are called "documentary," while those without such documents are called "clean." Many collections are covered by the current version of ❮Uniform Rules for Collections (URC)❯, a set of rules created by the ❮International Chamber of Commerce (ICC)❯ for use worldwide. Since the URC is not law, it must be specified in order to apply. However, it is in such common use that reference to it is often pre-printed on the collection letterforms commonly used by banks.

collection fees The charges banks impose for handling collections.

collection letter 🏛 A letter or form that conveys the ❮drawer❯'s instructions to the ❮presenting bank❯. While there are many variations, collection letters identify the drawer, ❮drawee❯, and any case-of-need party, and typically contain a series of boxes that apply to various instructional points. There are two kinds of collection letter: those originating from the drawer's bank and those originating from the drawer or its agent, called direct collection letters. Either way, the presenting bank receives the collection letter, endeavours to follow its instructions, and reports to the drawer's bank.

🛩 Insurance 🆑 Letters of credit ⚓ Liner vessel shipping 📄 Sales contracts 📃 Vessel chartering

C

Colombo Plan (= Colombo Plan for Cooperative Economic Development in South and South-East Asia). Established in 1951 to promote economic and social development among members in Asia and the Pacific, the Plan is headquartered in Colombo, Sri Lanka.

combination freight rate Two or more freight rates used in a single shipment by two or more ⟨carrier⟩s.

combined transport document (CTD) A transport document indicating more than one mode of transportation.
Examples
1. A "received for shipment" ⟨marine B/L⟩ indicating that pre-carriage from an inland originating point as well as main carriage transport were handled by the main ⟨carrier⟩.
2. An ⟨air waybill⟩ showing that pre-carriage from the shipment originating point as well as main carriage were handled by the main carrier.

COMESA ⟨Common Market for Eastern and Southern Africa⟩

Comité Européen de Normalisation (CEN) The European Committee for Standardization promotes technical harmonization in Europe in conjunction with worldwide bodies and its partners in Europe. While voluntary in theory, compliance with applicable CEN norms is obligatory for sales within Europe of non-electrical products that require the CE Mark.
> For more information, visit the CEN website at www.cenorm.be.

Comité Européen de Normalisation Electrotechnique (CENELEC) The European Committee for Electrotechnical Standardization promotes technical harmonization in Europe in conjunction with worldwide bodies and its partners in Europe. While voluntary in theory, compliance with applicable CENELEC norms is obligatory for sales within Europe of electrical products that require the CE Mark.
> For more information, visit the CENELEC website at www.cenelec.org.

commercial attaché The commercial expert on the diplomatic staff of a country's embassy or large consulate.

commercial counterfeiting The production or marketing of goods with the intent of defrauding the purchaser by falsely conveying, directly or indirectly, that the goods are produced by a known or reputable manufacturer.

commercial invoice A document recording a transaction between a seller and a buyer. Commercial invoices are normally prepared by

---

⟨see entry in dictionary⟩ ✈ Air transport 🏛 Bank collections @ e-commerce ⊞ Incoterms

sellers, and should include the following information:
- a unique invoice number
- the date the invoice is prepared
- the identities and addresses of the seller and buyer
- a "ship to" location (if other than the buyer's address)
- a buyer purchase order number and date (if any)
- the terms of sale (preferably Incoterms 2000)
- the terms of payment
- a complete description of all line items including their unit costs and line item totals
- an itemized list of all non-product services provided by the seller for the buyer's account, with their prices
- the grand total
- any certifications required by the import authorities of the buyer's country
- either packing details, or a cross reference to a separate packing list
- a signature by an authorized person at the seller's company, if required by the buyer's government.

commercial paper Short-term financial instruments that can be bought and sold, particularly promissory notes that call for the payment of specified amounts of money at specified times.

commercial risk The possibility of non-payment caused by such buyer-related problems as insolvency or bankruptcy, as opposed to problems encountered by the buyer's country. Commercial risk is often called "buyer risk."

commercial treaty An agreement between two or more countries setting forth the conditions under which business between or among the countries may be transacted. It may outline tariff privileges, terms on which property may be owned, the manner in which claims may be settled, etc.

commercial value The actual price at which a product is sold either to unrelated parties or to related parties at arm's length.

> This is the opposite of "no commercial value," a statement that should be shown on invoices covering shipments of samples that are being furnished without charge and are not intended for resale.

commission Compensation given by a principal to a party representing it. Sales commission, a percentage of the selling price to be paid to the sales agent or representative, is the most commonly used commission arrangement in foreign trade. ⟨Principal⟩s using commission agents or representatives normally increase their selling prices to provide for

C

such commission payments.

Sales commission agreements often provide that the commissions are not earned and payable until such time as the buyer has paid the principal, thereby assuring that the agent or representative will assist with any necessary collection effort.

commodity Broadly speaking, any article exchanged in trade, but commonly used to refer to raw materials and bulk-produced agricultural products.

commodity index The section of a freight tariff where commodity types are listed in alphabetical order.

commodity stockpiles ⟨buffer stocks⟩

common carrier ✈ ⚓ A company providing regularly scheduled transportation to the general public, as opposed to ⟨contract carriers⟩ that work as employees, sub-contractors or agents of a manufacturer or shipper.

common external tariff (CET or CEXT) A uniform tariff adopted by a customs union listing duties assessed on imports entering the union from countries outside the union.

common fund An international institution designed as the centrepiece of the ⟨UNCTAD⟩ Integrated Programme for Commodities. It operates from two accounts. The first account provides funds to help maintain buffer stocks maintained under international commodity agreements. The second account supports research and development and ⟨export⟩ promotion for selected commodities.

common market A group of two or more countries with a common external tariff, preferential tariffs and possibly provisions for mobility of labour and common economic policies among member countries.

Common Market for Eastern and Southern Africa (COMESA) In 1994, COMESA replaced the former Preferential Trade Area. COMESA supports area economic development and cooperation (agriculture, communications, customs, industry, monetary affairs, natural resources and trade) through its Trade & Development Bank, Clearing House, Association of Commercial Banks, Leather Institute and Re-Insurance Company.

For more information, visit the COMESA website at www.comesa.int.

Commonwealth of Independent States (CIS) Established in December 1991 as an association of republics of the former Soviet Union.

C

Community Research and Development Information Service (CORDIS) A service offering access to a wide range of information on ‹European Union› research and innovation activities provided at no charge by the European Commission's Innovation/SMEs programme.

For more information, visit the CORDIS website at www.cordis.lu.

Compagnie Française d'Assurance pour le Commerce Extérieur (COFACE) A French company acting as commercial ‹export› finance agency by insuring short-term political and commercial risk and by facilitating the financing for export credits. COFACE works in a quasi-official capacity for the French Government and also insures exports from other countries.

For more information, visit the COFACE website at www.coface.com.

comparative advantage A central concept in international trade theory that a country or region should specialize in the production and ‹export› of those goods and services that it can produce relatively more efficiently than other goods and services, and import those goods and services in which it has a comparative disadvantage.

compatible cargo A ‹hazardous materials› term for cargoes that may safely travel together.

compensation (tariff) The principle, central to GATT and the ‹WTO›, that any country that raises a tariff above its bound rate, that withdraws a binding on a tariff, or otherwise impairs a trade concession, must lower other tariffs or make other trade concessions to compensate for the disadvantage suffered by countries whose ‹export›s are affected.

Compensatory and Contingency Financing Facility (CCFF) An ‹International Monetary Fund› facility which provides resources to an IMF member for a shortfall in ‹export› earnings or an excess in cereal import costs which is due to factors largely beyond the member's control, and which is temporary.

compensatory finance A loan or transfer of resources on concessional terms to a country when its ‹export› receipts fall below a predetermined level. This can apply to either total export receipts or those derived from one or several predetermined commodities. Such arrangements exist under the ‹International Monetary Fund› and the ‹Lome Convention›.

composite currency peg An exchange system whereby a country pegs its currency to a basket of major trading partners' currencies

---

Ⓘ Insurance 🆔 Letters of credit Ⓛ Liner vessel shipping Ⓢ Sales contracts Ⓟ Vessel chartering

C

to make the pegged currency more stable than if only a single currency were used. The weights assigned to the currencies in the basket may reflect the geographical distribution of the pegging country's trade, services, or capital flows, or may be standardized as in ⟨special drawing rights⟩.

compound duty The combination of ⟨ad valorem⟩ (percentage) and specific import duty. Example: The import duty for a product classified under ⟨Harmonized System⟩ 381120 is 2.5 per cent ad valorem plus USD 0.08 per kilo.

concealed damage Damage to the contents of a package that externally appears undamaged.

concession A grant of a right or privilege by one party to a negotiation to induce the other party or parties to yield an equivalent privilege or right.

condensation (sweating). Moisture formed on cargo by a change of temperature, as from a cooler to a warmer environment. The temperature at which this occurs is called the "dew point."
Although commonly associated with transport by vessel, condensation can also occur with air shipments, as temperatures may change quickly with changes in altitude.

conditionality The set of conditions attached to the use of its resources by the ⟨International Monetary Fund⟩, involving undertakings and adjustment policies that will restore a sustainable balance-of-payments position within a one- to three-year period.

conference (liner) ⊥ A formal agreement among ship lines serving the same markets to establish common pricing and provide common discounts to shippers in return for loyalty commitments. Member ship lines are called conference carriers while non-members serving the same area are called independents. Some conferences are "closed", i.e.; they reserve the right to refuse membership to applying carriers.
Changes in national legislation permitting carriers and shippers to individually negotiate freight agreements have put the effectiveness of traditional conferences in question, particularly where such freight agreements may be kept confidential. Some conferences, in fact, have liquidated.

confirmed ⎣C⎦ A letter of credit that bears the additional guarantee of a financial institution other than the one that opened it.

confirming bank ⎣C⎦ A bank that adds its undertaking to a ⟨letter of credit⟩ in addition to that of the ⟨issuing bank⟩.

confirming house A trading company that represents the interests of foreign buyers. Confirming houses typically negotiate purchases on behalf of their overseas ⟨principal⟩s, place their domestic orders in the suppliers' countries, arrange for ⟨export⟩ handling and transportation to the buyer, and locally pay the suppliers.

confiscation Seizing of property by a government, usually as a penalty.

Conformité Européene (= CE Mark). The CE Mark signifies that a product meets specific ⟨European Union⟩ conformity assessment regulations. The mark does not endorse the quality or durability of a product, only that it satisfies mandatory technical requirements. The CE Mark is required for sale of products that become subject to European Union directives issued by the ⟨Comité Européen de Normalisation (CEN)⟩, whose website is www.cenorm.be or the ⟨Comité Européen de Normalisation Electrotechnique (CENELEC)⟩, whose website is www.cenelec.org.

congestion surcharge (= port congestion surcharge) 🔱 An additional charge added to the base rate ocean freight cost, reflecting the additional expenses that ship lines incur when calling at congested ports.

consignee ✖ 🅟 🔱 The intended receiver of a shipment; the named party having the legal right to claim the goods from the ⟨carrier⟩ at destination; the party whose name appears in the "consignee field" of a transport document.

consignment ① A shipment handed over to a ⟨carrier⟩. ② An arrangement whereby ⟨goods⟩ are placed at the disposal of a buyer under the condition that payment is to be made when they are resold.

consignor A party who enters into a ⟨contract of carriage⟩ with a ⟨carrier⟩ for shipment. This term is often synonymous with "shipper."

consolidation (= groupage) ✖ 🔱 Combining cargo from more than one shipper and/or to more than one ⟨consignee⟩ for shipment together, usually in a single shipping container. On arrival, the container is unloaded, and each individual shipment may be claimed by its appropriate consignee. The same scenario applies when a single shipper or consignee consolidates small shipments for its own use, or arranges that this be done by a third-party logistics provider. The advantages include lower pilferage potential, possibly lower freight costs and reduction in required ⟨export⟩ packing. The disadvantages include possible delay of an individual shipment awaiting sufficient

C

additional cargo to fill a container, possible problems resulting from incompatible cargo travelling in close proximity, and possible duplicate freight costs should the consolidator fail to pay the ⟨undercarrier⟩. Firms providing consolidation services often act as ⟨carrier⟩s, providing their own (house) transport documents that are supported by a (master) transport document issued by the undercarrier for the entire consolidated shipment. See also ⟨air freight consolidator⟩, ⟨non-vessel operating common carrier⟩ and ⟨third party logistics provider⟩.

consolidator (= groupage agent). A party that performs consolidation services. See also ⟨consolidation⟩.

consortium An association, particularly of businesses.

constructive total loss A marine insurance term for situations where the cost of repairing damaged insured goods exceeds their value.

consular documentation (= visaed = legalized documentation). Prescribed forms that have been presented to a consulate, usually of the buyer's government and usually in the country from which a shipment originates. While each country requiring consular documentation establishes its own fee schedule and procedures, ⟨commercial invoices⟩, ⟨certificates of origin⟩ and/or copies of transport documents are commonly used. Typically, importers in countries with such regulations are required to present the consularized documents to their authorities in order to clear customs. It is important to carefully prepare documents for consularization, since corrections are often both time consuming and expensive. Further, consulates are normally closed on their own national holidays as well as the holidays of their host countries. See also ⟨letter of correction⟩.

consular fee A fee charged by a consulate for performing services, such as signing ⟨consular documentation⟩.

consulate An office of a government located within the territory of another country. Consulates are the commercial equivalents of embassies.

container ① ⚓ A single, non-disposable structure to be filled with smaller objects to facilitate transportation. Containers are used extensively in waterborne, air and rail transport, and come in a variety of configurations to suit various kinds of loads. Typical container specifications for vessel transport include 20 foot and 40 foot dry freight, 20 foot and 40 foot open top, 20 foot and 40 foot refrigerated, 40 foot high cube refrigerated, 20 foot and 40 foot flat rack, 40 foot collapsible flat rack, 40 and 45 foot high cube, and 20 foot tank container. (Actual vessel container internal and external dimensions vary from manufacturer to manufacturer and from carrier to carrier.)

Airfreight containers, often called "igloos," are available in a variety of shapes and sizes. Rail containers are available for such specialized cargoes as metal coils.

Important notes on containerization:
Since all carriers do not always provide the full range of containers, it is important to check for availability when planning for a containerized shipment. Although container use may reduce the level of ⟨export packing⟩ required for damage-free shipment, the containers themselves must be carefully packed. Cargo must be secured to prevent in-transit shifting, and maximum container capacities must be observed.

② Any exterior packaging used for transportation.

container freight station (CFS) ⚓ ① At ports of shipment, designated areas for delivery of less-than-containerload cargo for container loading. ② At arrival ports, secure locations for container unloading and cargo delivery.

container rental surcharge ⚓ An additional fee for the use of a ⟨carrier⟩'s container, usually charged only for destinations with little outward cargo volume or high risk of loss or damage to the container.

container seal A pre-numbered device affixed to the locking device of a container in such a way that it must be broken for the container to be opened. Usually affixed by the party loading the container, seals both deter theft and indicate if a container has been opened while in transit. Each seal has a unique number, which should be recorded on the relevant transport document.

container yard (CY) ⚓ Carrier-designated locations at port areas for receiving, storing and delivering loaded containers, as well as for empty container pickup.

contingency insurance 🛡 Insurance coverage taken out by a party to an international transaction to insure against insurance coverage taken out by the ⟨counterparty⟩. The contingent ⟨insurer⟩ pays its beneficiary and attempts to collect from the primary insurer. For example, a pre-paying buyer purchasing on an ⟨Incoterm⟩ requiring the seller to insure (⟨CIP⟩ or ⟨CIF⟩) may purchase contingency insurance from his or her local insurer. Should there be a covered loss, the buyer's insurer would advance payment to the buyer, and assume the buyer's rights against the seller's insurer. Conversely, sellers can purchase contingency insurance from their

c

insurers for ‹export›s when buyers arrange the primary insurance cover. Should a buyer not pay because of failure of his or her insurer to honour a claim for a covered loss, the seller would claim on the contingency insurance. The contingency insurer would advance payment to the seller, and would bear the loss should the buyer's insurer never pay.

> **Contingency insurance does not replace primary insurance. It works only when the counterparty provides primary cover and the primary carrier fails to pay a covered loss.**

contract An agreement between parties to do or refrain from doing a specific act or acts.

contract carrier A non-common carrier that transports for compensation under individual contracts or agreements.

contract guarantee An agreement by a third party to be responsible for the performance of a contracting party. There are three major types of contract guarantee tender bonds, performance guarantees and repayment guarantees. See also ‹Uniform Rules for Contract Guarantees› and ‹Uniform Rules for Demand Guarantees›.

contract of carriage ‹carriage contract›

contracting parties ① Parties that have entered a contract with each other. ② Countries that are members of the General Agreement on Tariffs and Trade, or its successor, the ‹World Trade Organization›, and therefore have accepted the specified obligations and privileges.

Convention on Contracts for the International Sale of Goods ‹United Nations Convention on Contracts for the International Sale of Goods›

conversion A legal term for unauthorized assumption and exercise of rights of ownership over property belonging to another.

convertible currency (= hard currency). A currency of a nation that may be exchanged for that of another nation without restriction. Countries with hard currency typically have sizable exchange reserves so that their currency is generally considered to be low risk.

cookies Small files that are automatically downloaded from a web server and installed on the personal computer of someone browsing a website. Information stored in cookies can then be accessed any time that computer returns to the website. Cookies allow websites to "personalize" their appearance by identifying visitors, storing passwords, tracking preferences, and other possibilities. Users may control the downloading of cookies to their personal computers in the control section of their ‹browser›s.

COPANT ⟨Pan American Standards Commission⟩

C

copyright The exclusive right to make copies, license and otherwise exploit a literary, musical or artistic work.

> ⟨Trade Related Aspects of Intellectual Property⟩ and ⟨World Intellectual Property Organization⟩ for information on international copyright protection.

CORDIS ⟨Community Research and Development Information Service⟩

core labour standards Basic human rights agreed by the ⟨International Labour Organization⟩ to include freedom of association, the right to organize and bargain collectively, a prohibition on forced labour, a prohibition on discrimination in employment and a prohibition on exploitive child labour.

cornerboard A reinforcing piece designed to fit around the corner of a pallet to provide support for strapping and to prevent strapping damage to the contents.

Corp. (Corporation) ⟨limited liability⟩

Corporación Andina de Fomento (CAF) A multilateral financial institution, which supports the sustainable development of its shareholder countries.

> For more information, visit the CAF website at www.caf.com.

corporation (corp.) ⟨limited liability⟩

correspondent bank A bank-to-bank relationship between two banks that includes the exchange of signatures, test keys and settlement of funds agreement. This relationship is essential in the ⟨letter of credit⟩ process of advising, confirming and negotiating.

Cost and Freight (CFR)... named port of destination (Incoterms 2000) ⊞ An ⟨Incoterm⟩ designed for vessel transport where the seller arranges and pays for main carriage to the agreed port on the buyer's side, but ceases to be responsible for the condition of the goods once they cross the ship's rail at the port of embarkation.

Cost and Insurance (C&I) A loosely defined sales term whereby the seller provides the goods and the insurance cover, but the buyer is responsible for transportation.

> Since C&I is not an ⟨Incoterm⟩, it does not enjoy their worldwide acceptance. Parties using this term should be sure to clearly define their respective responsibilities elsewhere in the sales contract.

Cost, Insurance and Freight (CIF)... named port of destination

---

🛈 Insurance   🄻🄲 Letters of credit   🄻 Liner vessel shipping   🄢 Sales contracts   🄿 Vessel chartering

C

(Incoterms 2000) ⊞ An ⟨Incoterm⟩ designed for vessel transport where the seller arranges and pays for ⟨main carriage⟩ to the agreed port on the buyer's side, and provides at least minimum insurance cover, but ceases to be responsible for the condition of the goods once they cross the ship's rail at the port of embarkation.

Cost, Insurance, Freight & Commission (CIF&C) A loosely defined sales term whereby the seller provides the goods and arranges and pays for ⟨main carriage⟩ to the agreed port on the buyer's side, and provides at least minimum insurance cover, but ceases to be responsible for the condition of the goods once they cross the ship's rail at the port of embarkation. The price also includes any commissions payable.

> Since CIF&C is not an ⟨Incoterm⟩, it does not enjoy their worldwide acceptance. Parties using this term should be sure to clearly define their respective responsibilities elsewhere in the sales contract.

Council of Europe An intergovernmental organization of European countries that aims to protect human rights, pluralist democracy and the rule of law while promoting European cultural identity and diversity and seeking solutions to European societal problems.

> For more information, visit the Council of Europe website at www.coe.int.

counterparty The opposite party to a transaction. Sellers are the counterparties of buyers, and vice versa.

counterpurchase An arrangement whereby exporters agree to purchase a quantity of goods from a country in exchange for that country's purchase of the exporter's product. The goods being sold by each party are typically unrelated but may be of equivalent value. This is one of the most common forms of ⟨countertrade⟩.

countertrade An umbrella term for several kinds of trade in which the seller is required to accept goods, services, or other instruments of trade in partial or total payment for its products. Forms include barter, buy back, ⟨offset⟩ requirements, ⟨swap⟩, ⟨switch⟩ or ⟨triangular trade⟩, and/or evidence of bilateral clearing accounts.

> Some authorities include offsets as a form of countertrade; others make a distinction based on the view that countertrade is a reciprocal exchange of goods and services used to alleviate foreign exchange shortages on the part of importers, and that offsets are used as a means for advancing industrial development and may include equity investments.

countervailing duty (CVD) An extra charge that a country places on imported goods to counter the subsidies or bounties granted to the exporters of goods by their home governments. This duty is allowed by the Code on Subsidies and Countervailing Duties negotiated at the GATT Tokyo Round, if the importing country can prove that the subsidy would cause injury to domestic industry. See also ❬illustrative list❭, ❬subsidy❭ and ❬subsidies and countervailing measures, WTO Agreement❭.

country of destination The nation in which exported goods are to be used or consumed, as known to the shipper at the time of ❬export❭.

country of origin The nation in which referenced goods were grown, manufactured or produced (or for some origin criteria, substantially transformed).

country risk (= political or economic risk). The possibility of non-payment caused by such buyer-country related problems as political instability, war, arbitrary government action and exchange inconvertibility, as opposed to problems that could be encountered by the buyer such as insolvency or bankruptcy. See also ❬commercial risk❭.

cover note (= broker's cover note). An insurance document indicating coverage of a particular shipment under an open policy. This is distinguished, particularly regarding presentation under a documentary ❬letter of credit❭, from an ❬insurance policy❭ or ❬insurance certificate❭.

CPT ❬Carriage Paid to❭

crate A rigid slatted shipping container of wood or possibly plastic or metal.

> **To prevent introduction of non-native pests, some jurisdictions prohibit the importation of non-treated coniferous wood packing materials from certain originating countries.**

crawling peg system A procedure in which a currency exchange rate is altered frequently (multiple times a year) generally to adjust for rapid inflation. Between changes, the exchange rate for the currency remains fixed.

credit A promise of future payment in exchange for present delivery of ❬money❭, ❬goods❭ or ❬services❭.

credit application ① General: a request for the granting of credit. ② Banking: a request that a ❬letter of credit❭ be opened.

credit risk insurance Insurance designed to cover the risk of non-payment for delivered goods.

CSP ❬certification service providers❭

🖅 Insurance   🆔 Letters of credit   ⬇ Liner vessel shipping   🖅 Sales contracts   🅿 Vessel chartering

C

CT ⟨countertrade⟩

CTD ⟨combined transport document⟩

currency The circulating media of exchange in a country, including ⟨money⟩ and such financial instruments as ⟨cheques⟩.

currency adjustment charge (CAC = currency adjustment factor CAF) ⬇ An additional charge added to the base-rate ocean freight cost which is raised or lowered to reflect changes in the exchange rate of the currency in which the freight costs are billed. This charge is separate from the base rate because exchange rates fluctuate more often than freight costs do.

currency forward exchange contract/option ⟨forward exchange contract⟩ and ⟨forward exchange option⟩.

currency future ⟨future contract⟩

currency risk ⟨exchange risk⟩

customs That agency of a government charged with the primary responsibility for regulating imports.

customs area A geographic area, usually identical to one or several contiguous national political jurisdictions, applying a particular tariff schedule on goods entering or leaving the area.

customs broker An individual or company who represents the importer in ⟨customs clearance⟩ procedures. Customs brokers take on some degree of responsibility to their local authorities, and for this reason many countries require that they be licensed. A power of attorney authorizing the broker to act on behalf of the importer is another common requirement.

customs classification The particular category in a tariff nomenclature in which a product is classified for duty purposes (also, the procedure for determining it). Most major trading nations classify imported goods in conformity with the Harmonized Commodity Description and Coding System, also called the ⟨Harmonized System⟩.

customs clearance (= import clearance). The act of complying with the import regulations of an importing country. Generally, governments require some sort of import declaration (commonly called an entry). Depending on the country and the product, additional supporting documentation such as origin certificates, ⟨consular documentation⟩ and product-related health and safety certification may also be required. Payment or agreement to pay any applicable import duty and taxes often accompanies customs clearance.

Customs Cooperation Council (CCC) ⟨World Customs Organization⟩

C

customs duty A tax levied by a government on imported goods. The three most commonly used duties are ⟨ad valorem⟩ (percentage of value), ⟨specific⟩ (per imported unit) and ⟨compound⟩ (a combination of ad valorem and specific).

customs entry An import declaration made for the purpose of obtaining ⟨customs clearance⟩ by the importer or a ⟨customs broker⟩ authorized to represent the importer. Depending on the country and the product, additional supporting documentation such as origin certificates, ⟨consular documentation⟩ and product-related health and safety certification may also be required.

customs free zone ⟨free trade zone⟩

customs union An agreement between two or more countries to remove trade barriers with each other and to establish common tariff and non-tariff policies with respect to countries outside of the agreement. The ⟨European Union⟩ is the best-known example. The two primary trade effects of a customs union are: (1) Trade creation – the shift from consumption of purely domestic production towards the consumption of member country production. (2) Trade diversion – the shift from trade with non-member countries in favour of trade with member countries.

customs valuation The amount of money required to be shown on the ⟨customs⟩ entry according to the importing country's regulations. Since many products are assessed duty on an ⟨ad valorem⟩ basis, the correct customs value is necessary to determine the correct duty obligation. Countries have differing methods to determine customs valuation; for instance, some countries do not include the cost of transportation from the exporting countries, while others do. Some countries increase the value by the cost of so-called ⟨assist⟩s rendered by the importer to the foreign producer. Many countries have comparative formulas for testing customs values, such as the value of similar goods and/or estimates of the production cost, transportation costs and manufacturer/exporter profit. Accurate customs valuation is also important to determine whether the pricing of imported goods violates the importing country's ⟨anti-dumping⟩ regulations.

Customs Valuation Code, WTO Agreement A ⟨World Trade Organization⟩ agreement that is the successor to the Tokyo Round Customs Valuation Code, created to establish a uniform, fair and predictable international system for the valuation of goods for customs purposes and to preclude the arbitrary use of national valuation systems as non-tariff barriers to trade.

CD

cut-off date ⟨closing date⟩

CVD ⟨countervailing duty⟩

CWO ⟨cash with order⟩

CXT ⟨common external tariff⟩

CY ⟨container yard⟩

D/A ⟨documents against acceptance⟩

D/P ⟨documents against payment⟩

DAF ⟨Delivered at Frontier⟩

damage Injury or harm.

damage in transit Harm befalling goods between the shipment and arrival points.

> **⟨Carrier⟩s should perform at least superficial inspection when they accept goods for transport either from a shipper or another carrier. ⟨Consignee⟩s should do the same when receiving goods. Since any apparent damage is recorded on the transport document, a paper trail describing the condition of the goods is created.**

damages Estimated money equivalent for sustained injury or harm.

dangerous goods ⟨hazardous materials⟩

Dangerous Goods Declaration Shippers of dangerous goods are required to declare them to ⟨carrier⟩s per the ⟨International Air Transport Association⟩ and ⟨International Maritime Organization⟩ and any applicable additional local regulations. Also ⟨hazardous materials⟩.

DANIDA ⟨South Group, Danish Ministry of Foreign Affairs⟩

database A file or file system containing organized information and, most commonly, a filing and retrieval system for storing information. Most database software also includes tools for data analysis. Examples of database software include Oracle, Sybase, Microsoft Access, and Microsoft Sequel Server.

database search The process of using a search engine to search through a database to find information by a defined key, tag or keyword. A popular method to locate potential trading partners in e-marketplaces or on-line exchanges. See also ⟨search engine⟩.

data freight receipt (= data freight release) ⬇ An electronic (paperless) version of a ⟨sea waybill⟩. Instructions for the disposition of shipped cargo are electronically transmitted from the

D

〈carrier〉's office or agent on the seller's side to its counterpart on the buyer's side.

data protection directive (EU) Directive of the 〈European Union〉, enforcing the concept that data processing systems, including e-commerce, respect the fundamental right to privacy of individuals.

date of issuance 〈issue date〉

daylight exposure (= daylight credit = intraday credit). Credit extended for a period of less than one business day.

DDP 〈Delivered Duty Paid〉

DDU 〈Delivered Duty Unpaid〉

dead freight Compensation for cargo agreed to be shipped but unshipped (usually because it was unavailable for loading). In liner terms, dead freight can also mean compensation due to a ship line because the shipper failed to meet a pre-agreed quantity commitment under a service contract.

deceptive package A container designed to hold less than, or an entirely different product to what its appearance indicates. Deceptive packaging is illegal in many countries.

deck cargo Goods that are shipped on a ship's deck rather than in its hold. Generally, cargo shipped on-deck is at greater risk, which could be a major consideration for some types of goods. Further, the insurance premium payable for on-deck shipments may be greater than for those stowed below deck. 〈Carrier〉s clause their relevant marine transport documents for deck cargo in either of two ways a provision that the goods may be carried on-deck, or a statement that they were loaded on-deck. This is an important distinction for 〈letters of credit〉 that do not expressly permit on-deck shipment, as the first version does not in itself constitute an automatic discrepancy while the second version does.

declaration of dangerous goods 〈dangerous goods declaration〉

deductible A sum by which an insurance claim is reduced by prior agreement, often in return for a lower premium. Deductibles may be either a fixed amount or a percentage of the loss.

deferred payment L/C 〈LC〉 A 〈letter of credit〉 that is not payable at sight but at a future time.

DEG 〈German Financing Company for Investments in Developing Countries〉

del credere agent As relates to international commercial agency

---

🛩 Insurance   🔲 Letters of credit   ⬇ Liner vessel shipping   📝 Sales contracts   🅿 Vessel chartering

D

relationships a del credere agent is one who guarantees the ability to pay of prospective clients he or she has brought to the ⟨principal⟩. In return, the del credere agent is usually accorded a higher percentage of commission than that of a regular agent.

delay clause Wording found in many ⟨marine cargo insurance⟩ policies that loss caused solely by delay is not recoverable, even if caused by a covered peril.

Delivered at Frontier (DAF)... named place (Incoterms 2000) 🔠 An ⟨Incoterm⟩ used when the parties want delivery to occur at a land border. The seller arranges and pays all charges to get the goods to the named border point and is responsible for the condition of the goods until they arrive there. DAF is usually used for ground transport.

Delivered Duty Unpaid (DDU)... named place of destination (Incoterms 2000) 🔠 An ⟨Incoterm⟩ designed for omnimodal use, where the seller arranges and pays for all costs to the agreed place on the buyer's side, excluding import clearance, and remains responsible for the condition of the goods until they reach that place.

Delivered ex Quay (DEQ)... named port of destination (Incoterms 2000) 🔠 An ⟨Incoterm⟩ designed for vessel transport, where the seller arranges and pays for ⟨main carriage⟩ to the agreed port on the buyer's side, and remains responsible for the condition of the goods until they have been unloaded onto the wharf.

> **In Incoterms 2000, the responsibility for import clearance was changed from the seller to the buyer.**

Delivered ex Ship (DES)... named port of destination (Incoterms 2000) 🔠 An ⟨Incoterm⟩ designed for vessel transport, where the seller arranges and pays for ⟨main carriage⟩ to the agreed port on the buyer's side, but ceases to be responsible for the condition of the goods once the vessel arrives at port, i.e., before unloading.

delivery Transferring property or services from one party to another, such as from seller to buyer, shipper to ⟨carrier⟩, carrier to ⟨consignee⟩.

demand The quantity of a good or service that would be bought at a given price at a given time in a specific market.

demand guarantee A guarantee usually issued by a bank, under which the beneficiary is required only to make a demand in order to receive payment. In contrast to the conditional or surety guarantee, which requires the beneficiary to provide proof of the

D

⟨principal⟩'s default, a demand guarantee only requires that the beneficiary make a simple claim. Unless the guarantee requires a statement or a document substantiating the breach, the beneficiary will be entitled to claim payment without asserting, let alone providing proof, that the principal is in breach of his obligation. It is therefore relatively risky in terms of exposure to an unjustified demand on the beneficiary's part. Some protection against such an unfair demand can be obtained by making the guarantee subject to the current version of the ⟨Uniform Rules for Demand Guarantees⟩.

Demand guarantees issued by financial institutions are akin to standby ⟨letters of credit⟩.

demand schedule A chart of the quantities of a good or service that would be bought at all possible prices at a particular time in a specific market.

demise charter ⟨bareboat charter⟩

demurrage (= detention charge) 🅿 🅛 A charge for undue delay, either in loading /unloading or in detaining a piece of transportation equipment.

DEQ ⟨Delivered ex Quay⟩

derivatives Leveraged instruments that are linked to either specific financial instruments or indicators (such as foreign currencies, government bonds, share price indices or interest rates) or to particular commodities (such as gold, sugar, or coffee) that may be purchased or sold at a future date. Derivatives may also be linked to a future exchange of one asset for another, according to contractual agreement.

DES ⟨Delivered ex Ship⟩

desiccant Material that will absorb moisture, thereby protecting cargo from moisture damage. See also ⟨condensation⟩.

despatch money ⟨dispatch money⟩

detention charge ⟨demurrage⟩

devaluation The reduction of a currency's value in relation to other currencies. The exchange values of freely traded currencies are determined by market action. However, governments that interfere with market action can manipulate the value of their currency by fiat.

devanning (= stripping = unstuffing). Unloading, as in unloading a container or truck.

D

developed countries A term used to distinguish the more industrialized nations – including most ⟨OECD⟩ member countries – from developing or less-developed countries.

developing countries A broad range of countries that generally lack a high degree of industrialization, infrastructure and other capital investment, sophisticated technology, widespread literacy and advanced living standards among their populations as a whole.

Development Assistance Committee The OECD body that reviews and assesses resource transfers from ⟨developed countries⟩ to ⟨developing countries⟩. ⟨Organization for Economic Cooperation and Development⟩.

deviation clause ⟨✈⟩ An insurance term meaning that coverage will apply even if the vessel or voyage or interested parties are unintentionally stated incorrectly; or if actual transportation deviated from the intended routing, or was interrupted through no fault of the assured.

dew point ⟨condensation⟩

differential export tax A multi-tier ⟨export⟩ tax usually structured so that the tax on exports of a raw material exceeds the tax (if any) on exports of goods made from the raw material, thereby creating an incentive to process the raw material locally.

digital Involving or using numerical digits, as in computing. This word has become a commonly used prefix meaning related to computer use (such as "⟨digital cash⟩," "⟨digital signature⟩," etc).

digital cash (= digital money) ⟨@⟩ In order to turn the internet into a giant shopping centre, companies have developed software to provide complete and secure order fulfilment. Digital cash is either downloaded in "digital coins" from a participating bank to a user's computer, or an account is set up for payments through the bank. Once a purchase is made, either digital coins or permission to debit the bank account are transferred to the online merchant as payment.

digital receipt infrastructure (DRI) ⟨@⟩ A ⟨hierarchically assigned document⟩ that validates a communication occurring between two parties. It is a non-refutable communication between two parties who can verify the authenticity and authorization of each other, can ensure the integrity of the time and content of the communication, and can present this evidence to a third party should a dispute arise and recourse become necessary sometime in the future.

For more information, visit the DRI White Paper website at www.differential.com/dri_whitepaper.html or www.valicert.com

---

⟨see entry in dictionary⟩   ✈ Air transport   🏛 Bank collections   @ e-commerce   ⊞ Incoterms

D

digital signature (= authentication = ensure) @ A message encrypted by means of a private key, which is never shared, and a public key, which is shared with everyone. The result is a digital guarantee that a file has not been altered, as if it were carried in a digital envelope. See also ⟨general usage in international digitally ensured commerce⟩, ⟨open network systems⟩, and ⟨public key infrastructure⟩.

> **For more information, visit the GUIDEC website at www.iccwbo.org/home/guidec/guidec.asp**

dimensional weight (dimwt) A factor used in freight calculation comparing cargo size (volume) to weight.

> **The commonly used factors can be found in ✈ and ⤓**

direct investment Defined by the ⟨International Monetary Fund⟩ as "investment that is made to acquire a lasting interest in an enterprise operating in an economy other than that of the investor, the investor's purpose being to have an effective voice in the management of the enterprise."

direct tax A tax that is levied on wealth or income.

Direction des Relations Economiques Extérieures (DREE) The main French Government policymaking agency for ⟨export⟩ promotion and credit activities.

> **For more information, visit the French Ministry of the Economy, Finance and Industry website at www.commerce-exterieur.gouv.fr.**

dirty float (managed float). A system in which exchange rates are partially determined by government intervention or restriction to limit appreciation or depreciation.

discount ① A deduction from an amount due given in consideration of such circumstances as prompt or early payment or an order of unusually large quantity. ② Selling a receivable or accepted draft at a price below face amount for net present value.

discrepancy LC Failure to comply with a letter of credit requirement.

discrimination (trade). Inequality of treatment accorded imports from different countries, such as preferential tariff rates for imports from particular countries or trade restrictions targeted against particular countries.

discussion room (chat room). A program run within a website that allows users to post text messages, in sequence, with other users within the chat room. Chat room discussions are conducted "live", in real time, and are rarely saved for historic review by users. See also ⟨bulletin board system⟩.

✈ Insurance   LC Letters of credit   ⤓ Liner vessel shipping   ◁ Sales contracts   ⼂ Vessel chartering

D

dishonour The failure to comply with an obligation, such as failure to pay or accept a ‹draft› when due.

dispatch money (despatch money) 🅿 An incentive payment offered by a shipowner to a ‹charterer› in exchange for completing loading or unloading in less time than is specified in the ‹charterparty›.

Dispute Settlement, WTO Understanding on Rules and Procedures (DSU) A ‹World Trade Organization› agreement that provides a mechanism for settling disputes. The DSU sets forth actions WTO members may take in response to nullification or impairment of their rights under any of the WTO agreements.

distribution A method of supply through wholesalers (called distributors), who purchase quantities of product for their own account for local resale.

distributor An independent person or legal entity which sells goods locally on behalf of a ‹principal›. Distributors can be distinguished from sales agents or representatives because they buy the goods for their own account, then re-sell them at prices which they have some liberty to set. Distributorship is frequently based on a contract that grants the distributor exclusivity for a specific territory. By buying for their own account, distributors reduce the degree of account maintenance on the part of the principal. Further, as distributors normally import in quantity and maintain a local inventory rather than importing against specific orders, their activities tend to minimize freight and handling costs.

> **Prudent principals acquaint themselves with the applicable law of the distributor's country before assigning exclusivity. In some markets (such as the ‹European Union›), exclusive territories must be carefully structured to avoid breaking local law.**

dock A place where cargo is loaded/unloaded, often used as a synonym for wharf or pier. (A "loading dock" is the part of a shipping facility where trucks are loaded.)

dock receipt ⚓ A document indicating that a given shipment has arrived at a ship line terminal or elsewhere at a port on a particular date. This ‹receipt› transfers accountability from the delivering domestic ‹carrier› to the vessel owner. Since the ‹checker› at the port will note any apparent damage or shortage on the document itself, a clean dock receipt evidences good receipt. Dock receipts are normally prepared by ‹forwarder›s or ‹shipper›s, and are either faxed to the ship line's terminal or given to the delivering carrier to accompany the shipment.

documentary collection 🏛 A set of documents sent to a bank for

---

‹see entry in dictionary› ✈ Air transport 🏛 Bank collections @ e-commerce 🔲 Incoterms

D

handling in accordance with instructions provided in an enclosed letter or form.

documentary letter of credit 🔲 A ⟨letter of credit⟩ requiring presentation of supporting documents to evidence compliance with its conditions.

documents Paper instruments (or electronic message units) that prove certain events have taken place. For convenience, the documents commonly used in foreign trade may be grouped by function into five categories

- **commercial** the invoice and ⟨packing list⟩.
- **transport** ⟨air waybill⟩, ⟨dock receipt⟩, ⟨mate's receipt⟩, ⟨forwarder's receipt⟩, ⟨marine (ocean) B/L⟩, ⟨rail waybill⟩, ⟨sea waybill⟩, ⟨shipper's letter of instructions⟩ to ⟨forwarder⟩ or ⟨carrier⟩, ⟨truck⟩ (lorry) ⟨bill of lading⟩ (or waybill).
- **legal** Those documents that satisfy a governmental requirement, such as ⟨certificates of origin⟩, ⟨clean reports of findings⟩, ⟨consularized documents⟩, ⟨export declarations⟩, import entries, ⟨hazardous materials⟩ certifications and quota visas.
- **insurance** proof of insurance.
- **payment** ⟨collection letter⟩ of instructions, ⟨draft⟩ (although technically a draft is a financial instrument) ⟨letters of credit⟩.

documents against acceptance (D/A) 🏛 Collection terms of payment that require the ⟨drawee⟩ to accept a ⟨draft⟩ or drafts drawn for future maturity at the ⟨presenting bank⟩ prior to receiving the accompanying documents. Typically, such collections include a document that restricts possession or ownership, thereby forcing the drawee to accept the draft in order to obtain the relevant goods. The presenting bank then conveys the acceptance and maturity date(s) to the drawer through its bank, and presents the draft(s) for payment when due. There are two kinds of time drafts: those payable at a predetermined time from the day shown on the face of the draft (date drafts), and those payable at a predetermined time from the date the draft was accepted (time-sight drafts). As the date shown on drafts normally corresponds to the date of the transport document, date drafts extend time from shipment. Time-sight drafts, however, are normally accepted once the goods have arrived and thereby extend time from arrival. The net difference, therefore, is which party finances the goods during transit.

> The question of ⟨protest⟩ should be addressed when considering these payment terms.

documents against payment (D/P or **SD/DP)** 🏛 Collection terms of payment that require the ⟨drawee⟩ to pay a ⟨draft⟩ prior to

D

receiving the accompanying documents. Typically, such collections include a document that restricts possession or ownership, thereby forcing the drawee to honour the draft in order to obtain the relevant goods. While it is possible to protest for non-payment of sight drafts, the benefit is questionable, as the drawee will not have received the contract goods.

domain name A designation, using characters of a written language, for particular location on the internet. A domain name is the web address (URL, or "Uniform Resource Locator") that is used to find a website, e.g. www.YourCompany.com. Domain names work alongside IP addresses.

They are recorded by an official registrar, and a list of registrars is available from www.icann.org/registrars/accredited-list.html.

domicile ① A place of permanent residence. ② A place where a ⟨draft⟩ is made payable.

door-to-airport ✈ A ⟨contract of carriage⟩ whereby a single ⟨carrier⟩ undertakes transportation responsibility from the point where the shipment originates (usually the seller's door) to a designated airport on the buyer's side. Unless the seller is physically located at an airport, door-to-airport transportation includes pre-carriage and main carriage, but does not include on-carriage.

door-to-door ✈ ⚓ A ⟨contract of carriage⟩ whereby a single ⟨carrier⟩ undertakes transportation responsibility from the point where the shipment originates (usually the seller's door) to the point where final delivery takes place (usually the buyer's door). Unless one of the parties is physically located at a port or an airport, door-to-door transportation includes pre-carriage, main carriage and on-carriage.

door-to-port ⚓ A ⟨contract of carriage⟩ whereby a single ⟨carrier⟩ undertakes transportation responsibility from the point where the shipment originates (usually the seller's door) to a designated port on the buyer's side. Unless the seller is physically located at a port, door-to-port transportation includes pre-carriage and main carriage, but does not include on-carriage.

double column tariff A tariff schedule listing two duty rates for some or all commodities. Under such arrangements, imports may be taxed at a higher or lower rate, depending on the importing country's trade relationships with the exporting country.

downstream dumping A situation where producers sell at below cost to another producer in the same country, who further processes and exports the products to another country. See also ⟨dumping⟩.

draft 🏛 A financial instrument indicating debt of one party (the ⟨drawee⟩) to another (the ⟨drawer⟩). Drafts may be drawn ⟨at "sight"⟩ for immediate payment, at X time "date" for payment X days from the date shown on the face of the draft itself, or at X "time sight" for payment X days from the date the draft is accepted. Drafts are normally handled in two ways either as required by ⟨letters of credit⟩, or for presentation with ⟨collections⟩ In the latter case, they are sent with instructions to a bank in the drawee's country for presentation. The ⟨presenting bank⟩ reports their disposition to the party that sent the collection (usually the drawer's bank). Drafts accepted by parties other than banks are called trade acceptances. Drafts accepted by banks are called banker's acceptances, and enjoy preferred status in many financial markets.

drawback The refund by a government, in whole or in part, of customs duties assessed on imported goods that are subsequently exported. Drawback may also often be claimed for duty paid on the imported material content of domestically produced goods that are exported. Drawback regulations and procedures vary among countries.

drawee 🏛 The party upon whom a ⟨draft⟩ is drawn, that is, the party responsible for payment.

drawer 🏛 The party who draws a ⟨draft⟩, normally the party to whom payment is due.

drawing A term used to describe the payment of a ⟨letter of credit⟩ based on a presentation of documents that comply with the terms and conditions of the letter of credit.

drayage ⟨cartage⟩

DREE ⟨Direction des Relations Economiques Extérieures⟩

DRI ⟨digital receipt infrastructure⟩

drop test A testing method for packaging by dropping a packed item of a known weight from a known height to determine its durability. **Drop testing is particularly important in the classification of packing for hazardous materials shipment.**

drum A cylindrical shipping container.

dry charter Rental of an aircraft without fuel and typically without crew or supporting equipment or staff.

DSU ⟨Dispute Settlement, WTO Understanding on Rules and Procedures⟩

⚓ Insurance 🆘 Letters of credit ⚓ Liner vessel shipping 📝 Sales contracts 🅿 Vessel chartering

D

dual pricing Selling identical products at different prices in different markets.

dumping The sale of a commodity in a foreign country at less than fair value. Dumping is generally recognized as unfair because the practice can disrupt markets and injure producers of competitive products in an importing country. With price-to-price dumping, the foreign supplier can use its sales in the high-priced market (which is usually its home market) to subsidize its sales in the low-priced ‹export› market. The price difference is often due to government protection in the high-priced market. Price-cost dumping often indicates that the foreign supplier has a special advantage, as sustained sales below cost are normally possible only through subsidies.

dunnage Materials used to prevent cargo shifting or sweating, or to divide it into separate lots.

DUNS number An international numbering system provided by Dun & Bradstreet for identifying companies.

dutiable An imported item that is subject to ‹customs duty›.

duty ‹customs duty›

duty free An imported item that is not subject to customs duty. There are several reasons for this (1) A country could unilaterally exempt a particular class of product from duty. (2) A product originating in a participating country could be covered by a bilateral or multinational free trade agreement. (3) A product is being imported into a ‹bonded warehouse› or ‹free trade zone›, and remains conditionally duty-free until it is brought into the commerce of the importing country. (4) A product falls within the importing country's limits of purchases imported as accompanied baggage. (5) A product falls within the importing country's limits on the value of gifts or samples or unaccompanied baggage. (6) The product is purchased by or for the government of the importing country itself, or by an accredited diplomatic office of a foreign country located within the importing country.

duty free zone ‹free trade zone›

duty paid A price that includes the cost of ‹import› clearance. See the ‹Delivered Duty Paid Incoterm›.

> Sellers should be sure that they know the ‹import› regulations of the destination country, and that they know the cost of compliance before quoting duty-paid pricing. Further, sellers and buyers should agree on payment of such non-duty costs as value added taxes, since these are often collected at the point of importation.

‹see entry in dictionary›   ✈ Air transport   🏛 Bank collections   © e-commerce   ⊞ Incoterms

DE

duty suspension A unilateral non-application of a customs duty, or its application at a reduced level, usually on a temporary basis.

e-commerce ⟨electronic commerce⟩

e-mail ⟨electronic mail⟩

e-mail address ⟨electronic mail address⟩

e-marketplace ⟨electronic marketplace⟩

e-store ⟨electronic store⟩

eUCP ⟨Uniform Customs and Practice for Documentary Credits – Supplement for Electronic Presentation⟩

E&OE ⟨errors and omissions excepted⟩

East African Development Bank (EADB) Founded in 1967 and headquartered in Kampala, Uganda, the EABD was created to promote economic development among Kenya, Tanzania and Uganda.
> For more information, visit the EADB website at
> www.transafrica.org/eadb/main.htm

Eastern Caribbean Central Bank (ECCB) Established in 1983 and headquartered in Basseterre, St Kitts, the ECCB promotes economic development, monetary stability and credit and exchange among its eight member nations.

EBRD ⟨European Bank for Reconstruction and Development⟩

EbXML ⟨electronic business extensible markup language⟩

EC European Community ⟨European Union⟩

ECA ⟨United Nations Economic Commission for Africa⟩

ECB ⟨European Central Bank⟩

ECCB ⟨Eastern Caribbean Central Bank⟩

ECDC ⟨Economic Cooperation among Developing Countries⟩

ECGF ⟨Export Credit Guarantee Fund⟩

ECLAC ⟨United Nations Economic Commission for Latin America and the Caribbean⟩

eco-label A voluntary mark awarded by the ⟨European Union⟩ to producers who can show that their product is significantly less harmful to the environment than similar products.

Economic Cooperation among Developing Countries (ECDC) Attempts by developing countries, especially the ⟨Group of 77⟩, to

E

increase South-South trade and other economic relationships among themselves. See also ⟨Global System of Trade Preferences⟩.

Economic Community of Central African States (CEEAC) The CEEAC was created in 1985 by the Central African Customs and Economic Union to promote regional economic cooperation, eliminate trade restrictions, and establish a ⟨Central African Common Market⟩ headquartered in Libreville, Gabon.

> **For more information, visit the appropriate ⟨United Nations⟩ webpage at www.un.org/Depts/dpko/training/region3.htm.**

Economic Community of the Great Lakes Countries (CEPGL) The CEPGL was created in 1976 to promote regional economic cooperation and integration.

> **Their address is PO Box 58, Gisenyi, Rwanda, phone (250) 40228.**

Economic Community of West African States (ECOWAS) Established in 1976 with goals of establishing a customs union and promoting social and cultural fellowship, ECOWAS is headquartered in Abuja, Nigeria.

> **For more information, visit the ECOWAS website at www.ecowas.int.**

economic development The process of growth in total and per capita income, especially in developing countries, more industrial activity, improved agricultural practices, rising literacy, broadened employment opportunities and diminishing reliance on official development assistance.

economic interest grouping (= groupement d'intérêt economique = GIE). A joint venture that has the features of both a partnership and a corporation. See also ⟨limited liability⟩.

economic risk ⟨country risk⟩

economic sanctions Economic penalties used by governments for foreign policy purposes; such as prohibiting trade, stopping financial transactions, or barring economic and military assistance.

ECOSOC ⟨United Nations Economic and Social Council⟩

ECOWAS ⟨Economic Community of West African States⟩

ECTA ⟨European Competitive Telecommunications Association⟩

EDF ⟨European Development Fund⟩

EDI ⟨electronic data interchange⟩

E

EDIFACT ⟨electronic data for administration, commerce and transportation⟩

EEA ⟨European Economic Area⟩

EEZ ⟨exclusive economic zone⟩

EFT ⟨electronic funds transfer⟩

EFTA ⟨European Free Trade Association⟩

EIB ⟨European Investment Bank⟩

EICTA ⟨European Information and Communications Technology Industry Association⟩

EISA ⟨European Information Technology Services Association⟩

EITO ⟨European Information Technology Observatory⟩

electronic business extensible markup language (ebXML) A modular suite of specifications for standardizing XML globally in order to facilitate trade between organizations, regardless of size. The specification gives businesses a standard method to exchange XML-based business messages, conduct trading relationships, communicate data in common terms and define and register business processes.

electronic commerce (e-commerce) @ Any activity that utilizes some form of electronic communication in the inventory, exchange, advertisement and distribution of and the payment for ⟨goods⟩ and ⟨services⟩. The term includes internet marketing, buyer/seller matching, ⟨banner advertising⟩, electronic trade leads, virtual trade shows, etc.

electronic data interchange (EDI) @ The electronic communication of business transactions such as orders, confirmations and invoices between organizations. This is done on a closed-system basis.

> **For more information, visit the GUIDEC website at www.iccwbo.org/home/guidec/guidec.asp.**

Electronic Data Interchange for Administration, Commerce and Transportation (EDIFACT) @ An international syntax used in the interchange of electronic data.

electronic funds transfer (EFT) @ The electronic exchange between computer applications of commercial entities (in some cases also public administrations), in a standard format, of data relating to a number of message categories, such as orders, invoices, customs documents, remittance advices and payments. EDI messages are sent through public-data transmission networks or banking system

---

🛪 Insurance   🆔 Letters of credit   ⚓ Liner vessel shipping   🖊 Sales contracts   🅿 Vessel chartering

E

channels. Any movement of funds initiated by ⟨EDI⟩ is reflected in payment instructions flowing through the banking system.

electronic mail (e-mail) @ Internet communications among parties that have electronic mail addresses, normally registered with ⟨Internet service providers⟩. E-mail may consist of text only, or ⟨HTML⟩, allowing images to be imbedded within the text.

electronic mail (e-mail) address @ The routing directions on how to access an ⟨e-mail⟩ subscriber. The individual party account precedes the @ character, while the service provider is identified after the @ character. For example, in the e-mail address fjr424@aol.com, fjr424 is an individual account identifier while aol.com is the internet service provider America On Line.

electronic mail (e-mail) attachments Files attached to ⟨e-mail⟩ communications which may be downloaded, opened and saved by recipients. Popular attachment files are Word, Excel, PowerPoint, and ⟨Portable Document Format (PDF)⟩.

electronic marketplace (e-marketplace) A presence hosted by an entity on the internet, accessed by potential buyers and sellers via their web browsers, where ⟨e-commerce⟩ is conducted. Also referred to as "online exchanges" and "vertical business portals". ⟨B2B⟩ e-marketplaces are typically categorized by industry, and offer potential traders online ⟨catalogs⟩, advertising, and match-making services, as well industry news and information.

electronic store (e-store) A website containing ⟨e-commerce⟩ software, available on a public network, such as the internet, which offers ⟨goods⟩ and ⟨services⟩ for sale. An online storefront is the equivalent of a store or place of business that a customer would visit to purchase goods and services. E-stores often contain credit-card processing modules for online payments of merchandise.

electronic trade transaction (URGETS) URGETS, the ⟨ICC⟩ Uniform Rules and Guidelines for Electronic Trade and Settlement, covers only ⟨Business to Business (B2B)⟩ transactions. It is not for ⟨Business to Consumers (B2C)⟩ transactions or for personal, family or household purposes. URGETS is also supported by other ICC products such as the International Model Sales Contract, e-Terms and ⟨GUIDEC⟩ (General Usage for International Digitally Ensured Commerce).

electronic trading opportunity (ETO) Offers to buy and sell, entered through the ⟨United Nation⟩'s World Trade Point Federation program, the Global Trade Point Network. These offers may be entered at no charge into the ETO system, which then e-mails the opportunities to over 10 000 recipients on a daily basis.

E

See also ⟨trade leads⟩.

embargo ① In international trade, a government action limiting or prohibiting imports and/or exports of ⟨goods⟩ and/or ⟨services⟩ from or to a country. Embargoes may also be applied only against trade in certain products, regardless of origin, such as the ban on trade in ivory. ② An order suspending the acceptance or routing of cargo at certain points because of emergency, strike, etc.

EMC ⟨export management company⟩

enabling clause The Decision on Differential and More Favorable Treatment, Reciprocity, and Fuller Participation of Developing Countries made at the GATT Tokyo Round permits developed ⟨WTO⟩ members to extend preferences to ⟨developing countries⟩ without violating ⟨most-favoured-nation⟩ treatment agreements.

encryption The basis of network security. Encryption encodes network packets to prevent anyone except the intended recipient from accessing the data. The term for altering data or text into meaningless code for transmission. Only someone with the correct decoding information or key can read and use it.

endorsee The party in whose favour a document and/or the rights contained therein is transferred by the signature of the ⟨endorser⟩.

endorsement Transfer of a document and/or the rights contained therein by signature of the transferring party. See also ⟨endorser⟩.

endorser The party executing transfer of a document and/or the rights contained therein by affixing his or her signature.

English terms ① An insurance term used to distinguish conditions of English policies from those of other countries. ② An exchange rate showing the number of currency units per pound sterling.

enhanced structural adjustment facility (ESAF) A system by which the ⟨International Monetary Fund⟩ lends concessional resources to assist poor countries.

ensure (as used in open network communications). See also ⟨digital signature⟩

entrepot An intermediary storage facility where ⟨goods⟩ are kept temporarily for distribution within a country or for re-export.

entrepreneur a person who assumes responsibility for a commercial activity, such as a business firm.

Insurance   Letters of credit   Liner vessel shipping   Sales contracts   Vessel chartering

E

EOTC ‹European Organization for Testing and Certification›

EPC ‹European Patent Convention›

equilibrium A state in which economic forces that are likely to change in opposing directions are in perfect balance, making change unlikely.

equity ① Fairness, justice. ② The value of property beyond the total amount owed on it.

errors and omissions excepted (E&OE) Indicates a disclaimer of responsibility for spelling, typographical or clerical errors, when appended to a signature on a shipping document.

ESA ‹European Space Agency›

ESAF ‹Enhanced Structural Adjustment Facility›

ESC ‹European Shippers' Council›

ESCAP ‹United Nations Economic and Social Commission for Asia and the Pacific›

escape clause ‹safeguard measures›

ESCB ‹European System of Central Banks›

escrow account In countries with exchange controls, a special bank account in which earnings from sales (i.e., ‹convertible currency› proceeds from exports) are accumulated. These revenues are set aside for subsequent acquisition of ‹goods› and ‹services› from foreign suppliers.

ESCWA ‹United Nations Economic and Social Council for Western Asia›

ESI ‹European Software Institute›

estimated time of arrival (ETA) ✈ 🏛 ⬇ The anticipated date or time that a ‹carrier› will arrive at destination.

estimated time of departure (ETD) ✈ 🏛 ⬇ The anticipated date or time that a ‹carrier› will leave the port or airport of loading.

ETA ‹estimated time of arrival›

ETC ‹export trading company›

ETD ‹estimated time of departure›

ETNO ‹European Public Telecommunications Network Operators Association›

ETO ‹electronic trading opportunity›

ETSI ⟨European Telecommunications Standards Institute⟩

ETUC ⟨European Trade Union Confederation⟩

EU ⟨European Union⟩

EURATOM ⟨European Atomic Energy Community⟩

EUREKA ⟨European Research Coordination Agency⟩

EURL (sole ownership limited liability company). ⟨limited liability⟩

euro The common currency of those ⟨European Union⟩ countries that have elected to participate in the third stage of economic and monetary union. The euro was launched on 1 January 1999, with eleven participating countries converting their national currencies at irrevocably fixed conversion rates.

EUR-LEX @ A single internet entry portal to ⟨European Union⟩ legal texts. EUR-LEX is a first step in bringing together the whole body of EU texts for online consultation in a streamlined environment.
For more information, visit the EUR-LEX website at http//europa.eu.int/eur-lex

euro zone The geographic area of the participating countries in the ⟨euro⟩.

European article numbering system (EAN) ⟨bar coding⟩

European Atomic Energy Community (EURATOM) The ⟨European Union⟩ agency in charge of nuclear resources coordinates the research and development programmes of member states, while regulating the free flow of nuclear raw materials, equipment, investment capital and specialists within the community. It has wide authority over contracts, raw materials and standards to protect workers and the general population against the dangers of radiation.

European Bank for Reconstruction and Development (EBRD) Founded in 1991 and headquartered in London, England, EBRD provides assistance through direct loans, of which at least 60 per cent must contribute to the privatization of state-owned enterprises.
For more information, visit the EBRD website at www.ebrd.com.

European Central Bank (ECB) The common central bank, located in Frankfurt, Germany, of the ⟨European Union⟩ countries that use the common single currency, the ⟨euro⟩. The ECB in combination with the national central banks of the ⟨euro zone⟩ countries form the ⟨European System of Central Banks (ESCB)⟩.

European Committee for Electrotechnical Standardization ⟨Comité Européen de Normalisation Electrotechnique⟩

E

European Committee for Standardization ⟨Comité Européen de Normalisation⟩

European Community ⟨European Union⟩

European Competitive Telecommunications Association (ECTA) An industry association of new entrant European telecommunications network operators.

> For more information, visit the ETNO website at www.ectaportal.com.

European Consumers' Organization (BEUC) The federation of independent national consumer organizations from all ⟨EU⟩ member states and other European countries.

> For more information, visit the BEUC website at www.beuc.org.

European Development Fund (EDF) Established in 1958, the EDF is the principal means by which the ⟨European Union⟩ provides aid, concessionary finance and technical assistance to ⟨developing countries⟩.

European Economic Area (EEA) A "single market" agreement consisting of the ⟨European Union⟩ and three of the four ⟨European Free Trade Association⟩ member countries (Iceland, Liechtenstein and Norway).

> For details, visit the European Free Trade Association website www.efta.int and the European Union website www.europa.eu.int

European Free Trade Association (EFTA) An international organization comprising four states: Iceland, Liechtenstein, Norway and Switzerland. EFTA's activities can be divided into three main areas:

- monitoring and managing relationships among the EFTA member states
- developing third-country relations with non-⟨European Union⟩ countries
- maintaining the relationship of three of the four EFTA member countries (Iceland, Liechtenstein and Norway) with the European Union in the European Economic Area.

> For more information, visit the EFTA website www.efta.int.

European Information and Communications Technology Industry Association (EICTA) An association bringing together 22 national information and communications technology industry associations from 16 European countries and 31 large information and communications technology corporations with major operations in Europe.

> For more information, visit the EICTA website at www.eicta.org.

E

European Information Technology Observatory (EITO) A European organization providing an extensive overview of the European market for information and communication technology, and services to this industry, users and public authorities.

For more information, visit the EITO website at www.eito.com.

European Information Technology Services Association (EISA) A group of software products and associated service supplier trade associations from 16 European countries.

For more information, visit the EISA website at www.eisaweb.org.

European Institute A Washington DC-based policy organization devoted to transatlantic affairs, providing an independent forum for US and European interests.

European Investment Bank (EIB) Established in 1957 and headquartered in Luxembourg, the EIB is an independent public institution providing loans and guarantees to EU companies and public institutions to finance regional and structural development.

For more information, visit the EIB website at www.eib.org.

European Organization Conformity Assessment (EOTC) Established in 1990 and headquartered in Brussels, Belgium, the EOTC promotes mutual recognition of tests, test and certification procedures and quality systems within the European private sector for product areas not covered by EU legislative requirements.

For more information, visit the EOTC website at www.eotc.be.

European Patent Convention (EPC) Created in 1977, the EPC established a single European patent which, once granted by the European Patent Office (EPO), matures into a bundle of individual patents – one in each member country designated by the patent applicant.

For more information, visit the EPC website at www.epo.co.at/legal/epc.

European Public Telecommunications Network Operators' Association (ETNO) An industry association of established European telecommunications network operators.

For more information, visit the ETNO website at www.etno.belbone.be.

European Research Coordination Agency (EUREKA) Created in 1985 and headquartered in Brussels, Belgium, EUREKA coordinates advanced technology being carried out by European industry.

For more information, visit the EUREKA website at www3.eureka.be/home.

Insurance   Letters of credit   Liner vessel shipping   Sales contracts   Vessel chartering

E

European Shippers' Council (ESC) An organization representing companies that ship ‹goods› into, from, and within Europe, as well as a number of European commodity trade associations.

For more information, visit the ESC website at
www.europeanshippers.com.

European Software Institute (ESI) An association of European software producers for software process improvement, based in Zamudio, Spain.

For more information, visit the ESI website at www.esi.es.

European Space Agency (ESA) designs and coordinates construction of satellite systems among member European countries.

For more information, visit the ESA website at www.esa.int.

European System of Central Banks (ESCB) The term used for the organization composed of the ‹European Central Bank (ECB)› and the National Central Banks (NCBs) of all ‹European Union› member states.

For more information, visit the ECB website at www.ecb.int.

European Telecommunications Standards Institute (ETSI) A non-profit organization for telecommunications standards, providing a forum for over 700 members from 50 countries, including governments, network operators, manufacturers, service providers and users.

For more information, visit the ETSI website at www.etsi.org.

European Trade Union Confederation (ETUC) Established in 1973 and headquartered in Brussels, Belgium, the ETUC is the primary organization that speaks for European trade unions.

For more information, visit the ETUC website at www.etuc.org.

European Union (EU) A customs union comprised of fifteen states. Austria, Belgium, Denmark, Finland, France, Germany, Greece, Ireland, Italy, Luxembourg, Netherlands, Portugal, Spain, Sweden and the United Kingdom. The EU maintains a common external ‹tariff›, a growing number of common standards and certification criteria (‹Conformité Européene›), and has eliminated customs borders among the member states.

For further information, visit the EU website at www.europa.eu.int.

European Virtual Private Network Users' Association (EVUA) An association of over 70 multinational companies for the purpose of encouraging the creation of cost effective virtual private network services for its members and to act as a management forum for service quality.

For more information visit the EVUA website at www.evua.org.uk.

E

Eurosystem The term used to refer to the European Central Bank (ECB) and the National Central Banks (NCBs) of the member states that have adopted the ⟨euro⟩. The NCBs of member states that do not participate in the euro area, however, are members of the ESCB with a special status – while they are allowed to conduct their respective national monetary policies, they do not take part in the decision-making with regard to the single monetary policy for the euro area nor in the implementation of such decisions. The primary objective of the Eurosystem is to maintain price stability. Without prejudice to this objective, it supports the general economic policies in the Community and acts in accordance with the principles of an open-market economy. The basic tasks to be carried out by the Eurosystem are:

- to define and implement the monetary policy of the euro area;
- to conduct foreign exchange operations;
- to hold and manage the official foreign reserves of the member states; and
- to promote the smooth operation of payment systems.

In addition, the Eurosystem contributes to the smooth conduct of policies pursued by the competent authorities relating to the prudent supervision of credit institutions and the stability of the financial system.

For more information, visit the ECB website at www.ecb.int/about/escb.htm.

evergreen 🅛🅒 A ⟨letter of credit⟩ that automatically renews itself beyond its stated expiration.

EVUA ⟨European Virtual Private Network Users' Association⟩

EX (from) ⊞ When used in pricing such as ⟨Ex Works⟩, it signifies that the price quoted applies only at the point where shipment originates.

Ex Factory, Ex Mill (Ex Works, Ex Warehouse) ⟨Ex Works⟩

Ex Quay (EXQ) A pre-1990 ⟨Incoterm⟩ that has been replaced by ⟨Delivered Ex Quay (DEQ)⟩.

Ex Ship (EXS) A pre-1990 ⟨Incoterm⟩ that has been replaced by ⟨Delivered Ex Ship (DES)⟩.

Ex Works (EXW) ... named place (Incoterms 2000) ⊞ An ⟨Incoterm⟩ whereby the seller is responsible only for having the ordered ⟨goods⟩ available for pickup at the agreed place, which is usually the seller's own premises. The seller is also usually responsible for export packing to the extent that the transportation particulars are made available. EXW represents the minimum seller responsibility under Incoterms.

🗗 Insurance 🅛🅒 Letters of credit ⬇ Liner vessel shipping ◪ Sales contracts ⊟ Vessel chartering

E

> **Under the EXW Incoterm, the buyer is responsible for loading the collecting vehicle and export clearance – tasks that may be difficult for a foreign buyer to accomplish.**

EXCEL ⟨export credit enhanced leverage⟩

excess value An increase in liability provided by a ⟨carrier⟩, usually in return for an additional fee.

exchange control A government policy of regulating access to foreign currency. Typically, countries resort to exchange control because of chronic shortages of foreign currency, particularly so-called "hard" (freely convertible) currency. There are several ways governments implement exchange control. ⟨Import licensing⟩ limits the kind and quantity of products that may be legally imported. A second and often concurrent practice is to restrict foreign currency transactions to the government central bank or selected banks under government supervision.

exchange permit A permit required by governments using exchange control regulations to enable an importing firm to convert its national currency into foreign currency to pay for authorized imports.

exchange rate The price of one currency in terms of another, i.e., the number of units of one currency that may be exchanged for one unit of another. Influences on exchange rates include differences between interest rates and other asset yields between countries, investor expectations about future changes in a currency's value, ⟨arbitrage⟩ and central bank exchange rate support.

exchange risk The possibility of receiving less or paying more because a receivable or a payable is denominated in a foreign currency.

> **Countries with shortages of ⟨convertible (hard) currency⟩ reserves often resort to ⟨exchange controls⟩. Under these conditions, delays in payments often occur even after buyers have paid, while the central bank allocates the corresponding foreign exchange.**

excise A selective tax levied on certain ⟨goods⟩ produced within or imported into a country. See also ⟨indirect tax⟩.

exclusive economic zone (EEZ) The EEZ refers to the right of coastal nations to control the living and non-living resources of the sea for 200 nautical miles off their coasts while allowing freedom of navigation to other states beyond 12 nautical miles. It also gives the coastal nations the responsibility of managing the conservation of all natural resources within the 200-nautical mile limit.

E

EXIMBANK ‹Export-Import Bank of the United States›

expiry date [LC] The date at which the commitment of a ‹letter of credit›'s ‹opening› and ‹confirming bank› (if any) ends.

export The sale and/or movement of ‹goods› or ‹services› from one nation to another.

export broker An individual or company that brings together buyers and sellers located in different countries for a fee without taking part in actual sales transactions.

export clearance The act of complying with the ‹export› regulations of an exporting country.

export commission house ‹confirming house›

export controls Measures taken by a government to regulate ‹export›s. See also ‹export declaration›, ‹export licence›.

export credit guarantee facility (ECGF) A plan developed in the ‹United Nations› Conference on Trade and Development that would enable developing country exporters to refinance their ‹export› credits extended to importers in other countries under an international guarantee.

Export Credit Enhanced Leverage (EXCEL) Developed in 1990 by the ‹World Bank› and the International Union of Credit and Investment Insurers, the EXCEL provides ‹export› credits at consensus rates for private-sector borrowers in highly indebted countries which otherwise would have been too great a risk for insurers to cover.

Export Credits Guarantee Department The United Kingdom Government agency that provides support for banks that finance UK exports.

export credit insurance Special insurance coverage for ‹export› receivables to protect against ‹commercial risk› and ‹political risks›. Export credit insurance is available from insurance underwriters as well as from government agencies.

export declaration (= shipper's export declaration = SED). A formal statement containing such particulars as the exporting country's authorities require.

export disincentives Government policies such as sanctions and ‹export› controls that deter that country's exports.

Export-Import Bank of Japan (JEXIM) ‹Japan Bank for International Cooperation›

E

Export-Import Bank of the United States (EXIMBANK) Chartered in 1934, EXIMBANK offers ⟨export⟩ programmes to support the financing of US exports.

> **For more information, visit EXIMBANK's website at www.exim.gov.**

export incentives Assistance provided by governments to enable or assist their suppliers in securing foreign markets. Incentives take many forms. Some, such as assisting exporters in locating foreign importers through a country's foreign service posts or providing government-sponsored credit insurance, do not distort markets. Others, such as cash subsidies, promote unfair competition and violate ⟨World Trade Organization⟩ rules. A third class of incentives – reduced taxation of export-related profits – is highly controversial, and government programmes are referred to the World Trade Organization for rulings on a regular basis. See also ⟨countervailing duty⟩, ⟨illustrative list⟩, ⟨subsidy⟩ and ⟨Subsidies and Countervailing Measures, WTO Agreement⟩.

export licence A government document granting the licensee the right to export a specified quantity of a commodity to a specified country (or a specified party in a specified country). Such licences may be required in some countries for most or all exports and in other countries only under special circumstances.

export management company (EMC) A private firm that serves as the export department for several manufacturers, soliciting and transacting export business on behalf of its clients in return for a commission, salary, or retainer plus commission. EMCs maintain close contact with their clients and are supply-driven. While some EMCs take title to the ⟨goods⟩ that they sell, most do not, but work on sales commissions instead.

export marks Words or symbols placed on the outside of export-packed ⟨goods⟩ to indicate the shipment's destination. Typical marks for vessel shipments include the buyer's name or symbol, destination port, gross weight and dimensions, while marks for air or ground shipments usually include the buyer's full address. In all cases, marks should include the sequential number of the particular shipping piece (box, drum, package etc.) followed by a slash and the total number of shipping pieces. For example, a box marked 1/7 would indicate that it is the first piece of a shipment totaling seven boxes.

> **1. Each shipping piece number should correspond to the packing list entry for that piece.**
> **2. ⟨shipper⟩s of goods with a "street value" should refrain from using marks that disclose the shipment's contents.**

E

export merchant A party that purchases ⟨goods⟩ and exports them under its own private label.

export packing The preparation of ⟨goods⟩ for international shipping. The degree of export packing required greatly depends on the kind of product, the mode of transportation, and the facilities at the shipment and destination port or airport. Shipments made by vessel typically require extensive packing and moisture protection because of longer transit time, exposure to a humid environment, and the fact that they are usually handled and re-handled more than with other transport modes. Although containerization may reduce the need for crating, it does not remove the need for robust packing and careful container loading. Shipments made by air may require a lesser degree of export packing than vessel shipments because the transit times are shorter and air cargo itself tends to be of a lighter weight. However, changes in temperature and altitude may cause condensation, so effective moisture protection is often required. Ground-only shipments made among countries connected by first class infrastructure may often be treated as domestic shipments, unless long distances or ⟨multi-modal transport⟩ (truck-rail-truck) is involved. Sometimes, rail cars bump into each other in marshalling yards as trains are assembled.

> 1. Every ⟨Incoterm⟩ tasks the seller with export packing, except as otherwise agreed or for goods that do not require it.
> 2. ⟨Shippers⟩ of fragile products or those receiving frequent complaints of in-transit damage should consider consulting a surveyor for specific packing recommendations.
> 3. To prevent introduction of non-native pests, some jurisdictions prohibit the importation of non-treated coniferous wood packing materials from certain originating countries.

export promotion Public- or private-sector support for foreign sales through such activities as trade missions and trade fairs.

export quota A specific restriction or target objective on the value or volume of exports of a specified good imposed by the government of the exporting country. This restraint may be intended to protect domestic producers from temporary shortages of certain materials, or as a means to moderate world prices of specified commodities. Commodity agreements sometimes contain explicit provisions to indicate when export quotas should go into effect among producers. Export quotas are also used in connection with orderly marketing and voluntary restraint agreements.

export restraint Quantitative restrictions imposed by exporting countries to limit exports to specified foreign markets, usually pursuant to a formal or informal agreement concluded at the request of the importing country.

export subsidies Government payments or other economic inducements given to domestic producers of ‹goods› that are sold in foreign markets.

Export Trading Company (ETC) A private firm that serves as the export department for manufacturers, soliciting and transacting export business on behalf of its clients. ETCs maintain close contact with their clients and are supply-driven. Export trading companies differ from ‹export management companies› in that most ETCs take title to the ‹goods› they sell and derive their profits on markups. In doing so they obligate themselves to pay their domestic suppliers on domestic terms of payment, thereby taking on the export shipment and payment risks. This can be a great benefit to domestic suppliers that are not familiar with foreign trade.

EXQ ‹Ex Quay›

EXS ‹Ex Ship›

extensible markup language (XML) A specification developed by the ‹W3C›. XML is a pared-down version of ‹SGML›, designed especially for web documents. It allows designers to create customized "meta-tags" for electronic information, allowing an additional level of description for data, which enables the definition, transmission, validation, and interpretation of data between applications and between organizations.

EXW ‹Ex Works›

FAC ‹as fast as the vessel can›

factor table A table provided by ‹insurer›s to determine declared values for insurance at various insurance premiums.

factoring The discounting of receivables that does not involve a ‹draft›. The seller transfers ‹title› to some or all of its accounts receivable to a factoring house for cash at a discount from their face values. Factoring is often done without recourse to the seller. Non-recourse export factoring often allows an exporter to ship on ‹open account› payment terms, avoiding the need for a payment guarantee (‹letter of credit›), as the factor assumes the collection process and export-credit risk.

factoring houses Companies that purchase export receivables at discounted prices.

FAK ‹freight of all kinds›

F

FAO ⟨Food and Agriculture Organization⟩

FAQ ⟨frequently asked questions⟩

FAS ⟨Free Alongside Ship⟩

fathom 1.8288.8 metres (6 feet)

FBL ⟨FIATA B/L⟩

FCA ⟨Free Carrier⟩

FCL ⟨full container load⟩

FCN ⟨Freedom, Commerce and Navigation Treaty⟩

FCR ⟨forwarder's certificate of receipt⟩

feeder vessel ⏚ A ship that transports cargo from a major port (often called a ⟨base port⟩) to smaller ports within a given range. This is akin to the ⟨hub and spoke⟩ system used in air transport.

FEU ⟨forty-foot equivalent unit⟩

FHEX ⊟ A term meaning that Fridays and holidays are excluded in calculating the laytime for vessel chartering. See also ⟨laydays⟩.

FHINC ⊟ A term meaning that Fridays and holidays are included in calculating the laytime for vessel chartering. See also ⟨laydays⟩.

FIATA ⟨International Federation of Freight Forwarders' Associations⟩.

FIATA B/L (FBL) A negotiable combined transport ⟨bill of lading⟩ issued by freight ⟨forwarders⟩ acting as ⟨carrier⟩s, per the ⟨International Federation of Freight Forwarders' Associations⟩ format and subject to the ⟨International Chamber of Commerce⟩ Rules for a Combined Transport Document.

FIFO ⟨first in, first out⟩

fighting ship A vessel used in a particular trade by an ocean ⟨common carrier⟩ or conference for the purpose of excluding, preventing or reducing competition by driving another ocean common carrier out of that trade.

file transfer protocol (FTP) A set of standard codes for transferring files over the internet. An application program that uses TCP/IP internet works as a medium for transferring files; one of the many protocols used to copy files from one computer to another on the internet. FTP is usually used for retrieving large files or files that cannot be displayed through a ⟨browser⟩. Windows FTP, Cute FTP and Fetch are examples of FTP software.

⏚ Insurance 🆔 Letters of credit ⏚ Liner vessel shipping ⊠ Sales contracts ⊟ Vessel chartering

F

film (packaging). Packaging film can produce a tightly wrapped package and is particularly useful in unitizing smaller packages on pallets. There are two types in common use, shrink film and stretch film. Shrink film, also called shrink wrap, contracts when heated after packing. Stretch film attempts to return to its original dimensions after packing without the necessity of heat application.

FILO ① For chartering, ‹free in, liner out›. ② For inventory control, ‹first in, last out›.

FIO ‹free in and out›

FIOST ‹free in, out, stowed and trimmed›

first in, first out (FIFO) Inventory management and/or accounting procedure whereby the earliest arriving ‹goods› of their kind (first in) are shipped prior to those that have arrived more recently.

first in, last out (FILO) Inventory management and/or accounting procedure whereby the earliest arriving ‹goods› of their kind (first in) are shipped after those that have arrived more recently (last out).

first of exchange For many years, trade practice was to draw ‹draft›s in original and duplicate for fear that originals could become lost in the mail. The first of exchange is the original, and is valid only if the ‹second of exchange› is unpaid.

flag carrier A vessel registered under the flag of a particular nation.
> Some countries support their merchant marine industry by limiting certain types of cargo to vessels registered in their nationality, such as government-financed purchases or foreign aid. See also ‹preferential cargo›.

flag of convenience A ship registered under the flag of a nation that offers a minimal degree of control in the areas of taxes, crew and safety requirements.

floating exchange rate A rate of exchange that is determined by market forces. See also ‹clean float› and ‹dirty float›.

floating policy 🗗 ‹open marine cargo insurance policy›

Florence Agreement (Agreement on the Importation of Educational, Scientific and Cultural Materials) At the request of the ‹United Nations› Educational, Scientific and Cultural Organization, this agreement providing duty-free entry under certain conditions for educational, cultural and scientific materials, came into force in 1952.

flotsam Wreckage of a ship or cargo found floating on the water.

FOB ‹Free on Board›

F

FOB Airport A former ⟨Incoterm⟩ that has been replaced by ⟨Free Carrier⟩.

FOB/FAS insurance ⟨⟩ An insurance option permitting sellers to insure shipments from their point of origin to the point where the buyer assumes ⟨title⟩ and/or risk for the ⟨goods⟩. This is intended to dovetail buyer-provided coverage that begins only at the point where the buyer assumes title and/or risk. Thus, an unpaid seller using the ⟨FOB⟩ ⟨Incoterm⟩ has no obligation to the buyer to insure, but may wish for coverage to the point where the goods pass the ship's rail at the port of loading.

Food and Agricultural Organization (FAO) Founded in 1945 and headquartered in Rome, Italy, the FAO is a specialized ⟨UN⟩ agency that combats hunger and malnutrition.

> **For more information, visit the FAO website at www.fao.org.**

FOR/FOT ⟨free on rail/free on truck⟩

force majeure Circumstances that compel a party to behave contrary to its own volition. For instance, a storm may cause a vessel to seek refuge at a port in which it would normally be unwelcome, or a civil disturbance may cause it to avoid a scheduled port of call.

foreign access zone Japanese term for ⟨free trade zone⟩.

foreign exchange (FX = FOREX). A foreign country's currency or financial instruments; also, transactions for the purchase or sale of same.

foreign exchange earnings The proceeds from a country's exports of ⟨goods⟩, ⟨services⟩ and ⟨capital⟩, normally denominated in ⟨convertible currencies⟩.

foreign freight forwarder ⟨forwarder⟩

foreign trade zone ⟨free trade zone⟩

FOREX ⟨foreign exchange⟩

forfaiting A form of trade finance in which an exporter surrenders title to ⟨export⟩ receivables by selling them at a discount to a forfaiter, in exchange for cash. These receivables are usually in the form of ⟨drafts⟩ or ⟨promissory notes⟩ that have been guaranteed by a bank in the importer's country and that often carry the guarantee of a foreign government. They are easily transferable and can be sold on the secondary market. In a typical forfaiting operation, the exporter approaches a forfaiter before completing the transaction's structure. Once the forfaiter commits to the deal and sets the discount rate, the exporter can incorporate the discount cost into the selling price.

⟨⟩ Insurance   LC Letters of credit   ⟨⟩ Liner vessel shipping   ⟨⟩ Sales contracts   ⟨⟩ Vessel chartering

F

Forfaiting differs from export ⟨factoring⟩ in the following three ways:

1. Factors usually want access to all or a large percentage of an exporter's business, while most forfaiters will work on a transaction-by-transaction basis.

2. Forfaiters usually work with medium- and long-term receivables of 180 days to years, while factors work with short-term receivables of up to 180 days. Since payment terms usually reflect the type of product involved, forfaiters usually work with sales of capital ⟨goods⟩, commodities and large projects, while factors work mostly with sales of consumer goods.

3. Most factors do not have strong capabilities with developing parts of the world where legal and financial frameworks are inadequate and credit information is not available through affiliate factors. However, most forfaiters are willing to work with sales to such countries because they usually require bank or sovereign guarantees.

forfeit ① Something in which a right is lost. ② A penalty.

forklift truck A motorized truck equipped with two hydraulically powered forks that can lift, move and position skidded or palletized cargo.

forty-foot equivalent unit (FEU) ⬇ A practice in marine commerce of expressing cargo quantity in terms of forty-foot container loads. One FEU = two ⟨twenty-foot equivalent units (TEUs)⟩.

forward exchange contract A contract for the delivery of a specified amount of a named currency at a specified future date, in return for a specified amount of another named currency. Forward exchange contracts enable importers and exporters who will make or receive payment in a foreign currency at a future time to protect themselves from fluctuations in the rate of exchange. In contrast to currency future contracts, forward exchange contracts are accomplished for variable amounts and time periods and are transacted through banks and exchange houses.

forward exchange option A contractually agreed right to buy (put) or to sell (call) a specific amount of one currency for a specified amount of another at a predetermined future date (European option) or up to a predetermined future date (American option). Like ⟨forward exchange contracts⟩, forward exchange options enable importers and exporters who will make or receive payment in a foreign currency at a future time, to protect themselves from fluctuations in the rate of exchange. However, unlike foreign exchange contracts, the option holder is not obligated to perform the exchange transaction if doing so is not to his or her advantage.

⟨see entry in dictionary⟩ ✈ Air transport 🏛 Bank collections @ e-commerce 🔳 Incoterms

forwarder ✈ ⚓ A person or company that arranges transportation, usually on behalf of the party contracting for ⟨main carriage⟩. Many forwarders provide additional services, such as assistance with country-specific documentary requirements, insurance, storage, and even customs brokerage. Some forwarders also act as ⟨carriers⟩ (air freight consolidators or NVOCCs). Typically, forwarders obtain brokerage commission income from the carrier(s) they select. This minimizes the fees that they charge their clients, and makes using forwarders cost-competitive. Some countries require that forwarders obtain a licence, at least to be eligible for brokerage income.

forwarder's certificate of receipt (FCR) ⚓ A document issued by a ⟨forwarder⟩ stating that it has received or controls certain cargo for shipment. These quasi-transport documents can provide security for buyers when issued by buyer-appointed forwarders.

forwarding agent ⟨forwarder⟩

forwarding instructions ⟨shipper's letter of instructions⟩

foul transport document ✈ �</ ⚓ A receipt for shipped ⟨goods⟩ tendered by a ⟨carrier⟩ (such as a ⟨dock receipt⟩, or marine, air or ground transport document) that indicates shortage or damage to one or more of the shipping pieces. When cargo is first picked up for shipment, or is handed off from one carrier to another, it is inspected by the receiving carrier for obvious shortage or damage. Any such problems are noted on the carrier's receipt, thereby exonerating it from causing the problem. This creates a paper trail that can be followed backwards to determine where the damage or shortage took place and thereby assign responsibility on the carrier that caused it. ⟨Clean transport documents⟩ are those that bear no damage or shortage notations, and are the opposite of foul transport documents.

FPA ⟨free of particular average⟩

FPAD (freight payable at destination). ⟨freight collect⟩

franc zone (ZF) A monetary union among countries whose currencies are linked to the French franc at a fixed rate of exchange.

franchising A system based on the licensing of the right to duplicate a successful business format or industrial process. The franchiser (licensor) permits the franchisee to employ its business processes, ⟨trademarks⟩, trade secrets and know-how in a contractually specified manner for the marketing of ⟨goods⟩ or ⟨services⟩. The franchiser usually supports the operation of the franchisee's business through provision of advertising, accounting, training and related services, and in many instances also supplies products

F

required by the franchisee for operation of the franchise. The franchisee, in return, pays certain monies to the franchiser in terms of fees and percentage commissions, and agrees to respect contractual provisions dealing with such topics as quality of performance. The two principal kinds of franchise contracts are:

- master franchise agreements, under which the franchiser grants another party the right to sub-franchise within a given territory;
- direct or unit franchise agreements, which are direct contracts between the franchiser or sub-franchiser and the operator of the franchise unit.

FRC ⟨Free Carrier⟩

Free Alongside Ship (FAS)... named port of shipment (Incoterms 2000) 🔳 An ⟨Incoterm⟩ designed for vessel transport where the seller's costs and responsibility for the condition of the ⟨goods⟩ end when the goods are placed next to the vessel at the port of embarkation.

> In Incoterms 2000, the responsibility for export clearance was changed from the buyer to the seller.

Free Carrier (FCA)... named place (Incoterms 2000) 🔳 An ⟨Incoterm⟩ designed for ⟨omnimodal⟩ use where the seller's costs and responsibility for the condition of the ⟨goods⟩ end when the goods are handed over to the buyer-designated ⟨carrier⟩, ⟨forwarder⟩ or agent on the seller's side.

> Under the FCA Incoterm, the seller loads the collection vehicle (or provides pre-carriage to the buyer-designated carrier) and arranges for ⟨export clearance⟩. Since it is usually easier for the seller than for the buyer to accomplish these tasks, FCA provides a useful alternative to EXW.

free domicile An antiquated shipping term under which the seller arranges and pays all charges to the buyer's premises, usually including ⟨import clearance⟩. Free Domicile has been largely replaced by the ⟨Delivered Duty Paid⟩ ⟨Incoterm⟩.

free in and out (FIO) 🄵 Chartering term whereby the vessel owner is not responsible for the costs of loading or unloading. This is the opposite of ⟨gross terms⟩.

free in, liner out (FILO) 🄵 Chartering terms whereby the vessel owner is not responsible for the costs of loading but is responsible for the costs of unloading.

free in, out, stowed and trimmed (FIOST) 🄵 An elaboration of the ⟨free in and out⟩ chartering terms whereby the vessel owner is not responsible for the costs of loading, unloading, ⟨stowage⟩ or

⟨trimming⟩. This is the opposite of ⟨gross terms⟩.

free of capture and seizure A provision in standard commercial insurance coverage that exclude loss due to war and warlike acts. This peril can be mitigated by war ⟨risk coverage⟩, which is usually available at an additional premium cost.

free of particular average (FPA) 🗗 A type of ⟨marine cargo insurance⟩ providing minimum cover in the US market. ⟨London Institute of Underwriters "C" Clauses⟩ offer virtually the same coverage in other markets. Free of particular average covers:

a. Total or partial loss from stranding, sinking, burning or collision. (Under English terms partial loss is payable if any of these events occur. Under American terms, partial loss is payable only if caused by these events.)

b. Total loss from errors in vessel management, boiler bursting, defects in hull or machinery and explosion.

> **1.** This coverage is usually inadequate for shipments of ⟨goods⟩ of more than nominal value.
> **2.** Both ⟨Incoterms 2000⟩ and the current version of the ⟨ICC⟩'s ⟨Uniform Customs and Practice for Documentary Credits⟩ accept minimum-cover insurance as the seller's compliance with its obligation to insure in the absence of any agreement to the contrary. Therefore, the seller and buyer should carefully define the coverage that they want, and should clearly agree that the responsible party provide it.
> **3.** FPA is the opposite of ⟨all risks⟩ and ⟨London Institute of Underwriters Clauses A⟩, which provide maximum cover, especially when augmented to include war, ⟨strike, riot and civil commotion⟩ perils.

Free on Board (FOB)... named port of shipment (Incoterms 2000) 🗐 An ⟨Incoterm⟩ designed for vessel transport, where the seller's costs and responsibility for the condition of the ⟨goods⟩ end when the goods cross the ship's rail at the port of embarkation.

Free on Rail/Free on Truck (FOR/FOT) An obsolete ⟨Incoterm⟩ that has been replaced by ⟨Free Carrier⟩.

free port A form of ⟨free trade zone⟩ that usually encompasses an entire port area.

free time 🗗 🗓 The allowable time that shippers and/or consignees can use equipment or leave ⟨goods⟩ on a ⟨wharf⟩ or at a ⟨carrier⟩'s premises without incurring ⟨demurrage⟩ charges.

free trade A theoretical concept that assumes international trade unhampered by government measures, such as ⟨tariff⟩s or non-tariff barriers.

🗗 Insurance 🆑 Letters of credit 🗓 Liner vessel shipping 🖺 Sales contracts 🗐 Vessel chartering

F

free trade agreement (FTA) An arrangement that establishes unimpeded exchange and flow of ⟨goods⟩ and ⟨services⟩ between trading partners, regardless of national borders of member countries. FTAs do not address labour mobility across borders, common currencies, uniform standards or other common policies, such as taxes. Member countries apply their own individual ⟨tariff⟩ rates to countries outside the free trade area.

free trade area A group of countries that agree to eliminate ⟨tariff⟩s and other import restrictions on each others' ⟨goods⟩, while each participating country applies its own independent schedule of tariffs on ⟨imports⟩ from countries that are not members.

Free Trade Area of the Americas (FTAA) Concepted in 1994, FTAA is an effort to unite the economies of the Western Hemisphere into a single free trade arrangement. Negotiating groups include ⟨market access⟩, investment, services, ⟨government procurement⟩, ⟨dispute settlement⟩, agriculture, intellectual property, subsidies, and competition policy.

> **For more information, visit the FTAA website at www.ftaa-alca.org.**

free trade zone (= customs free zone, duty free zone, foreign trade zone). A generic term referring to a special commercial or industrial area at which special customs procedures allow the importation of foreign merchandise (including raw materials, components, and finished ⟨goods⟩) without the requirement that duties be paid immediately. If the merchandise is later exported, duty-free treatment is given to the re-exports. Merchandise brought into these areas may be stored, exhibited, assembled, processed or used in manufacture prior to re-export or entry into the national customs territory. Manufacturing activity occurring in free trade zones usually involves a combination of foreign and domestic materials, and usually requires special governmental approval. Free trade zones are usually located near ports or airports, (although lately there has been a growing trend toward allocating portions of inland facilities as "sub-zones").

freedom, commerce and navigation treaty (FCN) A bilateral treaty defining the legal and commercial rights of citizens of each country under the laws of the other. This is a generic term and does not refer to a specific treaty.

freely convertible currency ⟨convertible currency⟩

freely negotiable [LC] A ⟨letter of credit⟩ that can be presented with conforming documents at any bank.

freight ① Transportation charges. ② ⟨Goods⟩ being transported.

F

freight collect ✈ ⬇ A shipping arrangement whereby the ⟨carrier⟩ collects its ⟨freight⟩ charges from the ⟨consignee⟩ rather than from the shipper. This usually happens when the ⟨contract of carriage⟩ is between the carrier and the consignee.

freight forwarder ⟨forwarder⟩

freight of all kinds (FAK) ⬇ A ⟨freight⟩ rate that is not restricted to a particular commodity. FAK freight rates are quoted primarily by ⟨undercarriers⟩ to ⟨consolidators⟩ (NVOCCs and airfreight consolidators) who fill shipping containers with different kinds of cargoes received either from different shippers or for different consignees or both. While the consolidator may charge its clients on a commodity-specific basis, it pays the undercarrier a pre-determined FAK rate.

freight payable at destination (FPAD) ⟨freight collect⟩

freight prepayable (= freight to be prepaid). Terminology designed by ⟨carrier⟩s to provide transportation documentation indicating that ⟨freight⟩ charges are for the account of the shipper, while not stating that payment has actually been received.

> This situation usually arises with ⟨letters of credit⟩ requiring freight-prepaid transport documents. "Freight prepayable," "freight to be prepaid," or similar verbiage does not satisfy such a requirement unless specifically permitted by the individual L/C.

freight prepaid ✈ ⬇ A shipping arrangement whereby the ⟨carrier⟩ is paid its ⟨freight⟩ charges by the ⟨shipper⟩ rather than by the ⟨consignee⟩ This usually happens when the ⟨contract of carriage⟩ is between the shipper and the carrier.

freight rebate ✈ ⬇ A refund of a portion of previously paid transportation charges, usually in return for the ⟨shipper⟩'s tendering a certain volume of ⟨freight⟩ to the ⟨carrier⟩.

> Freight rebating is illegal in some countries such as the United States. This can have the unintended consequence of making legitimate claims against carriers difficult, since they must be fully documented to prove that they are not actually rebates in disguise.

frequently asked questions (FAQ) A section of a work (often instructional) that anticipates and answers questions that are most often asked.

frustrated cargo Cargo that although in the custody of a ⟨carrier⟩ cannot be moved or delivered because of carrier error or situations beyond the carrier's control, such as ⟨embargo⟩ or detention by customs.

✈ Insurance   LC Letters of credit   ⬇ Liner vessel shipping   ✍ Sales contracts   ⊟ Vessel chartering

FG

FTA ⟨free trade agreement⟩ or ⟨free trade area⟩

FTAA ⟨Free Trade Area of the Americas⟩

FTP ⟨file transfer protocol⟩

full container load (FCL) A shipment of sufficient volume or weight to justify the exclusive use of a shipping container.

fungible goods ⟨Goods⟩ that are commercially identical and interchangeable.

future contract A contract for the future delivery of a commodity, currency or security on a specific date. Currency future contracts are for standard quantities over standard periods of time and are primarily traded on exchanges (and in this way differ from ⟨forward exchange contracts⟩).

FX ⟨foreign exchange⟩

G-3 ⟨Treaty on Free Trade among Colombia, Mexico and Venezuela⟩

G-8 ⟨Group of 8⟩

G-77 ⟨Group of 77⟩

GA ⟨general average⟩

GAB ⟨general arrangements to borrow⟩

gateway ① A port or airport where ⟨customs clearance⟩ takes place. ② In the context of travel and transportation activities, a major airport or seaport.

GATS ⟨General Agreement on Trade Services⟩

GATT ⟨General Agreement on Tariffs and Trade⟩

gauger A party that measures, gauges or otherwise inspects. Customs services may require that imported ⟨goods⟩ be inspected by an approved commercial gauger for classification-verification purposes.

GBDe ⟨Global Business Dialogue on Electronic Commerce⟩

GCC ⟨Gulf Cooperation Council⟩

GDP ⟨gross domestic product⟩

General Agreement on Tariffs and Trade (GATT) The GATT was replaced on 1 January 1995 by the ⟨World Trade Organization (WTO)⟩.

General Agreement on Trade Services (GATS) A ⟨World Trade Organization⟩ agreement that is the first multilateral agreement to provide legally enforceable rules covering all international trade and investment in the service sector (except for those services provided in the exercise of governmental authority). GATS is designed to reduce or eliminate governmental measures that prevent services from being freely provided across national borders or that discriminate against locally established service firms with foreign ownership. Thus, GATS expands generally accepted notions of international trade in ‹goods› to trade in ‹services›. GATS consists of a framework agreement that lays out the general principles and obligations for trade in services (including ‹most-favoured-nation treatment›, ‹market access›, and ‹national treatment›) that apply to all WTO members, in the same way that WTO does for trade in goods. Attached to this framework agreement are annexes dealing with rules for specific service sectors (movement of natural persons, air transport, financial services, maritime and telecommunications). National schedules list each member's specific undertakings with respect to its service sectors. The agreement also provides for exceptions to the principles of national treatment and most-favoured-nation treatment. First, governments can choose the services in which they make market access and national treatment commitments; second, they can limit the degree of market access and national treatment they provide; third, they can take exceptions even from the most-favoured-nation obligation, in principle only for ten years, in order to give more favourable treatment to some countries rather than to all WTO members in general. Finally, GATS provides a forum for further negotiations to open service markets around the world.

General Arrangements to Borrow (GAB) Established in 1962 and subsequently amended, the GAB is an agreement under which the ‹International Monetary Fund› may borrow monies from major industrial countries (Belgium, Canada, France, Germany, Italy, Japan, the Netherlands, Sweden, Switzerland, United Kingdom, United States).

general average (GA) 🛦 A voluntary sacrifice or extraordinary expense incurred during waterborne transit to protect all interests from an impending peril. The main principle behind general average is that when a sacrifice is made to save the interests of all parties involved in transportation, the party who makes the sacrifice must be compensated by all the parties who stand to benefit from the sacrifice or expenditure. For instance, when cargo is jettisoned to save a vessel from sinking, all parties whose cargo was not thrown overboard must contribute to reimburse those parties whose cargo was. ‹Carriers› will require some form of security

---

🛦 Insurance   🄻🄲 Letters of credit   ⬇ Liner vessel shipping   📑 Sales contracts   🄿 Vessel chartering

G

(‹promissory note› or insurance company guarantee bond) prior to releasing cargo, in order to enforce each party's contribution. While this can be a burden for owners of uninsured cargo, insurance companies provide such guarantees for cargoes they insure.

> The ‹York–Antwerp Rules› provide a uniform basis for adjusting general average claims for nations that subscribe to them.

general average contribution The amount each party involved in a ‹general average› must contribute.

general average security A general average ‹bond›, deposit, or ‹underwriter›'s guarantee placed to obtain release of shipped ‹goods› by the shipowner. It replaces the lien imposed on shipped goods for general average purposes. See also ‹general average› and ‹general average contribution›.

general order ① A place of storage for imported ‹goods› that have not been promptly customs-cleared. The length of time goods may await clearance varies from country to country and port to port. ② A penalty fee for goods so described.

> General order storage can be extremely expensive, which is why timely ‹carrier› arrival notice is so important.

general rules of interpretation ‹harmonized system›

general tariff A ‹tariff› that applies to ‹imports› from other countries that do not enjoy either preferential or most-favored-nation tariff treatment. Where the general tariff differs from the ‹most-favoured-nation› rate, the general tariff is usually older and higher.

General Usage in International Digitally Ensured Commerce (GUIDEC) An ‹International Chamber of Commerce (ICC)› project toward establishing a framework for the ensuring and certification of digital messages, based on existing law and practice in different legal systems. See also ‹digital signature›, ‹open network systems› and ‹public key infrastructure›.

> For more information, visit the GUIDEC website at www.iccwbo.org/home/guidec.guidec.asp.

generalized system of preferences (GSP) A framework under which ‹developed countries› give preferential ‹tariff› treatment to ‹goods› imported from certain ‹developing countries›. GSP is one element of a coordinated effort by the industrial trading nations to bring developing countries more fully into the international trading system. Twenty-seven industrialized nations now maintain GSP programmes. Also ‹enabling clause›.

German Financing Company for Investments in Developing Countries (DEG) The DEG promotes direct private-sector investment in ‹developing countries› and provides advisory services in planning and implementing jointly-financed and managed companies. Operations emphasize matching small- and medium-sized German companies with similar counterparts in developing countries.

G

Ges.mbH (Gesellschaft mit beschränkter Haftung) ‹limited liability›

Gesellschaft mit beschränkter Haftung (GmbH) ‹limited liability›

Gesellschaft mit beschränkter Haftung & Co kommandit-gesellschaft (GmbH & Co KG) ‹limited liability›

GIE (Groupement d'Intérêt Economique) ‹Economic Interest Grouping›

GIIC ‹Global Information Infrastructure Commission›

GIP ‹Global Internet Project›

Global Business Dialogue on Electronic Commerce (GBDe) @ A worldwide, CEO-driven private sector effort to develop policies that promote ‹electronic commerce› for the benefit of businesses and consumers.
For more information, visit the GBDe website at www.gbde.org.

Global Information Infrastructure Commission (GIIC) An independent, non-governmental initiative involving leaders from developing and industrialized countries to foster private-sector leadership and private–public-sector cooperation in development of information networks.
For more information visit the GIIC website at www.giic.org.

Global Internet Project (GIP) An international group of senior executives from Asia, Europe and North America fostering continued growth of the internet.
For more information, visit the GIP website at www.gip.org.

global quota A quota on the total imports of a product from all countries. See also ‹import quota›.

Global System of Trade Preferences (GSTP) An objective developed by the ‹Group of 77› within the ‹United Nations› Conference on Trade Development, toward the negotiation of special intra-developing country preferences and the reduction of ‹non-tariff barriers› impeding South-South trade. See also ‹economic cooperation among developing countries›.

G

Global Telecommunications Society A non-profit professional association with chapters in Amsterdam, London, Texas and Washington DC, promoting dialogue on the technological, social and business aspects of global communications.
For more information, visit the Society's website at www.gtswashington.org

GmbH (Gesellschaft mit beschränkter Haftung) ⟨limited liability⟩

GmbH & Co KG (Gesellschaft mit beschränkter Haftung & Co kommanditgesellschaft) ⟨limited liability⟩

GMT ⟨Greenwich Mean Time⟩

goods and services tax (GST or **TPS)** ⟨value added tax⟩

good ship ⊡ A term used in vessel chartering to mean seaworthy.

goods Inherently useful and relatively scarce articles or commodities produced by manufacturing, mining, construction and agricultural sectors of the economy. Goods are important economically because they may be exchanged for ⟨money⟩ or other goods or ⟨services⟩.

government procurement The means and mechanisms through which official government agencies purchase ⟨goods⟩ and ⟨services⟩. Government procurement policies and practices may constitute ⟨non-tariff barriers⟩ to trade if they discriminate in favour of domestic suppliers when competitive imported goods are cheaper or of better quality. The GATT Government Procurement Code sought to reduce, if not eliminate, "buy national" bias by improving transparency and equity in national procurement policies, and by ensuring effective recourse to dispute settlement procedures. Also ⟨Government Procurement (GPA), WTO Agreement⟩.

Government Procurement (GPA), WTO Agreement A ⟨World Trade Organization⟩ agreement that went into effect 1 January 1996, replacing the GATT Government Procurement Code. This agreement is "plurilateral" rather than multilateral, and as such is binding only on member countries that have acceded to it rather than on the entire WTO membership.

GPA ⟨Government Procurement, WTO Agreement⟩

graduation The presumption that individual ⟨developing countries⟩ are capable of assuming greater responsibilities and obligations in the international community – within the context of the ⟨WTO⟩ or the ⟨World Bank⟩, for example – as their economies advance, as through industrialization, export development and rising living standards.

G

grandfather clause A provision in a legal instrument, such as the GATT, that allows countries that accede to it to maintain pre-existing domestic legislation inconsistent with the provision of that instrument.

gray market goods Genuine trademarked products that are imported by a party other than the ‹trademark› holder or authorized importer.

green clause ⟦LC⟧ A ‹letter of credit› provision permitting advances against security interests in the contract ‹goods›.

Greenwich Mean Time (GMT) The time of day at the prime meridian (zero degrees longitude), at which Greenwich, England is located.

gross charter ‹gross terms›

gross domestic product (GDP) ‹Gross national product› excluding payment on foreign investments.

gross national product (GNP) The total market value of all ‹goods› and ‹services› produced within a country within a given period, usually a year.

gross sales The total amount received or receivable for ‹goods› sold, before any allowances for returned goods or sales discounts.

gross terms (= gross charter) ⟦↻⟧ Chartering terms whereby the vessel owner is responsible for the costs of loading, ‹stowing›, ‹trimming› and unloading. Many voyage ‹charters› are handled on this basis.

gross vehicle weight The total weight of a vehicle as loaded, including the weight of the vehicle and all accessories and fuel.

gross weight The total scale weight of a shipment, including the ‹goods› and their packing.

Group of 8 (G-8) The heads of state of the leading industrial democracies have met annually since 1975 to coordinate economic policies to achieve sustained economic growth with price stability, to foster stability in exchange markets, and to promote adjustments in external imbalances. The group also addresses other pressing issues that affect global economic performance. Beginning as the Group of 5 with France, Germany, Japan, UK and US, it has grown to its present size with the addition of Canada, Italy and Russia. Recently, representatives of the ‹European Union› have attended as observers.

Group of 77 (G-77) The 77 countries represented at the ‹United Nations Conference on Trade and Development UNCTAD›-1 in 1964 established the precedent of meeting together in an attempt to

---

⟦🖪⟧ Insurance   ⟦LC⟧ Letters of credit   ⟦⚓⟧ Liner vessel shipping   ⟦✇⟧ Sales contracts   ⟦↻⟧ Vessel chartering

GH

develop common positions on major conference agenda items in advance of plenary UNCTAD meetings. The Group of 77 presently includes 132 ‹developing country› members from Africa, Asia and Latin America. See also ‹economic cooperation among developing countries› and ‹global system of trade preferences›.

groupage ‹consolidation›

groupage agent ‹consolidator›

groupement d'intérêt economique (GIE) ‹economic interest grouping›

Grupo Andino ‹Andean Group›

GSP ‹Generalized System of Preferences›

GST ‹Goods and services tax›. See also ‹value added tax›.

GSTP ‹Global System of Trade Preferences›

guaranteed freight Freight charges that are not prepaid but are payable whether the cargo is delivered or not, provided that failure to deliver resulted from causes beyond the ‹carrier›'s control.

guarantor A party that provides a guarantee.

GUIDEC ‹General Usage in International Digitally Ensured Commerce›

Gulf Cooperation Council (GCC) Established in 1981 and headquartered in Riyadh, Saudi Arabia, the GCC seeks to strengthen cooperation in areas such as agriculture, industry, investment, security and trade among its Arab member states.
For more information, visit the GCC website at www.gcc-sg.org.

GVW ‹gross vehicle weight›

HAB (= HAWB). ‹house air waybill›

Hague Rules 🗏 ⬇ Formally titled "The International Convention for the Unification of Certain Rules of Law relating to Bills of Lading 1924", the Hague rules are internationally agreed standard conditions that apply to marine-carriage contracts. These, or the ‹Hague–Visby› or ‹Hamburg Rules›, are often incorporated as a paramount clause in marine ‹contracts of carriage›.

Hague–Visby Rules 🗏 ⬇ Formally titled "The Hague Rules as Amended by the Brussels Protocol of 1968," Hague-Visby is a revision of the internationally agreed standard conditions that apply to marine carriage contracts originally found in the Hague rules. These, or the ‹Hague› or ‹Hamburg Rules›, are often incorporated as a paramount clause in marine ⟨contracts of carriage⟩.

H

Hamburg Rules 🅰 ⬇ Formally titled "The United Nations Convention on the Carriage of ⟨goods⟩ by Sea 1978," the Hamburg Rules are internationally agreed standard conditions that apply to marine ⟨carriage contracts⟩, and are considered more equitable to cargo interests (as opposed to shipowners) than either the ⟨Hague⟩ or ⟨Hague–Visby Rules⟩. These, or Hague or Hague-Visby Rules, are often incorporated as a paramount clause in marine contracts of carriage.

> **1. For the full text, visit the ⟨United Nations⟩ Commission on International Trade Law's web page www.uncitral.org/english/texts/transport/hamburg.htm.**
> **2. For a list of participating countries, visit the United Nations Commission on International Trade Law web page www.uncitral.org/english/status/status-e.htm.**

hard currency ⟨convertible currency⟩

harmonized system (HS) The Harmonized Commodity Description and Coding System (or Harmonized System) is a method of classifying ⟨goods⟩ in international trade developed by the Customs Cooperation Council (now the ⟨World Customs Organization⟩). The core system contains 96 chapters and classifies at the six-digit level, with the first two numbers indicating the appropriate chapter, the second two indicating the appropriate heading within the chapter, and the third two indicating the appropriate sub-heading within the heading. There are also six General Rules of Interpretation to be followed in order in the classification process.Beginning 1 January 1988, the new HS numbers replaced previously used import ⟨tariff⟩ schedules in over 50 countries, and many more countries have joined since.

> **1. Many countries place additional digits after the six-digit HS number to achieve greater classification precision. For example, the United States uses ten-digit numbers for export and import classification, of which the first six digits are "harmonized."**
> **2. For an up-to-date list of countries that participate in the harmonized system, visit the World Customs Organization's website at www.wcoomd.org. Select the "Conventions" section, and then select the "Convention on the Harmonized Commodity Description and Coding System."**

HAWB (= HAB). ⟨house air waybill⟩

hazardous materials (HAZMAT) Any substance or material that has been determined to be capable of posing an unreasonable risk to health, safety and commerce, and has been so designated by:
1. the ⟨International Maritime Organization (IMO)⟩, a ⟨United Nations⟩ agency,

---

H

2. the ⟨International Air Transport Association (IATA)⟩,

3. any appropriate government agency(ies).

There are many types of hazard (or hazmat) classes, based on the risk or risks that particular substances or materials may pose in transportation. Further, some materials may be considered hazardous for one mode but not for others. Possible incompatibility of hazardous substances shipped together is yet another factor, so ⟨carriers⟩ must be made aware of all hazmat shipments. ⟨Shipper⟩s and carriers must know the legally shippable quantities, required packing, required warning labels and required documentation for each class of hazard they handle. Regulations for international air shipments are published by IATA in the current edition of its Dangerous Goods Regulations. Regulations for international shipments by vessel are found in the IMO's International Marine Dangerous Goods Code (IMDG ode or IMGGC). Shippers bear the primary responsibility for determining the correct hazard class and compliant handling of hazmat shipments. Some countries, such as the United States, require certified training for employees who are responsible for hazardous materials shipments.

> While many countries adopt IATA and IMGGC regulations and even incorporate them into their national law, some jurisdictions have differing or additional regulations. Shippers and ⟨consignee⟩s should determine that they are aware of and compliant with any such regulations prior to shipment.

head charterer 🅰 A vessel ⟨charterer⟩ who makes a vessel that he or she has chartered available to other charterers (called sub-charterers).

heavy lift Cargo that exceeds the weight capacity or is too large to be loaded by the carrying breakbulk vessel's gear (traditionally around 5000 kilos). While containerized cargo is not subjected to heavy lift charges, it may be assessed excess weight charges.

hedging Purchasing a future contract for delivery of a commodity or currency to reduce the risk of adverse price changes occurring from the present to the time performance is due.

hierarchically assigned document An encrypted, time-stamped, tamperproof, digital receipt that encapsulates an electronic communication created by a trusted third party to ensure non-repudiation of a communication.

high cube 🅻 A vessel shipping container with interior and exterior height dimensions greater than the standard container nominal dimensions of 7 feet 6 inch and 8 feet. Many high cube containers have a 9 foot 6 inch exterior height dimension.

⟨see entry in dictionary⟩   ✈ Air transport   🏛 Bank collections   @ e-commerce   ⊞ Incoterms

H

> **Actual vessel container internal and external dimensions vary from manufacturer to manufacturer and from ⟨carrier⟩ to carrier.**

hire-purchase Payment by regular instalments.

hold A space in the lower part of a ship or aircraft in which cargo is stowed.

holder in due course A party that has received a ⟨negotiable instrument⟩ in good faith and without notice that it is overdue, or that there is any prior claim, or that there was a defect in the ⟨title⟩ of the party that negotiated it.

homologation Certification by a country that a vehicle or boat conforms to its safety and emission standards.

horizontal tariff reductions ⟨linear tariff reductions⟩

house air waybill (HAB = HAWB) ✈ A transport document for air carriage issued by a ⟨carrier⟩ other than the ⟨undercarrier⟩. This is the opposite of a ⟨master air waybill⟩, which is issued by the carrier actually transporting the cargo.

house bill of lading ⚓ A transport document for marine carriage issued by a ⟨non-vessel-operating common carrier (NVOCC)⟩ instead of the ⟨undercarrier⟩.

HS ⟨Harmonized System⟩

HTML ⟨hypertext markup language⟩

HTTP ⟨hypertext transfer protocol⟩

hub and spoke ✈ ⚓ A transport network system in which a ⟨carrier⟩ routes long and heavily trafficked flights or voyages among a few large air or sea ports called hubs or base ports, rather than making direct calls on smaller ones. The respective hinterlands of each hub are called spokes and are served with smaller equipment such as commuter aircraft, feeder vessels, barges or ground transport. The concept resembles wheels, with the spokes radiating from their central hubs. See also ⟨base port⟩ and ⟨feeder vessel⟩.

hull The body or frame of a ship, flying boat, etc.

hull insurance Insurance placed on a vessel (typically covering hull, machinery and complete equipment), rather than on cargo.

husbanding A general term used for managing the affairs of a ship while in port, including such tasks as customs formalities, fueling, supplies, repairs and any requirements of the crew. Husbanding is normally handled by ship line employees, or vessel owners or their agents.

✈ Insurance   🆑 Letters of credit   ⚓ Liner vessel shipping   📑 Sales contracts   🅿 Vessel chartering

HI

hyperlink A hypertext connection that takes the user to another document or another web page. On the ⟨world wide web⟩, hyperlinks appear as underlined text or pictures that are highlighted. To follow a hyperlink, click the highlighted material.

hypertext A type of database system in which objects (text, images, audio/video files, programs, etc.) can be linked to each other. Users can navigate from one object to another, even though they might have very different forms.

hypertext markup language (HTML) @ The lingua franca for describing the contents and appearance of pages on the ⟨world wide web⟩. HML is non-proprietary, and can be processed in a wide range of tools.

hypertext transfer protocol (HTTP) @ The protocol used to transmit and receive all data over the ⟨world wide web⟩, FTP sites and other areas of the internet.

hypothecation letter ⟨letter of hypothecation⟩

IAB (Internet Architecture Board). ⟨Internet Society⟩

IACAC ⟨Inter-American Commercial Arbitration Commission⟩

IADB ⟨Inter-American Development Bank⟩

IAEA ⟨International Atomic Energy Agency⟩

IAF ⟨International Accreditation Forum⟩

IAIGC ⟨Inter-Arab Investment Guarantee Corporation⟩

IATA ⟨International Air Transport Association⟩

IAU ⟨International Accounting Unit⟩

IBOR ⟨Interbank Offered Rate⟩

IBRD ⟨International Bank for Reconstruction and Development⟩

ICANN ⟨Internet Corporation for Assigned Names and Numbers⟩

ICAO ⟨International Civil Aviation Organization⟩

ICC ⟨International Chamber of Commerce⟩

ICC Arbitration ⟨ICC International Court of Arbitration⟩

ICC International Court of Arbitration Created in 1923 as the arbitration body of the ⟨International Chamber of Commerce (ICC)⟩, the ICC International Court of Arbitration has administered nearly 12,000 cases involving parties and arbitrators from some 170 countries. ICC arbitration has been conceived specifically for business disputes in an international context. However, it may also be used in non-international cases. The ICC International Court of Arbitration supervises arbitrations held under the ICC Rules of Arbitration. It meets weekly in Paris and monitors the work of ICC arbitral tribunals, which conduct procedures in countries on all continents. The ICC Court is assisted by a Secretariat, which closely follows all cases and acts as a neutral link between parties, arbitrators and the ICC Court.

> **Further information may be found on the ICC Court's website at www.iccarbitration.org. The ICC Court also provides ICC Dispute Resolution Services, which cover arbitration (www.iccarbitration.org), ADR (www.iccadr.org), expertise (www.iccexpertise.org) and documentary credit dispute resolution, otherwise known as Docdex (www.iccdocdex.org). Each service has its corresponding rules which are available on their respective websites.**

ICCR ⟨International Confederation of Container Reconditioners⟩

ice clause A standard clause in vessel chartering, dictating the course that a vessel master may take if the ship is prevented from entering the loading or discharge port because of ice, or if the vessel is threatened by ice while in port. The clause establishes the rights and obligations of both vessel owner and ⟨charterer⟩ if these events occur.

ICFTU ⟨International Confederation of Free Trade Unions⟩

ICGB ⟨International Cargo Gear Bureau⟩

ICHCA ⟨International Cargo Handling Coordination Association⟩

ICJ ⟨International Court of Justice⟩

ICSID ⟨International Centre for Settlement of Investment Disputes⟩

ICTF ⟨intermodal container transfer facility⟩

IDA ⟨International Development Association⟩

IDB ⟨Inter-American Development Bank⟩

IDENTRUS @ A private-sector company providing infrastructure for authentication, confidentiality, integrity and non-repudiation of ⟨electronic commerce⟩ transactions.

> **For more information, visit the IDENTRUS website at www.identrus.com.**

IEC ⟨International Electrotechnical Commission⟩

IETF ⟨Internet Engineering Task Force⟩

🛈 Insurance   📄 Letters of credit   ⚓ Liner vessel shipping   🗋 Sales contracts   📁 Vessel chartering

I

IFAD ⟨International Fund for Agricultural Development⟩

IFC ⟨International Finance Corporation⟩

IIC ⟨Inter-American Investment Corporation⟩

IICL ⟨International Institute of Container Lessors⟩

Illustrative List A list is contained in Annex 1 to the WTO agreement on Subsidies and Countervailing Measures. It enumerates certain practices that constitute countervailable export subsidies within the terms of the agreement, when provided or mandated by a government or special institution controlled by a government with respect to ⟨goods⟩ produced for export. These include:

- direct subsidies to a firm or industry, contingent upon export performance, currency retention schemes, and other practices that involve a bonus;
- preferential internal transport and freight charges on export shipments;
- remission of direct taxes specifically related to exports;
- provision of services or goods on preferential terms for use in the production of exported ⟨goods⟩;
- export credit guarantees.

See also ⟨countervailing duty⟩, ⟨subsidy⟩, ⟨Subsidies and Countervailing Measures, WTO Agreement⟩.

ILO ⟨International Labour Organization⟩

ILPF ⟨Internet Law and Policy Forum⟩

IMF ⟨International Monetary Fund⟩

IMO ⟨International Maritime Organization⟩

import The process of bringing into a country ⟨goods⟩ that originate in one or more other countries.

> **Some countries also consider the return of domestically produced goods as imports.**

import clearance ⟨customs clearance⟩

import duty ⟨customs duty⟩

import licence A document required and issued by some national governments authorizing the importation of ⟨goods⟩.

Import Licensing Procedures, WTO Agreement A ⟨World Trade Organization⟩ agreement implemented to prevent import licensing procedures from unnecessarily reducing or distorting international trade flows. It is the successor to the GATT Tokyo Round Import Licensing Code.

import quota (absolute & tariff rate). A quota is a limit on the quantity of a good that can be legally imported into a country. There are two types of quota in general use.
1. Absolute quota: a fixed limit to the legally importable quantity. All additional quantities will be denied entry until the opening of the next available quota period.
2. Tariff rate surcharge: a system whereby a certain quantity will be admitted at the normal duty. Additional quantities will also be admitted upon payment of additional duty.

import relief Alleviation of competitive pressures on a domestic industry through restrictions on the inflow of ⟨goods⟩ into the relevant market from other countries, as through the imposition of ⟨tariff⟩s or quantitative restrictions on imports. Also ⟨import quota⟩ and ⟨safeguard measures⟩.

import restrictions Regulations placed by a government for the purpose of limiting imports. These include ⟨exchange control⟩, ⟨import quotas⟩, ⟨tariff⟩s, ⟨prior import deposits⟩, import surcharges, ⟨embargoes⟩, and outright prohibitions of various categories of imports.

import substitution An economic strategy that encourages the development of domestic industry by emphasizing the replacement of imports with domestically produced ⟨goods⟩ rather than the production of goods for export.

importer A party responsible for customs clearance of imported ⟨goods⟩.

> Some countries define importer as the party responsible for payment of duty on imported goods, or an authorized agent acting on behalf of that party.

Inc. (Incorporated) ⟨limited liability⟩

Incoterms 2000 🔡 A set of 13 international standard trade terms (also known as delivery terms), created and maintained by the ⟨International Chamber of Commerce (ICC)⟩. Incoterms 2000 allow the seller and buyer to designate a point at which the costs and risks of transport are precisely divided between them. Incoterms also allocate responsibility for ⟨customs clearance⟩ between sellers and buyers. Since Incoterms are not law but are contractually standard terms, they do not necessarily apply to a given transaction unless the parties specifically incorporate them by referencing "Incoterms 2000." Incoterms are elements of the contract of sale, which may be derived from the seller's ⟨tender⟩ or ⟨proforma invoice⟩. Thus, Incoterms apply only to the seller and the buyer, one of whom will assume the role of ⟨shipper⟩ and enter into a ⟨contract of carriage⟩. The resulting contract of carriage should dovetail with the Incoterm in terms of allocation of transport costs and risks, but this will depend on the shipper giving precise directions to the ⟨carrier⟩ to ship according to the constraints of the given Incoterm.

1. While Incoterms should be specified in order to apply to a given sales contract, they may apply in exceptional cases regardless of explicit mention, if there is a custom of trade or prior course of dealing that indicates reliance on Incoterms, or if the local jurisdiction creates a presumption in favour of applicability of Incoterms.

2. Selection of carriers and service providers such as ⟨forwarders⟩ can be extremely important to parties requiring precise attention to detail for document-driven payment terms.

indemnity Protection against damage or loss, or compensation for damage or loss sustained. See also ⟨letter of indemnity⟩.

indent ⟨purchase order⟩

independent carrier ⚓ A ship line that does not belong to a conference for a particular trade route. See also ⟨conference (liner)⟩.

Independent Regulators Group Information Sharing (IRGIS) An organization to aggregate specific information on the European telecommunications sector, including licences, legislation, market information, consumer issues and statistics.

For more information, visit the IRGIS website at http//irgis.icp.pt.

indirect tax A tax that is levied on expenditure, such as a sales tax imposed at the retail level. Also ⟨excise tax⟩, ⟨sales tax⟩ and ⟨value added tax⟩.

inducement ⚓ A modification found in ship line schedules that a named vessel will call on a named port only if a sufficient amount of profitable cargo has been booked.

industrial policy Traditional governmental policies intended to provide a favourable economic climate for the development of industry in general or specific industrial sectors. Instruments of industrial policy may include tax incentives to promote investments or exports, direct or indirect subsidies, special financing arrangements, protection against foreign competition, worker training programmes, regional development programmes, assistance for research and development, and measures to help small business firms.

infant industry argument The view that "temporary protection" for a new industry or firm in a particular country through ⟨tariff⟩ and ⟨non-tariff barriers⟩ to ⟨imports⟩ can help the industry or firm to become established and eventually competitive in world markets. Historically, new industries that are soundly based and efficiently run have experienced declining costs as output expands and production experience is acquired. However, industries that have been established and operated with heavy dependence on direct or indirect government subsidies have sometimes found it difficult to relinquish the support.

inflation A general increase in the prices of most ⟨goods⟩ and ⟨services⟩ within a market, resulting in diminishing purchasing power of a given sum of the currency used in that market. Inflation results when demand for goods and services increases faster than their supply.

informatics @ A term used to describe the complex of industries and products based on digital information processing technologies.

Information Technology (ITA), WTO Agreement @ A ⟨World Trade Organization⟩ agreement to eliminate ⟨tariff⟩s on a wide range of information technology products. Coverage includes computers and computer equipment, semiconductors and integrated circuits, computer software products, telecommunications equipment, semiconductor manufacturing equipment and computer-based analytical instruments. The ITA is the only global sectoral agreement to date in which participating governments have agreed to eliminate duties on an identical list of products.

inherent vice (of goods) A defect in a product that could in itself result in damage without external cause.

inland bill of lading A ground transport ⟨bill of lading⟩ used in transporting ⟨goods⟩ either from the place where they originate to a port or airport for export, or from an arrival port or airport to the place of ultimate delivery. Although a through transport document can sometimes be used, it can be necessary to use separate ground transport documents in the absence of door-to-door transportation. See also ⟨pre-carriage⟩ and ⟨on-carriage⟩.

inland clearance depot (= inland dry port). A combination transport terminal and ⟨customs clearance⟩ centre at a location other than a port.

inland freight ⟨on-carriage⟩ and ⟨pre-carriage⟩

inland marine cargo insurance Cargo insurance that excludes ocean coverage. See also ⟨marine cargo insurance⟩.

🛧 Insurance 🆔 Letters of credit ⬇ Liner vessel shipping 📑 Sales contracts 📠 Vessel chartering

I

inland waterway A navigable body of water such as a river or canal, as opposed to the sea.

Institute of International Container Lessors (IICL) Established in 1971, the IICL's membership engages in leasing marine-cargo containers to ship operators and others, claiming roughly half of the world's container fleet. The institute is active in governmental, regulatory, customs, tax, educational, technological and environmental fields.

> **For more information, visit the IICL's website at www.iicl.org.**

Institute of Telecom Retailers in Europe, Middle East, India, Asia and Africa (ITRE) A non-profit organization offering globally competitive telecom companies a one-stop location with marketing, networking and education.

> **For more information, visit the ITRE website at www.itre.org**

insurable interest 🗗 A principle of insurance that in order to obtain coverage on a shipment, a party must have a legal relationship to either the transportation (entitlement to freight cost or wages) or to the insurable property (the ‹carrier› itself, or the cargo). This means that if the insurable property is safe or arrives safely at its destination, the party itself will benefit. Conversely, if there is loss or damage or detention to the insurable property, the party will suffer some detriment. Typical parties with insurable interests include those responsible for the condition of the ‹goods› while in transit, unpaid sellers, and buyers who have prepaid. See also ‹party at risk›. The insurable interest principle was established to prevent the macabre and often fraudulent practice of "gaming policies," i.e. speculation on the fate of shipments by unrelated parties through the purchase of insurance.

insurance 🗗 An agreement or contract (commonly called a policy) between the assured and an insurer that, in return for a premium, promises compensation if the assured suffers specified losses.

insurance certificate (= special cargo policy) 🗗 A document used to prove that coverage is provided to cover loss or damage to cargo while in transit when insurance is placed against an ‹open marine cargo policy›.

> **Insurance certificates are normally issued on a shipment-by-shipment basis, and should specify the levels of coverage and the insured amounts.**

insurance policy 🗗 Coverage by an insurance company for a shipment or shipments.

> **Policies covering only one shipment are called special risk**

policies while those covering multiple shipments are called open policies.

insurance premium 🔝 ‹Money› paid or to be paid for insurance coverage.

insurer (= underwriter) 🔝 A party that accepts a risk for a fee.

integrated carrier A ‹carrier› that has both air and ground fleets, or other combinations such as sea, rail and truck, thereby retaining control of the cargo from door to door. Since integrated carriers usually handle thousands of small parcels per hour, they are often less expensive and provide more diverse services than regular carriers. UPS and FedEx are examples of integrated carriers.

Integrated Programme for Commodities (IPC) A programme established by ‹UNCTAD›-IV to promote stabilization for 18 commodities of particular interest to ‹developing countries›.

intellectual property rights (IPR) A generic phrase encompassing intangible property rights, including, among others, ‹patents›, service and ‹trade marks›, ‹copyrights›, industrial designs, rights in semiconductor chip layout designs, rights in trade secrets, etc.

Inter-American Commercial Arbitration Commission (IACAC) Established in 1934 and headquartered in Washington, DC, USA, the IACAC administers a system for arbitrating and conciliating international commercial disputes throughout the Western Hemisphere. The Commission, associated with the ‹Organization of American States›, follows provisions of the ‹United Nations Commission on International Trade Law›.

Inter-American Development Bank (IADB or IDB) Established in 1960 and headquartered in Washington, DC, USA, the IADB is a regional financial institution that helps accelerate economic and social development in Latin America and the Caribbean. Besides regional member countries, IADB membership includes 16 nations located outside the Western Hemisphere.

For more information, visit the IADB website at www.iadb.org.

Inter-American Investment Corporation (IIC) Established in 1986, headquartered in Washington, DC, USA, and affiliated with the ‹IADB›, the IIC is a multilateral investment corporation that promotes the economic development of Latin American and Caribbean member countries by stimulating the establishment, expansion and modernization of private enterprises, especially small- and medium-sized organizations.

For more information, visit the IADB website at www.iadb.org.

🔝 Insurance   LC Letters of credit   ⬇ Liner vessel shipping   ◩ Sales contracts   ℗ Vessel chartering

I

Inter-American Telecommunication Commission (CITEL) Part of the ⟨Organization of American States⟩, where governments, regulators, operators and others meet to discuss telecommunications issues.

For more information, visit the CITEL website at www.citel.oas.org.

Inter-Arab Investment Guarantee Corporation (IAIGC) Established in 1965 and headquartered in Kuwait, the IAIGC stimulates capital transfer among members by providing investment risk coverage and supporting development studies.

For more information, visit the IAIGC website at www.iaigc.org.

interbank offered rate (IBOR) The rate of interest at which banks lend to other prime banks.

interest ⟨Money⟩ charged for the use of borrowed capital, usually expressed as a percentage.

intermediary A party that works between two other parties. For example, a sales agent is an intermediary between a seller and a buyer.

intermediate consignee Any party shown in the "⟨consignee⟩" field of a transport document other than the party for whom the shipment is destined. Typical intermediate consignees include buyer-appointed ⟨customs brokers⟩ or banks taking a security interest in shipped ⟨goods⟩.

intermodal ⟨multimodal transport⟩

Intermodal container transfer facility (ICTF) A site where cargo is transferred from one mode of transportation to another, such as from rail to ship.

international accounting unit (IAU) A unit of measure used by the ⟨North Atlantic Treaty Organization⟩ for its infrastructure projects. It is based on the exchange rates of NATO member countries as reevaluated every six months.

International Accreditation Forum (IAF) Created in 1993, the IAF is a group of international accreditation bodies that promote international recognition of accreditation for quality-systems registrars. Signatories include representatives of accrediting bodies in Australia, Canada, Japan, Mexico, the Netherlands, New Zealand and the United States.

international agreement A broad term for legally binding arrangements covered by international law between or among countries. Such arrangements are variously titled as treaties, conventions, protocols, annexes, accords and memoranda of understanding, notes, pacts, declarations, statutes, constitutions and processes-verbal. The title is not an important factor in making distinctions among arrangements.

International Air Transport Association (IATA) Established in 1945 and headquartered in Geneva, Switzerland, IATA is a trade association serving air carriers, passengers, ⟨shipper⟩s, travel agents and governments. The association promotes safety, standardization of forms (baggage checks, tickets, waybills and hazardous material declarations) and aids in establishing international air fares.

For more information, visit the IATA website at www.iata.org.

International Arrangement on Export Credits An agreement among the 22 ⟨OECD⟩ governments that they will not lower interest rates for export credits below specified levels or offer most tied-aid credits without informing other OECD governments.

International Atomic Energy Agency (IAEA) This specialized ⟨United Nations⟩ agency is the principal international organization that enforces safeguards to ensure that non-nuclear weapons states do not divert sensitive nuclear-related equipment from peaceful applications to the production of nuclear weapons. It also gives advice and technical assistance to ⟨developing countries⟩ on nuclear power development, nuclear safety, radioactive waste management and related efforts. IAEA was established in 1957 and is headquartered in Vienna, Austria.

For more information, visit the IAEA website at www.iaea.org.

International Bank for Reconstruction and Development (IBRD) Part of the ⟨World Bank Group⟩ and headquartered in Washington, DC, USA, the IBRD was established in 1945 to assist with postwar reconstruction. It now assists developing member countries by lending to government agencies and guaranteeing private loans for such projects as agricultural modernization and infrastructure development.

For more information, visit the IBRD website at
www.worldbank.org/htm/extdr/backgrd/ibrd.

International Cargo Gear Bureau, Inc. (ICGB) A New York, USA-based membership not-for-profit corporation established in 1954, ICGB provides registration, inspection, certification, documentation, design, evaluation and consulting services throughout the world for materials handling equipment ashore, offshore and afloat.

For more information, visit the ICGB website at www.icgb.com.

International Cargo Handling Coordination Association (ICHCA)
Headquartered in London, England, the ICHCA:
a. collects, edits and disseminates technical information relating to cargo handling by all modes of transport;
b. maintains consultative status with the ‹International Organization for Standardization (ISO)› for the development of standards relating to cargo handling equipment (such as hooks, containers, wire slings, spreaders and pallets);
c. maintains a library for members' use, and
d. represents members' interests on an international basis.

> **For more information, visit the ICHCA website at www.ichca.org.uk.**

International Centre for Settlement of Investment Disputes (ICSID) Headquartered in Washington, DC, USA, with its ‹World Bank› parent, the ICSID provides facilities for conciliation and arbitration of investment disputes between Contracting States and nationals of other Contracting States. While it does not itself mediate or arbitrate, it assists the initiation of such proceedings.

> **For more information, visit the ICSID website at www.worldbank.org/icsid.**

International Chamber of Commerce (ICC) Founded in 1919 and headquartered in Paris, France, ICC is the world business organization. Its role is to promote free trade and private enterprise, and to represent business interests at national and international levels. ICC has drawn up a number of widely accepted rules that govern the conduct of business across borders – some of its best known products include ‹Incoterms 2000›, the current version of ‹Uniform Customs and Practice for Documentary Credits (UCP)›, ‹Uniform Rules for Collections›, arbitration services, and publications such as the one you are reading. The ‹ICC International Court of Arbitration› is one of the best-known services provided by ICC. The organization has over 7000 members in more than 130 countries throughout the world and is coordinated by national committees in the world's major capitals.

> **For more information, visit the ICC website at www.iccwbo.org.**

International Civil Aviation Organization (ICAO) A ‹United Nations› agency promoting international civil aviation standards and regulations.

> **For more information, visit the ICAO website at www.icao.org.**

International Confederation for Agricultural Credit (ICAC)
Established in 1932 and headquartered in Zurich, Switzerland, the ICAC coordinates documentation and information improvements

---

‹see entry in dictionary› ✈ Air transport 🏛 Bank collections @ e-commerce 🔡 Incoterms

pertaining to agricultural credits. Confederation members are agricultural credit banks and other institutions that provide or study agricultural credits.

International Confederation of Container Reconditioners (ICCR) A worldwide group comprised of trade associations representing reconditioners in Europe, Japan and North America. It represents its member organizations before international agencies including the ⟨United Nations⟩.

For more information, visit the ICCR website at www.reusablepackaging.org.

International Confederation of Free Trade Unions (ICFTU) Founded in 1949 to promote the trade union movement, ICFTU organizes and educates free-trade unions in the developing world through its three regional organizations APRO for Asia and the Pacific, AFRO for Africa and ORIT for Latin America. ICFTU is headquartered in Brussels, Belgium.

For more information, visit the ICFTU website at www.icftu.org.

International Container Bureau (BIC) Established in 1933 under ⟨International Chamber of Commerce (ICC)⟩ auspices and headquartered in Paris, France, BIC is the main organization for promoting and forming international links for the development of containerization and combined transport. It developed the BIC-CODE, a unique registration system for containers.

The BIC is located at 167 rue de Courcelles, F-75017 Paris, France, fax (33) (1) 47660891.

International Court of Justice (ICJ) Founded in 1945 and headquartered in The Hague, Netherlands, the ICJ is the principal judicial organ of the ⟨United Nations⟩ It decides cases submitted by states, and gives advisory opinions on legal questions submitted by the UN General Assembly, Security Council, and specialized agencies.

For more information, visit the ICJ website at www.icj-cij.org.

International Development Association (IDA) Headquartered in Washington, DC, USA, with its ⟨World Bank⟩ parent, the IDA lends ⟨money⟩ to ⟨developing countries⟩ at no interest for long repayment periods.

For more information, visit the IDA website at www.worldbank.org/ida.

International Electrotechnical Commission (IEC) The IEC was established in 1906 to deal with questions related to international standardization in the electrical and electronic engineering fields. The

---

🔨 Insurance   🔠 Letters of credit   ⚓ Liner vessel shipping   📑 Sales contracts   📃 Vessel chartering

members of the IEC are the national committees, one per country, which are required to be as representative as possible of all electric interests in each country concerned manufacturers, users, governmental authorities, teaching and professional bodies. They are composed of representatives of various organizations dealing with questions of electrical standardization at the national level. Most of them are recognized and supported by their national governments.

For more information, visit the IEC website at www.iec.ch.

International Federation of Freight Forwarders Associations (FIATA) A non-governmental organization founded in 1926 representing the freight forwarding industry worldwide. FIATA has three main divisions, called institutes, covering airfreight, customs facilitation and multimodal transport. Each has its own advisory bodies and working groups. In addition, it has created the following documents to establish a uniform worldwide standard for freight forwarders

- FIATA FCR (Forwarders Certificate of Receipt)
- FIATA FCT (Forwarders Certificate of Transport)
- FIATA FWR (Warehouse Receipt)
- FIATA FBL (Negotiable Multimodal Transport Bill of Lading)
- FIATA FWB (Non-negotiable Multimodal Transport Waybill)
- FIATA SDT (Shipper's Declaration for the Transport of Dangerous ⟨goods⟩)
- FIATA SIC (Shipper's Intermodal Weight Certificate)
- FIATA FFI (Forwarding Instructions)

For more information, visit FIATA's website at www.fiata.com.

International Finance Corporation (IFC) Headquartered in Washington, DC, USA with its ⟨World Bank⟩ parent, the IFC promotes private investment in ⟨developing countries⟩.

For more information, visit the IFC website at www.ifc.org.

International Fund for Agricultural Development (IFAD) Established in 1977 and headquartered in Rome, Italy, the IFAD provides financial support for programs that improve agricultural policies and increase food production among members.

For more information, visit the IFAD website at www.ifad.org.

International Institute for the Unification of Private Law (UNIDROIT) UNIDROIT studies methods to coordinate and unify the private and trade laws of member countries. Originally established in 1926 as a League of Nations affiliate, the institute is now independent and headquartered in Rome, Italy.

For more information, visit the UNIDROIT website at www.unidroit.org.

International Labour Organization (ILO) Established in 1919, the ILO became a specialized ⟨United Nations⟩ agency in 1946. It seeks to promote improved working and living conditions by establishing standards that reduce social injustice in such areas as employment, pay, health, working conditions and freedom of association among workers. It is headquartered in Geneva, Switzerland.

For more information, visit the ILO website at www.ilo.org.

International Maritime Organization (IMO) Established as a specialized ⟨United Nations⟩ agency in 1948 and headquartered in London, England, the IMO facilitates cooperation on technical matters affecting merchant shipping and traffic, including improved maritime safety, dangerous ⟨goods⟩ and prevention of marine pollution.

For more information, visit the IMO website at www.imo.org.

International Monetary Fund (IMF) Established in December 1945, the IMF is a specialized ⟨United Nations⟩ agency that promotes international monetary harmony, monitors the exchange rate and monetary policies of member nations, and provides credit for member countries that experience temporary balance of payments deficits. Each member nation has a quota, expressed in ⟨special drawing rights⟩, which reflects both the relative size of the member's economy and that member's voting power in the fund. Quotas also determine members' access to the financial resources, and their shares in the allocation of special drawing rights by the fund. The IMF, funded through members' quotas, may supplement its resources through borrowing. Over 175 countries belong to the IMF.

For more information, visit the IMF website at www.imf.org.

international nautical mile 1,852 metres (6076.12 feet).

International Organization of Employers (IOE) Established in 1920 and headquartered in Geneva, Switzerland, the IOE consists of over 120 employer organizations and represents the interests of businesses in the fields of labour and social policy.

For more information, visit the IOE website at www.ioe-emp.org.

International Organization for Standardization (ISO) ⟨International Standards Organization⟩

International Road Transport Union (IRU) With members in 68 countries, the IRU assists bus, coach, taxi and truck operators throughout the world by briefing them on developments affecting their business.

For more information, visit the IRU website at www.iru.org.

⊼ Insurance [LC] Letters of credit Ⓛ Liner vessel shipping ⊠ Sales contracts Ⓟ Vessel chartering

International Road Transportation Convention (CMR) The Convention on the Contract for the International Carriage by Road was adopted at Geneva in 1956. This convention applies when ‹goods› are taken from one country to another and at least one of these countries is a party to the convention.

International Ship Suppliers Association (ISSA) A London, England based organization of more than 1800 ship suppliers operating in over 80 countries.

For more information, visit the ISSA website at www.shipsupply.org.

International Standards Organization (ISO = International Organization for Standardization). Established in 1947, the ISO is a worldwide federation of national bodies representing approximately 90 member countries. The scope of the ISO covers standardization in all fields except electrical and electronic engineering standards, which are the responsibility of the ‹International Electrotechnical Commission (IEC)›. Together, the ISO and IEC form the specialized system for worldwide standardization – the world's largest non-governmental system for voluntary industrial and technical collaboration at the international level. The result of ISO technical work is published in the form of international standards.

For more information, visit the ISO website www.iso.ch.

International Standby Practices (ISP) LC The ‹International Chamber of Commerce (ICC)› rules governing standby L/Cs.

International Telecommunications Union (ITU) A ‹United Nations› agency within which governments and the private sector coordinate global telecom networks and services.

For more information, visit the ITU website www.itu.int.

International Telecommunications Users Group (INTUG) A non-profit organization promoting users' interests at the international level to ensure that their voice is heard wherever telecommunications policies are decided. INTUG liaises with numerous other telecommunications organizations which can be found on their website.

For more information, visit the INTUG website at www.intug.net.

International Trade Centre (= UNCTAD/WTO/ITC). A quasi-autonomous, Geneva-based organization within the ‹United Nations› system (reporting to both the ‹WTO› and the UN Conference on Trade and Development) that provides a wide range of technical assistance to ‹developing countries› seeking to expand and promote their export potential.

‹see entry in dictionary›   ✈ Air transport   🏛 Bank collections   @ e-commerce   🔠 Incoterms

> **For more information, visit the ITC website at www.intracen.org.**

International Union of Railways (UIC) A worldwide organization for cooperation among railway companies and development of rail transport.

> **For more information, visit the UIC website www.uic.asso.fr.**

internet architecture board 〈Internet Society〉

Internet Corporation for Assigned Names and Numbers (ICANN) @ A technical coordination body for the internet that assumes responsibility for internet domain names, IP address numbers and protocol parameter and port numbers, as well as coordination of the stable operation of the internet's root server system.

> **For more information, visit the ICANN website at www.icann.org.**

Internet Engineering Task Force (IETF) @ A large international community of network designers, vendors and researchers concerned with the evolution of internet architecture and the smooth operations of the internet. See also 〈Internet Society〉

> **For more information, visit the Task Force's website at www.ietf.org.**

Internet Law and Policy Forum (ILPF) @ An international organization dedicated to promoting global growth of electronic commerce by contributing to a better understanding of the particular legal issues that arise from the cross border nature of the electronic medium.

> **For further information, visit the ILPF website at www.ilpf.org.**

Internet service provider (ISP) @ A party that links individual users to the internet.

Internet Society The Internet Society is a professional membership society with more than 150 organizations and 6000 individual members in 100 countries. It provides leadership in addressing issues that confront the future of the internet, and is the organization home of the 〈Internet Engineering Task Force (IETF)〉 and the Internet Architecture Board (IAB).

> **For more information, visit the Society's website at www.isoc.org.**

intraday credit 〈daylight exposure〉

Intranet 〈closed network communications〉

INTUG 〈International Telecommunications Users Group〉

inventory ① A complete listing of stock on hand. ② The objects represented on such a list.

IJ

invisible trade Items such as freight costs, ⟨insurance⟩ and financial services that are included in a country's ⟨balance-of-payments⟩ accounts, even though they are not recorded as physically visible ⟨exports⟩ and ⟨imports⟩. Also ⟨visible trade⟩.

invoice ⟨commercial invoice⟩ or ⟨proforma invoice⟩

IOE ⟨International Organization of Employers⟩

IPC ⟨Integrated Programme for Commodities⟩

IPR ⟨intellectual property rights⟩

IRGIS ⟨Independent Regulators Group⟩

irrevocable L/C 🄻🄲 A letter of credit that cannot be cancelled or changed by any party without the unanimous consent of all other parties.

IRU ⟨International Road Transport Union⟩

IsDB ⟨Islamic Development Bank⟩

Islamic Development Bank (IsDB) Established in 1975 and headquartered in Jeddah, Saudi Arabia, the IsDB finances economic aid and social development in member countries.
For more information, visit the IsDB website at www.isdb.org.

ISO ⟨International Standards Organization⟩

ISP ⟨Internet service provider⟩ or ⟨International Standby Practices⟩

ISSA ⟨International Ship Suppliers Association⟩

issue date 🄻🄲 The date a ⟨letter of credit⟩ was opened, or the date an amendment was issued.

issuing bank (= opening bank) 🄻🄲 The financial institution that opens a ⟨letter of credit⟩.

ITA ⟨Information Technology, WTO Agreement⟩

ITC ⟨International Trade Centre⟩

ITCF ⟨Intermodal Container Transfer Facility⟩

ITRE ⟨Institute of Telecom Retailers in Europe, Middle East, India, Asia and Africa⟩

ITU ⟨International Telecommunications Union⟩.

IVA ⟨value added tax⟩

J curve An economic phenomenon whereby a real reduction in the exchange value of a country's currency may cause a temporary worsening in the ⟨balance of trade⟩. This is because it takes time for import growth to decline because of the exchange rate change. It is called a "J curve" because the curve of the downward movement of the balance of trade is followed by an upward movement, resembling the letter J.

Japan Bank for International Cooperation (JBIC) Japan's official provider of export credits.

> **For more information, visit the JBIC website at www.jbic.go.jp.**

Japan External Trade Organization (JETRO) This Ministry of International Trade and Industry agency administers the export and import promotion programmes of the Japanese Government.

> **For more information, visit the JETRO website at www.jetro.go.jp.**

Japanese Federation of Economic Organizations ⟨Keidanren⟩

JBIC ⟨Japan Bank for International Cooperation⟩

JETRO ⟨Japan External Trade Organization⟩

jetsam ⟨Goods⟩ deliberately cast overboard as to lighten a vessel in emergency.

jettison 🗹 Throwing cargo overboard to avert disaster by lightening a ship, as in a storm.

jetty ⟨wharf⟩

JEXIM ⟨Japan Bank for International cooperation⟩

joint rate Two or more ⟨carriers⟩ providing a single rate for a shipment.

joint venture A form of business partnership involving joint management and the sharing of risks and profits.

just in time A distribution method where the buyer receives products as and when required, and is thereby relieved of the cost of maintaining large inventories. This is accomplished through careful advance planning, tight scheduling and closely monitoring production and transportation.

> **Note: Although excellent in theory, this often results in sellers holding larger inventories in order to supply their customers on an uninterrupted, just-in-time basis. In this respect, it reflects the relative bargaining positions of sellers and buyers as well as the overall availability of the products in question.**

KD ⟨knocked down⟩

Keidanren (Japanese Federation of Economic Organizations) Established in 1946, this powerful private non-profit economic

---

🗹 Insurance   🄻🄲 Letters of credit   ⬇ Liner vessel shipping   🅐 Sales contracts   🄿 Vessel chartering

K

organization represents virtually all branches of Japanese economic activity.

For more information, visit the Keidanren website at www.keidanren.or.jp.

keiretsu The horizontally and vertically linked industrial structure of post-war Japan. Horizontally linked groups include a broad range of industries linked by banks and trading companies. Vertically linked groups are centred around parent companies, with subsidiaries frequently serving as suppliers, distributors and retailers.

key currency ⟨reserve currency⟩

KFAED ⟨Kuwait Fund for Arab Economic Development⟩

KFT ⟨limited liability⟩

KFTA ⟨Korea Foreign Trade Association⟩

KfW ⟨Reconstruction Loan Corporation (German)⟩

KG (Kommanditgesellschaft) ⟨limited liability⟩

KGaA (Kommanditgesellschaft auf Aktien) ⟨limited liability⟩

knocked down (KD) Merchandise that is supplied complete with all parts, but in an unassembled state.

knot A measure of ship's speed. One knot = one international nautical mile (1852 metres) per hour.

know-how Knowledge of how to do something, expertise.

known Loss Loss or damage that was discovered before delivery.

KOM. PTI (kommandit pirket) ⟨limited liability⟩

kommandit pirket (KOM. PTI) ⟨limited liability⟩

Kommanditgesellschaft (KG) ⟨limited liability⟩

KOOP. (Kooperatif) ⟨limited liability⟩

Kooperatif (KOOP.) ⟨limited liability⟩

Korea Foreign Trade Association (KFTA) Headquartered in Seoul, Republic of Korea, KFTA is a non-profit private business organization of South Korean companies, providing information and services concerning trade, both for members and foreign businesses.

Korea Trade Promotion Corporation (KOTRA) Established in 1962 and headquartered in Seoul, Republic of Korea, KOTRA is a government-owned corporation promoting foreign trade and investment with South Korea.

> **For more information, visit the KOTRA website at www.kotra.or.kr/eng.**

KOTRA ⟨Korea Trade Promotion Corporation⟩

Kuwait Fund for Arab Economic Development (KFAED) Established in 1961 and headquartered in Safat, Kuwait, the KFAED is a Kuwaiti independent public institution that assists Arab and other ⟨developing countries⟩ in expanding their economies through concessional loans and financing feasibility studies.

> **For more information, visit the KFAED website at www.kuwait-fund.org.**

Kyoto Convention on the Simplification and Harmonization of Customs Procedures A 1973 international convention with the goal of the development of compatible national customs procedures in different countries as a means of encouraging and facilitating international trade.

L/C ⟨letter of credit⟩

LAES ⟨Latin American Economic System⟩

LAFTA ⟨Latin American Integration Association⟩

lagan In times of peril, a vessel may need to lighten its load by jettisoning cargo or equipment. Lagan is such jettison to which a ship's marker or buoy is attached. Should any such ⟨goods⟩ later be recovered, they must be returned to the indicated owner in return for a ⟨salvage⟩ payment.

LAIA ⟨Latin American Integration Association⟩

laissez passer A document accorded by a host government to foreign diplomatic personnel, which permits them to pass freely across the border of that country.

landbridge 🛈 Multi-modal transportation where containerized cargo is brought to a port on one coast, unloaded to ground transport, transported to a port on another coast, and loaded on to another vessel. Example a seller in Japan ships a full container, which goes by vessel from Yokohama to Seattle, USA, where it is loaded on a train for transport to Baltimore, USA, where it is again loaded on a vessel for further transport to Felixstowe, England. Usually, a single ⟨carrier⟩ (often the provider of ⟨main-carriage⟩ transportation) takes responsibility for the entire shipment.

landed value The value of cargo at the arrival point on the buyer's

Insurance   Letters of credit   Liner vessel shipping   Sales contracts   Vessel chartering

L

side; i.e., cost of ⟨goods⟩, packing, forwarding fees, ⟨pre-carriage⟩, ⟨main carriage⟩ and ⟨insurance⟩.

landlocked Having no direct access to the sea.

LASH (lighter aboard ship) An ocean-going vessel designed to carry specially configured barges which are used much as shipping containers. Although LASH service is limited to a few ship lines, it is practical for shallow ports.

last in, first out (LIFO) Inventory management and/or accounting procedure whereby the most recently arrived ⟨goods⟩ of their kind (last in) are shipped prior to those that have arrived before (first out).

Latin American Association of Development Financing Institutions (ALIDE) Founded in 1968 and headquartered in Lima, Peru, the Association promotes cooperation among its 24 member countries in ways that support the integration of member economies.

> For more information, visit the ALIDE website at
> www.alide.org.pe.

Latin American Economic System (LAES = SELA) Founded in 1975 and headquartered in Caracas, Venezuela, LAES promotes economic and social integration among its 26 member countries and seeks to promote a united view for Latin America to agencies of the ⟨European Community⟩ and the ⟨United Nations⟩.

> For more information, visit
> www.itcilo.it/english/actrav/telearn/global/ilo/blokit/sela.htm.

Latin American Export Bank ⟨Banco Latinamericano de Exportaciones⟩

Latin American Free Trade Association (LAFTA) ⟨Latin American Integration Association⟩

Latin American Integration Association (LAIA) Originally created in 1960 as the Latin American Free Trade Association, LAIA was restructured in 1980 as a more flexible alternative. It is headquartered in Montevideo, Uruguay.

> For more information, visit the LAIA website at www.aladi.org.

laydays (= laytime) 🄿 The time allowed by a shipowner to the ⟨charterer⟩ or ⟨shipper⟩ in which to load or discharge the cargo. This may be expressed in days or hours or tons per day. Laydays may be set in running days (every calendar day), working days (excluding Sundays and port holidays) or weather days (which exclude days where operations are prevented by bad weather). It

---

may be contractually provided that when the charterer or shipper loads/unloads more quickly than is necessary, he or she will be eligible for payment of an incentive called ⟨dispatch money⟩. However, if the loading or unloading time is excessive, the charterer or shipper may have to pay a penalty called ⟨demurrage⟩.

LCL ⟨less than container load⟩

LDC ⟨least developed countries⟩

lead time The amount of time required for something to happen. For example, production lead time would be the length of time required to produce a good once the work order has been placed at the factory, including any lead times for materials that must be ordered.

League of Arab States (= Arab League). Established in 1945 and headquartered in Cairo, Egypt, the League of Arab States is a regional grouping aimed at improving relations among Arab nations.

> **For more information, visit the Arab League website at www.leagueofarabstates.org.**

least developed countries (LLDC) Forty-eight of the world's poorest countries, considered by the ⟨United Nations⟩ to be the "least-developed" of the ⟨less-developed countries⟩.

legal weight The weight of ⟨goods⟩ and their immediate packing with which they are normally sold, but excluding the weight of any export packing.

legalized documents ⟨consular documentation⟩

less developed countries (LDC) Countries with low per-capita ⟨gross national product⟩.

less than container load (LCL) A shipment too small to justify the use of a shipping container.

less than truckload (LTL) A shipment too small to fill a truck.

lessee A party to whom a lease is granted.

lessor A party who grants a lease.

letter of correction A document addressed to a consulate containing such data as needed to resolve any necessary corrections in ⟨consular documentation⟩.

letter of credit (L/C) A guarantee on the part of a financial institution that a stipulated party will be paid a stipulated value at a stipulated time, provided that all terms and conditions stated

---

Insurance   Letters of credit   Liner vessel shipping   Sales contracts   Vessel chartering

L

within the L/C have been complied with.

letter of hypothecation 🏛 Banks that discount ‹drafts› for exporters may require an interest in the shipped ‹goods›, in addition to the drafts they receive as collateral. A letter of hypothecation provides possession rights to the goods themselves. When attached to a draft, it authorizes the discounting bank's overseas correspondent to sell the goods if the draft is not honoured.

letter of indemnity (LOI) ✉ ⚓ ① General: A document in which one party promises to protect another party against damage or loss. ② Steamer guarantee: A document used in international trade to allow a ‹carrier› to release ‹goods› to a receiver who is not yet in possession of the original (negotiable) marine ‹bill of lading›. An LOI is in essence a guarantee, which the receiver provides to the carrier assuring the carrier that it will not suffer any financial loss by having released the goods in the absence of the bill of lading.

> **Carriers often require that LOIs be supported by surety bonds or bank guarantees.**

letter of intent (LOI) A written statement of the intention to enter a formal agreement.

levy To assess or impose a tax or ‹tariff›, or as a noun, the charge itself.

lex mercatoria Internationally accepted general trade practices; the international, informal law of merchants.

liability ① An obligation or debt. ② Something disadvantageous. ③ Potential risk of responsibility because of injury or damage to others.

LIBID ‹London Interbank Bid Rate›

LIBOR ‹London Interbank Offered Rate›

licence ① A revocable privilege granted by a government for activities that would otherwise be illegal (example import licence). ② A contractual agreement whereby a party (licensee) receives another party's right to manufacture, distribute and/or sell ‹goods› or services (example a licensed Coca Cola bottler).

licensee A party that has been granted a licence.

licensing Code A GATT Tokyo Round code aimed at simplifying import licensing procedures and at ensuring their fair and equitable application. The ‹WTO› Agreement on Import Licensing Procedures is the successor to the Licensing Code. Also ‹Import Licensing Procedures, WTO Agreement›.

L

licensor A party granting a ⟨licence⟩.

lien A right over another's property to protect a debt charged on that property.

LIFFE ⟨London International Financial Futures and Options Exchange⟩

LIFO ① For chartering, ⟨Liner in, free out⟩. ② For inventory control, ⟨last in, first out⟩.

lighter aboard ship ⟨LASH⟩

lighterage Barge transport from pier to vessel or vessel to pier at ports that are too shallow to permit vessels to berth directly at piers. ⟨Goods⟩ subject to lighterage provide one of the few instances where they are actually placed directly alongside a vessel as defined in the ⟨Free Alongside Ship (FAS)⟩ ⟨Incoterm⟩.

LIMEAN ⟨London Interbank Mean Rate⟩

limited ⟨limited liability⟩

limited liability A situation whereby the liability of a party within a company is limited to some extent. There are many forms of limited liability enterprises. For instance, corporations normally limit shareholder liability to the amount invested in a business, while limited partnerships may hold only one or several designated partners personally liable yet limiting the liability of other partners. Most jurisdictions require that a business with limited liability indicate this by using a recognized symbol, such as Incorporated (Inc.), Corporation (Corp.), Limited (Ltd), Sociedad Anomina (S.A.), etc.

limited pirket (LTD PTI) ⟨limited liability⟩

line haul The direct movement of cargo on a single ship between two ports of call.

linear tariff reduction (= horizontal tariff reduction). A reduction by a given percentage of all ⟨tariff⟩s maintained by countries participating in trade negotiations, with or without exceptions for products deemed to be "sensitive."

liner in, free out (LIFO) 🅿 Chartering terms whereby the vessel owner is responsible for the costs of vessel loading but not for vessel unloading.

liner service ⬇ Regularly scheduled marine transportation provided by a ⟨carrier⟩ having a fixed port rotation and advertising it as such. Liner service is done on ⟨liner terms⟩, where the shipowner provides vessel loading and unloading.

🅰 Insurance 🄻🄲 Letters of credit ⬇ Liner vessel shipping 🅢 Sales contracts 🅿 Vessel chartering

L

liner terms ⬇ ✉ Marine transportation agreements whereby shipowners or operators take responsibility for vessel loading and unloading. Liner terms may apply to vessel ⟨charters⟩, and normally apply to ship lines offering ⟨liner service⟩ (regularly scheduled service among ports where they have facilities to receive, load, unload and dispatch cargo).

liner waybill ⟨sea waybill⟩

LLDC ⟨least developed countries⟩

logistics Planning, implementing and controlling the efficient movement of ⟨goods⟩, ⟨services⟩ and information from origin point(s) to the point or points where they will be used.

logo A symbol of an identifying company name, ⟨trademark⟩, etc., often stylized.

LOI Depending on the context, see either ⟨letter of indemnity⟩ or ⟨letter of intent⟩.

Lome Convention An agreement covering aid and trade preferences between the ⟨European Union⟩ and approximately seventy African, Caribbean and Pacific (APC) countries, of which most are former colonies of EU members.

London Institute of Underwriters "A" Clauses 📄 The broadest type of standard marine insurance coverage generally available (called "⟨all risks⟩" in the US market). This does not include coverage for the perils of ⟨war risk⟩, ⟨strike, riot and civil commotion⟩ These additional coverages are available for most markets, usually at modest additional premiums.

London Institute of Underwriters "B" Clauses 📄 Marine insurance coverage that expands all the perils covered under ⟨London Institute of Underwriters "C" Clauses⟩ to include partial losses for heavy weather, and covers the following additional perils lightning, seawater as a result of heavy weather and ⟨jettison⟩. With average (also called ⟨with particular average⟩) provides virtually the same coverage in the US market.

London Institute of Underwriters "C" Clauses 📄 A type of marine cargo insurance providing minimum cover. ⟨Free of Particular Average (FPA)⟩ provides virtually the same coverage in the US market.
London "C" Clauses cover:
- Total or partial loss from stranding sinking, burning or collision. (Under English Terms partial losses are payable if any of these events occur. Under American Terms, partial loss is payable only

if caused by these events.)

- Total loss from errors in vessel management, boiler bursting, defects in hull or machinery and explosion.

L

> **1. This coverage is usually inadequate for shipments of ⟨goods⟩ of more than nominal value.**
> **2. Both ⟨Incoterms 2000⟩ and the current version of ⟨ICC⟩'s ⟨Uniform Customs and Practice for Documentary Credits⟩ accept minimum-cover insurance as the seller's compliance with its obligation to insure in the absence of any agreement to the contrary. Therefore, the seller and buyer should carefully define the coverage that they want, and should clearly agree that the responsible party provide it.**
> **3. London C is the opposite of ⟨London Institute of Underwriters clause A⟩, (called "⟨all risks⟩" in the USA) which provides maximum cover, especially when augmented to include war, ⟨strike, riot and civil commotion⟩ perils.**

London Interbank Bid Rate (LIBID) The rate of interest paid for funds in the London Interbank Market.

London Interbank Mean Rate (LIMEAN) The mid-point of the ⟨London Interbank Bid Rate⟩ and the ⟨London Interbank Offered Rate⟩.

London Interbank Offered Rate (LIBOR) The most prominent of the interbank offering rates, LIBOR is the rate of interest at which banks in London lend funds to other prime banks in London. LIBOR is frequently used as a basis for determining the rate of interest payable on Eurocurrency loans, i.e. LIBOR plus a markup negotiated between lender and borrower.

London International Financial Futures and Options Exchange (LIFFE) Established in 1982, LIFFE is Europe's leading exchange trading in futures contracts, including short-term interest rates, government bonds, stock indices and traded options on these instruments.

> **For more information, visit the LIFFE website at www.liffe.com.**

long date forward A forward exchange contract whose maturity exceeds one year. See also ⟨forward exchange contract⟩.

loro account ⟨vostro account⟩

loss Deprivation, detriment, injury.

> **In both insurance and transport the word "loss" has two meanings**
> **1. As a general term, that something bad happened to a shipment resulting in deprivation. This could be either damage to shipped ⟨goods⟩ or failure of some or all of them to arrive.**
> **2. As a particular term, that all or part of a shipment failed to arrive (disappearance).**

LM

LTD (Limited) ⟨limited liability⟩

LTD. PTI. (Limited Pirket) ⟨limited liability⟩

LTL ⟨less than truckload⟩

lump sum charter 🅿 Renting a fixed capacity of a vessel in return for a fixed sum, as opposed to payment of a freight rate.

lump sum freight charge ⊥ An all-inclusive price for transportation. Lump sum totals typically include the base-rate freight cost and all applicable surcharges (such as fuel and currency adjustment factors and terminal handling charges).

lusophone countries Those countries whose official language is Portuguese.

MAB (= MAWB). ⟨master air waybill⟩

Maastricht Treaty This treaty created the ⟨European Union⟩ when it took force in 1993.

mafi A wheeled platform used for staging non-wheeled cargo on ⟨roll-on/roll-off⟩ vessels. Mafis are limited to ⟨wharf⟩ and vessel use.

Maghreb States (= Arab Maghreb Union). Algeria, Libya, Mauritania, Morocco and Tunisia.

main carriage International transportation, as from the departure point on the seller's side to the arrival point on the buyer's side.

managed float ⟨dirty float⟩

managed trade Attempts by governments at the national or international level to influence or control exports and imports based on the presumption that government perspectives are more likely to ensure optimal trade rather than relying on unmanaged market forces.

manifest (cargo). A listing of all cargo transported on a particular marine voyage or flight. The manifest prepared for cargo loaded at a given port or airport should equal the sum total of all transport documents (⟨B/Ls⟩, ⟨AWBs⟩) issued for cargo taken on at that port or airport.

maquiladora ("maquila") The Mexican in-bond industry programme that allows foreign manufacturers to ship components into Mexico for assembly and subsequent re-export.

> Although this programme originally permitted totally duty-free imports, Mexico's membership in free trade associations is causing some changes, so be sure to check the duty status of components you wish to use before establishing a maquiladora programme.

M

margin of preference The difference between the duty payable under a given system of ⟨tariff⟩ preferences and the duty that would be assessed in the absence of preferences.

marine bill of lading (= ocean bill of lading). ⟨bill of lading⟩

marine cargo insurance 🏹 Broadly speaking, marine cargo insurance covers loss of or damage to ⟨goods⟩ at sea, although many marine cargo insurance policies are written to also cover air and multimodal shipments. Levels of coverage differ. See also ⟨all risks⟩, ⟨free of particular average⟩, ⟨war risk⟩, ⟨strike, riot, and civil commotion⟩ and ⟨open marine cargo insurance policy⟩.

market access The ability of providers of ⟨goods⟩ and ⟨services⟩ in one country to penetrate a related market in a foreign country.

market disruption A situation where a surge in imports of a type of good causes sales of domestically produced ⟨goods⟩ to drop to an extent that domestic producers and their employees suffer major economic hardship. See also ⟨safeguard measures⟩.

market economy The national economy of a country that relies on market forces to determine levels of production, consumption, investment and savings without government intervention.

market risk The possibility that results at the time a product is delivered may differ from expectations held at the time it was ordered. For instance, the market price may have increased or decreased, or the product may be in greater or lesser demand than was the case when the order was placed.

Deteriorating markets may cause buyers to seek escape from sales contracts. This can result in refusals to accept meaningless discrepancies in ⟨letter of credit⟩ documentation or short extensions in previously agreed shipment or delivery times. On the other hand, buyers who find themselves in appreciating markets tend to be more forgiving.

master One who commands a merchant vessel.

master air waybill ✈ (MAB = MAWB). An air transport document issued by an ⟨undercarrier⟩. This is the opposite of a ⟨house air waybill⟩, which is issued by a ⟨carrier⟩ other than the undercarrier.

master form A central document in export administrative systems under which all necessary information is entered into a single master document or computer file, which is then used to generate all export-related documents.

mate's receipt 🅿 A transport document acknowledging receipt of cargo for transport issued by a responsible ship's officer after the

M

cargo has been tallied into the vessel. The mate's receipt can be taken to the master or his representative and exchanged for a ‹bill of lading›.

For modern ports, mates' receipts are used only for ‹charter› shipments. Shipments made on ‹"liner" terms› (where the ship line handles vessel loading and unloading) are covered by ‹dock receipts› signed when the ‹goods› are delivered to the ship line's terminal. The dock receipts are then replaced by marine transport documents issued on a "‹received for shipment›" or "‹on-board›" basis.

maturity date The date an obligation becomes due. In ‹bank collections›, the due date of an accepted ‹draft›.

MAWB (= MAB). ‹master air waybill›

MDB ‹multilateral development banks›

measurement ton the volume component of a formula used for calculating the number of revenue tons in a shipment. See also ‹revenue ton›.

mediation An attempt to resolve a dispute through discussions under the auspices of a neutral third party (mediator) where the contending parties are not obliged to accept the offered solution. This is in contrast to binding ‹arbitration›, where the contending parties are usually obligated to accept the offered solution.

Mercado Comun del Sur ‹MERCOSUR›

MERCOSUR (= Mercado Comun del Sur). A common market established in 1991 and comprised of nations located in South America's southern region. It anticipates the formation of a full customs union by 2006.

For more information, visit the MERCOSUR website at www.mercosur.com.

merger A combination of two or more business enterprises into a single enterprise.

MFN ‹most favoured nation›

micro landbridge ⚓ (microbridge). ‹Multimodal transportation› where containerized cargo is brought by ground from and/or to inland points that are not ports. A seller in Paris, France ships a full container, which goes by rail to Le Havre, France, where it is loaded on a vessel for further transport to Baltimore, USA. Usually, a single ‹carrier› (often the provider of ‹main-carriage› transportation) takes responsibility for the entire shipment.

microbridge ‹micro landbridge›

M

micropayment transfer protocol (MTP) A W3C-defined software-based system for micropayments, this protocol is "optimized for use in low-value transfers between parties who have a relationship over a period of time." See also ⟨W3C⟩.

middleman A trader who handles a product between its producer and its consumer.

MIF ⟨Multilateral Investment Fund⟩

MIGA ⟨Multilateral Investment Guarantee Agency⟩

mini landbridge (minibridge = MLB) ⚓ Multimodal transportation where containerized cargo is brought by ground transport across a continent for further transport by sea. For example, a seller in New York ships a full container, which goes by rail to Portland, USA, where it is loaded on a vessel for further transport to Kaohsiung, Taiwan. Usually, a single ⟨carrier⟩ (often the provider of main-carriage transportation) takes responsibility for the entire shipment.

Ministry of International Trade (MITI) A powerful Japanese Government agency responsible for formulating and implementing Japan's trade and industrial policies.

MITI ⟨Ministry of International Trade⟩

mixed credit The practice of combining concessional and market-rate export credits as an export promotion mechanism.

MLB ⟨mini landbridge⟩

MMCF ⟨multimedia communications forum⟩

money Any medium of exchange that is widely accepted in payment for ⟨goods⟩ and ⟨services⟩ or to settle debts. Money also serves as a standard of value in measuring the relative worth of different goods and services, and as a means of storing wealth.

money laundering The process whereby criminals seek to "wash" illicit funds (generally garnered from international terrorism or drug dealing). By moving funds around from country to country, a fraudster's intention is to conceal the source of the funds and make them appear legitimate.

money order An instrument used to remit money to a named ⟨payee⟩, often used by parties who do not hold a current account with a banking institution to pay bills or transfer ⟨money⟩ to another party. There are three parties to a money order: the remitter (payer), the payee and the ⟨drawee⟩. Drawees are usually financial institutions or post offices.

🗂 Insurance 🆑 Letters of credit ⚓ Liner vessel shipping 📑 Sales contracts 📂 Vessel chartering

M

Montreal Convention ✈ A convention for the uniformity of certain rules of international carriage by air.

Montreal Protocol A multilateral agreement negotiated in 1988 to reduce and eventually eliminate the use of chlorofluorocarbons and halogens, so as to prevent the erosion of the ozone layer.

most favoured nation treatment (MFN) A commitment by a country that it will extend to another country the lowest ⟨tariff⟩ rates it applies to any other country. All contracting parties undertake to apply such treatment to one another under Article I of the GATT (now ⟨WTO⟩). When a country agrees to cut tariffs on a particular product imported from one country, the tariff reduction automatically applies to imports of this product from any other country eligible for most favoured nation treatment. This principle of nondiscriminatory treatment of imports appeared in numerous bilateral trade agreements prior to the establishment of GATT. A country is under no obligation to extend MFN treatment to another country unless both are parties to the WTO or when MFN is specified in a bilateral agreement to which the country subscribes.

> **Some countries such as the United States use the term "normal trade relations" in place of MFN, so as to extend this treatment to countries without endorsing their non-trade behaviour.**

MRA ⟨Mutual Recognition Agreements⟩

MTO ⟨Multimodal Transport Operator⟩

multilateral Having a number of participating parties, members, or countries. In the context of the ⟨World Trade Organization⟩, "multilateral" has a special meaning. Multilateral agreements of the WTO are binding on all member countries, in contrast to ⟨plurilateral⟩ WTO agreements, which are binding only on those WTO members that have affirmatively acceded to such agreements.

multilateral agreement An international compact in which three or more parties participate. Multilateral agreements are usually open to all qualifying nations.

multilateral aid Development assistance given by donors to recipient countries through international institutions.

multilateral development banks (MDB) There are five multilateral development banks: ⟨African Development Bank⟩, ⟨Asian Development Bank⟩, ⟨European Bank for Reconstruction and Development⟩, ⟨Inter-American Development Bank⟩ and ⟨World Bank⟩.

Multilateral Investment Fund (MIF) A special fund, administered by the Inter-American Development Bank, that was established in 1993 to accelerate private-sector development and help improve the climate for private investment in Latin America and the Caribbean.

Multilateral Investment Guarantee Agency (MIGA) Established in 1993 and headquartered in Washington, DC, USA with its World Bank parent, MIGA encourages equity and other direct investment flows to ⟨developing countries⟩ through the mitigation of non-commercial investment barriers. The agency offers investors guarantees against non-commercial risk; advises developing-member governments on the design and implementation of policies, programmes and procedures related to foreign investments; and sponsors a dialogue between the international business community and host governments on investment issues.
For more information, visit the MIGA website at www.miga.org.

multilateral trade negotiations A term describing the rounds of negotiations held under the auspices of the General Agreement on Tariffs and Trade since 1947 and, more recently, the ⟨World Trade Organization⟩.

Multimedia Communications Forum (MMCF) An international non-profit research and development organization of telecom-munications service providers, end users and multimedia application and equipment developers.
For more information, visit the MMCF website at www.mmcf.org.

multimodal transport Transport by more than one means. For instance, in door-to-door transport one might use ground transport for ⟨pre-carriage⟩ to the port or airport on the seller's side, ⟨main carriage⟩ by vessel or air to the arrival point on the buyer's side, and ground transport for ⟨on-carriage⟩. Multimodal transport occurs when a ⟨carrier⟩ provides more than one of these movements.

multimodal transport document A document issued or signed by a ⟨carrier⟩ indicating carriage by more than one means of transportation. For example, a multimodal transport document for a door-to-port shipment with ⟨main carriage⟩ by vessel might indicate pickup at the place where the shipment originates (often the seller's premises) with ⟨pre-carriage⟩ by truck and main carriage from the named port of loading to the named port of discharge by a named vessel. Depending on how the ⟨contract of carriage⟩ was drafted, this document could be issued either on a "⟨received for shipment⟩" basis at any time after the ⟨goods⟩ entered the control of the main carrier, or on an "⟨on-board⟩" basis after the goods were loaded on the named vessel. If in our example it were the ship line that contracted for door-to-port transport, it would be

---

⤢ Insurance   🆁🅲 Letters of credit   ⚓ Liner vessel shipping   📧 Sales contracts   🅵 Vessel chartering

MN

responsible for both pre-carriage and main carriage.

As some ship lines accept liability only while the cargo is on their vessel, it is important to carefully read the contract of carriage.

Multimodal Transport Operator (MTO) A ⟨carrier⟩ providing transport by more than one means, and for which the MTO accepts liability as a carrier.

multinational corporation (= transnational corporation). A large commercial organization with affiliates operating in a number of different countries; sometimes referred to (especially in the ⟨United Nations⟩) as a transnational corporation.

Mutual Recognition Agreements (MRAs) Mutual Recognition Agreements are negotiated on a sectoral basis (such as telecommunications, medical devices, pharmaceuticals, chemicals, processed foods) and allow countries to accept each other's final test results, although quality assurances may be required. Under MRAs, the entire testing and certification process may occur outside the importing country. For instance, under MRAs with the ⟨European Union⟩, a US firm would obtain product certification on an EU-wide basis, enabling the firm to market its product throughout the EU. Based on private law contractual negotiations, subcontracting permits a notified body of the EU to delegate some of its testing responsibilities to a third-country testing lab or quality assessment body. However, the notified body retains ultimate responsibility for final decisions relating to EU certification.

mysterious disappearance Cargo that is missing for unknown reasons.

Naamloze Vennootschap (NV) ⟨limited liability⟩

NADBank ⟨North American Development Bank⟩

NAFTA ⟨North American Free Trade Agreement⟩

NAICS ⟨North American Industry Classification System⟩

named perils policy Any ⟨marine cargo insurance policy⟩ that limits coverage to perils specifically listed within the policy.

named place Sales terms such as ⟨Incoterms⟩ must be accompanied by a geographic location, such as
- named airport of departure,
- named departure point,
- named departure port,
- named vessel,
- named place of delivery at frontier,

⟨see entry in dictionary⟩   ✈ Air transport   🏛 Bank collections   @ e-commerce   🔳 Incoterms

N

- named destination place,
- named destination point,
- named destination port.

National Industrial Transportation League (NITL) The largest organization in the United States representing the transportation policy interests of those companies that place freight of all kinds onto any mode of transportation.

> **For more information, visit the NITL website www.nitl.org.**

national treatment National treatment affords individuals and firms of foreign countries the same competitive opportunities, including market access, as are available to domestic parties.

NATO ⟨North Atlantic Treaty Organization⟩

nautical mile, international 1852 metres (6076.12 feet).

NCND ⟨non-circumvention, non-disclosure agreement⟩

negotiable B/L (= order B/L) 🅿 ⬇ A marine (or ocean) transport document showing that shipment has been made with a designated ⟨carrier⟩ that includes the word ORDER in the "⟨consignee⟩" field. Once signed by the carrier and endorsed by the ⟨shipper⟩ or whoever's name follows the word ORDER, a negotiable B/L becomes a bearer instrument of ⟨title⟩ to the shipped ⟨goods⟩. A second feature of negotiable B/Ls is that they permit goods to be sold and resold while in transit by the simple expedient of endorsing and passing on the original B/L to the new owner(s). For these reasons, the carrier will insist upon surrender of the original negotiable B/L prior to releasing the goods.

> **Marine B/Ls are frequently issued in sets of three originals claused "one original being accomplished the others are void" (or similar terminology). As any one of the originals serves to release the ⟨goods⟩, unpaid sellers should carefully control the accessibility of all three originals.**

negotiable instrument A written, signed, unconditional promise or order to pay a fixed amount of ⟨money⟩ to order or bearer at a definite time or on demand.

negotiating bank 🄻🄲 Any bank other than the ⟨opening bank⟩ that gives value for presentation of conforming documents against a ⟨letter of credit⟩.

negotiation ① The act of giving value for documents presented against a ⟨letter of credit⟩. ② Bargaining.

NESOI ⟨not elsewhere specified or indicated⟩

🄰 Insurance   🄻🄲 Letters of credit   ⬇ Liner vessel shipping   🄰 Sales contracts   🅿 Vessel chartering

N

nested ⟨Goods⟩ packed within one another to reduce volume.

net price The price paid or payable after all discounts and rebates have been applied.

net terms ⊟ Vessel chartering terms under which the vessel owner is not responsible for the cost of loading, ⟨stowing⟩, ⟨trimming⟩ and unloading the vessel. See also ⟨free in and out (FIO)⟩ and ⟨free in, out, stowed and trimmed (FIOST)⟩.

net weight The weight of only the ⟨goods⟩ in a shipment, exclusive of any packing materials.

NetGlos Internet Glossary @ A website that provides basic internet terminology definitions in 14 languages.

> **For more information, visit the NetGlos website at http//wwli.com/translation/netglos/netglos.html.**

network As in electronic communications, two or more computers that are connected. Typical networks include local area networks (LAN), wide area networks (WAN) and the internet, which is the world's largest network.

neutral marks Cargo marks that agree with the relevant ⟨packing list⟩ but which do not indicate either the ⟨shipper⟩ or the ⟨consignee⟩. Neutral marks are commonly used to reduce theft, when either the shipper or ⟨consignee⟩ is generally known to be involved with products having a "street value."

newly industrialized countries This term, originated by the ⟨Organization for Economic Cooperation and Development⟩, describes nations that have enjoyed rapid economic growth and can be described as "middle-income" countries.

NGO ⟨non-government organization⟩

NIB ⟨Nordic Investment Bank⟩

NITL ⟨National Industrial Transportation League⟩

no show Cargo that has failed to physically arrive for loading after having been booked for a particular vessel and voyage.

non-aligned movement A loose coalition of ⟨developing countries⟩ that met at the head-of-state level between the 1950s and 1980s, and now meet under the auspices of the ⟨Group of 77⟩.

non-circumvention non-disclosure agreements (NCND) A type of contract frequently requested by international brokers or middlemen in order to prevent buyers from going around the broker to deal directly with suppliers.

⟨see entry in dictionary⟩   ✈ Air transport   🏛 Bank collections   @ e-commerce   ⊞ Incoterms

non-government organization (NGO) A private sector, non-profit organization that contributes to economic improvement in ⟨developing countries⟩ through such activities as infrastructure cooperation projects, financial aid, material aid, dispatch of personnel, trainee instruction and development education. In this context, NGOs are accredited by the ⟨United Nations⟩ or its specialized agencies, and can lobby and do business with them.

non-market economy A national economy in which the government seeks to determine economic actively largely through a mechanism of central planning.

non-negotiable B/L (= straight B/L) 🄿 ⬇ A transport document showing that shipment has been made with a designated ⟨carrier⟩. For vessel shipments, the "⟨consignee⟩" field will not contain the word ORDER, but will include the name of the party entitled to claim the cargo. Since a non-negotiable B/L is not a bearer instrument of ⟨title⟩, the carrier will release the shipped ⟨goods⟩ to the named party only upon identification, often without insisting upon surrender of the original B/L. Goods shipped against a straight B/L cannot be sold in transit, and only the party named in the consignee field is entitled to receive the shipped goods.

> Some countries hold that marine transport documents must be negotiable to qualify as ⟨bills of lading⟩. In such countries, a straight B/L would be termed a ⟨sea waybill⟩.

non-tariff barriers (NTBs) Market access barriers that result from prohibitions, restrictions, conditions or specific requirements and make importing products difficult and/or costly. The term covers any restriction or quota, charge, or policy, (other than traditional customs duties), domestic support programmes, discriminatory labelling and health standards, and exclusive business practices that limit the access of imported ⟨goods⟩. NTBs may result from government- or private-sector actions.

non-vessel operating common carrier (NVOCC) ⬇ A marine ⟨carrier⟩ that does not own or operate vessels, but pledges quantities of cargo to operating carriers (ship lines, also called ⟨undercarriers⟩) in return for lower "⟨freight of all kinds (FAK)⟩" freight rates. Supported by these lower freight rates, the NVOCC then resells transportation at higher and often commodity-specific freight rates. NVOCCs typically consolidate smaller "⟨less than container load (LCL)⟩" shipments to fill shipping containers. This serves the ⟨shipper⟩s because it often reduces the need for heroic export packing. It also serves the undercarriers, who prefer to receive cargo pre-packed in shipping containers. The NVOCC

N

profits from the difference between the low freight cost it has negotiated with the undercarrier and the higher freight cost it charges. NVOCCs issue their own ❮"house" bills of lading❯ to each shipper. These are, in turn, backed up by master bills of lading for full container loads issued to the NVOCCs by the undercarriers. NVOCCs can provide cost savings and convenience, particularly to LCL shippers. However, there can be downsides, such as:

1. Incompatible cargoes could be located near each other for long sea voyages. While hazardous cargo must be handled appropriately, certain non-hazardous items may not travel well in close proximity; for instance, scented products and blotter paper.

2. Transit time may be longer. Since NVOCCs charge per LCL shipment and pay by full container load, they naturally prefer to completely fill each container they ship. ❮Goods❯ arriving at the NVOCC facility immediately after a container has been shipped may languish awaiting sufficient additional cargo to fill the next container. Some NVOCCs alleviate this concern by committing to a frequency of shipments, regardless of whether there is sufficient cargo to fill every container.

3. NVOCCs typically have and require less capital than undercarriers, so weaker NVOCCs could be more likely to go out of business during adverse conditions. Payment of freight charges to a defunct NVOCC that fails to pay the undercarrier does not satisfy the undercarrier's right to payment, and shippers have been forced to pay freight costs twice in such situations.

NOR ❮notice of readiness❯

NORAD ❮Norwegian Agency for Development❯

Nordic Council Established in 1952, and headquartered in Stockholm, Sweden, the Nordic Council supports cooperation among Nordic countries in communications, cultural, economic, environmental, fiscal, legal and social areas. Members include Denmark, Finland, Iceland, Norway and Sweden.

> **For more information, visit the Nordic Council website at www.norden.org.**

Nordic Investment Bank (NIB) Founded in 1975 and headquartered in Helsinki, Finland, the NIB promotes economic cooperation and development by providing resources and guarantees for exports and for capital investment projects. Bank members include Denmark, Finland, Iceland, Norway and Sweden.

> **For more information, visit the NIB website at www.nibank.org.**

normal value (NV) A customs term meaning the price at which merchandise is sold or offered for sale in the principal markets of the country from which it is exported.

> In some countries a comparison of the price paid or payable by a local importer with the same item's normal value can provide the basis for an ⟨anti dumping⟩ investigation.

North American Development Bank (NADBank) An institution established under the auspices of the North American Free Trade Agreement to finance environmental infrastructure projects along the US–Mexico border, as well as community adjustment and investment in both nations.

North American Free Trade Agreement (NAFTA) A free trade agreement established in January 1994 comprising Canada, Mexico and the United States. NAFTA provides for progressive elimination of import duties among the three countries and national treatment for their products and services. It also provides protection for foreign investors of each member country within the other members.

> For recent developments, visit the following NAFTA websites www.nafta-sec-alena.org and www.nafta-customs.org.
> For the entire NAFTA treaty, visit the OAS website at www.sice.oas.org/trade/nafta/naftatce.asp

North American Industry Classification System (NAICS) An economic classification system developed jointly by Canada, Mexico and the United States and implemented in 1997 to provide a uniform mechanism for collecting and analyzing industry statistics across North America. NAICS supercedes Standard Industrial Classification (SIC) codes.

North Atlantic Treaty Organization (NATO) Originally a defence treaty among Canada, the United States, and western European countries, NATO's role in the post-cold-war world is being defined and its membership is being expanded.

Norwegian Agency for Development (NORAD) Established in 1968 and headquartered in Oslo, Norway, NORAD provides financing for project exports from Norway to ⟨developing countries⟩, for economic undertakings that can be sustained without future external assistance.

NOS ⟨not otherwise specified⟩

nostro account An account held by a bank with its foreign correspondent bank, in the currency of that foreign country.

not elsewhere specified or indicated (NESOI) (= not otherwise specified (NOS)). An item that is not mentioned elsewhere in a

---

⚓ Insurance   🅛🅒 Letters of credit   🅛 Liner vessel shipping   🅢 Sales contracts   🅟 Vessel chartering

NO

classification system, such as a customs or freight ⟨tariff⟩.

not otherwise specified (NOS) (= not elsewhere specified or indicated (NESOI)). An item that is not mentioned elsewhere in a classification system, such as a customs or freight ⟨tariff⟩.

notice of readiness (NOR) 🅐 A term used in vessel chartering to indicate that a ship has arrived and is ready for loading or unloading.

notified body A party designated to maintain certain records at the disposal of local authorities under the ⟨European Union⟩'s ⟨Conformité Européene (CE Mark)⟩ programme.

notify party 🅧 🅛 The party to which a ⟨carrier⟩ should send notice of a shipment's arrival. This information is normally shown on the transport document or its electronic equivalent.

As many carriers are notoriously negligent in advising arrivals, the party contracting transportation with the carrier should keep the party awaiting arrival informed as the shipment progresses. This can be done by e-mail and/or sending copies of all relevant documents including the transport document, clearly marked COPY. Otherwise, ⟨demurrage⟩ charges can quickly accrue for shipments unclaimed because the carrier failed to inform the notify party.

NSG ⟨Nuclear Suppliers Group⟩

NTB ⟨non-tariff barrier⟩

Nuclear Suppliers Group (NSG) An organization of nuclear supplier nations, which coordinates exports of nuclear materials and equipment with the ⟨International Atomic Energy Agency⟩ inspection regime.

NV ⟨normal value⟩

NV (Naamloze Vennootschap) ⟨limited liability⟩

NVOCC ⟨non-vessel operating common carrier⟩

OAS ⟨Organization of American States⟩

OAU ⟨Organization of African Unity⟩

ocean bill of lading (= marine bill of lading). ⟨bill of lading⟩

ocean transportation intermediary (OTI) ① In general, a party engaged in arranging transportation by vessel. ② In the United States, specifically an ocean freight ⟨forwarder⟩ or a ⟨non-vessel operating common carrier⟩

ODA ⟨official development assistance⟩

OECD ❬Organization for Economic Cooperation and Development❭

OECF ❬Overseas Economic Cooperation Fund❭

O

offer list A list of market concessions that a country participating in trade negotiations is willing to make, in return for comparable concessions from its trading partners. Also ❬request list❭.

official development assistance (ODA) Economic or technical assistance extended to ❬developing countries❭ by the governments of ❬developed countries❭ and by international organizations, as contrasted with private-sector financed gifts, loans and investments.

offsets An umbrella label for a broad range of industrial and commercial compensation packages required as a condition of purchase in commercial or government-to-government sales. Typically, offsets involve overseas production resulting in the creation or expansion of industrial capacity in the importer's country.

offshore manufacturing The production of ❬goods❭ overseas by a domestic country primarily to be imported to the domestic market.

OHG (Offene Handelsgesellschaft) An unlimited partnership.

OIC ❬Organization of the Islamic Conference❭

OMA ❬orderly marketing agreement❭

omnimodal 🏏 Those ❬Incoterms❭ that can be used for all modes of transport (❬EXW❭, ❬FCA❭, ❬CPT❭, ❬CIP❭, ❬DAF❭, ❬DDU❭ and ❬DDP❭).

on-board B/L 🅿 ⚓ A marine transport document indicating that the shipped ❬goods❭ have been loaded on the carrying vessel.

on-board notation 🅿 ⚓ Loading information shown on ❬on-board B/Ls❭. The on-board notation should show the date that the ❬goods❭ were actually loaded, and should be initialed by an employee or agent of the ❬carrier❭.

on-carriage The movement from the arrival point on the buyer's side to the place where transportation will end, often the buyer's premises. On-carriage is often called "inland freight on the buyer's side."

on-deck A notation on marine transportation documents that the shipped cargo was loaded on the deck of the carrying vessel as opposed to within the ship's hold ("under deck"). On-deck shipments are more susceptible to in-transit damage, and normally command a higher insurance premium. Further, on-deck shipments

---

🛧 Insurance   🆻 Letters of credit   ⚓ Liner vessel shipping   🖳 Sales contracts   🅿 Vessel chartering

O

constitute automatic discrepancies for ‹letters of credit› that do not specifically permit them.

> Occasionally, ‹carrier›s will post a notation on their transport documents that ‹goods› "may be shipped on-deck". Such notations are not considered definitive for letter of credit purposes, and therefore do not cause a discrepancy, except for credits specifically prohibiting them.

online exchange ‹electronic marketplace›

OPEC ‹Organization of Petroleum Exporting Countries›

open account A payment term under which the buyer promises to pay the seller within a predetermined number of days, and the seller does not restrict the availability of documents that control possession rights to the ‹goods›. In practice, required documentation is sent directly to the buyer or the buyer's ‹customs broker›. Buyers requesting open account payment terms for sums in excess of their sellers' comfort levels can be accommodated by opening ‹standby letters of credit› in favour of the sellers. However, this is prudent only when a buyer has absolute confidence that the seller will not wrongfully draw on the standby. Export credit insurance may also increase open-account sellers' comfort levels.

open marine cargo insurance policy (= blanket policy = floating policy) ⬚ A type of ‹insurance policy› intended to cover an indefinite number of future individual shipments. The insurance contract remains in force until cancelled. Under the open policy, individual successive shipments are periodically reported or declared to the insurer and reported shipments are automatically covered on or after the policy's inception date. Open policies can provide efficiency and savings for all parties concerned, especially when the insured conducts a significant volume of highly similar transactions.

open network systems @ Electronic communications through such non-restricted media as the internet that are open to previously unrelated parties. Unlike closed network systems, which are typically structured around existing trading partners, open systems offer the possibility of broadening market access to new participants. However, lacking the limited access and agreed structure found in closed network systems, open network systems require new methods of providing information security and authentication. See also ‹digital signature›, ‹public key infrastructure› and ‹General Usage in International Digitally Ensured Commerce›.

> For more information, visit the GUIDEC website at www.iccwbo.org/home/guidec/guidec.asp.

‹see entry in dictionary›   ✈ Air transport   🏛 Bank collections   @ e-commerce   ▦ Incoterms

O

open policy ⟨open marine cargo insurance policy⟩

opening bank ⟨issuing bank⟩

OPIC ⟨Overseas Private Investment Corporation⟩

order ⟨purchase order⟩

order B/L ⟨negotiable B/L⟩

order of shipper ⟨negotiable B/L⟩

orderly marketing agreement (OMA) An international compact negotiated between two or more governments, in which they agree to restrain the growth of trade in a specified "sensitive" product or products, usually through the imposition of export quotas.

Organization for Economic Cooperation and Development (OECD) An international agency that promotes the economic and social welfare of its 24 member countries and stimulates efforts on behalf of developing nations. Its Business and Industry Advisory Committee (BIAC) brings together the advice and business counsel of the business communities of OECD member countries.

> For more information, visit the OECD website www.oecd.org. or the BIAC website at www.biac.org.

Organization of African Unity (OAU) Founded in 1963 and headquartered in Addis Ababa, Ethiopia, the OAU aims to further African unity and solidarity, to coordinate political, economic, social, scientific and defence policies, and to eliminate colonialism in Africa.

> For more information, visit the OAU website at www.oau-oua.org/.

Organization of American States (OAS) Founded in 1951 and headquartered in Washington, DC, USA, the OAS promotes Western Hemisphere economic and social development.

> For more information, visit the OAS website at www.oas.org.

Organization of Petroleum Exporting Countries (OPEC) Founded in 1960 and headquartered in Vienna, Austria, OPEC is an association of world oil-producing countries, whose chief purpose is coordination of member petroleum policies.

> For more information, visit the OPEC website at www.opec.org.

Organization of the Islamic Conference (OIC) Established in 1971 and headquartered in Jeddah, Saudi Arabia, the OIC promotes cooperation in cultural, economic, scientific and social areas among Islamic nations.

> For more information, visit the OIC website at www.oic-un.org.

🛈 Insurance 🄻🄲 Letters of credit 🚢 Liner vessel shipping 📃 Sales contracts ⚓ Vessel chartering

OP

origin rules Procedures that governments use to determine the origin of imported products. Rules of origin play an important part in international trade because the application of duties and other restrictions on entry often depend on the deemed source of the ⟨imports⟩.

Origin Rules WTO Agreement A ⟨World Trade Organization⟩ agreement providing for harmonization in the practices of WTO members in the rules that determine the country of origin of an imported product.

OTI ⟨ocean transportation intermediary⟩

overdraft ① A deficit in a bank account caused by drawing more ⟨money⟩ than is credited to it. ② A line of credit arrangement permitting this situation, also called "overdraft protection."

Overseas Economic Cooperation Fund (OECF) Established in 1961 and headquartered in Tokyo, the OECF is a Japanese Government development financial institution providing grants and long-term, low-interest loans to ⟨developing countries⟩ and areas.

Overseas Private Investment Corporation (OPIC) Established in 1971 and headquartered in Washington, DC, USA, OPIC is a US Government corporation that assists US private investment in less-developed nations, by providing direct loans and loan guarantees.
    For more information, visit the OPIC website at www.opic.gov.

OY ⟨limited liability⟩

P&I CLUB ⟨Protection and Indemnity Club⟩

Pacific Economic Cooperation Council (PECC) Established in 1980, PECC is aimed at promoting economic cooperation in the Asia-Pacific region.
    For more information, visit the PECC website at www.pecc.org.

Pacific Island Forum Established in 1971 as the South Pacific Forum, the Pacific Island Forum is a regional arrangement for convening 15 area governments and territories for deliberations on issues of mutual interest.
    For more information, visit their website at www.forumsec.org.fj/.

Pacific rim An informal, flexible term referring to countries bordering the Pacific Ocean.

Pacific Telecommunications Council (PTC) An international, non-profit, non-governmental membership organization to promote the development of telecommunications and related industries throughout the Pacific region with emphasis on ⟨developing countries⟩.
    For more information, visit the PTC website at www.ptc.org.

⟨see entry in dictionary⟩   ✈ Air transport   🏦 Bank collections   @ e-commerce   ⊞ Incoterms

P

packaging, labelling and marking requirements The requirement, usually by an importing country, that imported ⟨goods⟩ be packaged, labelled, or marked according to particular guidelines.

packing ⟨export packing⟩

packing list A seller-prepared commercial document indicating the net and gross weights, dimensions and contents of all shipping pieces (boxes, crates, bundles, etc.) in a shipment. Each packing list should reference the shipment for which it is made, and the line item totals should agree with the relevant commercial invoice. A packing list should be made for all shipments consisting of more than one shipping piece for the following reasons:
- They aid in identifying lost cargo, especially for ⟨carrier⟩ and insurance claims.
- They permit selective inspection by customs authorities, and many governments require them for large shipments.
- They provide a "map" of the shipment, enabling the buyer to easily unpack and stock the shipped ⟨goods⟩.

pallet A shallow portable platform used to facilitate handling of ⟨goods⟩ by ⟨forklift trucks⟩. Often, packages are packed together on a pallet and then over-packed or shrink-wrapped to form a unitized load. Pallets are commonly made of wood, plastic or fiberboard.

1. A four-way pallet is particularly useful, as it is constructed to enable forklift truck tines to engage from any of its four sides.
2. To prevent introduction of non-native pests, some jurisdictions prohibit the importation of non-treated coniferous wood packing materials from certain originating countries.

Pan American Standards Commission (COPANT) Headquartered in Buenos Aires, Argentina, COPANT coordinates the activities of all institutes of standardization in Latin American countries. It develops all types of product standards, standardized test methods, terminology and related matters.

For more information, visit the COPANT website at www.copant.org.

par value An official fixed rate of exchange between two currencies, or between a currency and a basket of currencies or a specific weight of gold.

parallel imports ⟨Imports⟩ made by parties other than the factory-authorized importer.

paramount clause (= clause paramount). The pre-eminent clause in a legal document. For example, many ⟨bills of lading⟩ or ⟨charterparty⟩ contracts include a paramount clause citing the

---

⊼ Insurance   🆗 Letters of credit   ⬇ Liner vessel shipping   📧 Sales contracts   ꟼ Vessel chartering

P

general terms and conditions such as ⟨Hague⟩ or ⟨Hague-Visby Rules⟩, or the US COGSA 1936 for shipments involving US ports.

parcel post receipt ⟨postal receipt⟩

Paris Convention for the Protection of Industrial Property First adopted in 1883, the Paris Convention is the major international agreement providing basic rights for protecting industrial property. It covers ⟨patents⟩, industrial designs, ⟨service marks⟩, ⟨trade names⟩, and indications of source and unfair competition. The treaty provides two fundamental rights:
- The principle of national treatment provides that nationals of any signatory country shall enjoy in all other countries of the union the advantages that each country's laws grant to its own nationals.
- The right of priority enables any resident or national of a member country to first file a patent application in any member country, and thereafter to file a patent application for the same invention in any of the other member countries within 12 months of the original filing, and receive the benefit of the original filing date. The resident or national of a member country can also claim the filing date of a trademark application or industrial design filed in another member country within six months of the filing date in his or her own country or country of residence. See also ⟨Patent Cooperation Treaty⟩.

partial shipment A portion of less than the total quantity of an order. See also ⟨back order⟩.

particular average ⟨⟩ Insurance coverage against partial damage or loss caused by covered perils.

party at risk ⟨⟩ Between the seller and the buyer, that party who has the most to lose in the event of damage or loss to a shipment, such as:
1. Unpaid sellers, especially if the problem occurs before the point where their responsibility for the condition of the shipped ⟨goods⟩ has passed. See also ⟨Incoterms⟩.
2. Buyers who have prepaid, especially if the problem occurs after the point where the seller's responsibility for the condition of the goods ends. See Incoterms.
3. Whichever party is shown as ⟨shipper⟩ for the purpose of general average.

It is this party who should normally be most interested in having adequate insurance coverage.

pass through A foreign country's use of one country in a trade bloc as a means of gaining preferential treatment from other countries in the bloc.

P

patent The grant by a government to an inventor of the exclusive right to manufacture, use or sell an invention.

Patent Cooperation Treaty (PCT) Established in 1978 and open to any ⟨Paris Convention⟩ member country, the PCT addresses procedural requirements in order to simplify the filing, searching and publication of international patent applications.

pay ton ⟨revenue ton⟩

payee The party designated to receive payment of a ⟨negotiable instrument⟩. In a ⟨cheque⟩ or ⟨draft⟩, it is the party shown after the words "pay to the order of."

paying bank LC The bank designated in a ⟨letter of credit⟩ as the party that will honour ⟨drafts⟩ drawn under the L/C.

payment at sight 🏛⟨cash against documents⟩ and ⟨documents against payment⟩.

payment in advance ⟨cash with order⟩

payment terms 🖋 That part of an agreement that defines when, where, to whom and in what currency the underlying obligation is to be discharged.

payment under reserve LC Provisional payment made against a non-compliant or questionable presentation under a ⟨letter of credit⟩, against which the ⟨beneficiary⟩ agrees to repay if reimbursement is not received from the ⟨opening bank⟩ within a specified time.

PCT ① ⟨Patent Cooperation Treaty⟩ ② Abbreviation for percent.

PDF ⟨portable document format⟩

PECC ⟨Pacific Economic Cooperation Council⟩

PEFCO ⟨Private Export Funding Corporation⟩

per diem By the day.

performance bond (guarantee). A bond or guarantee that has been issued as security for one party's performance. If that party, known as the ⟨principal⟩, fails to perform, the ⟨beneficiary⟩ may obtain payment under the bond guarantee. A performance bond may be of either the demand or conditional variety, which means that the beneficiary may or may not be required to prove default by the principal in order to obtain payment. See also ⟨surety/surety-ship bond/guarantee⟩.

performance requirements Activities mandated by some governments that foreign investors must undertake, usually as a

---

🛈 Insurance   LC Letters of credit   ⬇ Liner vessel shipping   🖋 Sales contracts   🅿 Vessel chartering condition of establishment or operation in a particular country.

P

perils of the sea A marine insurance term used to designate heavy weather, stranding, lightning, collision and sea water damage.

permanent normal trade relations ⟨most favoured nation treatment⟩

persona grata A diplomatic representative who is acceptable to the government of the country where he or she is assigned.

persona non grata A diplomatic representative who is no longer acceptable to the government of the country where he or she is assigned.

PFP ⟨policy framework paper⟩

pH A numerical representation of the acidity or alkalinity of an aqueous solution. Seven is neutral. Decreasing numbers from seven to zero indicate increasing acidity, while increasing numbers from seven to fourteen indicate increasing alkalinity.

> **pH can be an important factor in determining whether an item is considered hazardous for transportation.**

phytosanitary certificate An inspection certificate issued by a competent governmental authority to show that a particular shipment has been inspected and, if necessary, has been treated to be free from harmful pests and plant diseases.

pier ⟨wharf⟩

piggyback ⟨trailer on flat car⟩

pilferage Theft of a small portion of shipped cargo, rather than a large portion or the entire shipment.

> **some marine ⟨insurance policies⟩ do not cover pilferage, so if desired, it must be added as an additional peril at an additional premium.**

pipeline protection A term that broadly refers to protection accorded by a country for inventions that already existed prior to that country's making ⟨patent⟩ protection available for such inventions.

> **This often applies to pharmaceutical or agricultural products.**

PKI ⟨public key infrastructure⟩

placard A notice prominently posted on the outside of a truck, rail car or shipping container that it contains a particular hazardous material or materials.

PLC (public limited company) ⟨limited liability⟩

plurilateral An international agreement embracing a restricted number of countries (as opposed to multilateral, which is open to all qualifying nations). See also ⟨international agreement⟩.

P

> Some multilateral agreements have plurilateral sections; for example, the ⟨WTO⟩ treaty is multilateral, but in some respects differentiates between ⟨developed countries⟩ and ⟨developing countries⟩, and in these cases is plurilateral.

policy ⟨insurance policy⟩

policy framework paper (PFP) A plan outlining the steps a country will take while receiving structural adjustment assistance from the ⟨International Monetary Fund⟩.

political risk ⟨country risk⟩

port congestion surcharge ⟨congestion surcharge⟩

port of discharge (unloading). The port where a shipment is unloaded from a vessel.

port of loading (lading) The port where a shipment is loaded aboard a vessel.

port shopping The practice of exporters and importers choosing particular ports on the basis of their assessment of customs treatment, rather than on port quality or physical facilities.

port-to-port 🄰 🄻 ⟨Main carriage⟩ vessel transportation only from the ⟨port of loading⟩ to the ⟨port of discharge⟩, i.e., excluding ⟨pre-carriage⟩ and ⟨on-carriage⟩.

portable document format (PDF) Virtually any electronic file from any application (i.e. images, word processing, spreadsheets) may be converted to PDF files, which generally allow only read-only rights to the recipient. These files are created by Adobe's Acrobat software, and are read using Adobe's Acrobat Reader. A popular and efficient method to download information from internet ⟨websites⟩.

portal A ⟨website⟩ or service connected to the internet which may offer a broad range of resources and services, such as ⟨e-mail⟩, ⟨bulletin boards⟩, chat rooms, information, ⟨search engines⟩, and ⟨e-stores⟩.

postal receipt (= parcel post receipt). A stamped (or signed) and dated form from a postal facility, acknowledging receipt of a parcel for shipment.

power of attorney The authority to act for another in legal or financial matters. Some countries require that a ⟨customs broker⟩ and/or ⟨forwarder⟩ have a power of attorney in order to represent a ⟨principal⟩ for import or export control purposes.

P

pratique Permission from a port's health officer for a vessel to enter and use a port.

pre-advice LC An official notice from an ⟨issuing bank⟩ that it is opening a referenced ⟨letter of credit⟩, either concurrently or within a reasonable time.

pre-carriage Transportation from the place where a shipment originates to the departure point on the seller's side. Pre-carriage brings the ⟨goods⟩ to the ⟨main carrier⟩, and is often called "inland freight on the seller's side."

pre-shipment inspection (PSI) The requirement that a shipment be inspected prior to leaving the exporting country. This requirement may be the result of a seller-buyer agreement or a requirement of the buyer's government. In the case of seller-buyer agreements, inspections would be done by a mutually agreed upon third party and would cover whatever issues the parties determine to be important. When required by the buyer's country, inspections are performed by a government-designated inspection service, such as S.G.S., and typically include price verification and physical inspection of the ⟨goods⟩ to determine that they conform in quantity and kind to the importation approval. See also ⟨clean report of findings⟩.

Pre-shipment Inspection (PSI), WTO Agreement A ⟨World Trade Organization⟩ agreement that applies to government-mandated pre-shipment inspection activities carried out in the territory of member countries (that is, in the country of export prior to exportation).

preferences Special advantages extended by importing countries to exports from particular trading partner countries, usually by admitting their ⟨goods⟩ at ⟨tariff⟩ rates below those imposed on imports from other supplying countries.

preferential cargo Cargo that by the rules of the exporting or importing country must be transported by a particular ⟨flag carrier⟩.

Preferential Trade Area for Eastern and Southern African States (PTA) ⟨Common Market for Eastern and Southern Africa⟩

preliminary notice of claim A written notice informing a ⟨carrier⟩, ⟨insurer⟩ or ⟨bailee⟩ that a claim is pending based on discovery of loss or damage to a particular shipment. See also ⟨time bar⟩.

premium ⟨insurance premium⟩

presentation date LC The date on which compliant documents were given to the ⟨issuing bank⟩ or any other institution permitted under a ⟨letter of credit⟩.

⟨see entry in dictionary⟩   ✈ Air transport   ▥ Bank collections   ⓔ e-commerce   ▦ Incoterms

presentation date (latest) LC The latest date at which compliant documentation must be given to the ⟨issuing bank⟩ or any other institution permitted under a ⟨letter of credit⟩.

presenting bank 🏛 In bank ⟨collections⟩, the ⟨collecting bank⟩ that deals directly with the ⟨drawee⟩ (and is often the drawee's bank of account).

price ⟨purchase price⟩

prima facie At first sight, self-evident.

prima facie evidence Evidence sufficient to establish a fact or raise a presumption of fact unless rebutted.

primary commodity A commodity in its raw or unprocessed state, such as iron ore. By contrast, pig iron is considered a semi-processed product, and a steel girder is a manufactured item.

principal In bank collections, the party entrusting the handling of a ⟨collection⟩ to a bank.

principal parties in interest Those persons in a transaction that receive the primary benefit, monetary or otherwise, of the transaction – normally the seller and buyer.

> This term has particular significance for exports from the United States in view of changes to its export reporting regime.

prior import deposit A deposit required by a government of a specified sum, in domestic or foreign currency, usually corresponding to a certain percentage of the value of the imported product. Such deposits are characteristically held without interest, sometimes for many months – from the time an order is placed until after the import transaction is completed – and represent real costs to importers. The purpose of prior deposits is usually to discourage ⟨imports⟩, particularly for ⟨balance of payment⟩ reasons, and they are generally recognized as ⟨non-tariff barriers⟩ to trade.

Private Export Funding Corporation (PEFCO) A private company that works with the ⟨Export Import Bank of the United States⟩ in using private capital to finance US exports.

> For more information, visit the PEFCO website at www.pefco.com.

private key @ The secret part of a two-key encryption system used with digital signatures in open network communications. See also ⟨digital signature⟩, ⟨open network systems⟩, and ⟨public key infrastructure⟩.

> For more information, visit the GUIDEC website at www.iccwbo.org/home/guidec/guidec.asp.

🛧 Insurance   LC Letters of credit   ⬇ Liner vessel shipping   ◿ Sales contracts   ▱ Vessel chartering

P

private sector The part of a national economy comprising privately owned enterprises, individuals, and non-profit making organizations, as contrasted with government and government-controlled entities.

private voluntary organizations (PVOs) Non-profit, non-governmental organizations comprised of private citizens, whose purpose is to engage in voluntary, charitable and development operations. As such, some governments consider them eligible to receive foreign aid and developmental assistance funding.

procurator An agent or proxy, especially one who has ‹power of attorney›.

proforma invoice ✍ An offer to sell from a seller to a prospective buyer; a price quotation rendered in invoice form. Proforma invoices should include the following information:
- a unique proforma invoice number,
- the date the proforma invoice is prepared,
- the estimated date of shipment should an order result,
- the identities and addresses of the seller and prospective buyer,
- a "ship to" location (if known, and if other than the buyer's address),
- the proposed terms of sale (preferably ‹Incoterms 2000›),
- the proposed terms of payment,
- the applicable body of law under which the offer is made,
- a complete description of all line items including their unit costs and line-item totals,
- an itemized list of all non-product services that the seller proposes to provide for the buyer's account, with their estimated prices,
- the grand total,
- any certifications required by the import authorities of the buyer's country,
- the validity period of the quotation,
- a signature by an authorized person at the seller's company, if required.

> When accepted in their entirety by buyers, proforma invoices often become the "offer" halves of ‹sales contracts›. For this reason, prospective sellers should take care to quote pricing and delivery information that they can live with for any order received from the prospective buyer during the validity period of the quotation.

promissory note An unconditional written promise to pay a specified sum of ‹money› on demand or at a specified date to, or to the order of, a specified person, or to bearer. Promissory notes are ‹negotiable instruments› and perform more or less the same function as accepted ‹drafts›.

P

property An asset whose ownership gives the right to present or future material benefit as protected by law.

protection Government measures – including ⟨tariff⟩ and ⟨non-tariff barriers⟩ – that raise the cost of imported ⟨goods⟩ or otherwise restrict their entry into a market, and thus strengthen the competitive position of domestically produced goods.

Protection and Indemnity Club (P&I Club) A mutual association of shipowners and/or vessel ⟨charterers⟩ that provides ⟨liability⟩ insurance for members.

protest The act of formalizing the dishonour of a ⟨draft⟩. Laws differ from country to country, but in general the procedure works as follows:
1. The principal has instructed that dishonoured drafts be protested.
2. A draft matures for payment and is not paid.
3. Whatever applicable grace period in the ⟨drawee's⟩ country expires.
4. The banker, often accompanied by a public notary, formally presents the draft for payment. Notice of the dishonour is recorded by the notary.

The results of a protested draft vary from country to country, but the net result is often akin to the recording of a judgment entry. Knowledge of the default can become widespread in the local market, adversely affecting the drawee's local credit. Certainly, the drawee's bank is aware of the situation, as it participated in the protest procedure. Further, in some countries, protested drafts enjoy preferred status over non-protested drafts in case of bankruptcy liquidation.

Although protest procedures exist for both non-acceptance and non-payment, they are usually reserved for non-payment of ⟨time drafts⟩. Since acceptance usually happens in exchange for documents, drawees who have not accepted time drafts (or have not paid ⟨sight drafts⟩) normally have not received the shipped ⟨goods⟩. While not taking the goods may breach the sales contract, it becomes questionable whether the drawee actually owes the full value of goods it has not taken.

Some countries require that drafts covered by ⟨avals⟩ (third party guarantees) be protested if defaulted at maturity. This assures that the guarantor receives due notice that its contingent liability may be called.

PSI ① ⟨pre-shipment inspection⟩ (or ⟨Pre-shipment Inspection, WTO Agreement⟩). ② Pounds per square inch.

PTA ⟨Common Market for Eastern and Southern Africa⟩

⊼ Insurance LC Letters of credit ⊥ Liner vessel shipping ◁ Sales contracts ⊟ Vessel chartering

PQ

PTC ⟨Pacific Telecommunications Council⟩

public key infrastructure (PKI) @ A registration system for public keys, one of two components of digital signature authentication (ensuring) of electronic messages in an open network system. Public keys are shared with everyone, and the identities of their holders are certified by public key certification service providers, who in turn are certified by certification authorities. See also ⟨certification service providers⟩, ⟨digital signature⟩, ⟨General Usage in International Digitally Ensured Commerce⟩, and ⟨open network systems⟩.

> **For more information, visit the GUIDEC website at www.iccwbo.org/home/guidec/guidec.asp.**

public limited company (PLC) ⟨limited liability⟩

public sector The part of a national economy accounted for by government expenditures and state-owned or state-controlled enterprises.

public warehouse A warehouse that will store ⟨goods⟩ for a fee, regardless of who owns them.

purchase order ✒ An offer from a buyer to a seller for the purchase of specified ⟨goods⟩ at specified pricing and under specified terms and conditions. The purchase order is often the buyer's half of a ⟨sales contract⟩.

> **Also ⟨proforma invoice⟩ for points typically covered in purchase orders.**

purchase price The price paid or payable for merchandise or ⟨services⟩.

purchasing agent A party acting on behalf of a buyer, often outside of the buyer's country.

purchasing power parity An economic theory that states that exchange rates between currencies are in equilibrium when their purchasing power is the same in each of the two countries.

pure freight ⟨base rate⟩

PVOs ⟨private voluntary organizations⟩

quantitative restrictions Explicit limits, or quotas, on the quantity of a good that can be imported or exported during a specified time period. Also ⟨export quota⟩, ⟨export restraint⟩, ⟨global quota⟩, ⟨import quota⟩.

quarantine, sanitary, and health laws and regulations Government measures to protect consumer, animal, and plant health by regulating the import and/or use of items presenting a risk or perceived risk. Also ⟨Phytosanitary Certificate and Sanitary and Phytosanitary Measures, WTO Agreement⟩.

quay ⟨wharf⟩

quota ⟨export quota⟩, ⟨global quota⟩, and ⟨import quota⟩

quotation An offer to sell ⟨goods⟩ or ⟨services⟩ In international trade, offers to sell goods are often prepared in a ⟨proforma invoice⟩ format.

R/T ⟨revenue ton⟩

ramp A railway location where containers are loaded onto and unloaded from flat cars.

range In shipping, range means extent or scope of places. ⟨Carriers⟩, particularly ship lines, quote ⟨base rate⟩ freight costs based on services from the places they serve that are located within one range to the places they serve that are located within another range. Example: "X dollars per revenue ton from US Northeast Coast Ports to the Bordeaux-Hamburg Range" means that x dollars in base rate freight would be charged for each revenue ton of a given commodity shipped from any port the ship line calls located on the US Northeast Coast to any port it calls located from Bordeaux, France to Hamburg, Germany.

> Since different ports have different capabilities, cargo handling procedures and ⟨terminal handling charges⟩, ship lines quote only base rate freight on a range-to-range basis, and add a terminal handling charge that depends on which ports are actually used.

rate A charge or fee, usually expressed either as a fixed sum per unit as in ⟨freight⟩ rate or as a percentage of value, as in "⟨ad valorem⟩" duty or interest.

rate of exchange ⟨exchange rate⟩

rated transport document A transport document specifying the cost of ⟨freight⟩ and any accessorial charges.

re-exports Exports of foreign-origin merchandise that had previously been imported.

> For export control purposes, the United States considers re-exports to be shipments of US-origin products from one foreign country to another.

receipt A written acknowledgment given in exchange for taking ⟨goods⟩ into one's possession.

Insurance   LC Letters of credit   Liner vessel shipping   Sales contracts   Vessel chartering

R

received for shipment B/L ⬇ A marine transport document indicating that the shipped ‹goods› have been handed over to the control of the ‹main carrier›, but not necessarily loaded on the carrying vessel. This is the opposite of an ‹on-board B/L›.

reciprocity The reduction of a country's import duties or other trade restraints in return for comparable trade concessions from another country.

Reconstruction Loan Corporation (German = KfW). The KfW provides assistance to ‹developing countries› in the form of loans, grants, materials and services. It promotes the establishment and promotion of new technologies by German companies in developing countries.
For more information, visit the KfW website at www.kfw.de.

red clause L/C LC A ‹letter of credit› permitting disbursements prior to shipment.

reefer Refrigerated transport equipment.

reefer cargo Cargo that must be kept at a low temperature, which has to be specified on the transport document.

reimbursing bank LC A bank nominated by the ‹opening bank› to pay a ‹negotiating›, ‹accepting› or ‹paying bank› in a letter of credit transaction.

reinstatement (of a revolving L/C) LC ‹Revolving letters of credit› come back to life for repeated drawings after being used. There are two methods: automatic reinstatement and reinstatement by amendment only. Only the former is truly a revolving L/C, as under the latter the applicant or ‹issuing bank› could forestall the reinstatement process by simply refusing to provide the required amendment.

reinsurance The practice of one insurance carrier purchasing supplemental coverage from another ‹insurer› for a particularly high value or high risk commitment.

related parties Parties that are identical, or have more than a certain equity interest in each other, or are owned or controlled by the same party, or in the case of natural persons are closer than a certain degree of kindred.

relay vessel ‹feeder vessel›

remittance ‹payment›

remittance instructions (remittance detail). Instructions on how a

R

payment is to be applied.

remitting bank In <collections>, the bank to which the <principal> (<drawer>) has entrusted the handling of a collection. In practice, this is usually the drawer's bank of account.

representative <agent>

request list A list of market concessions which a country participating in trade negotiations desires from its trading partners. Also <offer list>.

reservation of title <retention of title>

reserve currency (= key currency). A national currency such as the US dollar or British pound sterling, or international basket of currencies such as <special drawing rights>, used by many countries to settle debit balances in their international accounts. Central banks generally hold a large portion of their monetary reserves in reserve currencies, which are sometimes called "key currencies."

residual restrictions Quantitative restrictions maintained by governments since they became contracting parties to GATT or members of <WTO>, despite the general GATT or WTO prohibitions against such measures.

restricted negotiation LC A <letter of credit> that limits negotiation to a specific bank or banks.

restrictive business practices Actions in the private sector, such as collusion among the largest international suppliers, designed to restrict competition and keep prices relatively high.

retaliation Action taken by a country whose exports are adversely affected by the raising of <tariffs> or other trade-restricting measures by another country.

retention of title (= reservation of title = ROT) **clause** An agreement between seller and buyer that the seller will continue to own the contract <goods> even after they are delivered to the buyer. Such agreements should be incorporated into the <contract of sale>.

Many jurisdictions have procedures which must be followed to record a seller's continued interest in delivered <goods>. Failure to observe them could jeopardize title retention.

revenue ton (= pay ton = R/T) A unit of measure used in marine transport to compare the volume and weight of a shipment. <Freight> rates are usually expressed in terms of cost per revenue ton. There are three different formulas in general use for

R

determining the total number of revenue tons in a given shipment when the freight is calculated on a weight or measurement basis:

a. The greater of the total number of cubic metres versus the total number of metric tons;
b. The greater of total cubic feet / 40 versus the total gross weight in pounds / 2000;
c. The greater of total cubic feet / 40 versus the total gross weight in pounds / 2240.

Occasionally, <carrier>s will assign a per-unit freight cost to a particular type of cargo, for instance, locomotives up to "x tons" and "y cubic metres" might pay a fixed amount of USD 8000.00 per locomotive.

As there are different formulas that produce different results, it is important that the carrier and the party contracting for carriage clearly understand which one applies.

reverse preferences <Tariff> preferences once offered by <developing countries> to <imports> from certain <developed countries> that granted them preferences in return.

Revised American Foreign Trade Definitions <American Foreign Trade Definitions>

revocable L/C LC A <letter of credit> that can be cancelled or changed by any party at any time without the consent of any other parties.

revolving L/C LC A <letter of credit> that, once used, comes back to life for repeated drawing(s).

rider A form containing special provisions that are not contained in the basic <insurance policy> contract.

Rio Group A political forum of Latin American and Caribbean countries that promotes regional political, social and economic cooperation.

For more information, visit the Rio Group website at www.ibge.gov.br/poverty/.

risk ① The possibility of gain or loss depending upon the success or failure of a commercial venture. ② The possibility that a loan or other obligation will be defaulted.

roll-on/roll-off (RORO) Vessels configured to accept wheeled cargo loaded by ramp rather than by crane. These are typically used to transport autos, trucks, boats on trailers, but can also accommodate cargoes without wheels by placing them on open (flat rack) containers or smaller wheeled open container-like conveyances called <mafis>.

RS

RORO ⟨roll-on/roll-off⟩

ROT ⟨retention of title⟩

rounding 🛫 ⚓ ① In vessel shipments, the practice of rounding up length, width and height dimensions to the nearest whole centimetre or inch in calculating the dimensional weight factor for revenue tons. ② In air freight shipments, the practice of rounding up the entire shipment's dimensional or actual gross weight to the nearest whole kilo or pound.

rounds Cycles of multilateral trade negotiations under the ⟨General Agreement on Tariffs and Trade⟩ and the ⟨World Trade Organization⟩, culminating in simultaneous agreements among participating countries to reduce ⟨tariff⟩ and ⟨non-tariff trade barriers⟩.

routed transaction A transaction in which a buyer arranges for export, usually through an agent in the seller's country.

routing order Instructions specifying the use of a particular ⟨carrier⟩ or ⟨forwarder⟩, usually given by a buyer to a seller.

royalties ① Compensation or portion of the proceeds paid to the owner of a right for its use, as in a ⟨patent⟩ or mineral right. ② A portion of the income from a work payable to its author or composer.

RT ⟨limited liability⟩

rules of origin The criteria applied by an importing country to determine the origin of a good.

> The question of origin is becoming more complex because many ⟨goods⟩ contain materials of mixed origin and many preferential trade agreements employ different origin criteria. Until uniform origin rules are adopted by the ⟨World Trade Organization⟩, importers should be sure that they understand the particular rules that their governments apply.

ruling A decision made by a judge or other authorized official.

running days 🗗 A vessel chartering term meaning days that run consecutively after each other.

S-HTTP ⟨secure hypertext transfer protocol⟩

SA (Sociedad Anoníma or Société Anonyme) ⟨limited liability⟩

SA de CV (Sociedad Anomína) ⟨limited liability⟩

SAARC ⟨South Asian Association for Regional Cooperation⟩

🛫 Insurance   🄻🄲 Letters of credit   ⚓ Liner vessel shipping   🖾 Sales contracts   🗗 Vessel chartering

S

sack A receptacle of flexible material with an opening at the top. Sacks are usually made from heavier material than bags; for instance, gunny sacks are made from jute.

SACU ⟨Southern African Customs Union⟩

SADC ⟨Southern Africa Development Community⟩

SAE (Société Anonyme Egyptienne) ⟨limited liability⟩

safe harbour privacy principles An agreement worked out between the US Department of Commerce and the European Commission regarding ⟨e-commerce⟩ privacy issues, necessary as ⟨EU⟩ citizens have privacy rights that exceed those of US citizens. See also ⟨data protection directive⟩.

safeguard measures (= escape clause). Emergency measures taken when increased imports of particular products cause or threaten to cause serious injury to the importing country's domestic industry.

Safeguard Measures, WTO Agreement The ⟨World Trade Organization⟩ agreement setting forth the rules governing the application of safeguard measures involving the suspensions of concessions or obligations under WTO agreements. This agreement requires that, at a minimum, safeguard measures be temporary, imposed only when imports are found to cause or threaten to cause serious injury to a domestic industry, applied on a ⟨most-favoured nation⟩ basis, and be progressively liberalized while in effect.

said to contain (STC) (= said to weigh (STW) = shipper's load and count (S&C)) ⬇ These are caveat clauses applied to container-shipment transport documents, indicating that the ⟨carrier⟩ has no firsthand knowledge of what was loaded in the container. They do not deny that the quantity invoiced is actually the quantity shipped, and in themselves do not constitute discrepancies under ⟨letters of credit⟩.

sales agent ⟨agent⟩

sales contract ✍ An agreement between a seller and a buyer for the sale of ⟨goods⟩, real property or ⟨services⟩. Sales contracts should, at a minimum, identify the seller and buyer, the quantity and type of product, delivery time, price and conditions of payment. In addition, a well-constructed sales contract will reference the governing body of law, the forum where any disputes are to be resolved and the method of dispute resolution, such as arbitration as opposed to litigation. (For international sales of goods, the body of law will often be the ⟨UN Convention on Contracts for the International Sale of goods⟩.) Contracts for the international sale of goods should also indicate the terms of sale, preferably one of the 13 ⟨ICC⟩ ⟨Incoterms⟩.

Sales contracts covering goods that are not shipped under a ⟨negotiable marine bill of lading⟩ should also specify when (time or place) and/or how ownership passes from seller to buyer.

> **1. Often, international transactions are conducted without the benefit of a document called a sales contract. Instead, the seller provides a quotation (often in the form of a proforma invoice) and the buyer responds with a purchase order. When these substantially agree, a de-facto contract results (offer = acceptance). This may be sufficient for repeat sales between well-acquainted parties that have developed a basis of previous dealings. However, it can lead to unanticipated problems in case of disputes. Major issues not covered in the contract and without precedence in previous dealings between the parties will be "filled in" by the dispute resolving authority, often with surprising consequences.**
>
> **2. For background also ⟨Incoterms⟩, ⟨proforma invoice⟩, ⟨purchase order⟩, ⟨title⟩ and the ⟨United Nations Convention on Contracts for the International Sale of Goods⟩.**

sales representative ⟨agent⟩

sales tax A tax levied on the exchange of ⟨goods⟩ and ⟨services⟩ in the process of distribution. See also ⟨indirect tax⟩, ⟨value added tax⟩.

salvage ① Recovery of a ship or its cargo from sea peril. ② ⟨Goods⟩ so recovered. ③ Compensation for the party performing the recovery (salvor).

sample A portion or piece taken as a representative of a whole. When cost permits, sellers often provide samples to new customers, or of new products to existing customers. Either way, this is normally done at low or no charge to the customer.

> **1. Sample shipments may present problems in international trade, as countries' rules differ in how they are treated for customs purposes. The safest procedure is to ask the buyer whether a commercial invoice is required and, if so, what verbiage should be used. For many countries, a "no charge" invoice stating the lowest defensible value and clearly indicating "samples – no commercial value – not for resale" works well.**
>
> **2. Importers find that samples are useful when requesting a classification ruling from their customs authorities.**

sanctions ① General approval. ② International coercive measures applied by a country or group of countries to force another country to obey international law.

sanitary measures Regulations that governments impose to restrict

---

S

imports for health protection reasons. See also ‹phytosanitary certificate›.

Sanitary and Phytosanitary Measures (SPS), WTO Agreement A ‹World Trade Organization› agreement establishing a set of rules, principles and benchmarks for WTO members, to ensure that sanitary and phytosanitary trade measures are justified and do not constitute disguised barriers to international trade.

SARL (société a responsibilité limitée) ‹limited liability›

SAS (société par actions) ‹limited liability›

SASO ‹Saudi Arabian Standards Organization›

Saudi Arabian Standards Organization (SASO) Established in 1972 as the sole Saudi Government standards organization, SASO issues import eligibility directives on class and testing procedures for many products.

> **For more information, visit the Saudi Arabia website at www.saudia-online.com.**

SD ‹short delivery›

SD/DP ‹sight draft, documents against payment›

SDRs ‹special drawing rights›

sea waybill ⊟ ⚓ A non-negotiable marine transport document indicating that shipment is to be made (received for shipment) or has been made (on-board) on a named vessel from and to named ports.

search engine A program within a host computer serving a ‹website›, which finds information from the website, from databases stored within the website, or from other websites. This is accomplished by searching for, and finding matches for, specific text keywords or meta-tags. See also ‹extensible markup language›.

seaworthy A vessel considered safe for a voyage at sea.

second advising bank In a ‹letter of credit› transaction, the seller usually prefers that the incoming letters of credit be advised through its bank of account. However, if the seller's bank lacks a correspondent banking relationship with the issuing bank, it is unable to authenticate the letter of credit. In such cases, the ‹issuing bank› will transmit the letter to its correspondent bank (the first advising bank) for authentication, with instructions to relay the credit to the seller's bank (the second advising bank).

second of exchange For many years, trade practice was to draw

S

⟨drafts⟩ in original and duplicate for fear that originals could become lost. The second of exchange is the duplicate copy, and is valid only if the first of exchange is unpaid.

secure hypertext transfer protocol (S-HTTP) A secure version of ⟨HTTP⟩, providing general transaction security services over the internet. Used especially in creating secure environments where credit card payments are processed.

secure electronic transaction (SET) @ A standard permitting secured internet credit card transactions. SET enables merchants to verify buyer identity through ⟨electronic signatures⟩, and directs buyer credit card numbers directly to the credit card issuers for verification and billing without revealing the numbers to the merchants.

> **For more information, visit the SETCO website at www.setco.org.**

security ① A document giving ⟨title⟩ to property as collateral for a loan. Also ⟨collateral and hypothecation letter⟩. ② A saleable income-yield paper such as bonds and shares.

SED (shipper's export declaration) ⟨export declaration⟩

SELA ⟨Latin American Economic System⟩

self insured (= uninsured). A shipment on which insurance coverage is not placed.

sensitive products Domestically produced goods considered economically important in a country whose competitive position would be threatened if protection against the imports of similar ⟨goods⟩ were reduced.

service contract A negotiated agreement between a ⟨carrier⟩ and ⟨shipper⟩, providing for ⟨freight⟩ charges and service conditions for a specified time period based on a quantity commitment.

service mark ⟨trademark⟩

services Economic activities – such as transportation, banking, insurance, tourism, telecommunications, advertising, entertainment, data processing and consulting – that normally are consumed as they are produced, as compared with economic ⟨goods⟩ that are more tangible.

SET ① @ ⟨secured electronic transaction⟩. ② A definition under the ⟨Harmonized System⟩ General Rule of Interpretation 3b, whereby articles of a different nature but retail-packaged together for a dedicated purpose are classified together.

🛪 Insurance 🆘 Letters of credit ⬇ Liner vessel shipping 📑 Sales contracts 📂 Vessel chartering

S

SGML ⟨standard generalized markup language⟩

sherka mosahema ⟨limited liability⟩

sherka zat masouleya mahdouda ⟨limited liability⟩

SHEX 🔲 A term meaning that Sundays and holidays are excluded in calculating the laytime for vessel ⟨chartering⟩. See also ⟨laydays⟩.

SHINC 🔲 A term meaning that Sundays and holidays are included in calculating the laytime for vessel ⟨chartering⟩. See also ⟨laydays⟩.

ship A vessel.

ship's gear Material handling equipment, such as cranes, that are permanently mounted on a vessel.

ship's hook ⟨ship's tackle⟩

ship's manifest ⟨manifest⟩

ship's rail 🔲 ⚓ A railing surrounding the outermost perimeter of most vessels. Although the ship's rail serves the very practical purpose of keeping people from falling off the vessel, it also defines the ship in place. For this reason, it is used as a risk-demarcation point for vessel loading in the ⟨FOB⟩, ⟨CFR⟩ and ⟨CIF⟩ ⟨Incoterms⟩.

- In the FOB Incoterm, the seller's costs and risk for the condition of the shipped ⟨goods⟩ end when they pass the ship's rail.
- In the CFR and CIF Incoterms, despite the fact that the seller's costs extend to payment of ⟨main carriage⟩, the sellers risk for the condition of the shipped ⟨goods⟩ ends when they pass the ship's rail.

At one time, the ship's rail provided an actual place where cargo was handed off from stevedores to the vessel crew during the loading process. Although everyone realizes that passing the ship's rail has little relevance for shipments of manufactured goods from modern ports, it does provide a place that can be measured, and the custom continues.

ship's stores A vessel's provisions excluding baggage.

ship's tackle (= ship's hook). The device connecting the cargo to the ship's gear during loading and unloading, often a hook.

shipbroker 🔲 In vessel chartering, a party who acts as a ⟨middleman⟩ in return for a fee or ⟨brokerage⟩, negotiating the terms of a contract between ⟨charterer⟩ and vessel owner.

shipment ✈ 🔲 ⚓ (as in consignment). The act of handing over cargo to a ⟨carrier⟩ or other transportation service provider for transport.

S

shipment ⊟ ⬇ (on board a vessel). The act of placing cargo on a vessel. This can be literally defined as passing the ship's rail. Once ⟨goods⟩ are successfully loaded, the ⟨carrier⟩ can issue a marine transportation document bearing an "on-board" notation.

shipment date The date a shipment takes place, which is usually the date of the relevant transport document.

> **For banking purposes, with shipments by vessel for which an on-board marine transport document is issued, the shipment date is considered to be the date of the ⟨on-board notation⟩ if it is the same date or later than the date on which the document is executed.**

shipment date (latest) ⌧ The last date specified in a ⟨letter of credit⟩ when shipment may take place, as determined by the date on the required transport document.

shipper ① As the party who contracts for carriage, the party who enters into a ⟨contract of carriage⟩ with a ⟨carrier⟩ and pays the carrier is in a position to give the carrier handling instructions. For freight-prepaid shipments this would usually be the seller; for freight-collect shipments, it would usually be the buyer. ② As the party who delivers ⟨goods⟩ to carrier, the party who hands over cargo for transport is called "shipper." However, in case of conflicting instructions, those given to the carrier by the counterparty may prevail when it is the counterparty who contracts for carriage.

shipper's dangerous goods declaration ⟨dangerous goods declaration⟩

shipper's export declaration ⟨export declaration⟩

shipper's letter of instruction (SLI) ✈ ⬇ Directions to a ⟨forwarder⟩ or ⟨carrier⟩ on how a shipment and its resulting documentation are to be handled. The party engaging the forwarder and/or contracting with the carrier should normally issue these instructions. Shippers entrusting cargo to carriers or forwarders with which they are not contract parties run the risk of having their instructions disregarded if they conflict with the wishes of the party actually contracting for carriage.

shipper's load and count (S&C) ⟨said to contain⟩

shippers' association ⬇ A group of unrelated vessel ⟨shipper⟩s who pool their volumes to achieve bargaining power with ⟨carrier⟩s.

shipping conference ⟨conference (liner)⟩

✈ Insurance   ⌧ Letters of credit   ⬇ Liner vessel shipping   ◿ Sales contracts   ⊟ Vessel chartering

S

shipping documents ✈ 📄 ⚓ Pieces of paper or electronic message units that detail how a shipment has taken or should take place. Typical shipping documents include truck (or lorry) ❬B/L❭ (or waybill), ❬air waybill❭, ❬marine B/L❭, ❬sea waybill❭ and ❬multimodal transport document❭.

shipping instructions ❬shipper's letter of instruction❭

shipping marks ❬export marks❭

shipping weight ❬gross weight❭

shopping cart Shopping cart software allows a credit cardholder to select items from an ❬electronic store❭ and place them in a "virtual" shopping basket or shopping cart. The shopping cart remembers which items are selected while the cardholder views other items within the e-store, keeps a running total, and may calculate taxes and shipping. The items in the shopping cart are eventually ordered if the cardholder chooses.

shore crane A crane located at shipside rather than on a vessel.

short delivery (SD) Non-delivery of cargo at the intended port. When reported, this will result in the ship's agent sending a cargo tracer to locate the missing cargo.

short form B/L A ❬bill of lading❭ that does not include the full terms and conditions of the ❬contract of carriage❭. Instead, it contains an abbreviated version of the ❬carrier❭'s conditions, with a reference to the full set of conditions.

short landed cargo ❬short delivery❭

short shipment A shipment whose total cargo was less than indicated on its covering documentation.

shrink film ❬film (packaging)❭

SIC (Standard Industrial Classification Codes) ❬North American Industry Classification System❭

SIDA ❬Swedish International Development Authority❭

sight draft, documents against payment (SD/DP) ❬documents against Payment❭

single column tariff A ❬tariff❭ schedule listing only one duty rate for each imported product classification.

single currency peg A country pegs its currency to one major currency (such as the US dollar or French franc), with infrequent adjustments to the parity. Akin to this is limited flexibility vis-a-vis the major currency, where the value is maintained within certain margins of the peg.

SITC ⟨Standard International Trade Classification⟩

skids Parallel runners attached to the underside of large packages to facilitate engagement by ⟨forklift truck⟩ tines.

> To prevent introduction of non-native pests, some jurisdictions prohibit the importation of non-treated coniferous wood packing materials from certain originating countries.

SL (sociedad de responsibilidad limitada) ⟨limited liability⟩

SLI ⟨shipper's letter of instructions⟩

slot charter ⊟ One ship line renting space on a vessel of another. See also ⟨vessel sharing⟩.

SM ⟨trademark⟩

small- and medium-sized enterprises (SMEs) While the definition varies, SMEs are generally considered to be companies that have no more than one-third of their capital held by a larger company and have up to 500 employees.

SMEs ⟨small- and medium-sized enterprises⟩

smuggling Unlawfully taking or sending of ⟨goods⟩, persons or information into or out of a country.

snapback A return to earlier and usually higher ⟨tariff⟩ levels.

SNC ⟨société en nom collectif⟩ and ⟨società in nome collettivo⟩.

sociedad anomina (SA) ⟨limited liability⟩

socieded anonima de capital variable (SA de CV) ⟨limited liability⟩

sociedad de responsibilidad limitada (SL) ⟨limited liability⟩

societa a responsabilita limitada (SRL) ⟨limited liability⟩

societa per azioni (SPA) ⟨limited liability⟩

société à responsabilité limitée (SARL) ⟨limited liability⟩

société anonyme (SA) ⟨limited liability⟩

société anonyme egyptienne (SAE) ⟨limited liability⟩

société en commandité simple ⟨limited liability⟩

société en nom collectif (SNC) A general partnership with no limit on the liability of the partners.

⊤ Insurance   LC Letters of credit   ⟁ Liner vessel shipping   ◪ Sales contracts   ⊟ Vessel chartering

S

société in nome collettivo (SNC) A general partnership, with no limit on the liability of the partners.

société par actions (SAS) ⟨limited liability⟩

Society for Worldwide Interbank Financial Telecommunications (SWIFT) @ A Brussels-based banking organization that provides for electronic transmission of financial messages. A "SWIFT" message is a correct play on words since transmission and reception is virtually simultaneous.

> **For more information, visit the Society's website at www.swift.com.**

soft currency A currency of a nation in which exchange may be made only with difficulty. Countries with soft currencies typically have limited exchange reserves so that their currency is generally considered to be high risk.

soft loan A loan from a government or a multilateral development bank with a long repayment period and below-market interest rate.

sole of exchange Wording on a ⟨draft⟩ that indicates that only an original has been issued, as opposed to an original and a copy. See also ⟨first of exchange⟩ and ⟨second of exchange⟩.

sole ownership limited liability company (EURL) ⟨limited liability⟩

South Asian Association for Regional Cooperation (SAARC) Founded in 1985, SAARC promotes economic, technical, scientific and social cooperation among member countries.

> **For more information, visit the SAARC website at www.saarc-sec.org.**

South Group, Danish Ministry of Foreign Affairs Replaced the Danish International Development Assistance (DANIDA) as the focus of Danish Governmental development assistance.

South Pacific Forum (SPF) ⟨Pacific Island Forum⟩

Southern African Customs Union (SACU) Established in 1910, SACU provides for the free exchange of ⟨goods⟩, a common external ⟨tariff⟩ and sharing of customs revenues within Botswana, Lesotho, Namibia, South Africa and Swaziland.

Southern Africa Development Community (SADC) Established in 1980, and headquartered in Gaborone, Botswana, SADC is a regional economic pact focusing on development.

> **For more information, visit the SADC website at www.sadc.int**

southern cone A geographic term for the southern part of South

America including Argentina, Brazil, Chile, Paraguay and Uruguay.

S

sovereign immunity The legal principle that a national government cannot be sued without its permission in its own courts or in the courts of other nations. This is particularly applicable for activities that are of a governmental rather than a commercial nature.

sovereign risk The reduced possibility of default because of the guarantee of a national government.

SPA (societa per azioni) ⟨limited liability⟩

space charter 🅟 The ⟨chartering⟩ of all or part of a vessel's cargo capacity without responsibility for operation.

special and deferential treatment The concept that ⟨export⟩s from ⟨developing countries⟩ should be given preferential access to the markets of ⟨developed countries⟩, and that developing countries participating in trade negotiations need not fully reciprocate concessions they receive. See also ⟨enabling clause⟩.

special cargo policy ⟨insurance certificate⟩

special drawing rights (SDRs) A supplemental monetary reserve asset created in 1969 by the ⟨International Monetary Fund (IMF)⟩. SDRs are available to governments through the IMF and may be used in transactions between the IMF and member governments. IMF member countries have agreed to regard SDRs as complementary to gold and reserve currencies in settling their international accounts.

special risk policy ⟨Marine cargo insurance⟩ written on a single shipment basis.

specific duty Duty or tax payable on a unit of imported product rather than as a percentage of value. Example USD 0.08 per kilo.

spot A vessel chartering term for a ship that can begin loading immediately after the ⟨charter⟩ agreement has been made.

spot rate The ⟨rate of exchange⟩ quoted for purchases and sales of a foreign currency for immediate delivery and payment. Spot is the "here and now" rate, as opposed to forward exchange contracts or options.

SPS ⟨Sanitary and Phytosanitary Measures, WTO Agreement⟩

SRCC ⟨strike, riot and civil commotion⟩

SRL (societa a responsibilita limitada) ⟨limited liability⟩

🅘 Insurance 🅛🅒 Letters of credit 🅛 Liner vessel shipping 🅢 Sales contracts 🅟 Vessel chartering

S

stale transport document `LC` A ⟨letter of credit⟩ term for a transport document over 21 days old.

standard generalized markup language (SGML) A system for organizing and tagging elements of a document. SGML was developed and standardized by the International Organization for Standardization (ISO) in 1986. SGML itself does not specify any particular formatting; rather, it specifies the rules for tagging elements. These tags can then be interpreted to format elements in different ways.

Standard Industrial Classification Codes (SIC) ⟨North American Industry Classification System⟩

Standard International Trade Classification (SITC) A numerical code developed by the ⟨United Nations⟩ for the classification of ⟨goods⟩.

standards Government regulations concerning performance, health and safety of regulated products. See also ⟨non-tariff barriers⟩ and ⟨Technical Barriers to Trade (TBT), WTO Agreement⟩.

standby L/C `LC` A ⟨letter of credit⟩ payable against beneficiary attestation rather than documentary evidence.

state trading enterprise (STE) Entities established by governments to import, export and/or produce certain products.

STC ⟨said to contain⟩

STE ⟨state trading enterprise⟩

steamer guarantee ⟨letter of indemnity⟩

stevedoring charges ⟨terminal handling charges⟩

stowage ⊟ The placing of ⟨cargo⟩ in a ship's hold in such a fashion as to assure safe and stable transport.

straight B/L ⟨non-negotiable B/L⟩

straight L/C `LC` A ⟨letter of credit⟩ payable only at the ⟨opening bank⟩ or at a bank specified within the credit.

strategic stockpiles Accumulated stocks of raw materials or other commodities deemed necessary for national defence.

stretch film ⟨film (packaging)⟩

strike, riot and civil commotion (SRCC) ⟲ Three perils, usually grouped together, that are not normally included in "⟨all risk⟩" (⟨London Institute of Underwriters clause A⟩) insurance cover.

Coverage is usually available for an additional premium.

stripping (= devanning = unstuffing). ⟨devanning⟩

stuffing Loading ⟨Goods⟩ inside a container or truck.

STW ⟨said to contain⟩

sub-charter 🄟 A vessel chartering situation under which a ⟨charterer⟩ (called the head charterer) makes the chartered vessel available to other charterers (called sub-charterers).

subrogation 🄸 The transfer of all rights to claim against third parties to an insurance company upon payment of a claim.

subsidiary A company controlled by another company, usually through ownership of 50 to 100 per cent of its shares, or through other organizational or managerial agreement.

subsidy Direct financial aid provided by a government to a private industrial undertaking. Government subsidies can be used to make products artificially price-competitive in foreign markets. See also ⟨countervailing duty⟩ and ⟨illustrative list⟩.

Subsidies and Countervailing Measures, WTO Agreement A ⟨World Trade Organization⟩ agreement that was concluded as the successor to the GATT Subsidies Code, providing that subsidies given by a government to a domestic industry should not be permitted to harm or threaten to harm one's trading partners. Unlike its predecessor, the WTO agreement is binding on all WTO members. See also ⟨countervailing duty⟩ and ⟨illustrative list⟩.

sue and labour clause 🄸 A provision found in many insurance contracts whereby the assured is obligated to keep any damaged ⟨goods⟩ from becoming further damaged, pending instructions from the ⟨insurer⟩ for their disposition. Storing damaged ⟨goods⟩ under cover and away from the elements is an example. The insurer normally reimburses any costs for this.

supplier The party furnishing ⟨goods⟩ or ⟨services⟩ in a transaction.

supply The quantity of a ⟨good⟩ or ⟨service⟩ that sellers will make available at a given price and at a certain time in a specific market.

supply chain logistics The management of various functions that must be performed to get a product or service from the supply point to the user. For example, a typical export shipment would include most or all of the following assembling the ordered ⟨goods⟩ for shipment, ⟨export packing⟩, ⟨pre-carriage⟩, ⟨export clearance⟩, ⟨main carriage⟩, ⟨import clearance⟩, ⟨on-carriage⟩ and probably insurance.

🄸 Insurance 🄻🄲 Letters of credit 🄻 Liner vessel shipping 🄰 Sales contracts 🄟 Vessel chartering

S

surcharge (= accessorial charge) ⚓ An additional charge for ⟨services⟩. ⟨Carrier⟩s typically assess surcharges for services that they provide, but for which the costs are not included in their base-rate freight prices. Typical transportation surcharges include ⟨congestion surcharges⟩ which compensate carriers for unusually long delays at crowded ports, ⟨currency adjustment factors (CAF)⟩, which compensate for exchange rate differentials, fuel adjustment factors, which cover unanticipated increases in the cost of fuel, and ⟨terminal handling charges⟩, which cover port-usage fees that are often port-specific.

surety/surety-ship bond/guarantee A surety bond is a guarantee, usually issued by an insurance or surety company, that a particular party will perform according to a contract. In order to collect payment under such a bond, the beneficiary normally must prove actual default on the part of the ⟨counterparty⟩, by furnishing a court judgement, arbitral award or official certificate. Surety-ship bonds may be issued subject to the ICC Uniform Rules for Contract Bonds. Surety bonds are commonly used in foreign trade as ⟨bid bonds⟩ (which cover the possibility of a successful bidder's failing to take up the contract) and ⟨performance bonds⟩.

surplus The amount of a commodity that cannot be absorbed in a given market at the existing price.

surveyor ⏚ An independent third-party expert who examines and ascertains the condition of ⟨goods⟩ or transport equipment (especially ships). Surveyors often participate in the insurance claim process by examining goods to determine the level of damage and often how it occurred.

swaps An umbrella term for the exchange of one type of asset or payment for another.

sweating ⟨condensation⟩

Swede Corp ⟨Swedish International Development Cooperation Agency⟩

Swedish International Development Cooperation Agency (SIDA = SwedeCorp). Established in 1991 and headquartered in Stockholm, Sweden, SwedeCorp is funded under Sweden's aid programme to support enterprise development through joint venture investments in ⟨developing countries⟩ and in Central and Eastern Europe.
For more information, visit the SIDA website at www.sida.se.

SWIFT ⟨Society for Worldwide Interbank Financial Telecommunications⟩

⟨see entry in dictionary⟩ ✈ Air transport 🏛 Bank collections @ e-commerce ⊞ Incoterms

ST

switch arrangements A form of ⟨countertrade⟩ in which unused purchase rights for unwanted ⟨goods⟩ received by a firm in a countertrade transaction are sold at a discount to third-party buyers.

TABD ⟨Transatlantic Business Dialogue⟩

TACD ⟨Transatlantic Consumer Dialogue⟩

tare weight The weight of a container and/or packaging materials without the weight of the ⟨goods⟩.

targeting A comprehensive mobilization of technology, capital and skilled labour involving direct or indirect government intervention in the marketplace in support of a specific industry.

tariff anomaly A ⟨tariff⟩ anomaly exists when the customs duty on raw materials or semi-manufactured ⟨goods⟩ is higher than the duty on the finished product.

tariff (customs). A schedule of items and their respective duty costs used by customs services. Most customs tariffs are numerically structured, and many are based on the 6-digit ⟨Harmonized System (HS)⟩ developed and administered by the ⟨World Customs Organization (WCO)⟩.

tariff (freight) ✈ ⬇ A price list issued by ⟨carriers⟩ for transportation services, often written on a commodity-specific basis.

tariff rate surcharge ⟨import quota⟩

tax A payment exacted on persons, corporations and other economic entities by a government, to pay for government operations or to discourage the consumption of ⟨goods⟩ or ⟨services⟩ on which the tax is applied.

TBL ⟨through bill of lading⟩

TBT ⟨Technical Barriers to Trade, WTO Agreement⟩

TC ⟨time charter⟩

Technical Barriers to Trade (TBT), WTO Agreement This ⟨World Trade Organization⟩ agreement attempts to ensure that standards and regulations imposed by governments and governmental authorities do not unnecessarily restrict or distort trade by imposing rules to reduce the risk of their being adopted simply to protect domestic industries. It is accompanied by a Code of Good Practice, which is designed to serve as a guide to bodies that prepare, adopt and apply standards.

technology transfer The movement of modern or scientific methods

---

✈ Insurance 🔲 Letters of credit ⬇ Liner vessel shipping 📄 Sales contracts 📁 Vessel chartering

T

of production or distribution from one enterprise, institution or country to another, as through foreign investment, international trade, licensing of patent rights, technical assistance or training. Technology may also be transferred by giving it away (technical journals, conferences, emigration of technical experts, technical assistance programmes), or by industrial espionage.

tender An offer of sale, usually made in response to a call for bids.

tenor The notation on the face of the ‹draft› indicating when it is to be paid. If at sight, payment is to be made immediately. If a ‹time draft›, it is the time upon which a draft's maturity is calculated.

term ① A condition, such as "term of sale" or "term of payment". ② Length of time as in "term bond".

terminal handling charge (THC) ⚓ A surcharge levied by ship lines that provide "‹liner terms›", whereby the shipowner is responsible for vessel loading and unloading. Since charges and methods of operation differ from port to port, terminal handling charges cannot be included in base rates for ‹carriage› to or from ranges of ports.

terms of trade The ratio of unit value prices of a country's exports to the unit value prices of its imports.

territory An area; in commercial usage an area in which a party operates, such as a "sales territory." A territory's size and the degree of exclusivity are often important commercial considerations in foreign trade.

TEU ‹twenty-foot equivalent unit›

Textiles and Clothing (ATC), WTO Agreement This ‹World Trade Organization› agreement superseded the Multi-Fibre Arrangement (MFA) which established quotas on imports of certain textile products. The ATC applies to all WTO members but not to non-WTO members, even those that were party to the MFA. Under the ATC, quotas will come to an end by 2005, and importing member countries will no longer be able to discriminate among exporters.

THC ‹terminal handling charge›

third country dumping A situation in which exports of a product from one country are being injured or threatened with injury as a result of exports of the same product from a second country into a third country at less than fair value.

third party logistics provider (3PL) A company that provides a full complement of services (such as transportation, storage, and scheduling) under contract. 3PLs usually replace individual company-owned traffic departments.

through bill of lading (TBL) A single ⟨bill of lading⟩ covering the receipt of ⟨cargo⟩ for shipment involving two or more modes of transport.

through rate A ⟨freight⟩ cost that includes ⟨pre-carriage⟩, ⟨on-carriage⟩ or both, in addition to ⟨main carriage⟩.

through transport Transportation including ⟨pre-carriage⟩, ⟨on-carriage⟩ or both, in addition to ⟨main carriage⟩.

tied aid credit The practice of providing grants and/or concessional loans, either alone or combined with export credits, linked to procurement from the donor country.

tied loan A loan made by a government agency that requires a foreign borrower to spend the proceeds in the lender's country.

time bar A limit in time as to when an action may be taken, such as claiming against a ⟨carrier⟩ for transit-related damage.

time charter (TC) A ⟨charter⟩ agreement providing the ⟨charterer⟩ with the use of a vessel for a stated length of time, or for one or consecutive voyages among ranges of ports.

time drafts ⟨Draft⟩s that are due at a future time.

TIR ⟨transport international routier⟩

title A legal term for property ownership.

> The concept of passing ownership from seller to buyer is often confused with several other related issues. It is possible to own property without possessing it, or conversely to possess property without owning it. It is likewise possible for one to be responsible for the condition of property without owning it, or to own property without being responsible for its condition. In international trade, passing of ownership can take place by expressed wording in the ⟨sales contract⟩, a ⟨negotiable marine bill of lading⟩ or operation of law. Possession is usually indicated through the manner in which the main carriage transport document is constructed; i.e., the party shown as "⟨consignee⟩". The point where the seller's responsibility for the condition of shipped ⟨goods⟩ ends is usually indicated by the governing sales term, particularly if ⟨Incoterms⟩ are used.

title transfer ⟨transfer of ownership⟩

TM ⟨trademark⟩

TOFC ⟨trailer on flat car⟩

TPRM ⟨trade policy review mechanism⟩

T

TPS (goods and services tax). ⟨value added tax⟩

tracer ① Request for an answer to a communication, commonly used by banks in the ⟨documentary collection⟩ process. ② Request to a ⟨carrier⟩ for the status of ⟨goods⟩ in transit.

trade acceptance ⟨draft⟩

trade barrier An impediment to trade, often included in one of the following classifications:
* ⟨tariffs⟩, quantity restrictions, import licensing
* restrictive standards
* restrictive government procurement
* export subsidies
* lack of intellectual property protection
* service barriers
* investment barriers
* ⟨embargoes⟩

trade diversion The situation in which ⟨imports⟩ from free-trade member countries increase, displacing imports from non-member countries.

trade fair A stage-setting event in which firms of several nationalities present their products or services to prospective customers. Trade fairs are normally larger than similar events such as ⟨trade shows⟩.

Trade L/C ⓒ An organization dedicated to automating international trade transactions, with the backing of a major international bank.

trade leads (online). Offers to buy or sell merchandise or services, posted on ⟨websites⟩, e-marketplaces and online exchanges, by potential suppliers or purchasers. These offers typically contain a brief description of the merchandise to be provided or required, as well as contact information. See also ⟨electronic trading opportunity⟩.

trade mission Experts and/or businesspeople sent by a government or commercial interests in one country to encourage ⟨exports⟩ to the market of another country.

trade name The name used by an enterprise to individually identify itself as a business.

Trade Policy Review Mechanism (TPRM) An annex to the ⟨World Trade Organization⟩ Agreement providing for periodic review of each WTO member's trade policy regime.

trade-related environmental issues Elements of environmental policy with important implications for or impacts on the trading system.

T

Trade Related Aspects of Intellectual Property (TRIPS), WTO Agreement A ⟨World Trade Organization⟩ agreement that obligates countries to provide minimum standards of intellectual property (IP) protection in national laws and to enforce minimum standards for protecting intellectual property. The TRIPS agreement covers copyright and related rights (that is, the rights of performers, producers of sound recordings, and broadcasting organizations); ⟨trademarks⟩, including service marks; geographical indications including appellations of origin; industrial designs; ⟨patents⟩, including the protection of new varieties of plants; the layout-designs of integrated circuits; and undisclosed information, including trade secrets and test data. The agreement sets out the minimum standards of protection to be provided by each member with respect to each of the main areas of intellectual property covered.

⟨Developed countries⟩ were required to have implemented all of the obligations under the agreement as of 1 January 1996. ⟨Developing countries⟩ were permitted a transitional period of an additional four years (until 1 January 2000). ⟨Least-developed country⟩ members are permitted a transitional period of an additional ten years (until 1 January 2006). In addition, developing countries that, as of 1995, were without patent protection for a given area of technology, especially pharmaceutical or agricultural inventions, have an additional five-year transition (until 1 January 2005) before being required to provide such protection.

Trade Related Investment Measures (TRIMS), WTO Agreement A ⟨World Trade Organization⟩ agreement that recognizes that measures and regulations that governments impose on investments and investors can reduce or distort international trade, and may function as disincentives for investors in situations where investment is needed.

The objectives of the TRIMS Agreement, as set forth in its preamble, include "the expansion and progressive liberalization of world trade and to facilitate investment across international frontiers, so as to increase the economic growth of all trading partners, particularly ⟨developing country⟩ members, while ensuring free competition." Under TRIMS, WTO member countries agreed to eliminate investment measures that limit or force certain types of investments, to offer national treatment to foreign investors and to eliminate quotas and other restraints. The agreement restricts the use of three TRIMS requirements: local content requirements, trade balancing requirements and ⟨foreign exchange⟩ balancing requirements.

trade show A stage-setting event in which firms of several nationalities present their products or services to prospective

---

⟨🔨⟩ Insurance ⟨LC⟩ Letters of credit ⟨🔱⟩ Liner vessel shipping ⟨📃⟩ Sales contracts ⟨🅿⟩ Vessel chartering

customers. Trade shows are normally smaller than ‹trade fairs›.

T

TradeCard @ An organization dedicated to automating international trade transactions. Trade Card has the backing of several major international banks.

> **For more information, visit the TradeCard website at www.tradecard.com.**

trademark (TM) (= service mark (SM)). A distinctive marking placed by a manufacturer on its products, or a distinctive name used for services. Trademarks and service marks are considered to be intellectual property. Since registration and protection differ from country to country, owners of valuable marks should take care to ensure that they are protected.

trailer on flat car (= piggyback = TOFC). Transportation of containers and truck trailers on railroad flatcars.

tramp (vessel). A vessel that does not operate under regular schedule, but calls on any port where cargo may be obtained.

tranche A term used to describe a loan taken by a borrower in partial payments, rather than a single payment at the beginning of the loan.

Transatlantic Business Dialogue (TABD) An informal process whereby European and US companies and business associations develop joint EU–US trade policy recommendations, working together with both governments.

> **For more information, visit the TABD website at www.tabd.org.**

Transatlantic Consumer Dialogue (TACD) A forum of EU and US consumer organizations that develops joint consumer policy recommendations to the EU and US Governments to promote consumer interests in policy making.

> **For more information, visit the TACD website at www.tacd.org.**

transfer of ownership (= title transfer) ✍ The act or point in place or time at which ownership of a thing is passed from one person to another. In foreign trade, this is usually specified in ‹sales contracts› by statements like:

- "Seller and buyer agree that title for the contract ‹goods› will pass to the buyer when they have been shipped from the seller's premises," or
- "Seller and buyer agree that title for the contract ‹goods› will pass to the buyer when they have arrived at (xxx)," or
- "Seller and buyer agree that the seller will continue to own the contract ‹goods› until such time as payment for them has been received,"

or similar verbiage. In some cases, a title-bearing document is created through the shipment process; for instance, shipments covered by a negotiable ⟨marine bill of lading⟩.

transferable L/C `LC` A ⟨letter of credit⟩ specifically permitting transfer from the original ⟨beneficiary⟩ to one or more secondary beneficiaries.

transit zone The area surrounding a port of entry in a coastal country that serves as a storage and distribution centre for the convenience of a neighbouring country – a ⟨landlocked⟩ country, for example – lacking adequate port facilities or access to the sea. A transit zone is administered so that ⟨goods⟩ in transit to and from the neighbouring country are not subject to ⟨customs duties⟩, import controls or many of the entry and exit formalities of the host country.

transnational corporation ⟨multinational corporation⟩

transparency The extent to which laws, regulations, agreements and practices affecting international trade are open, clear, measurable and verifiable.

transport international routier (TIR) A system used throughout Europe for sealed road transport of ⟨goods⟩. TIR carnets are transport documents used to cover international transport shipments on road vehicles such as trucks (lorries). Issued pursuant to the 1949 TIR Convention, these carnets allow trucks or other vehicles to pass through TIR-member countries without having to go through customs inspection until they reach the destination country.

transportation lien A lien that ⟨carriers⟩ may take on cargo to collect transport and other charges incurred by that cargo.

transshipment This term can have several meanings depending on the context in which it is used.
The literal definition is passing of shipped ⟨goods⟩ from one ⟨carrier⟩ to another. Under this strict definition, all through transport shipments would involve transshipment.
This thinking dates back to the time where every leg of a transport movement was covered by its own transport document; for instance, a truck ⟨bill of lading⟩ from factory to port and a port-to-port marine transport document plus perhaps another truck bill of lading from the arrival port to the buyer's premises.
A more practical definition might be that transshipment occurs whenever more than one of the same kind of conveyance is used for ⟨main carriage⟩. For example, transshipment would take place if goods bound for Hamburg are shipped on one vessel from New

T

York to London and then reloaded on a second vessel from London to Hamburg. However, a shipment made by truck to New York, where it is loaded on a vessel bound for Hamburg, would not be considered transshipped, since a single vessel accomplishes main carriage. The biggest problem with transshipment is that it subjects goods to additional risk and delay in extra unloading and reloading. This happens in the first example because two vessels are used. Contrast this with the second example, where the goods are vessel loaded and unloaded only once.

The issue of transshipment becomes critical with ⟨letters of credit⟩ that prohibit it. Because of the ⟨hub and spoke⟩ system widely used in vessel and air transport, transshipments frequently take place. When considering vessel shipments, banks consider only the information shown on the transport document, even though the fact that a feeder vessel is being used can be easily ascertained. Further, for air shipments, banks disregard the fact that an ⟨air waybill⟩ may show several different flight numbers and dates, as long as they are shown on only one document.

> **Because this term is used in several different ways, sellers and buyers should clearly indicate what they mean when they use it.**

Treaty on Free Trade Among Colombia, Mexico and Venezuela (G–3) A ⟨free trade agreement⟩ among these countries that was signed in 1990 to take effect 1 January 1995.

> **For more information, visit the Trade Agreements site map Organization of American States SICE website at www.sice.org**

triangular trade Related trade among three countries.

trimming ⊟ The operation of shoveling and spreading, within the ship's hold, dry bulk cargoes such as cement, ore or grains, so as to avoid weight imbalances that might hinder the ship's handling or unloading.

TRIMS ⟨Trade-Related Investment Measures, WTO Agreement⟩

TRIPS ⟨Trade-Related Aspects of Intellectual Property Rights, WTO Agreement⟩

trust receipt A document executed by a buyer in favour of a bank financing an import transaction, whereby the bank receives a security interest in the ⟨goods⟩ in exchange for releasing the documents required by the ⟨carrier⟩ for delivery. The buyer is obligated to maintain the goods or the proceeds from their resale at the disposal of the bank.

Trusted Third Party (TTP) ⟨Certification Service Provider⟩

⟨see entry in dictionary⟩   ☒ Air transport   🏛 Bank collections   @ e-commerce   ⊞ Incoterms

TU

TTP (Trusted Third Party) ‹Certification Service Provider›

turnkey A scope of supply whereby the contractor assumes total responsibility from design through completion of the project.

twenty-foot equivalent unit (TEU) ⚓ A practice in marine commerce of expressing cargo quantity in terms of twenty-foot container loads. Two twenty-foot equivalent units (TEUs) = one forty-foot equivalent unit (FEU).

UCC ‹Uniform Commercial Code›

UCP ‹Uniform Customs and Practice for Documentary Credits›

UIC ‹International Union of Railways›

ullage A measurement of space between the surface of liquid in a container and the top of the container's inner surface – commonly used in reference to tanks on vessels.

ultimate consignee The party shown on the transport document to whom final delivery of the ‹goods› will be made. This is normally the buyer of the shipped goods.

UMOA ‹West African Economic and Monetary Union›

UN ‹United Nations›

UNCID ‹Uniform Rules of Conduct for Interchange of Trade Data by Teletransmission›

UNCITRAL ‹United Nations Commission on International Trade Law›

unclean transport document ‹foul transport document›

unconfirmed L/C 🆔 A ‹letter of credit› that does not bear the undertaking of any financial institution bank other than the institution that issued it.

UNCTAD ‹United Nations Conference on Trade and Development›

under deck Cargo shipped in the hold of a vessel. This is the opposite of cargo shipped on-deck. Normally, all cargo shipped against a transport document lacking an on-deck notation may be considered under deck.

under reserve ‹payment under reserve›

undercarrier (underlying carrier) ✈ ⚓ The ‹carrier› performing actual transport in situations where another carrier contracts for carriage. This term is most commonly used with non-vessel operating common carriers, which contract for carriage with the ‹shipper› and subcontract for the actual transportation with a ship line. In this situation, the ship line is the undercarrier.

U

Understanding on Rules and Procedures Governing the Settlement of Disputes ‹Dispute Settlement, WTO Understanding on Rules and Procedures (DSU)›

underwriter ‹insurer›

UNDP ‹United Nations Development Programme›

UNECE ‹United Nations Economic Commission for Europe›

UNEP ‹United Nations Environment Programme›

unfair calling insurance Coverage to protect principals who have issued ‹demand guarantees› or bonds against an unfair or abusive call of the bond/guarantee i.e., one that is not truly based on non-performance by the principal.

unfair trade practices Unusual government support to firms, such as export subsidies, or certain anti-competitive practices of the firms themselves, such as ‹dumping›, that result in competitive advantages for those firms in international trade.

UNIDO ‹United Nations Industrial Development Organization›

UNIDROIT ‹International Institute for Unification of Private Law›

Uniform Commercial Code (UCC) The codification of United States commercial law, followed in a substantially uniform fashion by all US states. Article 5 of the UCC deals with ‹letters of credit› Article 2 deals with terms of sale.

> Sellers and buyers should use ‹Incoterms› in their contracts for international sales of ‹goods›, rather than those shown in the UCC, as Incoterms are more likely to be understood by both parties. There are similar words and abbreviations in both, but their meanings often differ.

Uniform Customs and Practice for Documentary Credits (UCP) [LC] The ‹International Chamber of Commerce (ICC)› rules that govern the use of most documentary ‹letters of credit› throughout the world. Since the UCP is not law, it must be specified in order to apply. However, it is in such common use that reference to it is often pre-printed on the letter of credit forms commonly used by banks. L/Cs advised by SWIFT are automatically.

Uniform Customs and Practice for Documentary Credits – Supplement for Electronic Presentation (eUCP) [LC] A supplement to the ‹International Chamber of Commerce's (ICC)› ‹Uniform Customs and Practice for Documentary Credits› to accommodate presentation of electronic records alone or in

---

combination with paper documents.

uniform resource locator (URL) @ These codes provide a short consistent way to name any resource on the internet. Although first designed for use only on the ‹world wide web›, they are used everywhere as a shorthand for ‹file transfer protocol› archives. For example, in the following website address www.iccwbo.org/home/guidec/guidec.asp, the "www.iccwbo.org" portion is the host name where the resource can be found (which happens to be the ‹International Chamber of Commerce (ICC)›) while the rest of the URL is the resource name on that host.

Uniform Rules for Collections (URC) 🏛 The ‹International Chamber of Commerce (ICC)› rules that govern the use of most ‹collections› throughout the world. Since the URC is not law, it must be specified in order to apply. However, it is in such common use that reference to it is often pre-printed on the collection forms commonly used by banks.

Uniform Rules for Contract Guarantees The ‹International Chamber of Commerce (ICC)› has established a set of contractual rules that may be used for contract guarantees to achieve a fair balance among the legitimate interests of the three parties involved in contract guarantees the ‹beneficiary›, the ‹principal› and the ‹guarantor› These rules are not law, and apply only if the parties to the contract guarantee so choose. Such choice needs to be expressed by a reference in the text of the guarantee. To some extent, these rules have been replaced by the ‹Uniform Rules for Demand Guarantees›.

Uniform Rules for Demand Guarantees The ‹International Chamber of Commerce (ICC)› has established a set of contractual rules that may be used for ‹demand guarantees› and counter-guarantees. These rules are not law, and apply only if the parties to the demand or counter-guarantee so choose. Such choice needs to be expressed by a reference in the text of the guarantee.

unilateral An action taken by a single country on its own initiative, and not in any way dependent upon or conditional upon the actions of any other country or countries.

unimodal transport Transport accomplished by one mode.

United Nations (UN) An international organization formed in 1945 to promote international peace, security and cooperation. There are a number of UN organizations having a direct bearing on foreign trade listed in this book.

For more information, visit the UN website at www.un.org.

🛪 Insurance   LC Letters of credit   ⬇ Liner vessel shipping   ✍ Sales contracts   ⏃ Vessel chartering

U

United Nations Commission on International Trade Law (UNCITRAL) Established in 1966 to aid in harmonizing and unifying international trade law, the commission has focused on four principal issues sales of ⟨goods⟩, payments, commercial arbitration and legislation pertaining to shipping.

> **For more information, visit the UNCITRAL website at www.uncitral.org.**

United Nations Conference on Trade and Development (UNCTAD) Established in 1964, UNCTAD promotes international trade and seeks to develop trade between ⟨developing countries⟩ and countries with different economic systems. UNCTAD also examines problems of economic development within the context of principles and policies of international trade, and seeks to harmonize trade, development, and regional economic policies.

> **For more information, visit the UNCTAD website at www.unctad.org.**

United Nations Convention on Contracts for the International Sale of Goods (= CISG = Vienna Convention) ⊠ The CISG is a 1980 international treaty that came into force in 1988. As it has been signed by most leading trading nations, the CISG amounts to a virtual commercial code for international sale-of-goods transactions, but excludes contracts for services, securities, electricity and some other items. Although the CISG is the default body of contract law when both the seller and buyer are nationals of countries that have ratified it, parties may opt out by explicitly stating so in their sales contract. A separate but related agreement, the United Nations Convention on the Limitation Period on the International Sale of Goods, took place in 1974 and also came into force in 1988. It covers time limits for buyer or seller claims of breach, termination, or invalidity arising from contracts of international sales of goods.

> **1. Parties desiring to opt out of either convention should specify the body of law they wish to use instead. Care must be taken when doing so, as the conventions may be part of the body of law that the parties wish to use.**
> **2. An up-to-date list of participating countries is available from the ⟨United Nations Commission on International Trade Law⟩'s web-page www.uncitral.org/english/status/status-e.htm.**

United Nations Convention on the Carriage of Goods by Sea ⟨Hamburg Rules⟩

United Nations Convention on the Limitation Period in the International Sale of Goods ⟨United Nations Convention on Contracts for the International Sale of Goods⟩

United Nations Convention on the Recognition and Enforcement

⟨see entry in dictionary⟩ ✈ Air transport 🏛 Bank collections © e-commerce ▦ Incoterms

of Foreign Arbitral Awards This 1958 convention covers the status of arbitral awards of a country other than the country where recognition and enforcement is sought.

> An up-to-date list of participating countries is available from the <United Nations Commission on International Trade Law>'s web-page www.uncitral.org/english/status/status-e.htm.

United Nations Development Programme (UNDP) Established in 1965, the UNDP provides multilateral technical assistance including expert advice, training, and limited equipment to developing countries.

> For more information, visit the UNDP website at www.undp.org.

United Nations Economic and Social Commission for Asia and the Pacific (ESCAP) Originally established as the Economic Commission for Asia and the Far East in 1947, ESCAP is the main organization for United Nations activities in the Asian and Pacific region. Headquartered in Bangkok, Thailand, ESCAP comprises fifty-two member countries and nine associate members, which combine for approximately 60 per cent of the world's population. It concentrates on spreading the growth momentum from its more dynamic member countries to the rest of the region, with the goal of bringing some 830 million people into the world economic mainstream.

> For more information, visit the ESCAP website at www.unescap.org.

United Nations Economic and Social Commission for Western Asia (ESCWA) Originally established in 1973 as the Economic Commission for Western Asia, ESCWA promotes economic reconstruction and development among 14 member nations.

> For more information, visit the ESCWA website at www.escwa.org.lb.

United Nations Economic and Social Council (ECOSOC) The ECOSOC was established by the <UN> Charter under the authority of the General Assembly to promote:

- higher living standards, full employment and conditions of economic and social progress and development;
- solutions of international economic, social, health and related problems; and international cultural and educational cooperation;
- universal respect for, and observance of, human rights and fundamental freedoms for all without distinction as to race, sex, or religion.

U

The council consists of 54 members, elected for three-year terms by the General Assembly.

For more information, visit the ECOSOC website at www.un.org/documents/ecosoc.htm.

United Nations Economic Commission for Africa (ECA) Established in 1958 and headquartered in Addis Ababa, Ethiopia, the ECA is mandated to support the economic and social development of its 53 member States, foster regional integration, and promote international cooperation for Africa's development.

For more information, visit the ECA website at www.uneca.org.

United Nations Economic Commission for Europe (UNECE) The UNECE was established in 1947 to encourage greater economic cooperation among its member States. It focuses on economic analysis, environment and human settlements, statistics, sustainable energy, trade and enterprise development, timber and transport, with the participation of member-states and over 70 international professional and other non-governmental organizations.

For more information, visit the UNECE website at www.unece.org.

United Nations Economic Commission for Latin America and the Caribbean (ECLAC) First established as the Economic Commission for Latin America (ECLA) in 1948, ECLAC was expanded to include the countries of the Caribbean in 1984. It contributes to area economic development, coordinating actions directed toward this end, and reinforcing economic relationships both among the area countries and with other nations. The promotion of the region's social development was later added to its primary objectives. ECLAC's headquarters are in Santiago, Chile, and has sub-regional offices in Mexico City, Mexico, and Port of Spain, Trinidad & Tobago.

For more information, visit the ECLAC website at www.eclac.cl.

United Nations Environment Programme (UNEP) Established in 1972, the UNEP leads ‹United Nations› environmental activities and assists ‹developing countries› in implementing environmentally sound development policies. UNEP produced a worldwide environmental monitoring system to standardize international data.

For more information, visit the UNEP website at www.unep.org.

United Nations Industrial Development Organization (UNIDO) Established in 1967, UNIDO became a specialized ‹United Nations› agency in 1986. It promotes accelerated commercial development in ‹developing countries› and encourages industrial cooperation worldwide. As part of its activities, UNIDO identifies and brings promising entrepreneurs in the developing world to the attention of

---

‹see entry in dictionary›   ✈ Air transport   🏛 Bank collections   @ e-commerce   🔠 Incoterms

potential partners in industrialized countries through a network of Investment Promotion Services (ISP).

UV

For more information, visit the UNIDO website at www.unido.org.

United States Department of Commerce (USDC) The US Government agency in charge of many economics-related tasks including export promotion and most of export control compliance.

For more information, visit the Commerce Department's website at http//home.doc.gov.

unitization (cargo) The consolidation of a quantity of cargo into one large shipping unit for easier handling, as in palletizing or containerization.

Universal Postal Union (UPU) Founded in 1874, the UPU is a 189-member specialized ⟨United Nations⟩ organization regulating postal service throughout the world.

For more information, visit the UPU website at www.upu.int.

Universal Product Code (Uniform Product Code = UPC) ⟨bar coding⟩

unstuffing (= devanning = stripping) ⟨devanning⟩

UPC ⟨bar coding⟩

upstream subsidies Subsidies provided to a manufacturer's supplier of inputs for a product that will be exported.

UPU ⟨Universal Postal Union⟩

URC ⟨Uniform Rules for Collections⟩

URGETS ⟨electronic trade transaction⟩

URL ⟨uniform resource locator⟩

USAID ⟨Agency for International Development⟩

usance The time upon which an obligation's maturity is calculated.

usance drafts ⟨time drafts⟩

usance L/C 🔲 A ⟨letter of credit⟩ payable at a predetermined time after the presentation of conforming documents. These are also called time L/Cs or deferred payment L/Cs, and are the opposite of L/Cs payable at sight.

USDC ⟨United States Department of Commerce⟩

valuation ⟨customs valuation⟩

valuation clause The clause in a ⟨marine cargo insurance⟩ policy

---

🔲 Insurance   🔲 Letters of credit   🔲 Liner vessel shipping   🔲 Sales contracts   🔲 Vessel chartering

V

that contains the agreed basis for determining the value of covered ⟨goods⟩. This sets the amount due under any claim for loss or general average contribution.

value What something is worth. There are several values frequently used in foreign trade:
- Transaction value – the price paid or payable for a good or service.
- Value for customs – the value on which import duty should be assessed where there is no transaction value, as in the case of no-charge samples or replacement parts provided under warranty.
- Value for carriage – the amount of liability the ⟨carrier⟩ assumes, (normally used for shipments not otherwise insured and when ⟨goods⟩ are worth more than the carrier's minimum liability coverage).

value added tax (VAT = IVA = GST). A tax assessed on the increased value of ⟨goods⟩ as they pass from the raw material stage through the production and distribution processes to final consumption. The tax on processors or merchants is levied on the amount by which they increase the value of the items they purchase. Also ⟨indirect tax⟩ and ⟨sales tax⟩.

value dating The practice of remitting payment with a future effective date; i.e., the funds are not actually available until the stipulated "value" date. This provision is often found in ⟨letters of credit⟩, and some banks offer discounts to L/C applicants for including it. However, while the applicant may be indifferent, value dating adversely affects the beneficiary's cash flow.

variable levy A ⟨tariff⟩ subject to alterations as world market prices change. The alterations are designed to assure that the import cost after the payment of the duty will equal a predetermined "gate" price.

VAT ⟨value added tax⟩

vessel operating common carrier (VOCC) A ⟨carrier⟩ that operates its own vessels. See also ⟨non-vessel operating common carrier⟩.

vessel sharing An agreement among ⟨vessel operating carriers⟩ to share space on each other's vessels. See also ⟨slot chartering⟩.

Vienna Convention ⟨United Nations Convention on Contracts for the International Sale of Goods⟩

virtual storefront ⟨electronic store⟩

virtual tradeshow An online collection of electronic catalogues,

VW

usually hosted by an online exchange or industry-specific e-marketplace, where potential purchasers may view the merchandise of suppliers, similar to an actual trade fair. Virtual Tradeshows have evolved to include audio/video presentations created by the suppliers.

visaed documents ⟨consular documentation⟩

visible trade Imports, exports and re-exports of merchandise. Also ⟨invisible trade⟩.

VOCC ⟨vessel operating common carrier⟩

vostro account (= loro account). An account held by a bank with its foreign correspondent bank in the currency of the account-owning bank. This may be compared to a ⟨nostro account⟩, where the account is in the currency of the foreign bank.

voyage A trip made by a vessel to specified ports. Most voyages are numbered, and the reference number usually appears on the marine transport document along with the document number, vessel name and ⟨ports of lading and discharge⟩. For example Good Ship Lollypop, V 23, B/L 107, Baltimore/Genoa.

voyage charter ⊡ A ⟨charter⟩ agreement providing the ⟨charterer⟩ with the use of a vessel for a single voyage between ports or within a range of ports.

WA ⟨with particular average⟩

W3C ⟨World Wide Web Consortium⟩

WADB ⟨West African Development Bank⟩

WAEMU ⟨West African Economic and Monetary Union⟩

waiver A formal exemption of a right to claim.

WAND ⟨World Access Network of Directories⟩

WAP ⟨Wireless Application Protocol⟩

war risk ⊡ A peril that is normally excluded by a capture and seizure clause even in "⟨all risk⟩" (⟨London Institute of Underwriters clause A⟩) insurance cover. Coverage is usually available for an additional premium.

warehouse receipt A document issued by a warehouse for commodities received. There are two types:
* Negotiable – A warehouse receipt made out to the ORDER of a named party is a bearer instrument. As with ⟨order bills of lading⟩, ownership of the warehoused ⟨goods⟩ can be

W

transferred by endorsing and passing the document from party to party.

- Non-negotiable – A warehouse receipt lacking the word ORDER is similar to a ‹non-negotiable bill of lading›, as it permits delivery only to the named party.

warehouse-to-warehouse ⟨✈⟩ Marine insurance coverage from the point where a shipment originates to its destination point. There are often limitations, such as a limit on the time coverage is in force after the ‹goods› arrive on the buyer's side (but before final delivery takes place). Sellers and buyers should align warehouse-to-warehouse coverage with the terms of sale (‹Incoterms›) they use to ensure seamless coverage.

Warsaw Convention ⟨✈⟩ An international agreement defining the responsibilities and limiting the liability of air ‹carriers› involved in international transport.

Wassenaar Arrangement A multinational regime for the control of weapons proliferation, adopted by 33 countries in July 1996.

For further information, visit the US Government's Bureau of Export Administration website at www.bxa.doc.gov/Wassenaar.

waybill ⟨✈⟩ ⟨⚓⟩ ⟨📠⟩ A non-negotiable transport document issued for ocean carriage (‹sea waybill›), air transport (‹air waybill›) or rail transport (rail waybill).

WCN ‹World Chambers Network›

WCO ‹World Customs Organization›

weather permitting ⟨📠⟩ Agreement in a vessel ‹charterparty› that time during which weather prevents working will not count as ‹laytime›.

weather working day ⟨📠⟩ A vessel ‹chartering› term meaning a day or part of a day when weather does not prevent vessel loading or unloading.

web browser A software package used for locating, requesting and displaying web pages on the internet. The two most popular web browsers are Netscape Navigator and Microsoft Internet Explorer.

web page A single document forming a small part of a ‹website›, created using various programming languages such as ‹HTML›, ‹ASP›, Cold Fusion, Java Script and PERL. Web pages may consist of text, images, and links to programs, databases, and other pages and files on the web.

website A collection of related web pages and files, interlinked to each other, and usually associated with the same ‹URL›.

‹see entry in dictionary› ✈ Air transport ⟨⚓⟩ Bank collections ⟨©⟩ e-commerce ⟨⊞⟩ Incoterms

W

weight Heaviness, the amount that an object weighs. There are three kinds of weight most frequently used for cargo:

- **gross** the total scale weight of a shipment, including the ⟨goods⟩ themselves and their packing
- **net** the weight of only the goods in a shipment, exclusive of any packing materials
- **tare** the weight of a container and/or packing materials without the weight of the goods it contains.

The following weight-related terms are commonly used in foreign trade:

- long ton 1016.06 kilos. (2240 pounds)
- short ton 907.20 kilos (2000 pounds)
- metric ton 1000 kilos (2204.6 pounds)

The terms "dimensional weight" and "measurement ton" refer to the comparison of a shipment's weight to volume used to calculate freight costs.

The following units of weight apply to vessels:

- **deadweight tonnage** The total lifting capacity of a vessel, expressed in long tons. The cargo deadweight capacity is determined by deducting the weight of fuel, stores, crew and passengers. Deadweight tonnage is the difference between a vessel's loaded displacement and light displacement.
- **displacement ton** A unit approximately equal to the volume of a long ton weight of sea water (35 cubic feet), used in reckoning the displacement of vessels.
- **displacement tonnage** The weight in long tons of the volume of water displaced by the submerged portion of a floating vessel. It is measured in seawater at 35 cubic feet to the ton. Light displacement is the weight of the vessel with crew and ordinary stores aboard, but excluding cargo, fuel, and passengers. Loaded displacement is the weight of the vessel at her maximum draft with crew, stores, cargo, fuel and passengers.

West Africa Economic Community (CEAO) Established in 1974 and headquartered in Ouagadougou, Burkina Faso, the CEAO operates as a free-trade area for agricultural products and raw materials and as a preferential trading area for approved industrial products, with a regional cooperation tax replacing import duties and encouraging trade among members. A Community fund provides private lender Community participation in advancement of the Community's ⟨least- developed nations⟩ CEAO envisions eventual creation of a customs union and coordination of fiscal policies.

West African Clearing House (CCAO) Established in 1975 and

🛅 Insurance 🔲 Letters of credit 🛳 Liner vessel shipping 🗺 Sales contracts 🅿 Vessel chartering

W

headquartered in Freetown, Sierra Leone, the CCAO provides settlement-of-payments services among central banks and other monetary authorities in West Africa. Membership includes the Central Bank of West African States (representing Benin, Burkina Faso, Ivory Coast, Mali, Niger, Senegal and Togo), as well as The Gambia, Ghana, Guinea, Guinea-Bissau, Liberia, Mauritania, Nigeria and Sierra Leone.

West African Development Bank (WADB – BOAD) Established in 1973 and headquartered in Lome, Togo, the WABD promotes regional economic development and integration in West Africa. Members include Benin, Burkina Faso, Ivory Coast, Mali, Niger, Senegal and Togo.

> **For more information, visit the WADB website at www.boad.org.**

West African Economic and Monetary Union (WAEMU – UMOA) Founded in 1963, revised in 1973 and headquartered in Dakar, Senegal, the Union comprises seven French-speaking African countries (Benin, Burkina Faso, Ivory Coast, Mali, Niger, Senegal and Togo). They share a central bank, a common currency (CFA franc) that is fully convertible to the French franc, and a common regional development bank.

> **For more information, visit the WAEMU website at www.dakarcom.com/waemu.htm.**

wet charter ✈ A ⟨charter⟩ agreement whereby the owner supplies fuel and typically crew, ground support, etc. in addition to the aircraft itself. This is the opposite of ⟨dry charter⟩.

WFDFI ⟨World Federation of Development Financing Institutions⟩

wharf A port facility projecting from land to water or parallel to the shoreline where vessels berth for unloading and loading.

wharfage A charge assessed by a ⟨wharf⟩ owner for handling incoming or outgoing cargo. See also ⟨terminal handling charge⟩.

wharfinger ⟨checker⟩

WHO ⟨World Health Organization⟩

WIPO ⟨World Intellectual Property Organization⟩

Wireless Application Protocol (WAP) An emerging protocol whereby web-coded information is adapted for use in mobile access devices such as cellphones, pagers or PDAs. These devices will increasingly serve to connect small hand-held devices to the internet, and greatly increase ⟨e-commerce⟩.

with average ⟨with particular average⟩

---

with particular average (WPA) (= with average = WA) 🗹 A US marine insurance term meaning coverage that expands all the perils covered under ⟨free of particular average⟩ to include partial losses for heavy weather, and covers the following additional perils: lightning, seawater as a result of heavy weather and ⟨jettison⟩. ⟨London Institute of Underwriters "B" Clauses⟩ provide virtually the same coverage.

without reserve A term indicating that an agent or representative is empowered to make definitive decisions and adjustments without the approval of the ⟨principal⟩ represented. This is the opposite of ⟨advisory capacity⟩.

WITSA ⟨World Information Technology and Services Alliance⟩

World Access Network of Directories (WAND) A portal for directories that works like a classified telephone directory in sixteen languages.

For more information, visit the WAND website at www.wandinc.com.

World Bank Group The World Bank Group is a specialized ⟨United Nations⟩ agency dedicated to improving living standards in ⟨developing countries⟩ through facilitation and financing development and investment. There are five organizations within the group:

- ⟨International Bank for Reconstruction and Development (IBRD)⟩ provides low-cost developmental loans for reasonably creditworthy sovereign buyers by issuing bonds backed by its own triple-A rating.
- ⟨International Development Association (IDA)⟩ provides low cost developmental loans for less-developed nations from funds donated by nearly 40 countries.
- ⟨Multilateral Investment Guarantee Agency (MIGA)⟩ provides political risk coinsurance and reinsurance for investment in client-developing countries.
- ⟨International Finance Corporation (IFC)⟩ finances and advises for private-sector ventures and projects in developing countries.
- ⟨International Centre for Settlement of Investment Disputes (ICSID)⟩ provides facilities for conciliation and arbitration of disputes.

For information, visit the World Bank website at www.worldbank.com.

World Chambers Federation (WCF) An ⟨International Chamber of Commerce (ICC)⟩ specialized division for its chamber of commerce members worldwide. Through its extensive global support network,

---

🗹 Insurance   🆔 Letters of credit   🔱 Liner vessel shipping   🖾 Sales contracts   🅿 Vessel chartering

W

WCF runs the ⟨World Chambers Network (WCN)⟩ – a global internet platform fostering a comprehensive exchange of business information between chambers and their member companies throughout the world. WCF also manages the ⟨ATA Carnet System⟩.

World Chambers Network (WCN) Managed by ⟨ICC⟩'s ⟨World Chambers Federation (WCF)⟩, WCN provides a platform for the global chamber of commerce network, fostering a comprehensive exchange of business information and opportunities between chambers and their member companies throughout the world.

> For more information, visit the WCN website at
> www.worldchambers.com

World Customs Organization (WCO) Established in 1952 as the Customs Cooperation Council, the World Customs Organization is an independent, intergovernmental body whose mission is to enhance the effectiveness and efficiency of customs administrations. With over 90 member governments, it is the only intergovernmental worldwide organization competent in customs matters.

> For more information, visit the WCO's website at
> www.wcoomd.org.

World Economic Forum A non-governmental global institution capable of gathering world leaders in business, government and civil society to address the major challenges confronting humanity.

> For more information, visit the Forum's website at
> www.weforum.org.

World Federation of Development Financing Institutions (WFDFI) Established in 1979 and headquartered in Madrid, Spain, WFDFI promotes improved technical operations of, and coordination among, worldwide development banking activities.

World Health Organization (WHO) Headquartered in Geneva, Switzerland, the World Health Organization is a specialized agency of the ⟨United Nations⟩ that helps build better health systems throughout the world, especially in ⟨developing countries⟩. WHO establishes standards in many fields, such as food, biological and pharmaceutical ⟨goods⟩, diagnostic procedures and environmental health protection. It also helps name, classify and prevent diseases. The agency works with governments to provide safe drinking water, adequate sewage disposal and immunization against childhood diseases.

> For more information, visit the WHO website at www.who.int.

World Information Technology and Services Alliance (WITSA) A worldwide consortium of 41 information technology associations representing over 97 per cent of the world information technology market. WITSA liaises with a large number information technology resource organizations which can be found on its website.

WX

For more information, visit the WITSA website at www.witsa.org.

World Intellectual Property Organization (WIPO) A ⟨United Nations⟩ agency dedicated to helping ensure that the rights of creators and owners of intellectual property are protected worldwide, and that investors and authors are thus recognized and rewarded for their ingenuity. With a total membership of 175 nations, WIPO administers 21 international treaties (15 on industrial property and six on copyright).

For more information, visit WIPO's website at www.wipo.int.

World Trade Organization (WTO) Established by the Uruguay Round in 1995 as the successor to the ⟨General Agreement on Tariffs and Trade (GATT)⟩, the WTO is the only global international organization dealing with the rules of trade among nations. It is responsible for monitoring national trading policies, handling trade disputes and enforcing the GATT agreements. The mission of the WTO is also to reduce ⟨tariff⟩s and other international barriers and eliminate discriminatory treatment in international commerce. 135 countries belong to the WTO as of 2001.

For more information, visit the WTO's website at www.wto.org.

world wide web (WWW) @ A graphics standard that has become a virtual subset of the internet. Organizations, universities and companies maintain presences on the web with websites (home pages), which are much like animated telephone book advertisements. The information on the website may be highlighted (hypertext), in which case the viewer may click on the particular text to obtain access to another website, database or further information.

World Wide Web Consortium (W3C) @ The W3C was established in 1994 to lead the ⟨world wide web⟩ to its full potential by developing common protocols that promote its evolution and ensure its interoperability. It has over 500 member organizations from around the world.

For more information, visit the W3C website at www.w3c.org.

WPA ⟨with particular average⟩

WTO ⟨World Trade Organization⟩

WWW ⟨world wide web⟩

XML ⟨extensible markup language⟩

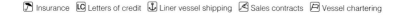
Insurance Letters of credit Liner vessel shipping Sales contracts Vessel chartering

YZ

York – Antwerp Rules (Y/A = YAR1994) 📄 A body of rules adopted by international convention to provide a uniform basis for adjusting general average claims. Some nations do not follow Y/A rules, and interested parties should refer to the ⟨carrier⟩ or the text of the marine transport document.

ZF ⟨franc zone⟩

A to Z

f international trade

Bank collections 🏛

e-commerce @

Incoterms ⊞

Insurance 🖘

Letters of credit LC

Liner vessel shipping ⚓

Sales contracts 🖎

Vessel chartering ⊟

Focus on Air Transport

Overview

In many respects, air transportation is less complicated than vessel transportation. Air cargo does not languish for days or weeks awaiting vessel loading from ports as is common with shipments by water. Transit time is short, seldom more than a few days – so shipments are less exposed to in-transit loss or damage. As the capacity of an aircraft is considerably smaller than that of a vessel, the volume of cargo per flight and the number of stops per trip are fewer. This, plus the faster transit time, results in fewer routing errors (and their faster detection), since they become obvious when goods fail to arrive on schedule.

The reduced stress and generally smaller size of air cargo, as opposed to shipments by vessel, often permit an adjustment in export packing. Lighter, smaller packaging is critical to lower airfreight costs. However, shippers must consider the nature of the commodity, conditions at destination, plus the fact that in-flight altitude and temperature fluctuations may cause moisture problems resulting from condensation.

While always a must for urgently needed cargoes, air transport has also become a cost-effective alternative to minimum-bill-of-lading (very small) vessel shipments, particularly for small and/or high value cargoes. Unlike seaports, airports can be built almost anywhere traffic demands, a fact that often reduces the cost of pre-carriage and on-carriage.

While comparatively less complicated than vessel transportation, airfreight has some peculiarities. There are far more hazardous materials restrictions with air shipments than with vessels, and generally lower limits on the allowable quantity of each type of hazard per shipment. Finally, the transport document for air shipments (called an air waybill) cannot be made in negotiable form, a situation that may lead to problems with cash against documents payment terms.

⟨see entry in dictionary⟩ ✈ Air transport 🏛 Bank collections © e-commerce 🔠 Incoterms

Practice

Types of carriers

The air transport industry is in a constant state of flux. Buyouts, mergers and alliances frequently occur, sometimes changing the nature of individual carriers.

As the name implies, all-cargo carriers handle cargo only. By contrast, combination carriers handle both cargo and passengers. Passengers normally take precedence in combination carrier operations. Integrated carriers like UPS, FcdEx, Airborne and BAX combine the use of their aircraft with supplemental service from the airlines, as required. Airfreight forwarders (consolidators) are indirect carriers that do not own their own aircraft, but combine smaller shipments to fill airfreight containers (groupage) for shipment by the airlines (undercarriers). They receive attractive volume "freight of all kinds" (FAK) rates from the undercarriers, and publish their own freight tariffs.

Some airlines and all "integrated" carriers provide forwarding services. All carriers may operate in one mode or another in different countries, as none has its own aircraft in service everywhere in the world. Integrated carriers tend to have their own ground transportation in many places, while other airlines have made arrangements with large trucking companies for their services. Airfreight forwarders usually have extensive country-specific information and documentation expertise.

Aircraft chartering is also available when large cargo units or remote locations require it.

Charter agreements may be made for one flight or may be longer term – ranging from equipment-only to all-inclusive, complete with crew, ground support, fuel, etc. (called wet charters).

Types of service

Integrated carriers typically offer door-to-door service, undertaking transportation responsibility from the point where the shipment originates to the point where final delivery takes place. They can also provide door-to-airport transportation from the point where the shipment originates to a designated airport on the buyer's side. Combination and all-cargo carriers usually provide airport-to-airport transportation from the departure airport on the seller's side to the arrival airport on the buyer's side, and the same is true of chartering. Airfreight forwarders, of course, use the other carriers as undercarriers.

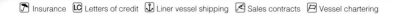

Insurance   Letters of credit   Liner vessel shipping   Sales contracts   Vessel chartering

Ground-air-ground

Because of the sophisticated hub and spoke system used by air carriers in countries with highly developed transportation infrastructures, many shipments made by airfreight actually have a ground-freight component. For instance, an air shipment made from a smaller city with a regional airport would likely go overnight by truck, rather than by air, to a city with an international gateway airport. The increase in transit time is minimal, because even if the shipment were to go to the gateway airport by air, it would have to be transferred from the domestic flight to the international flight. Both the contract of carriage and the resulting transport document are multimodal, and the air carrier takes responsibility for the entire journey.

Airfreight cost calculation

Air carriers maintain price lists called tariffs. When the tariff is available to the general public, the carrier is a common carrier. If not, it is a contract carrier, and the freight rates are negotiable. Freight rates are shown in the tariff by commodity or by class of commodities, and they indicate the price per shipping unit. The unit is normally expressed in kilos, but almost all tariffs provide for a comparison between weight and dimensions, and the freight rate is based on the greater of the two. The following two formulas are in general use for international airfreight:

1. Cubic inches /138 (dimensional pounds) versus gross scale weight in pounds
2. Cubic centimetres /5000 (dimensional kilos) versus the gross scale weight in kilos.

The cube, whether in metric or inches, is determined by multiplying the length, width and height dimensions.

One side or the other (volume versus weight) will produce a larger number, which is then multiplied by the freight rate from the tariff. Further, airfreight is always paid on a whole-unit basis, and fractions are always rounded up to the next whole unit.

Example: a shipment whose cube is 1660 cubic inches and gross weight is 8 pounds.
a. 1660/138 = 12.03 "dimensional pounds" which is greater than the 8 pound scale weight
b. 12.03 = 5.45 dimensional kilos
c. round up to 6 and multiply by the applicable freight rate per kilo.

Most air carriage tariffs provide a minimum charge, which applies if the freight as calculated is lower.

‹see entry in dictionary› ✈ Air transport 🏛 Bank collections @ e-commerce 🔲 Incoterms

Some integrated carriers do not issue commodity-based tariffs. Instead, they charge for volume or weight as above, using rates that are based solely on which area zones transportation begins and ends at.

Surcharges are intended to assist carriers in situations beyond their control. From time to time, air carriers impose them for such items as jet fuel, but there are nowhere near as many as in marine transport. Air carriers performing additional services such as origin pickup, destination delivery, insurance or even customs clearance will bill appropriate accessorial charges.

Freight rebating is the refunding of a portion of previously paid transportation, usually based on a certain quantity of shipments or revenue to the carrier over time. Freight rebating is legal in some countries; it is forbidden in others. Such prohibitions may have the unintended consequence of making legitimate claims against carriers difficult, since the claims must be fully documented to prove that they are not freight rebates in disguise.

Terms of sale

Airfreight shipments work best with Incoterms designed for use with all modes of transportation. These omnimodal sales terms include Ex Works (EXW), Free Carrier (FCA), Carriage Paid To (CPT), Carriage and Insurance Paid (CIP), Delivered Duty Unpaid (DDU) and Delivered Duty Paid (DDP).

Carrier liability

The Warsaw Convention covers carrier liability for air shipments. Currently, the liability limit is 17 Special Drawing Rights per kilo, which converts to approximately USD 20.00 per kilo. Many air carriers provide insurance as an additional service for an additional charge. As with all insurance, it is important to determine exactly where coverage begins and ends, e.g. warehouse-to-warehouse or airport-to-airport. This is particularly important with door-to-door or door-to-airport carriage contracts.

Documentation

Airfreight forwarders, integrated air carriers and airlines with forwarding divisions should be given handling instructions by means of a shipper's letter of instructions (SLI). Sometimes, shippers will complete the actual air waybill (airfreight forwarders always do). Air waybills issued by airlines are called master air waybills; those issued by airfreight forwarders are called house air waybills. Integrated carriers use their own air waybill versions. In all cases, the document

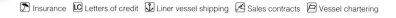

is consigned directly to a named party (consignee) and will identify the shipper (consignor), flight number or numbers (or integrator bar codes), shipment date, commodity, freight and accessorial charges as well as whether the freight is payable by shipper (freight prepaid) or by consignee (freight collect).

Like ocean transport documents, air waybills without adverse notations of damage or shortage are considered "clean," indicating that the carrier received the cargo in "apparent good order and condition." Air waybills bearing adverse notations are variously called "claused," "unclean" or "foul".

Because of the danger in transporting hazardous materials ("hazmat") by air, the industry attention and focus is extremely high. Movement and restrictions are subject to the UN International Civil Aviation Organization (ICAO) as stated in its publication *Technical Instructions for the Safe Transport of Dangerous Goods by Air.* They can be found in the current edition of the International Air Transportation Association's (IATA) *Dangerous Goods Regulations.* Some jurisdictions have more restrictive regulations and have adopted these regulations in whole or in part. When in doubt, it is good practice to check with a local competent authority.

Carriers must issue arrival notices in order that consignees will be aware of the position of the cargo and can quickly arrange for import clearance and on-carriage. With today's speed of communications, the arrival notices are frequently prepared upon "wheels up," that is, while the shipment is airborne. However, it is prudent for shippers or their forwarding agents to independently alert the consignees by fax or e-mail. Frequently, other documents are required for clearance, and the shipper or its agent must also supply them. Since air cargo arrives quickly, any delays in clearance may subject the consignee to demurrage, detention and/or storage costs.

Payment terms

As noted above in *Documentation,* air shipments cannot be consigned "to order," and air waybills therefore cannot be executed in negotiable form. A named party must appear in the "consignee" field. Non-negotiable transport documents can present a problem for airfreight shipments made on payment terms that rely on the exchange of documents for payment, such as sight draft, documents against payment or cash against documents. The question becomes how to keep the buyer from obtaining the shipped goods before authorizing payment at the bank at which the documents reside.

‹see entry in dictionary› ✈ Air transport 🏛 Bank collections @ e-commerce ▦ Incoterms

As with all payment term situations, nothing replaces confidence in the buyer's ability and willingness to honour its obligations. When this is present, the following procedure should provide the seller with adequate protection if the buyer's bank is willing to help.

1. Request the buyer to provide the name and physical address, fax and telephone number of its bank as well as the name of the account officer.
2. Armed with this information, the seller should have his or her BANK request permission from the buyer's bank to consign the shipment to the latter's care. Indicate the approximate amount and payment terms, and promise that the collection documents will be sent to the buyer's bank immediately after shipment.
3. If, and only if, the buyer's bank replies to the seller's bank that it agrees, the shipment can proceed. It should be consigned only to the buyer's bank, and the buyer's name should not appear anywhere on the air waybill unless local regulations indicate that it must (and if they do, never in the consignee field).
4. The air waybill should instruct the carrier to await instructions from the bank, and not attempt delivery until they are received.
5. The air waybill and collection documents should follow as soon as possible by the fastest means. Keep in mind that airfreight shipments usually arrive at destination within two days.

Incidentally, the reason communications should flow through banks is that they can authenticate messages between each other.

The following terms used in air transportation are defined in Key definitions AZ:

aerotropolis	consignor
air waybill	consolidation (= groupage)
aircraft agreement	container
airport-to-airport	data freight receipt (= data freight
apparent damage	release)
apparent good order and condition	dimensional weight
arrival notice (AN)	door-to-airport
carriage contract	door-to-door
carrier	estimated time of arrival (ETA)
charter	estimated time of departure (ETD)
charterer	flag carrier
clean transport document	forwarder
common carrier	forwarder's certificate of receipt
consignee	foul transport document
consignment	freight collect

Insurance   Letters of credit   Liner vessel shipping   Sales contracts   Vessel chartering

freight of all kinds (FAK)
freight prepaid
freight rebate
frustrated cargo
general cargo rate
gross weight
hazardous materials
house air waybill (HAB=HAWB)
hub and spoke
integrated carrier
International Air Transport
    Association (IATA)
International Civil Aviation
    Organization (ICAO)
main carriage
manifest (cargo)
master air waybill
Montreal Convention
multimodal transport

multimodal transport document
multimodal transport operator (MTO)
net weight
notify party
omnimodal
on-carriage
pre-carriage
shipment
shipment date
shipper
shipper's letter of instructions (SLI)
tariff (Freight)
through rate
through transport
transportation
transshipment
ultimate consignee
undercarrier
Warsaw Convention

Focus on Bank Collections

international trade

Air transport ✈

e-commerce @

Incoterms ⊞

Insurance ⟋

Letters of credit LC

Liner vessel shipping ⚓

Sales contracts ✍

Vessel chartering ⛴

Focus on Bank Collections

Overview

The International Chamber of Commerce (ICC) provides in its Uniform Rules for Collections a compilation of definitions and rules that banks may use in the handling of collections. Since these are in widespread use throughout the world, we turn to the current version (URC522 – ICC Publication No. 522) for our basic vocabulary. The article and sub-article numbers correspond to the full text, and are included here for further reference only.

Basic Definitions

Definition of a Collection (Article 2)

For the purpose of these articles:

a. COLLECTION means the handling by banks of documents (as defined below) in accordance with instructions received, in order to:
  i.   obtain payment and/or acceptance, or
  ii. deliver documents against payment and/or against acceptance, or
  iii. deliver documents on other terms and conditions

b. DOCUMENTS means financial documents and/or commercial documents:
  i.   "Financial documents" means bills of exchange, promissory notes, cheques or other similar instruments used for obtaining the payment of money
  ii. "Commercial documents" means invoices, transport documents, documents of title or other similar documents, or any other document whatsoever, not being financial documents.

c. CLEAN COLLECTION means collection of financial documents not accompanied by commercial documents.

d. DOCUMENTARY COLLECTION means collection of:
  i.   Financial documents accompanied by commercial documents
  ii. Commercial documents not accompanied by financial documents.

Parties to a collection (Article 3)

a. For the purposes of these Articles, the parties thereto are:

   i. the "principal" who is the party entrusting the handling of a collection to a bank;

   ii. the "remitting bank", which is the bank to which the principal has entrusted the handling of a collection;

   iii. the "collecting bank", which is any bank, other than the remitting bank, involved in processing the collection;

   iv. the "presenting bank", which is the collecting bank making presentation to the drawee.

b. The drawee is the one to whom presentation is to be made in accordance with the collection instruction.

Practice

Let's now apply these terms to trade practice. "Principals" are sellers, or others to whom payments for international sales are due. They can use the banking system to exchange papers for money or promises to pay at a pre-agreed future time through a process known as collection. It is important to note that although the banks involved in the collection process will follow established procedures such as URC522 and instructions provided by the principal, they do not examine the documents and do not guarantee eventual payment unless they specifically declare that they do so.

When drafts are used with collections, the party that draws them is usually called the drawer. Therefore, the terms "principal" and "drawer" are usually synonymous.

In all cases, the principal must provide the remitting bank (usually its bank of account) with clear instructions on how the collection is to be handled. These are normally given by means of a collection instruction letter or schedule, a basic format in general use by banks throughout the world. While details may vary from bank to bank, the following basic information should always be indicated:

1 Who is to pay? (In the case of drafts, this party is called the drawee.)

2 When is payment due? (In the case of drafts, this is called tenor.)

3 Where is the collection to be sent? (This will be the collecting bank, which in practice is usually also the presenting bank, and is often the drawee's bank of account.)

4 How is the principal to be informed of the status of the collection? (This could be electronic means or mail.)

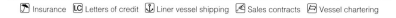

5   Other than informing the principal, what action should be taken in case the collection is not honoured as anticipated? (Should the draft be protested? Is there a guarantor that must be informed?)

6   Is there anyone representing the principal in the drawee's country that the presenting bank should contact for assistance? (Such party is called a "case of need.") If so, what is the scope of this party's authority?

7   Who is responsible for paying the collection fees of the remitting bank, the presenting bank or any other collecting banks involved in the collection process? What action should be taken if the responsible party declines these bank charges?

8   What action should be taken if the currency in which the collection is payable is not available at the time of payment? Should the presenting bank accept a local currency deposit?

9   How should the proceeds be remitted to the principal?

10 Any special instructions?

Most collection instructions provide for this by means of a series of boxes, which are either checked or left blank to indicate preference.

Initiation

Collections are initiated in one of two ways. The instructions and accompanying documents (if any) may be physically brought to the remitting bank by the principal, for transmission to the presenting bank or another designated collecting bank. A second, and more commonly used, way is for the principal to complete a pre-numbered direct collection form and send it along with the documents directly to the presenting bank, retaining a copy for follow-up purposes. Another copy is sent to the remitting bank, which then sets up a collection file. Thereafter, unless special instructions are given to the contrary, all correspondence will flow back and forth between the remitting bank and the presenting bank, just as though the remitting bank physically sent the collection.

Drafts

Drafts, also called bills of exchange, are financial instruments indicating debt of one party (the drawee) to another (the drawer). Drafts may be drawn at "sight" for immediate payment, at X time "date" for payment X time from the date shown on the face of the draft itself, or at X "time-sight" for payment X time from the date the draft is accepted. See *Sight versus time* below.

Drafts are normally handled in two ways: either as required by letters of credit (covered in *Focus on Letters of Credit*) or for presentation with collections.

Drafts accepted by parties other than banks are called trade acceptances. Drafts accepted by banks are called bankers' acceptances, and enjoy preferred status in many financial markets.

Documents

Documents may be defined as pieces of paper (or electronic message units) that prove that events have occurred. These events should correspond with the seller's obligation under the governing contract of sale. Typical documents include:

- a commercial invoice
- a transport document
- a certificate of origin
- an insurance certificate
- any required consular documentation
- any required pre-shipment inspection documentation (often called a clean report of findings)
- any additional documentation to which the seller and buyer have agreed.

One or more drafts are often drawn on the drawee to accompany the collection.

In addition to these commonly used documents, remitting banks that discount drafts for their exporting customers may require an interest in the shipped goods as well as the collections they receive as collateral. A hypothecation letter provides possession rights to the goods themselves. When attached to the covering draft (or drafts), it authorizes the remitting bank's overseas correspondent to sell the goods if the draft is not honoured. In this case, it can be important to the remitting bank to route such collections through its correspondents so that they become the collecting and/or presenting banks.

Documentary collections

These are collections accompanied by original documents. Often, some or all of the accompanying documentation is required for claiming the shipped goods from the carrier or for customs clearance. For instance, some types of transport documents can be structured to restrict possession rights and/or ownership. Instructions that documents not be released to the drawee until certain conditions are met force the drawee to deal with the collecting bank, in order to

obtain the goods. When the instructions are that the drawee must pay, such as cash against documents or sight draft documents against payment (D/P), the net result is a Cash-On-Delivery (C.O.D.) type situation. This is actually safer than C.O.D., since banks are more experienced at collecting and remitting payments than are carriers. (This fact has not gone unnoticed by the large integrated carriers, and some are developing enhanced C.O.D. services for international shipments.)

Certain transport documents ending with the term "waybill" cannot be structured to convey title. This presents a problem with documentary collections, particularly with air shipments, because the transport document is an air waybill. Since the carrier may release the goods without requiring surrender of the waybill document, the drawee could conceivably get the goods without dealing with a bank. One solution is that the principal request that the remitting bank contact the collecting bank and ask permission to consign the shipment to its care. If permission is granted, one should ship the goods and send the instructions to the collecting bank by the fastest means. It is imperative that such arrangements be made prior to shipment, because banks have no obligation toward goods consigned to their care unless they have first agreed to take on the role of "intermediate consignee." It is also important that these arrangements be done between the remitting bank and the collecting bank, rather than directly between the principal and the collecting bank, since only banks have means of verifying that communications are really sent from other banks.

Clean collections

These are collections that are not accompanied by documents that restrict possession or ownership to the shipped goods. They provide only limited security for principals, since drawees can usually obtain the goods without first dealing with the bank. For this reason, their use is largely restricted to the following situations:

1 Buyer preference, where the seller would be willing to extend open account terms, but the buyer prefers to pay by means of drafts presented at its bank. (This could be a buyer convenience in using its bank as its accounts payable department, or because the bank lends against the goods and maintains a security interest in them.)
2 Exchange control regulations, where the seller would be willing to extend open account terms, but the buyer's country requires that foreign currency payments be justified by certain documents.
3 Short transit time, when goods will arrive long before documents could possibly reach the collecting bank.

⟨see entry in dictionary⟩   ✈ Air transport   🏛 Bank collections   @ e-commerce   ⊞ Incoterms

Clean collections are also used to process cheques drawn on and payable at foreign banks located beyond the clearing range of the payee's country's banking system.

Sight versus time

Collections may provide for either immediate payment or payment at a future time.

In banking terminology, the word "sight" means right away, theoretically as soon as it is seen. Collections requiring immediate payment may either include a draft (sight draft/documents against payment, abbreviated D/P) or not (cash against documents abbreviated CAD). Either requires the drawee to pay prior to receiving the accompanying documents. Typically, such collections are documentary, and include a document that restricts possession or ownership, thereby forcing the drawee to deal with the bank in order to obtain the goods. In practice, sight drafts are considered promptly paid if settlement occurs within a few days of receipt by the presenting bank. Some drawees defer payment until the goods have arrived.

The opposite of sight collections are called "documents against acceptance (D/A) ", and require the drawee to accept a draft or drafts drawn for future maturity at the presenting bank, prior to receiving the accompanying documents. As with sight collections, these are often documentary, and include a document that restricts possession or ownership, thereby forcing the drawee to accept the draft in order to obtain the goods. The presenting bank then informs the acceptance and maturity date(s) to the drawer through the remitting bank, and presents the draft(s) for payment when due.

There are two types of drafts calling for payment at a future time: date and time-sight. The net difference is a question of which party finances the goods during transit.

1 Date drafts mature for payment on the stated number of days from the date on the face of the draft itself, regardless of when the draft was accepted. (However, even though the clock is ticking, there is no obligation of the drawee to pay until after he or she has accepted the draft.) Since drafts normally bear the date of the main carriage transportation document, date drafts extend time from date of shipment.

2 Time-sight drafts mature for payment on the stated number of days from the date of acceptance, regardless of the date on the face of the draft. Since drawees often postpone acceptance until they need the documents to collect the goods, acceptance dates normally coincide with arrival dates. For this reason, the time extended by

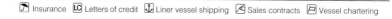

time-sight drafts normally begins shortly after the goods arrive on the drawee's side.

The difference between date and time-sight can be significant when transport times are long. Principals who are eager to know the maturity dates of obligations due them as soon as possible may be willing to grant a greater number of days in return for using date rather than time-sight drafts.

It is possible that a collection may call for several partial payments. Called split drafts, such collections may include a draft payable for a portion at sight and one or more time drafts calling for payment at a future time or times. Normally, split-draft collections are documentary, so the drawee would pay the sight draft and accept the time draft or drafts in order to obtain the documents from the presenting bank.

Avals

An aval is a guarantee provided by a third party that it will honour an obligation in case the drawee fails to do so. Drafts are normally used for aval situations, and the party guaranteeing the drawee's performance normally accepts the draft or drafts along with the drawee.

Correspondence

Depending on the instructions they receive, presenting banks will inform the status of unpaid collections to remitting banks by mail or electronic means. Typical notices include:

- acknowledgements of receipt of collection
- advice of acceptance with maturity date or non-acceptance with reasons for time drafts
- either advice of payment or of non-payment with reasons.

Principals may follow up on the status of outstanding drafts through remitting banks. Many remitting banks have their own systems for monitoring the status of pending collections, and send "tracer" follow-up notices to collecting banks as appropriate.

Protest

Protesting a draft means formalizing its dishonour. Laws differ from country to country, but in general the procedure works as follows:

1 The principal has instructed that dishonoured drafts be protested.
2 A draft matures for payment and is not paid.
3 Whatever applicable grace period in the drawee's country expires.

4 The banker, often accompanied by a public notary, formally presents the draft for payment. Notice of the dishonour is recorded by the notary.

The results of a protested draft vary from country to country, but the net result is often akin to the recording of a judgment entry. Knowledge of the default can become widespread in the local market, adversely affecting the drawee's local credit. Certainly, the drawee's bank is aware of the situation, as it participated in the protest procedure. Further, in some countries, protested drafts enjoy preferred status over non-protested drafts in case of bankruptcy liquidation.

Although protest procedures exist for both non-acceptance and non-payment, they are usually reserved for non-payment of time drafts. Since acceptance usually happens in exchange for documents, drawees that have not accepted time drafts (or have not paid sight drafts) normally have not received the goods. While not taking the goods may breach the sales contract, it becomes questionable whether the drawee actually owes the full value of goods it has not taken.

Some countries require that drafts covered by avals be protested if defaulted at maturity in order to protect the guarantee. This assures that the guarantor receives due notice that its contingent liability may be called.

Many countries employing protest procedures require that instructions to protest a draft be received by the presenting bank prior to the draft's maturity. In other words, defaulted drafts cannot be retroactively protested.

Since protest is a powerful tool, it should be used judiciously to avoid harming the very party that is responsible for payment. It works best with split-draft collections, where drawers that encounter default in earlier maturing drafts can quickly issue protest instructions for those that have not yet matured.

Risk/risk mitigation

In a collection transaction, both the buyer and seller are willing to take certain risks. These risks can be mitigated to varying degrees.

In a sight draft transaction, the seller's risk is that the buyer may refuse payment. In that case the seller may:

1 Re-negotiate the payment with the buyer.
2 Find another buyer, if possible in the same area to save shipping costs.

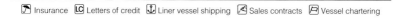

3 Return the goods, in which case they enjoyed a round trip at the seller's expense.

4 Abandon the goods, if all other options fail and the cost of returning the shipment is prohibitive.

In a sight draft transaction, the buyer's risk is that he or she is authorizing payment without seeing the goods, since the enabling documents will not be released until payment is made. This risk may be mitigated by having the goods inspected. This must happen at the port of exportation, since the goods cannot be inspected at the port of importation until the buyer gets the documents. The buyer will usually bear the expense of the inspection, and the inspection document would accompany the documents sent to the presenting bank.

In a time draft transaction, the seller's risk is that the buyer may not accept the draft. In that case the buyer does not obtain the documents, and therefore the seller has the same four options available as a denied sight draft (see above). If the buyer accepts the draft, the bank releases the documents based on a promise to pay at maturity. If the buyer then defaults, the seller has few options available since the buyer has already received the goods. The seller can protest non-payment of the draft (see "protest" above) or initiate litigation proceedings, both of which can be expensive with uncertain results. The seller's risk on a time draft transaction is essentially the same as with open account, except for two mitigating factors:

1 The accepted draft offers tangible evidence of a promise to pay, i.e., proof of debt.

2 Most solvent buyers are reluctant to demonstrate bad faith at their own bank as they probably borrow from the very same institution.

In a time draft transaction, the buyer's risk is that he or she is offering a commitment to pay by accepting the draft before seeing the goods, just like the buyer with sight draft terms. As with sight draft, this risk may be mitigated by having the goods inspected at the port of exportation.

The following terms used in bank collections are defined in Key definitions :

acceptance

acceptance date

acknowledgement

advice of payment/non-payment

at sight

at X days date or at X days sight

aval

case of need

cash against documents (cad)

clean collection

collecting bank

collection

collection letter

documentary collection

documents

documents against acceptance (d/a)

documents against payment (d/p)

draft

drawee

drawer

letter of hypothecation

maturity date

presenting bank

remitting bank

tenor

time drafts

Uniform Rules for Collections (URC)

usance

usance draft

A to Z
international trade

Air transport ✈

Bank collections 🏛

Incoterms ⊞

Insurance 🏹

Letters of credit LC

Liner vessel shipping ⚓

Sales contracts ✍

Vessel chartering ⬭

Focus on e-Commerce

Overview

Of the nine appendices in this book, our e-commerce coverage is truly a work in process. Most of the terms did not exist ten years ago, and new terms are being added daily. The same is true of software, including the programs with which this book was written and published.

Worldwide e-mail has made communication faster and more efficient than ever, at incredibly low cost. This provides a tremendous boon to legitimate business, personal communications and the exchange of ideas in general. However, it becomes a mixed blessing when one considers the quantity of unsolicited "SPAM" mail and pornography that we encounter daily. Add the scams that are now beyond number, and the constant threat of virus attack, and you find that for all its benefits today's computer linkages require caution and common sense.

Transportation carriers of all kinds now routinely track shipments with bar coding. Bolero and similar verification systems are closing in on their primary objective – secure electronic replacement of paper documentation, which will avoid those annoying delays while documents catch up to cargo. The enabling encryption has advanced by leaps and bounds, increasing the relative safety of financial transactions over the internet. (Remember, common sense and caution!) Even the venerable letter of credit is getting an e-commerce makeover with e-UCP. The downside is that criminals and terrorists can employ the same encryption techniques to everyone's disadvantage.

The enormous potential of e-commerce is quickly eliminating the distinctions between domestic and foreign trade. In fact, for software products delivered over the internet, this distinction has practically evaporated, and has become very porous for internet-ordered small packages. This, too, comes as a mixed blessing. It is great for consumers with access to credit cards that pay in hard currency. It also

⟨see entry in dictionary⟩   ✈ Air transport   🏛 Bank collections   @ e-commerce   ⊞ Incoterms

assists governments in clearing shipments, since pertinent information can be instantly provided by seller, buyer, carrier or customs broker. By the same token, internet-delivered software may provide problems for governments concerning duty, sales tax and compliance with export and/or import control regulations.

Perhaps the greatest beneficiaries are developing countries, as they can jump-start trade with sophisticated digital technology. Surely, the most obvious leaps in communication technology are found in places where it was most primitive until the advent of cell phones and e-mail. This means both new sources of supply and new markets, to the mutual advantage of buyers and sellers alike. Also, e-commerce serves to "level the playing field" for small- and mid-sized companies, allowing them resources and cost-saving global trade tools previously available only to huge multi-national firms while freeing them from layers of intermediaries.

Basic definition: e-commerce

Electronic commerce ("e-commerce") includes and describes commercial activities that use some form of electronic communication, chiefly the world wide web on the internet. For international purchasers and suppliers, conducting the various elements of trade over the internet offers low acquisition costs for orders and customers, incredibly wide marketing reach and exposure, increased processing efficiency and low communications expenses.

In addition to the revolutionary information and research capabilities offered by the internet, e-commerce includes a wide range of activities, including advertising, marketing, buyer/seller matching, party verification, logistics tracking and support services, product/service quotations as well as purchase and payment/collection.

International e-commerce is rapidly evolving toward "end-to-end" solutions that seek to encompass all the various trade activities in a single on-line experience. These solutions are being created as application service provider, or "ASP," models, with users requiring little more than an internet connection and a web browser.

e-commerce venues

The conduct of electronic commerce over the internet may be described in three distinct categories, each illustrating a unique venue for business. As these venues evolve, international groups are striving

⚓ Insurance   LC Letters of credit   ⚓ Liner vessel shipping   ⚓ Sales contracts   ⚓ Vessel chartering

to keep up with the policies, protocols and standards required to maintain order in the electronic marketplace.

business to business (B2B) These internet presences generally feature places where suppliers and purchasers may:

- discover potential business partners by searching through on-line databases of products, catalogues and companies;
- place and negotiate electronic offers to buy or sell;
- communicate with each other via e-mail, find links to company websites, use chat rooms and bulletin boards; and, ultimately,
- place orders and conduct transactions.

These include e-marketplaces, on-line exchanges, company portals and excess-inventory auction sites. Many of these sites are industry-specific, and include industry news and information. Most are evolving to include on-line trade services with third-party entities to provide on-line logistics, insurance, translation, payment/collection and other trade services.

business to consumer (B2C) These websites on the internet include consumer-oriented portals, hosted by retailers or auction sites, selling merchandise and services to non-business entities. Examples are Amazon.com and Ebay.com. These generally include e-stores, complete with product images and descriptions, shopping cart technology and credit card payment methods.

business to government (B2G) This category of e-commerce includes both the procurement of goods and services by government purchasing agencies, as well as the processing of reporting requirements by businesses to regulatory agencies. Governments have discovered that the efficiencies of dealing with businesses electronically save both human and financial resources, and result in more effective, faster service.

international organizations & protocols Government, industry and commercial organizations have come together to create and review policies and standards for international e-commerce. These bodies consider internet technology standards, electronic information security and privacy, protocols for electronic-funds transfers and international legal issues. Many of the organizations listed at the end of this appendix are in the forefront of such arrangements.

e-commerce activities

Global traders may engage in a variety of activities defined as e-commerce. At the most basic level, internet communication methods have revolutionized trade, compressing both distance and time and

---

reducing costs tremendously. Examples are e-mail and e-mail attachments, chat rooms, instant messaging, bulletin boards and electronic documents. One powerful example for global traders is the sending of electronic brochures and sales proposals in Adobe Acrobat PDF file format via e-mail attachments. The cost savings as opposed to printing and courier services are incredible, while delivery is nearly instantaneous.

On-line advertising and marketing have afforded exporters and importers incredibly wide exposure and reach, through company websites, banner advertising, electronic trade leads, directory listings and on-line catalogues. Buyer/seller matching capabilities found on e-marketplaces and exchanges allow for the worldwide discovery of potential trade partners by means of on-line database searches for products and companies.

Virtual trade shows allow potential buyers to visit a seller's electronic "booth" anywhere on earth, at any time. The potential cost savings as opposed to travel, lodging and time away from the office are tremendous. Add closed-circuit teleconferencing and you have face-to-face discussions for relationship building.

Finally, service providers are offering such on-line services as business credit reports, product inspection reports, party verification, carrier tracking, freight quotation and arrangement, payment and collection, translation, insurance quotations and government regulatory reporting. They have long provided the means of electronically processing paper, and have largely graduated to an all-electronic environment. This allows them to compete for and service clients outside their geographic locations, while reducing their processing and communications costs.

The synthesis of these e-commerce activities into electronic transactions will enable all participants – seller, buyer, service providers and government agencies – to share transactional information in a single seamless process.

Privacy and security issues

While e-commerce is proving to be immensely empowering and efficient for global traders, it also opens the door to fraud and information abuse. Both technological schemes and regulatory policies are evolving to ensure the security of electronic data, especially regarding on-line payments and the protection of private electronic information. Verification of trading partners is also becoming very important, as the internet becomes more pervasive and anonymous.

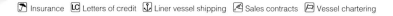
Insurance   LC Letters of credit   Liner vessel shipping   Sales contracts   Vessel chartering

As technology creates better, more secure methods of encrypting electronic data and transactions, various international bodies are meeting to create international protocols, which will serve to regulate and control fraud and abuse of information over the internet.

Basic e-commerce & internet terminology

E-commerce, like any new industry or process, has created its own language, rife with initials and abbreviations, and heavily based in the technology that created it. Some of these terms reflect the operational and technological aspects of the new electronic medium, while others describe the tools and functions required by users to work within this medium. A brief listing of the major terminology that on-line global traders may encounter as they embark upon e-commerce follows. Since websites often refer visitors to related websites, the information-gathering potential is immense.

The following terms used with e-commerce are defined in Key definitions AZ:

Acrobat Reader
Alliance for Global Business (AGB)
application service provider (ASP)
Association for International
    Business (AIB)
authentication (as used in open
    network communications)
banner advertising
Bolero
bulletin board system (BBS)
business to business (B2B)
business to consumer (B2C)
business to government (B2G)
catalog (On-line)
CCEWeb
certificate of authority (CA – as used
    in the public key infrastructure)
certification service providers
    (CSP)
cookies
data protection directive (EU)
database
database search
digital cash (= digital money)
digital receipt infrastructure (DRI)

digital signature (= authentication =
    ensure)
discussion room (chat room)
domain name
e-UCP
electronic business extensible
    markup language (ebXML)
electronic commerce (e-commerce)
electronic data interchange (EDI)
electronic data interchange for
    administration, commerce and
    transportation (EDIFACT)
electronic funds transfer (EFT)
electronic mail (e-mail)
electronic mail attachments
electronic marketplace
electronic store (e-store)
electronic trade transaction
    (URGETS)
encryption
EUR-LEX
European Competitive Telecom-
    munications Association (ECTA)
European Information and
    Communications Technology

Association (EICTA)
European Information Technology Observatory (EITO)
European Information Technology Services Association (EISA)
European Public Telecommunications Network Operators' Association (ETNO)
European Software Institute (ESI)
European Telecommunications Standards Institute (ETS)
European Virtual Private Network Users' Association (EVUA)
extensible markup language (XML)
file transfer protocol (FTP)
Global Business Dialogue on Electronic Commerce (GBD)
Global Information Infrastructure Commission (GIIC)
Global Internet Project (GIP)
Global Telecommunications Society (GTS)
hyperlink
hyperlink markup language (HTML)
hypertext transfer protocol (HTTP)
IDENTRUS
Independent Regulators Group (IRGIS)
Information Technology (ITA), WTO Agreement
Institute of Telecom Resellers in Europe, Middle East, India, Asia and Africa (ITRE)
Inter-American Telecommunication Commission (CITEL)
International Telecommunication Users' Group (INTUG)
Internet Corporation for Assigned Names and Numbers (ICANN)
Internet Engineering Task Force (IETF)

Internet Law & Policy Forum (ILPF)
Internet service provider (ISP)
Internet Society
Multimedia Communications Forum (MMCF)
NetGlos Internet Glossary
Pacific Telecommunications Council (PTC)
portable document format (PDF)
portal
private key
public key infrastructure (PKI)
safe harbour privacy principles
search engine
secure hypertext transfer protocol (S-HTTP)
secured electronic transaction (SET)
shopping cart
Society for Worldwide Interbank Financial Telecommunications (SWIFT)
standard generalized markup language (SGML)
trade L/C
trade leads (on-line)
TradeCard
uniform resource locator (URL)
virtual trade show
web browser
web page
website
wireless application protocol (WAP)
world access network of directories
World Information Technology and Services Alliance (WITSA)
world wide web (WWW)
world wide web consortium (W3C)

Focus on Incoterms 2000

of international trade

Air transport ✈

Bank collections 🏛

e-commerce @

Insurance 🏹

Letters of credit LC

Liner vessel shipping ⚓

Sales contracts ✍

Vessel chartering ⏹

Focus on Incoterms 2000

Overview

Incoterms (International Commercial Terms) are a set of international standard trade terms (also known as delivery terms), created and maintained by the International Chamber of Commerce (ICC). First published in 1936 and periodically revised thereafter, Incoterms have become the worldwide standard for describing seller-buyer responsibilities in international contracts for the sale of goods.

The most recent revision, Incoterms 2000, consists of thirteen terms. Each Incoterm comprises ten tasks, including any required export or import clearances, contracts of carriage, insurance, points of delivery and providing notices. These tasks are aligned in matching-column format between seller and buyer. Not only does this arrangement clearly indicate each party's responsibility to the task and to each other, but it also provides both sellers and buyers with handy checklists.

The thirteen Incoterms are also grouped into four classifications: Departure, Main Carriage Unpaid, Main Carriage Paid and Arrival. The seller's responsibility for the indicated tasks increases as one moves from the Departure to the Arrival groupings. The same is true of the point at which the seller's responsibility for the condition of the contract-goods ceases. Presumably, the selling price and the seller's control over the transaction also increase as the seller assumes more obligations.

Advantages

Probably the biggest advantage Incoterms offer is their universality. The official text, *Incoterms 2000* (ICC Publication No. 560), has been translated into over 20 languages. Its companion work, *ICC Guide to Incoterms 2000* (ICC Publication No. 620), provides both illustrations and commentary. Even more explanatory detail as well as an inter-active panorama and tutorial are available for computer use on a CD

ROM titled *Incoterms 2000 Multimedia Expert* (ICC publication No. 616). (For information, visit the ICC Publishing website at www.iccbooks.com.) All these venues make it increasingly likely that sellers and buyers throughout the world either already understand or can readily learn Incoterms 2000.

The use of well-established definitions like Incoterms can provide great savings in time and money in dispute resolution. Further, Incoterms fit in well with such other well-established trade codes as the UN Convention on Contracts for the International Sale of Goods (CISG) and the Uniform Customs and Practice for Documentary Collections (UCP).

Incoterms provide such convenience that it is easy to assume they cover everything in foreign trade. This is not the case, and users should keep their limitations in mind.

Incoterms speak only to the contract of sale. While some tasks require either the seller or the buyer to contract for carriage, Incoterms are not intended for use in such supplemental contracts. The resulting contract of carriage should dovetail with the Incoterm in terms of allocation of transport costs and risks, but this will depend on the contracting party providing the carrier with precise directions to ship according to the constraints of the given Incoterm.

What Incoterms do not do

Incoterms are not law. They are contractually standard terms. As such, they do not necessarily apply to a given transaction unless the parties specifically incorporate them by referencing "Incoterms 2000." It is true that Incoterms may apply in exceptional cases even when not explicitly mentioned, if there is a custom of trade or prior course of dealing that indicate reliance on Incoterms, or if the local jurisdiction creates a presumption in favour of applicability of Incoterms. However, it is best to specify Incoterms 2000 in sales contracts.

Incoterms do not convey ownership, a fact that may be difficult to grasp for those whose national law relates sales terms to title passage. The important question of when ownership passes from seller to buyer must be addressed either elsewhere in the sales contract, or in some cases by means of a transport document called a negotiable (or order) marine bill of lading.

Incoterms do not directly speak to possession rights. The answer to the question of to whom and under what conditions a carrier should hand over the contract goods is left largely to the instructions it receives from the party contracting for carriage (again with the

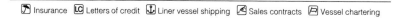

Insurance   Letters of credit   Liner vessel shipping   Sales contracts   Vessel chartering

exception of a negotiable marine bill of lading). However, Incoterms answer the question indirectly, by assigning the task of contracting carriage to either the seller or the buyer. The carrier is very likely to take its instructions from the party contracting (and usually paying) for its services.

Only two Incoterms (CIF and CIP) require that the seller provide insurance coverage, and none requires the buyer to insure. This does not mean that insurance is not required for the other eleven terms – only that sellers and buyers should arrange for it outside of the Incoterm. Further, under CIP and CIF, the seller complies with the Incoterm obligation to insure by providing minimum coverage (variously known as "London Institute of Underwriters Clause C" or "Free of Particular Average"). This does not mean that minimum coverage is adequate for most shipments. Rather, sellers and buyers should consider the appropriate level of coverage outside of the Incoterm.

Incoterms apply only to contracts for the sale of goods. They do not apply to services or intangibles.

Finally, Incoterms must accommodate the many variables found at ports worldwide and different practices found in different trades. To do so, they must sacrifice a degree of precision, which they do by deferring to "customs of the port or a particular trade."

The four groupings

As mentioned in the overview, Incoterms 2000 are divided into four groupings: Departure, Main Carriage Unpaid, Main Carriage Paid, and Arrival. The definitions with quote marks come from the preambles, as found in Incoterms 2000. Note that these preambles neither constitute the full text of Incoterms 2000 nor a summary of them, but simply present selected features of Incoterms.

> **Some of the preambles only work in conjunction with particular sections of the Introduction to Incoterms 2000 (see the end of 🔡 for details).**

Departure

There is only one Incoterm in the Departure group – Ex Works (EXW).

" **Ex Works (EXW) ...named place** (Incoterms 2000): "Ex works" means that the seller delivers when he places the goods at the disposal of the buyer at the seller's premises or another named place (i.e. works, factory, warehouse, etc.) not cleared for export and not loaded on any collecting vehicle.

"   This term thus represents the minimum obligation for the seller, and the buyer has to bear all costs and risks involved in taking the goods from the seller's premises.

"   However, if the parties wish the seller to be responsible for the loading of the goods on departure and to bear the risks and all the costs of such loading, this should be made clear by adding explicit wording to this effect in the contract of sale.[1] This term should not be used when the buyer cannot carry out the export formalities directly or indirectly. In such circumstances, the FCA term should be used, provided the seller agrees that he will load at his cost and risk."

[1] Refer to Introduction paragraph 11 – see end of .

EXW tasks the buyer with so many functions that it can become impractical, except when the buyer has a presence or is represented on the seller's side. It may be used for all modes of transport since, from the seller's perspective, it involves no transport at all.

Main Carriage Unpaid

There are three Incoterms in this group, all beginning with the letter F: Free Carrier (FCA), Free Alongside Ship (FAS) and Free On Board (FOB). In all cases, the place is somewhere on the seller's side and it is the buyer that arranges main carriage transportation.

"   **Free Carrier (FCA) ...named place** (Incoterms 2000): "Free Carrier" means that the seller delivers the goods, cleared for export, to the carrier nominated by the buyer at the named place. It should be noted that the chosen place of delivery has an impact on the obligations of loading and unloading the goods at that place. If delivery occurs at the seller's premises, the seller is responsible for loading. If delivery occurs at any other place, the seller is not responsible for unloading.

"   This term may be used irrespective of the mode of transport, including multimodal transport.

"   "Carrier" means any person who, in a contract of carriage, undertakes to perform or to procure the performance of transport by rail, road, air, sea, inland waterway or by a combination of such modes.

"   If the buyer nominates a person other than a carrier to receive the goods, the seller is deemed to have fulfilled his obligation to deliver the goods when they are delivered to that person."

FCA has two functional places: the seller's premises or anywhere else on the seller's side. Used with the seller's place, it often presents a

---

🛪 Insurance 🆔 Letters of credit ⬇ Liner vessel shipping ◀ Sales contracts 🅟 Vessel chartering

preferable alternative to EXW by tasking the seller with loading the collecting vehicle and arranging for export clearance.

" **Free Alongside Ship (FAS) ...named port of shipment** (Incoterms 2000): "Free Alongside Ship" means that the seller delivers when the goods are placed alongside the vessel at the named port of shipment. This means that the buyer has to bear all costs and risks of loss of or damage to the goods from that moment.

" The FAS term requires the seller to clear the goods for export.

" THIS IS A REVERSAL FROM PREVIOUS INCOTERMS VERSIONS WHICH REQUIRED THE BUYER TO ARRANGE FOR EXPORT CLEARANCE.

" However, if the parties wish the buyer to clear the goods for export, this should be made clear by adding explicit wording to this effect in the contract of sale[2].

" This term can be used only for sea or inland waterway transport."

[2] Refer to Introduction paragraph 11 – see end of

FAS is often not practical for use with liner service for several reasons. At modern ports, cargo is normally handed over to the carrier at a gateway or terminal some distance from the vessel. It also exposes the seller to risk regarding the condition of the contract goods from the time they have been handed over to the buyer-designated carrier until they have been placed alongside the vessel.

Further, although terminal handling charges at the loading port are for the seller's account under FAS, ship lines normally bill them to the party paying for main carriage transport (in this case, the buyer). Finally, the seller may have difficulty evidencing compliance, as ship lines do not normally issue documents confirming that cargo has been placed next to vessels.

" **Free on Board (FOB) ...named port of shipment** (Incoterms 2000): "Free on Board" means that the seller delivers when the goods pass the ship's rail at the named port of shipment. This means that the buyer has to bear all costs and risks of loss of or damage to the goods from that point. The FOB term requires the seller to clear the goods for export. This term can be used only for sea or inland waterway transport. If the parties do not intend to deliver the goods across the ship's rail, the FCA term should be used."

Although commonly used with liner service, FOB may present problems. First, it exposes the seller to the risk for the condition of the contract goods from the time they have been handed over to the buyer-designated carrier (at a port gateway or terminal) until they have been loaded aboard the vessel. Further, although terminal handling charges at the loading port are for the seller's account under FOB, ship lines normally bill them to the party paying for main carriage transport (in this case, the buyer).

Main Carriage Paid

There are four Incoterms in this group, all beginning with the letter C: Cost and Freight (CFR), Cost Insurance and Freight (CIF), Carriage Paid To (CPT) and Carriage and Insurance Paid (CIP). In all cases, the place is somewhere on the buyer's side and it is the seller that arranges main-carriage transportation. However, the seller's responsibility for the condition of the contract goods ends somewhere on the seller's side; that is, the seller is not responsible for their condition during main carriage. This places the buyer at risk while the goods are in the custody of the seller-appointed carrier.

" **Cost and Freight (CFR) ...named port of destination**
  (Incoterms 2000): "Cost and Freight" means that the seller delivers when the goods pass the ship's rail in the port of shipment.

" The seller must pay the costs and freight necessary to bring the goods to the named port of destination BUT the risk of loss of or damage to the goods, as well as any additional costs due to events occurring after the time of delivery, are transferred from the seller to the buyer.

" The CFR term requires the seller to clear the goods for export.

" This term can be used only for sea and inland waterway transport. If the parties do not intend to delivery the goods across the ship's rail, the CPT term should be used."

The seller remains responsible for the condition of the contract goods from the time they are handed over to the carrier until they are vessel-loaded, and it is the seller who contracts for main carriage and presumably selects the carrier. Since this term is vessel-restricted, the place will always be a port on the buyer's side.

" **Cost Insurance and Freight (CIF) ...named port of destination**
  (Incoterms 2000): "Cost, Insurance and Freight" means that the seller delivers when the goods pass the ship's rail in the port of shipment.

" The seller must pay the costs and freight necessary to bring the goods to the named port of destination BUT the risk of loss of or damage to the goods, as well as any additional costs due to events occurring after the time of delivery, are transferred from the seller to the buyer. However, in CIF the seller also has to procure marine insurance against the buyer's risk of loss of or damage to the goods during the carriage.

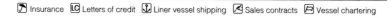

Insurance   Letters of credit   Liner vessel shipping   Sales contracts   Vessel chartering

" Consequently, the seller contracts for insurance and pays the insurance premium. The buyer should note that under the CIF term the seller is required to obtain insurance only on minimum cover[3]. Should the buyer wish to have the protection of greater cover, he would either need to agree as much expressly with the seller or to make his own extra insurance arrangement.

" The CIF term requires the seller to clear the goods for export.

" This term can be used only for sea and inland waterway transport. If the parties do not intend to deliver the goods across the ship's rail, the CIP term should be used."

[3] Refer to Introduction paragraph 9.3 – see end of

The seller remains responsible for the condition of the contract goods from the time they are handed over to the carrier until they are vessel-loaded. However, as with all "C" terms, it is the seller who contracts for main carriage and presumably selects the carrier. Further, the seller is providing insurance, which will reduce this risk if the coverage is greater than minimum. As with CFR, the place will always be a port on the buyer's side because this term is vessel-restricted.

" **Carriage Paid to (CPT) ...named place of destination** (Incoterms 2000): "Carriage paid to..." means that the seller delivers the goods to the carrier nominated by him but the seller must in addition pay the cost of carriage necessary to bring the goods to the named destination. This means that the buyer bears all risks and any other costs occurring after the goods have been so delivered.

" "Carrier" means any person who, in a contract of carriage, undertakes to perform or to procure the performance of transport, by rail, road, air, sea, inland waterway or by a combination of such modes.

" If subsequent carriers are used for the carriage to the agreed destination, the risk passes when the goods have been delivered to the first carrier.

" The CPT term requires the seller to clear the goods for export.

" This term may be used irrespective of the mode of transport including multimodal transport."

Since the seller's responsibility for the condition of the contract goods ends when they are handed over to the first carrier, the buyer relies on the performance of a seller-appointed carrier. This could represent additional risk, particularly if the pre-carrier is independent of any multimodal transportation arrangement.

‹see entry in dictionary›   ✈ Air transport   🏛 Bank collections   @ e-commerce   ⊞ Incoterms

Since CPT may be used with any mode of transport, the place will be anywhere on the buyer's side that the seller and buyer agree (a port, an airport, a border or an inland location).

" **Carriage and Insurance Paid to (CIP)...named place of destination** (Incoterms 2000): "Carriage and Insurance paid to..." means that the seller delivers the goods to the carrier nominated by him, but the seller must in addition pay the cost of carriage necessary to bring the goods to the named destination. This means that the buyer bears all risks and any additional costs occurring after the goods have been so delivered. However, in CIP the seller also has to procure insurance against the buyer's risk of loss of or damage to the goods during the carriage.

" Consequently, the seller contracts for insurance and pays the insurance premium.

" The buyer should note that under the CIP term the seller is required to obtain insurance only on minimum cover[4]. Should the buyer wish to have the protection of greater cover, he would either need to agree as much expressly with the seller or to make his own extra insurance arrangements.

" "Carrier" means any person who, in a contract of carriage, undertakes to perform or to procure the performance of transport, by rail, road, air, sea, inland waterway or by a combination of such modes.

" If subsequent carriers are used for the carriage to the agreed destination, the risk passes when the goods have been delivered to the first carrier.

" The CIP term requires the seller to clear the goods for export.

" This term may be used irrespective of the mode of transport, including multimodal transport."

[4] Refer to Introduction paragraph 9.3 – see end of 🔲

As with CPT, the buyer relies on the performance of a seller-appointed carrier, since the seller's responsibility for the condition of the contract goods ends when they are handed over to the first carrier. This could represent additional risk, particularly if the pre-carrier is independent of any multimodal transportation arrangement. However, the insurance provided by the seller may offer protection if the parties agree that it should exceed minimum coverage.

Since CIP may be used with any mode of transport, the place will be anywhere on the buyer's side that the seller and buyer agree (a port, an airport, a border or an inland location).

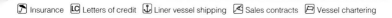
🔲 Insurance 🔲 Letters of credit 🔲 Liner vessel shipping 🔲 Sales contracts 🔲 Vessel chartering

Arrival

There are five Incoterms in this group, all beginning with the letter D: Delivered at Frontier (DAF), Delivered Ex Ship (DES), Delivered Ex Quay (DEQ), Delivered Duty Unpaid (DDU) and Delivered Duty Paid (DDP). With the exception of DAF, the place is somewhere on the buyer's side, and it is the seller that arranges main carriage transportation. However, unlike the Main Carriage Paid Group, the seller's responsibility for the condition of the contract goods continues up to the named place. (Under DAF, the place is a border location.)

" **Delivered At Frontier (DAF)...named place** (Incoterms 2000): "Delivered at Frontier" means that the seller delivers when the goods are placed at the disposal of the buyer on the arriving means of transport not unloaded, cleared for export, but not cleared for import at the named point and place at the frontier, but before the customs border of the adjoining country. The term "frontier" may be used for any frontier including that of the country of export. Therefore, it is of vital importance that the frontier in question be defined precisely by always naming the point and place in the term.

" However, if the parties wish the seller to be responsible for the unloading of the goods from the arriving means of transport and to bear the risks and costs of unloading, this should be made clear by adding explicit wording to this effect in the contract of sale[5].

" This term may be used irrespective of the mode of transport when goods are to be delivered at a land frontier. When delivery is to take place in the port of destination, on board a vessel or on the quay (wharf), the DES or DEQ terms should be used."

[5] Refer to Introduction paragraph 11 – see end of

Although DAF may be used for any mode of transport, the place must be a border location. This means that transport would normally be either ground or multimodal with the last leg as ground.

" **Delivered Ex Ship (DES) ...named port of destination** (Incoterms 2000): "Delivered Ex Ship" means that the seller delivers when the goods are placed at the disposal of the buyer on board the ship not cleared for import at the named port of destination. The seller has to bear all the costs and risks involved in bringing the goods to the named port of destination before discharging. If the parties wish the seller to bear the costs and risks of discharging the goods, then the DEQ term should be used.

" This term can be used only when the goods are to be delivered by sea or inland waterway or multimodal transport on a vessel in the port of destination."

DES does not fit well with liner service, where the carrier normally handles vessel loading and unloading.

" **Delivered Ex Quay (DEQ) ...named port of destination** (Incoterms 2000): "Delivered Ex Quay" means that the seller delivers when the goods are placed at the disposal of the buyer not cleared for import on the quay (wharf) at the named port of destination. The seller has to bear costs and risks involved in bringing the goods to the named port of destination and discharging the goods on the quay (wharf). The DEQ term requires the buyer to clear the goods for import and to pay for all formalities, duties, taxes and other charges upon import.

" THIS IS A REVERSAL FROM PREVIOUS INCOTERMS VERSIONS WHICH REQUIRED THE SELLER TO ARRANGE FOR IMPORT CLEARANCE.

" If the parties wish to include in the seller's obligations all or part of the costs payable upon import of the goods, this should be made clear by adding explicit wording to this effect in the contract of sale[6].

" This term can be used only when the goods are to be delivered by sea or inland waterway or multimodal transport on discharging from a vessel onto the quay (wharf) in the port of destination. However if the parties wish to include in the seller's obligations the risks and costs of the handing of the goods from the quay to another place (warehouse, terminal, transport station, etc.) in or outside the port, the DDU or DDP terms should be used."

[6] Refer to Introduction paragraph 11 – see end of 🔲

With liner service, arriving cargoes are usually removed from the quay to the carrier's terminal or other port location.

' **Delivered Duty Unpaid (DDU) ...named place of destination** (Incoterms 2000): "Delivered duty unpaid" means that the seller delivers the goods to the buyer, not cleared for import, and not unloaded from any arriving means of transport at the named place of destination. The seller has to bear the costs and risks involved in bringing the goods thereto, other than, where applicable[7], any "duty" (which term includes the responsibility for and the risks of the carrying out of customs formalities, and the payment of formalities, customs duties, taxes and other charges) for import in the country of destination. Such "duty" has to be borne by the buyer as well as any costs and risks caused by his failure to clear the goods for import in time.

"   However, if the parties wish the seller to carry out customs formalities and bear the costs and risks resulting therefrom as well as some of the costs payable upon import of the goods, this should be made clear by adding explicit wording to this effect in the contract of sale[8].

"   This term may be used irrespective of the mode of transport but when delivery is to take place in the port of destination on board the vessel or on the quay (wharf), the DES or DEQ terms should be used."

[7] Refer to Introduction paragraph 14 – see end of
[8] Refer to Introduction paragraph 11 – see end of

DDU differs from CPT in that the seller remains responsible for the condition of the contract goods until they arrive at the agreed place on the buyer's side. Since this Incoterm may be used with any mode of transport, the place will be anywhere on the buyer's side that the seller and buyer agree (a port, an airport, a border or an inland location).

"   **Delivered Duty Paid (DDP)...named place of destination** (Incoterms 2000): "Delivered duty paid" means that the seller delivers the goods to the buyer, cleared for import, and not unloaded from any arriving means of transport at the named place of destination. The seller has to bear all the costs and risks involved in bringing the goods thereto including, where applicable[9], any "duty" (which term includes the responsibility for and the risk of the carrying out of customs formalities and the payment of formalities, customs duties, taxes and other charges) for import in the country of destination.

"   Whilst the EXW term represents the minimum obligation for the seller, DDP represents the maximum obligation.

"   This term should not be used if the seller is unable directly or indirectly to obtain the import licence.

"   However, if the parties wish to exclude from the seller's obligations some of the costs payable upon import of the goods (such as value-added tax: VAT), this should be made clear by adding explicit wording to this effect in the contract of sale[10].

"   If the parties wish the buyer to bear all risks and costs of the import, the DDU term should be used.

"   This term may be used irrespective of the mode of transport but when delivery is to take place in the port of destination on board the vessel or on the quay (wharf), the DES or DEQ terms should be used."

[9] Refer to Introduction paragraph 14 – see end of
[10] Refer to Introduction paragraph 11 – see end of

DDP differs from CPT in that the seller remains responsible for the condition of the contract goods until they arrive at the agreed place on the buyer's side. Since this Incoterm may be used with any mode of transport, the place will be anywhere on the buyer's side that the seller and buyer agree (a port, an airport, a border or an inland location).

The 13 Incoterms according to transport mode

Ex Works (EXW): any mode (as transportation is not a factor of delivery under this term).

Free Carrier (FCA): all modes of transportation.

Free Alongside Ship (FAS): vessel only.

Free On Board (FOB): vessel only.

Cost and Freight (CFR): vessel only.

Cost, Insurance and Freight (CIF): vessel only.

Carriage Paid To (CPT): all modes of transportation.

Carriage and Insurance Paid (CIP): all modes of transportation.

Delivered at Frontier (DAF): all modes of transportation (provided the final leg is by ground).

Delivered Ex Ship (DES): vessel only.

Delivered Ex Quay (DEQ): vessel only.

Delivered Duty Unpaid (DDU): all modes of transportation.

Delivered Duty Paid (DDP): all modes of transportation.

Practice

Sellers and buyers include an Incoterm in their sales contract, preferably specifying it as an "Incoterm 2000." Ideally, sellers should prepare detailed price quotations (called proforma invoices), reflecting the costs of the product and any non-product services specified by the selected Incoterm. Ideally, buyers will indicate the same in their purchase orders. Once a sales contract has been established, each party follows his or her respective obligations as illustrated in the Incoterms 2000 matching column, where the A 1–10 column applies to sellers and the B 1–10 column applies to buyers.

Insurance   Letters of credit   Liner vessel shipping   Sales contracts   Vessel chartering

Incoterms are meant to be informative rather than adversarial. While not obligatory, sellers and buyers are encouraged to assist whenever unforeseen circumstances make compliance difficult for the counterparty. However, any such help is rendered at the recipient's cost and risk.

The following terms used with Incoterms are defined in Key definitions AZ

all risks (AR)C	demurrage
alongside	devanning
apparent good order and condition	dispatch money
arrival notice	documents
average	door-to-airport
booking	door-to-door
cargo	door-to-port
cargo insurance	duty free
carriage	duty paid
carrier	estimated time of arrival (ETA)
certificate of inspection	estimated time of departure (ETD)
charter	export
charterer	export clearance
charterparty	export declaration
claim	export licence
clean receipt	export marks
clean report of findings	export packing
clean transport document	export quota
closing date	forwarder
commercial invoice	foul transport document
consignee	free of particular average (FPA)
consignment	freight collect
consignor	freight prepaid
consular documentation	general average (GA)
contingency insurance	goods
contract	hazardous materials (HAZMAT)
contracting parties	import
counterparty	import licence
customs broker	import quota
customs clearance	import restrictions
customs duty	importer
customs entry	insurable interest
damage in transit	insurance
dangerous goods declaration	intermediate consignee
delivery	liner terms

⟨see entry in dictionary⟩   ✈ Air transport   🏛 Bank collections   @ e-commerce   ⊞ Incoterms

main carriage

marine cargo insurance

multimodal transport

named place

negotiable B/L

no show

notify party

on-board notation

on-carriage

packing list

port-to-port

pre-carriage

pre-shipment inspection

proforma invoice

purchase order

quay

received for shipment B/L

said to contain

sales contract

self insured

ship's rail

ship's tackle

shipment (on board a vessel)

shipment date

shipper

shipper's letter of instructions (SLI)

shipping documents

surcharge

terminal handling charge (THC)

through rate

through transport

title

transfer of ownership

transshipment

ultimate consignee

United Nations Convention on
Contracts for the International
Sale of Goods (CISG)

value

value added tax (VAT)

voyage

warehouse-to-warehouse

weight

wharf

Extracts from the Introduction to Incoterms 2000 (ICC publication No.560)

To be read in conjunction with the Preambles to Incoterms 2000

(see footnotes of preambles, as from page 32)

9. THE TERMS

9.3 The "C"-terms require the seller to contract for carriage on usual terms at his own expense. Therefore, a point up to which he would have to pay transport costs must necessarily be indicated after the respective "C"-term. Under the CIF and CIP terms the seller also has to take out insurance and bear the insurance cost. Since the point for the division of costs is fixed at a point in the country of destination, the "C"-terms are frequently mistakenly believed to be arrival contracts, in which the seller would bear all risks and costs until the goods have actually arrived at the agreed point. However, it must be stressed that the "C"-terms are of the same nature as the "F"-terms in that the seller fulfils the contract in the country of shipment or dispatch.

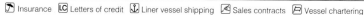

Insurance LC Letters of credit Liner vessel shipping Sales contracts Vessel chartering

Thus, the contracts of sale under the "C"-terms, like the contracts under the "F"-terms, fall within the category of shipment contracts.

It is in the nature of shipment contracts that, while the seller is bound to pay the normal transport cost for the carriage of the goods by a usual route and in a customary manner to the agreed place, the risk of loss of or damage to the goods, as well as additional costs resulting from events occurring after the goods having been appropriately delivered for carriage, fall upon the buyer. Hence, the "C"-terms are distinguishable from all other terms in that they contain two "critical" points, one indicating the point to which the seller is bound to arrange and bear the costs of a contract of carriage and another one for the allocation of risk. For this reason, the greatest caution must be observed when adding obligations of the seller to the "C"-terms which seek to extend the seller's responsibility beyond the aforementioned "critical" point for the allocation of risk. It is of the very essence of the "C"-terms that the seller is relieved of any further risk and cost after he has duly fulfilled his contract by contracting for carriage and handing over the goods to the carrier and by providing for insurance under the CIF- and CIP-terms.

The essential nature of the "C"-terms as shipment contracts is also illustrated by the common use of documentary credits as the preferred mode of payment used in such terms. Where it is agreed by the parties to the sale contract that the seller will be paid by presenting the agreed shipping documents to a bank under a documentary credit, it would be quite contrary to the central purpose of the documentary credit for the seller to bear further risks and costs after the moment when payment had been made under documentary credits or otherwise upon shipment and dispatch of the goods. Of course, the seller would have to bear the cost of the contract of carriage irrespective of whether freight is pre-paid upon shipment or is payable at destination (freight collect); however, additional costs which may result from events occurring subsequent to shipment and dispatch are necessarily for the account of the buyer.

If the seller has to provide a contract of carriage which involves payment of duties, taxes and other charges, such costs will, of course, fall upon the seller to the extent that they are for his account under that contract. This is now explicitly set forth in the A6 clause of all "C"-terms.

If it is customary to procure several contracts of carriage involving transhipment of the goods at intermediate places in order to reach the agreed destination, the seller would have to pay all these costs, including any costs incurred when the goods are transhipped from one means of conveyance to the other. If, however, the carrier exercised his rights under a transhipment – or similar clause – in order to avoid unexpected hindrances (such as ice, congestion, labour disturbances, government orders, war or warlike operations) then any additional cost resulting therefrom would be for the account of the buyer, since the seller's obligation is limited to procuring the usual contract of carriage.

It happens quite often that the parties to the contract of sale wish to clarify the extent to which the seller should procure a contract of carriage including the costs of discharge. Since such costs are normally covered by the freight when the goods are carried by regular shipping lines, the contract of sale will frequently stipulate that the goods are to be so carried or at least that they are to be carried under "liner terms". In other cases, the word "landed" is added after CFR or CIF. However, it is advisable not to use abbreviations added to the "C"-terms unless, in the relevant trade, the meaning of the abbreviations is clearly understood and accepted by the contracting parties or under any applicable law or custom of the trade.

In particular, the seller should not – and indeed could not, without changing the very nature of the "C"-terms - undertake any obligation with respect to the arrival of the goods at destination, since the risk of any delay during the carriage is borne by the buyer. Thus, any obligation with respect to time must necessarily refer to the place of shipment or dispatch, for example, "shipment (dispatch) not later than...". An agreement for example, "CFR Hamburg not later than..." is really a misnomer and thus open to different possible interpretations. The parties could be taken to have meant either that the goods must actually arrive at Hamburg at the specified date, in which case the contract is not a shipment contract but an arrival contract or, alternatively, that the seller must ship the goods at such a time that they would normally arrive at Hamburg before the specified date unless the carriage would have been delayed because of unforeseen events.

It happens in commodity trades that goods are bought while they are at sea and that, in such cases, the word "afloat" is added after the trade term. Since the risk of loss of or damage to the goods would then, under the CFR- and CIF-terms, have passed from the seller to the buyer, difficulties of interpretation might arise. One possibility would be to maintain the ordinary meaning of the CFR- and CIF-terms with respect to the allocation of risk between seller and buyer, namely that risk passes on shipment: this would mean that the buyer might have to assume the consequences of events having already occurred at the time when the contract of sale enters into force. The other possibility would be to let the passing of the risk coincide with the time when the contract of sale is concluded. The former possibility might well be practical, since it is usually impossible to ascertain the condition of the goods while they are being carried. For this reason the 1980 United Nations Convention on Contracts for the International Sale of Goods article 68 stipulates that "if the circumstances so indicate, the risk is assumed by the buyer from the time the goods were handed over to the carrier who issued the documents embodying the contract of carriage". There is, however, an exception to this rule when "the seller knew or ought to have known that the goods had been lost or damaged and did not disclose this to the buyer". Thus, the interpretation of a CFR- or CIF-term with the addition of the word "afloat" will depend upon the law applicable to the contract of sale. The parties are advised to ascertain the applicable law and any solution which might follow therefrom. In case of doubt, the parties are advised to clarify the matter in their contract.

Insurance   Letters of credit   Liner vessel shipping   Sales contracts   Vessel chartering

In practice, the parties frequently continue to use the traditional expression C&F (or C and F, C+F). Nevertheless, in most cases it would appear that they regard these expressions as equivalent to CFR. In order to avoid difficulties of interpreting their contract the parties should use the correct Incoterm which is CFR, the only world-wide-accepted standard abbreviation for the term "Cost and Freight (... named port of destination)".

CFR and CIF in A8 of Incoterms 1990 obliged the seller to provide a copy of the charterparty whenever his transport document (usually the bill of lading) contained a reference to the charterparty, for example, by the frequent notation "all other terms and conditions as per charterparty". Although, of course, a contracting party should always be able to ascertain all terms of his contract – preferably at the time of the conclusion of the contract – it appears that the practice to provide the charterparty as aforesaid has created problems particularly in connection with documentary credit transactions. The obligation of the seller under CFR and CIF to provide a copy of the charterparty together with other transport documents has been deleted in Incoterms 2000.

Although the A8 clauses of Incoterms seek to ensure that the seller provides the buyer with "proof of delivery", it should be stressed that the seller fulfils that requirement when he provides the "usual" proof. Under CPT and CIP it would be the "usual transport document" and under CFR and CIF a bill of lading or a sea waybill. The transport documents must be "clean", meaning that they must not contain clauses or notations expressly declaring a defective condition of the goods and/or the packaging. If such clauses or notations appear in the document, it is regarded as "unclean" and would then not be accepted by banks in documentary credit transactions. However, it should be noted that a transport document even without such clauses or notations would usually not provide the buyer with incontrovertible proof as against the carrier that the goods were shipped in conformity with the stipulations of the contract of sale. Usually, the carrier would, in standardized text on the front page of the transport document, refuse to accept responsibility for information with respect to the goods by indicating that the particulars inserted in the transport document constitute the shipper's declarations and therefore that the information is only "said to be" as inserted in the document. Under most applicable laws and principles, the carrier must at least use reasonable means of checking the correctness of the information and his failure to do so may make him liable to the consignee. However, in container trade, the carrier's means of checking the contents in the container would not exist unless he himself was responsible for stowing the container.

There are only two terms which deal with insurance, namely CIF and CIP. Under these terms the seller is obliged to procure insurance for the benefit of the buyer. In other cases it is for the parties themselves to decide whether and to what extent they want to cover themselves by insurance. Since the seller takes out insurance for the benefit of the buyer, he would not know the buyer's precise requirements. Under the Institute Cargo Clauses drafted by the Institute of London Underwriters, insurance is available in "minimum cover" under Clause C, "medium cover" under Clause B and "most extended cover" under Clause A. Since in the sale of commodities under the CIF term the buyer may wish to sell the goods in transit to a subsequent buyer who in turn may wish to resell the goods again, it is impossible to know the insurance cover suitable to such subsequent buyers and, therefore, the minimum cover under CIF has traditionally been chosen with the possibility for the buyer to require the seller to take out additional insurance. Minimum cover is however unsuitable for sale of manufactured goods where the risk of theft, pilferage or improper handling or custody of the goods would require more than the cover available under Clause C. Since CIP as distinguished from CIF, would normally not be used for the sale of commodities, it would have been feasible to adopt the most extended cover under CIP rather than the minimum cover under CIF. But to vary the seller's insurance obligation under CIF and CIP would lead to confusion and both terms therefore limit the seller's insurance obligation to the minimum cover. It is particularly important for the CIP-buyer to observe this: should additional cover be required, he should agree with the seller that the latter could take out additional insurance or, alternatively, arrange for extended insurance cover himself. There are also particular instances where the buyer may wish to obtain even more protection than is available under Institute Clause A, for example insurance against war, riots, civil commotion, strikes or other labour disturbances. If he wishes the seller to arrange such insurance he must instruct him accordingly in which case the seller would have to provide such insurance if procurable.

11 VARIANTS OF INCOTERMS

In practice, it frequently happens that the parties themselves by adding words to an Incoterm seek further precision than the term could offer. It should be underlined that Incoterms give no guidance whatsoever for such additions. Thus, if the parties cannot rely on a well-established custom of the trade for the interpretation of such additions they may encounter serious problems when no consistent understanding of the additions could be proven.

If for instance the common expressions "FOB stowed" or "EXW loaded" are used, it is impossible to establish a world-wide understanding to the effect that the seller's obligations are extended not only with respect to the cost of actually loading the goods in the ship or on the vehicle respectively but also include the risk of fortuitous loss of or damage to the goods in the process of stowage and loading. For these reasons, the parties are strongly advised to clarify whether they only mean that the function or the cost of the stowage and loading operations should fall upon the seller or whether he should also bear the risk until the stowage and loading has actually been completed. These are questions to which Incoterms do not provide an answer: consequently, if the contract too fails expressly to describe the parties' intentions, the parties may be put to much unnecessary trouble and cost.

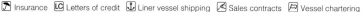

 Insurance   Letters of credit   Liner vessel shipping   Sales contracts Vessel chartering

Although Incoterms 2000 do not provide for many of these commonly used variants, the preambles to certain trade terms do alert the parties to the need for special contractual terms if the parties wish to go beyond the stipulations of Incoterms.

EXW   the added obligation for the seller to load the goods on the buyer's collecting vehicle;

CIF/CIP   the buyer's need for additional insurance;

DEQ   the added obligation for the seller to pay for costs after discharge.

In some cases sellers and buyers refer to commercial practice in liner and charter party trade. In these circumstances, it is necessary to clearly distinguish between the obligations of the parties under the contract of carriage and their obligations to each other under the contract of sale. Unfortunately, there are no authoritative definitions of expressions such as "liner terms" and "terminal handling charges" (THC). Distribution of costs under such terms may differ in different places and change from time to time. The parties are recommended to clarify in the contract of sale how such costs should be distributed between themselves.

Expressions frequently used in charterparties, such as "FOB stowed", "FOB stowed and trimmed", are sometimes used in contracts of sale in order to clarify to what extent the seller under FOB has to perform stowage and trimming of the goods onboard the ship. Where such words are added, it is necessary to clarify in the contract of sale whether the added obligations only relate to costs or to both costs and risks.

As has been said, every effort has been made to ensure that Incoterms reflect the most common commercial practice. However in some cases – particularly where Incoterms 2000 differ from Incoterms 1990 – the parties may wish the trade terms to operate differently. They are reminded of such options in the preamble of the terms signalled by the word "However".

14 CUSTOMS CLEARANCE

The term "customs clearance" has given rise to misunderstandings. Thus, whenever reference is made to an obligation of the seller or the buyer to undertake obligations in connection with passing the goods through customs of the country of export or import it is now made clear that this obligation does not only include the payment of duty and other charges but also the performance and payment of whatever administrative matters are connected with the passing of the goods through customs and the information to the authorities in this connection. Further, it has – although quite wrongfully - been considered in some quarters inappropriate to use terms dealing with the obligation to clear the goods through customs when, as in intra-European Union trade or other free trade areas, there is no longer any obligation to pay duty and no restrictions relating to import or export. In order to clarify the situation, the words "where applicable" have been added in the A2 and B2, A6 and

B6 clauses of the relevant Incoterms in order for them to be used without any ambiguity where no customs procedures are required.

It is normally desirable that customs clearance is arranged by the party domiciled in the country where such clearance should take place or at least by somebody acting there on his behalf. Thus, the exporter should normally clear the goods for export, while the importer should clear the goods for import.

Incoterms 1990 departed from this under the trade terms EXW and FAS (export clearance duty on the buyer) and DEQ (import clearance duty on the seller) but in Incoterms 2000 FAS and DEQ place the duty of clearing the goods for export on the seller and to clear them for import on the buyer respectively, while EXW – representing the seller's minimum obligation – has been left unamended (export clearance duty on the buyer). Under DDP the seller specifically agrees to do what follows from the very name of the term – Delivered Duty Paid – namely to clear the goods for import and pay any duty as a consequence thereof.

Focus on Insurance

international trade

Focus on Insurance

Caveat: This section contains generally applicable information, and is not to be considered legal advice. National law and insurance practices vary from country to country (e.g. the difference between American Terms and English Terms). Further, many insurers modify standard coverages to address customer needs on a case-by-case basis. For these reasons, it is best to refer any specific questions to the insurer before shipping.

Overview

Marine cargo insurance covers the agreed risks to goods shipped in international trade, regardless of the transportation mode. It also covers General Average (GA) if the ship's master voluntarily sacrifices cargo, equipment or funds to save the voyage. There are three basic types of marine cargo insurance: "free of particular average", "with average" and "all risk". Coverage levels and premiums differ substantially from one to another. There are additional perils that are not normally covered even in the broadest standard coverages. These, too, may be insured but at an extra premium.

Premiums are determined by such factors as the level of coverage, the type of goods, the places of origin and destination, the mode of transportation and the loss experience of the shipper. Coverage is provided by insurance companies through insurance agents and brokers. Insurance can also be purchased through most freight forwarders and/or customs brokers, or in some cases through the transportation carriers themselves.

The purpose of marine cargo insurance is, as far as possible, to protect the financial interests of the parties by restoring the assured party to the situation it would have enjoyed if a covered loss had not occured. For this reason, insurers will pay only the actual value plus a provision for out-of-pocket expenses (referred to by insurers as "sue & labour expenses"). Thus, most marine cargo insurance is

---

〈see entry in dictionary〉 ✈ Air transport 🏛 Bank collections © e-commerce ⊞ Incoterms

written for 110% of the total of the value of the goods plus the cost of transportation plus the cost of the insurance itself; i.e., 110% of the CIF or CIP value (which are identical). This practice is so widespread that it has become the default-insured amount in the International Chamber of Commerce Incoterms and Uniform Customs and Practice for Documentary Credits trade codes.

Anyone having an "insurable interest" in cargo may become an assured. Normally, this would include the owner of the goods – either the seller or buyer having responsibility for their condition under the sales contract (see focus on Incoterms 2000) – or a carrier or other bailee. The insurable interest requirement is to prevent disinterested parties from purchasing insurance purely for speculation (called gaming). Parties to a transaction may also purchase supplemental coverage for that part of the transportation for which they are responsible (i.e. inland marine), or against the possibility that insurance placed by the counterparty may fail to pay a covered loss. (The latter is called contingency insurance, and covers insurer nonperformance in responding to a legitimate covered loss.)

The fact that a shipment is insured does not eliminate seller-buyer responsibility for its well-being. In fact, assured parties are expected to behave as though shipments were not insured at all. Sellers are responsible for adequate export packing. Buyers are responsible for inspecting incoming shipments for signs of loss or damage, and, where appropriate, to claim against (at least) the delivering carrier. Since buyers are normally the first parties to unpack and examine their imported purchases, they are also required to notify the insurance company of any loss or damage, and take reasonable steps to keep a bad situation from getting worse.

There are some terms used in a unique way by the insurance industry. An "adventure" is a voyage. An "average" is a partial loss. "Fortuitous" means by chance rather than by design, and applies to both bad and good happenings. "Sue and labour" does not necessarily mean legal action – merely keeping a bad situation such as damaged goods from becoming worse. Some insurance provisions are referenced by vessel names such as "Inchmaree," which means that losses caused by vessel-equipment breakdown are covered.

Given the low limits to carrier liability, perhaps the most impressive thing about marine cargo insurance is its relatively low cost. Premiums for most shipments are well below one percent of the insured value, even for maximum coverage.

Practice

Basic types of marine cargo insurance

Free of particular average (FPA) provides the minimum level of coverage in the American insurance market. London Institute Cargo Clauses "C" provide similar minimum coverages in other markets. The following perils are normally covered:

a. Total or partial loss from stranding, sinking, burning or collision. Note that under English Terms partial losses are payable if any of these events occur. Under American Terms, partial losses are payable only if caused by these events.

b. Total loss from errors in vessel management, boiler bursting, defects in hull or machinery and explosion.

With average (WA, also called with particular average) expands all the perils covered under FPA to include partial losses for heavy weather, and covers the following additional perils: lightning, seawater as a result of heavy weather and jettison (throwing cargo overboard to protect a vessel from sinking). London Institute Cargo Clauses "B" provide similar coverages.

All risks (AR) and London Institute Cargo Clauses "A" provides the broadest level of coverage. In addition to the above perils, all risks covers additional perils such as: freshwater damage, ship's sweat, condensation, steam, improper carrier stowage, damage by hook, mud and grease, theft, pilferage, non-delivery, leakage and breakage. By contrast, most standard all-risk policies do not cover losses caused by the following: improper packing, abandonment of cargo, rejection by import authorities, inherent vice, delay, loss of market, nuclear damage, seagoing barge, on-deck shipment, or losses occurring to undelivered goods beyond time limits recited in the policy. All risk coverage and London Institute Cargo "A" Clauses also do not include loss or damage caused by war or strike, riot and civil commotion (SRCC), although coverage for these is normally available at modest additional premiums.

Note: All three levels of marine cargo insurance cover general average situations.

Who should insure, and why

There are thirteen Incoterms, but only two (CIF and CIP) require that either party insure. Under CIF and CIP, sellers are obliged to insure, but their obligation extends only to minimum cover (free of particular average or London "C" coverage). Since this level of coverage is inadequate for most shipments, sellers and buyers should address the insurance issue even under these terms.

There are two reasons for FPA being the default position. Both apply to limited situations, and both have to do with minimizing the premium spent on mandatory insurance. First, some countries require that all marine cargo insurance be placed with local insurers, and these may not be as reliable as the parties would like. In these situations, counterparties often also insure in their own countries. Second, goods are often sold while in transit, and each successive buyer may want to insure them. In both cases, it is to everyone's advantage to minimize the premium the seller must pay, provided that better coverage is obtained elsewhere.

The fact that only the CIF and CIP Incoterms require insurance should not be taken to mean that insurance is not necessary for the other eleven terms, only that it must be addressed outside the Incoterm.

While anyone having an insurable interest is eligible to be an assured, the security of adequate coverage is likely to be of more importance to some parties than to others. Although Incoterms clearly indicate the point where the seller's responsibility for shipped goods ends, unpaid sellers run a definite payment risk if uninsured or underinsured goods become lost or damaged in transit. Likewise, buyers who pre-pay or open irrevocable letters of credit in favour of their suppliers rely on loss- and damage-free deliveries, or the ability to place insurance claims when this doesn't happen. We call these parties "parties at risk," and since they have the most to lose if loss or damage occurs in transit, they should be concerned that adequate insurance coverage is in place.

Parties at risk relying on insurance protection provided by their counterparties face the possibility of non-performance by an insurer with which they have no direct relationship. This risk can be reduced through the purchase of contingency insurance, which works as follows (note that in all cases the primary insurance coverage is supplied by the counterparty):

- A pre-paying buyer whose claims for covered damage or loss are not honoured by the seller's insurer would be advanced payment by its contingency insurer, which would assume the buyer's rights against the primary insurer.
- A seller that is unpaid because of failure of the buyer's insurer to honour a claim for covered damage or loss would be advanced payment by its contingency insurer, which would assume the seller's rights against the primary insurer.

Insurance · LC Letters of credit · Liner vessel shipping · Sales contracts · Vessel chartering

Sometimes, sellers are parties-at-risk for only part of the transportation. For instance, the FOB Incoterm holds sellers responsible to their buyers for the condition of the shipped goods until they are loaded on the carrying vessel at the embarkation port. Insurance, called FOB/FAS coverage, is available for this portion of the shipment.

Sources of marine cargo insurance

Marine cargo insurance may be purchased from insurance companies on either a single-shipment or multiple-shipment basis. Single shipment policies are called special risk policies, while those covering multiple shipments are variously called "blanket," "floater" or "open" policies. Owners of blanket policies have the peace of mind of knowing that they have purchased insurance which provides automatic coverage on all shipments that they either are responsible for insuring (CIP or CIF sales), or on which they are responsible for loss or damage to the goods during the main carriage, plus any additional contingency or special coverages (e.g. FOB/FAS) they may have added to the basic policy.

Many freight forwarders and customs brokers own blanket policies, and can therefore arrange marine cargo insurance for their customers.

Some carriers also provide insurance, either through their own blanket policies or by increasing their carrier liability, in return for an additional fee. Caution should be used with the latter method, as it may not provide coverage for the goods after they leave that carrier's immediate control.

Regardless of the source from which the insurance is purchased, most blanket, or floater, or open policies require reporting of individual shipments as they take place. Reporting for exports is normally done by copy of a document called an insurance certificate (or special cargo policy), which also serves as proof of insurance for the buyer. Another document called a declaration is used to report import shipments. In both cases, premiums are billed for actual use.

Duration of insurance coverage on shipments

As important as the type of marine cargo insurance purchased and the source it is purchased from, is the time frame during which insurance is in effect on each shipment. Most insurance policies contain a warehouse-to-warehouse clause which states, essentially, that the insurance applies to a shipment from the time it leaves the point at which it originates to its arrival at the place to which it is to be delivered (with certain time periods after arrival on the buyer's side). However, the actual points at which the insurance coverage attaches

❮see entry in dictionary❯ ✈ Air transport 🏛 Bank collections @ e-commerce 🔠 Incoterms and terminates depends on the Incoterm applicable to the actual shipment. For example, under CIP named place of destination Incoterm, insurance is effected by the seller and will cover from the original place of shipment until the goods are delivered to the buyer at the agreed place on the buyer's side, often the buyer's own warehouse. Conversely, if the Incoterm is CIF named port of destination, insurance coverage will cease when the goods are delivered at the named port of destination, which is not usually the final destination of the goods.

Another example would be an assured buyer purchasing goods under the FOB named port of shipment Incoterm. Although the buyer's insurance may contain a warehouse-to-warehouse clause, coverage comes into effect only at the time the goods have been loaded onboard the vessel at the named port of shipment. Damage that can be identified as having occurred prior to that time would be the responsibility of the seller.

It is therefore important that the buyer and seller carefully review with their insurers the Incoterms on which they usually transact business to be sure they have appropriate coverages.

Calculating marine cargo insurance premiums and CIF/CIP amounts

The Cost Insurance and Freight (CIF) and Carriage and Insurance Paid (CIP) Incoterms require the seller to provide marine cargo insurance. Since these two terms include the same cost factors, the total amounts will be identical. The amount of insurance coverage should be 110% unless the seller and buyer specifically decide otherwise.

Many insurers provide their blanket policyholders with a factor table to assist with premium calculation. It will get you close enough for most purposes if used as follows:

1. Calculate the shipment's Cost and Freight (CFR) or Carriage Paid To (CPT) value by adding the total value of the goods and the total value of the freight costs and such non-freight shipping expenses as export packing and forwarding fees.
2. Determine the insurance premium rate.
3. Select the insurance factor that applies to the insurance premium rate. For instance, the factor for a premium of USD 0.15 per USD 100.00 would be 1.1018.
4. Multiply the CFR or CPT amount by the factor. This is the insured value to be declared on the insurance certificate.
5. To get the premium amount, multiply the insured value by the premium rate and divide the result by 100.

---

6. Add the insurance premium to the CFR or CPT total to get the CIF or CIP total.

Although the above method is generally acceptable, many letters of credit covering CIF or CIP shipments require that the insured value be no less than 110% of the CIF or CIP value, and even a slightly lower insured value would constitute a discrepancy. Since the insurance premium is included in the CIF and CIP values, a circular equation is needed for this level of precision:

1. Calculate the shipment's Cost and Freight (CFR) or Carriage Paid To (CPT) value by adding the total value of the goods and the total value of the freight costs and such non-freight shipping expenses as export packing and forwarding fees.
2. Increase by 110%.
3. Divide the total from step 2 by 100.
4. Add the total from step 3 to the CFR or CPT value.
5. Multiply the total from step 4 by 110%.
6. Divide the total from step 5 by 100.
7. Multiply the total from step 6 by the insurance premium rate.
8. Add the total from step 7 to the CFR or CPT amount
9. Multiply the total from step 8 by 110%
10. Divide the total from step 9 by 100
11. Multiply the total from step 10 by the insurance premium rate. The result is the insurance premium in money.
12. Add the insurance premium from step 11 to the CFR or CPT value to reach the CIF or CIP total.

13. Multiply the CIF or CIP total by 110% for the insured value to be declared on the insurance certificate.

Claims

Transportation is covered by a document or documents that carriers issue as they receive or deliver cargo. For instance, a shipment from an inland location may proceed to a port by truck or rail, and the first carrier should perform at least a casual inspection of the goods when picking them up. At the port, a checker examines non-containerized cargo for obvious damage or shortage, and the delivering carrier should do the same when picking up the shipment at the arrival port. Since each receiving carrier should note any apparent shortage or damage, a paper trail develops as cargo is handed over from one to another. (Obviously, this is less important when one carrier handles the entire transport.) Clean documentation indicates no apparent damage or shortage, while foul documentation pinpoints the place where any apparent problem was discovered, and probably the carrier that had custody of the goods when it occurred.

As the buyer will probably be the first to discover any problems with shipments covered by clean transport documents, there are steps that he or she must take to protect the right to claim:

1. Inspect incoming shipments and indicate any shortage or damage discovered at the time of delivery in writing on the delivering carrier's delivery receipt. Identify damaged shipping pieces individually. Any problems discovered after delivery must be claimed on all carriers within allowable time frames, which vary from country to country. Failure to act promptly could result in a claim becoming time-barred, thereby depriving the insurer of subrogation rights.

2. Segregate damaged goods and their shipping pieces (i.e., boxes, cartons, etc.) and packing materials.

3. Immediately notify the insurer. Most insurance certificates show names and addresses of authorized agents on the back. If there is none in the destination country, contact the nearest Lloyds surveyor or other underwriting organization representative as instructed on the insurance certificate. The insurer will want to have a surveyor examine the damage.

4. Avoid further damage by removing undamaged goods from wet packing, storing under cover, etc. Note: Most insurance policies have "sue and labour" clauses, which provide for reimbursement for such out-of-pocket costs.

5. Assemble the required documentation, including at a minimum the insurance certificate plus a copy of the following: the contract of carriage (transport document), commercial invoice, packing list, claim letters filed with carriers, carrier delivery receipt indicating loss or damage (or carrier confirmation of non-delivery for missing shipments), import clearance documentation, bills covering sue and labour expenses and the surveyor report. This should be sent to the insurer or its local agent along with the claim.

Sellers who provide insurance should inform their customers of these responsibilities.

General average (GA)

General average is a marine-transport provision that if a sacrifice is intentionally made to save the voyage, all parties (cargo owners and the vessel owner) will participate in the loss on a pro-rata basis. A typical general average situation would be the jettisoning of cargo in

---

🔌 Insurance   🔤 Letters of credit   🔱 Liner vessel shipping   📯 Sales contracts   📄 Vessel chartering

order to keep a vessel from sinking. In this case, all cargo owners and the vessel owner would bear a proportion of the loss.

If a general average is declared on a voyage, a general average adjuster is appointed to determine the extent of the loss and of each party's contribution. All cargo owners must place a suitable general average security in order to obtain their cargo. Since general average is covered by marine cargo insurance, this becomes the insurer's responsibility for insured shipments. For uninsured shipments, the security can be in the area of one-third of the value of the shipped goods, and unless an acceptable surety bond can be placed, this may need to be in cash. Although actual general average contributions are normally lower, adjusters set high security levels because of the length of time – normally years – it takes to fully resolve these situations. The mathematics for determining the actual general average contribution for a particular shipment is the value of the cargo divided by the total values of all cargoes and the vessel, multiplied by the total amount of the loss.

Naturally, the level of insurance coverage will determine whether an individual insurer will pay jettisoned-cargo owners.

Many countries use the York Antwerp Rules (YAR1994) for settling general averages.

The following terms used in marine cargo insurance are defined in Key definitions AZ

abandonment

act of God

actual total loss

adventure

all risks

american terms

apparent damage

apparent good order and
    condition

assured

average

average adjuster

beneficiary

brokerage

brokers cover note

captain's protest

cargo insurance

carriage and insurance paid to
    (CIP)…named place of
    destination (Incoterms 2000)

carrier liability limit

casualty

checker

claim

claimant

clean transport document

concealed damage

condensation (sweating)

constructive total loss

contingency insurance

Cost and Insurance (C&I)

Cost, Insurance and Freight
    (CIF)…named port of destination
    (Incoterms 2000)

Cost, Insurance, Freight &
  Commission (CIF&C)
cover note (=broker's cover note)
damage in transit
deck cargo
delay clause
desiccant
deviation clause
excess value
export marks
factor table
floating policy
force majeure
foul transport document
free of capture and seizure
free of particular average (FPA =
  London Institute of Underwriters
  Clause C)
general average (GA)
general average contribution
general average security
hull insurance
inherent vice (of goods)
inland marine cargo insurance
insurable interest
insurance
insurance certificate (=special cargo
  policy)
insurance policy
insurance premium
insurer (=underwriter)
International Civil Aviation
  Organization (ICAO)
International Maritime Organization
  (IMO)
jettison
known loss
London Institute of Underwriters
  Clauses A
London Institute of Underwriters
  Clauses B
London Institute of Underwriters
  Clauses C
loss

marine cargo insurance
mysterious disappearance
neutral marks
on-deck
open marine cargo insurance policy
  (= blanket policy = floating
  policy)
packing list
particular average
party at risk
preliminary notice of claim
Protection and Indemnity Club (P&I
  Club)
reinsurance
rider
risk
self insured
short delivery (SD)
short shipment
soft currency
special cargo policy
special risk policy
strike, riot and civil commotion
  (SRCC)
subrogation
sue and labour clause
surveyor
time bar
title
under deck
valuation clause
war risk
with particular average (WPA = with
  average = WA)
York–Antwerp Rules (Y/A=YAR1994)

Focus on Letters of Credit

Air transport ✈

Bank collections 🏛

e-commerce @

Incoterms ⊞

Insurance ☂

Liner vessel shipping ⚓

Sales contracts ✍

Vessel chartering ⌷

Focus on Letters of Credit (L/C)

Overview

A letter of credit (L/C or "credit") is a conditional undertaking by a financial institution that it will pay a specified amount or amounts at a specified time or times, provided that all terms and conditions described within the L/C have been observed.

- conditional undertaking means that the financial institution is obligated only if all terms and conditions of the letter of credit have been met.
- financial institution: most letters of credit are opened and handled by commercial banks.
- terms and conditions: time frames and performance criteria are normally stated within the letter of credit. These may include documentary evidence for documentary credits, or attestations for standby credits. Banks are not concerned with, or bound by, any underlying contracts for which letters of credit may be issued.

Irrevocable versus revocable

Irrevocable credits cannot be cancelled or amended without the consent of all parties to the credit, including the financial institution that opened it (called the issuing or opening bank), the party that caused it to be opened (called the applicant or account party) and the party in whose favour it is opened (called the beneficiary). For this reason, irrevocable credits provide real payment protection.

Note: In the case of confirmed credits, the confirming bank has the right to decide whether any subsequent amendments will be included in the scope of its confirmation.)

Revocable credits may be cancelled or amended by the issuing bank without the consent of the beneficiary, provided such notice is received before conforming documents have been presented. Revocable credits therefore provide very limited payment protection. Since beneficiaries have an aversion to this type of letter of credit, its use is very limited.

‹see entry in dictionary› ✈ Air transport 🏛 Bank collections © e-commerce ⊞ Incoterms

All credits covered by the current ICC Uniform Customs and Practice for Documentary Credits or International Standby Practices are irrevocable unless they clearly state otherwise.

Types of letters of credit

Documentary credits (also called "commercial" credits) require the presentation of documents that prove certain events have taken place. Common examples cover packing, transport, insurance, any documentation addressing country-specific regulations and a commercial invoice summarizing the transaction. Since presentation of conforming documentation activates the credit, it can be said that documentary credits are intended to be used and that they pay when events happen. Most documentary credits are covered by the current version of International Chamber of Commerce (ICC) Uniform Customs and Practice for Documentary Credits (UCP), but each credit should be checked for this provision, as these rules are not obligatory. All credits communicated by SWIFT are automatically covered by the UCP, but a specific reference to the UCP must be included in onward transmissions of such credits by advising or confirming banks.

Example: Company A instructs its bank to open an irrevocable letter of credit covering the purchase of 1000 widgets for shipment by 1 September from company B. As instructed by the credit, company B must submit to the issuing, advising or confirming bank the required documents in compliance with the letter of credit terms. Typical documents include as a commercial invoice, a packing list and a transport document evidencing shipment on or before 1 September.

Standby credits do not necessarily require the presentation of documentary evidence that events have happened, but rely on attestations. Since "standbys" normally do not guarantee specific performance, they do promise payment to the injured party in the event of nonperformance. For instance, a documentary credit requiring a transport document would pay only if shipment takes place, while a standby covering non-shipment of goods would pay against the beneficiary's attestation that shipment had not been made within the agreed time period.

Standbys are very versatile and may be structured to cover just about any imaginable circumstances. They are often used in lieu of bid bonds and performance bonds. Most standby credits are covered by either the current version of International Standby Practices or Uniform Customs and Practice for Documentary Credits, but each

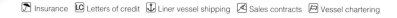

credit should be checked for this provision as these rules are not obligatory.

Example: In order to induce Company Y to supply one million dollars of product on open-account terms of payment, Company Z has its bank open a standby credit in favour of Company Y. The credit should be written to expire sometime after the open account due date(s), and should require Company Y to present a signed statement that Company Z failed to pay as agreed in order to draw and collect payment from the bank.

Confirmed versus unconfirmed

Confirmation is the adding of a separate undertaking by a financial institution to a letter of credit in addition to that of the issuing financial institution. By contrast, an unconfirmed letter of credit does not bear any undertaking other than that of the financial institution that issued it. All letters of credit lacking specific confirmation notices from any additional banks are considered unconfirmed.

Sight versus time

Letters of credit may be paid either promptly (sight) or at a future time (usance), based upon presentation of conforming documents.

Banks have a reasonable time (up to seven banking days from presentation) to determine whether or not to take up documents. As the term implies, sight letters of credit pay at sight against compliant presentations made to issuing or confirming banks. Banks receiving compliant presentations against credits that they have merely advised are not required to pay until/unless they have obtained reimbursement.

Usance letters of credit are payable at a predetermined time after the presentation of conforming documentation. There are two varieties – those calling for a draft to be accepted and those that do not. Those calling for a draft to be accepted by a bank create bankers' acceptances, which are drafts (demands for payment) accepted for maturity at a future time by banks. These financial instruments are considered low risk, and can usually be discounted without recourse for immediate payment at attractive rates.

Usance credits not requiring a draft do not in themselves give rise to a financial instrument.

Although not a type of letter of credit, value dating can affect when beneficiaries will be paid against compliant drawings. Value dating is the practice of remitting payment with a future effective date; i.e. the funds are not actually available until the stipulated "value" date, which could be some days after the remittance instructions.

Important dates

Letters of credit incorporate time lines that must be strictly observed.

Expiry date: The date on which the commitment of a letter of credit's opening and confirming bank (if any) ends. Unless a credit contains other requirements, it is also the latest date that conforming documents may be presented to the designated bank. All credits must have an expiry date. An expiry date that falls on a bank holiday or recognized non-working day in the designated bank's country is automatically extended to the next banking day.

(Latest) presentation date: The latest date that conforming documents may be presented to the bank designated in the credit. This may be the expiry date, or another date based on a formula contained within the credit such as: "Documents must be presented within fifteen days of the date of the shipping document." In the absence of such a formula, the documents must be presented not later than 21 days after the date of shipment or by the credit's expiry date, whichever occurs first.

(Latest) shipment date: The latest date that may appear as the shipment or on-board date on any transport documents required by a letter of credit. Unlike expiry dates, latest shipping dates do not extend because of holidays.

Amendments

An amendment is an advice by the issuing bank of any proposed change to the terms and conditions of a letter of credit. Any term of an irrevocable letter of credit can be changed or deleted, or new terms can be introduced, provided the change is acceptable to all parties. (Of course, issuing banks do not need to obtain agreement of other parties to amend a revocable L/C.)

The beneficiary and any confirming bank may choose to accept or reject any amendment(s) generated by the applicant. Conversely, if a beneficiary requires an amendment, the request must be communicated to the applicant who, if agreeable, would authorize the issuing bank to issue the amendment.

Governing rules

Uniform Customs and Practice for Documentary Credits (UCP):
These International Chamber of Commerce rules standardize the use

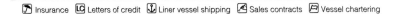

Insurance   Letters of credit   Liner vessel shipping   Sales contracts   Vessel chartering

of documentary L/Cs throughout the world. They are updated approximately every ten years to reflect current banking practice.

> **To apply to a particular L/C, UCP rules must be specifically cited. However, they are so frequently used that this citation is often pre-printed on the L/C form itself. As mentioned earlier, all credits communicated by SWIFT are automatically subject to the UCP.**

International Standby Practices (ISP): These International Chamber of Commerce rules standardize the use of many standby letters of credit throughout the world. The first version took effect on 1 January 1999.

> **To apply to a particular L/C, ISP rules must be specifically cited. Since ISP rules are rather new, it is possible to find standby L/Cs covered by the current version of the Uniform Customs and Practice for Documentary Credits (UCP).**

Bank participants

Issuing bank: The financial institution that opens a letter of credit is called the issuing or opening bank. It sends the L/C to its correspondent bank in the beneficiary's country, which will then forward it (with or without adding its confirmation) to the beneficiary. The issuing bank may also send a credit directly to the beneficiary. However, to avoid the possibility of fraud, care should be taken with credits issued abroad that are not routed through a bank in the beneficiary's country. See "The role of advising banks" below.

Correspondent bank: A bank that is engaged in a bank-to-bank relationship with another that includes the exchange of signatures, test keys and settlement of funds agreement. This relationship is essential in the L/C process of advising, confirming and negotiating credits.

Advising bank: An advising bank passes a letter of credit issued by another bank to the beneficiary or another designated third party, without adding its confirmation. According to the UCP, this bank's sole responsibility is to take reasonable care in establishing the apparent authenticity of the letter of credit it advises. If it does anything more, consider it good customer service.

> **It is possible for there to be more than one bank advising a credit. This happens most often when a beneficiary requests that a credit be advised through its own bank which does not have a correspondent relationship with the issuing bank. In such cases, the issuing bank will transmit the letter to its correspondent bank for authentication, with instructions to relay the credit on to the beneficiary's bank.**

Confirming bank: A confirming bank is one that adds its separate undertaking to that of the issuing bank. See "Confirmed versus unconfirmed" above.

Negotiating bank: Any bank other than the opening bank authorized within the letter of credit terms to give value for presentation of conforming documents against a letter of credit. This bank may be the advising or confirming bank.

Accepting bank: A financial institution that executes a banker's acceptance on a usance draft or time drafts drawn against a letter of credit. See "Sight versus time" above and "Banker's acceptance" below.

> **Although possibly designated as accepting banks in the texts of L/Cs, banks are not bound to accept drafts drawn against letters of credit that they did not issue or confirm, unless they otherwise indicate their willingness to do so.**

Paying bank: The bank designated in a letter of credit as the party that will honour drafts drawn under the L/C.

Reimbursing bank: A bank nominated by the issuing bank to pay a negotiating, accepting or paying bank in a L/C transaction. Typically, the opening bank has an account at the reimbursing bank, and the reimbursing bank will honour the reimbursement request with no liability as to the validity of the claim. Reimbursing banks are not interested in the terms and conditions of the underlying letter of credit.

The following terms also speak to bank participation:

Freely negotiable: A letter of credit that can be presented with conforming documents to any bank. With freely negotiable credits, any bank is considered authorized within the letter of credit terms to give value for presentation of conforming documents.

Restricted negotiation: A letter of credit that limits negotiation to a specified bank or banks. (It is the opposite of a freely negotiable L/C.)

Do not become overwhelmed by this array of different banking roles. We define them all as one or another may come into play, depending on the way the credit is structured and the relationships among the banks involved. The protection provided by a letter of credit depends on the issuing bank, any bank that adds its confirmation, and the beneficiary's ability to abide with its terms and conditions.

Practice

Issuing

A seller and buyer enter a sales contract, specifying payment terms involving an irrevocable letter of credit. The buyer (applicant) instructs

its bank to open and forward it to a correspondent bank in the seller's country.

At this point, the issuing bank may issue a pre-advice, an official notice usually via telecommunication, that it is opening the referenced L/C by hard copy, either concurrently or within a reasonable time. Pre-advices typically identify the issuing bank's reference number, the applicant, the beneficiary, the tenor and the amount and currency for which the L/C will be issued. Since most L/Cs today are issued electronically, the practice of giving pre-advice is declining. Instead, the issuing bank will probably issue the actual L/C in either paper or more commonly electronic form.

If requested, the corresponding bank may or may not decide to add its confirmation, but in any case will authenticate the credit.

Compliance

Since all letters of credit contain terms and conditions and require the presentation of some sort of documents for payment, beneficiaries should carefully examine them upon receipt. While documentary evidence of compliance is the very nature of documentary credits, even "standbys" require presentation of something and have expiry dates.

Documents are paper instruments (or electronic message units) that prove certain events have taken place. While a documentary credit may call for virtually any conceivable document, the following are commonly required: commercial invoice, packing list, transport document, insurance certificate, and country-specific documents such as origin certificate, consularized certification and pre-shipment clean report of findings. Applicants and beneficiaries should check to ensure that a credit's documentary requirements match the sales contract and do not conflict with each other.

Beneficiaries of documentary letters of credit should immediately send a copy to the forwarders and/or carriers that they plan to use. Often, credits have hidden problems that are obvious only to documentation and transportation experts. Finding them early enables the beneficiary to request any necessary amendments before shipping.

Unresolved discrepancies put payments at risk, since banks are not required to pay against discrepant presentations. A discrepancy occurs when one or more documents or dates do not comply with the L/C terms and conditions, or documents are inconsistent with each other, or where the current ICC Uniform Customs and Practice for Documentary Credits or International Standby Practices rules are broken. Common discrepancies include:

- presentation after the L/C expiration date

- shipment made after the latest permitted shipment date
- quantities shown on the commercial invoice that differ from the shipped quantities shown on the transport document
- weights and dimensions shown on the packing list that differ from the transport document
- more than 21 days have elapsed between the date of shipment indicated on the transport document and the date documents are presented
- spelling in one or more documents that differs from the letter of credit text
- drawings exceed the letter of credit amount
- failure to present one or more required documents
- partial shipment where prohibited by the L/C
- a required draft is drawn on the wrong party
- on-deck shipment not expressly permitted by the L/C
- insurance incorrectly calculated (recent ICC opinion reduces the likelihood of this happening).

There are several remedies for letter of credit discrepancies. Beneficiaries have the right to re-present corrected documents if this can be done within the letter of credit time constraints. If corrected documents cannot be re-presented in time, the beneficiary may ask the applicant to either amend the credit or authorize the issuing bank to pay despite the discrepancy (called permission to pay). Should neither of these work, the documents may be sent to the opening bank on approval with the stipulation that they not be released unless the applicant waives the discrepancy.

Given the importance of compliant documentation, many letter of credit beneficiaries have their presentations reviewed by their bankers even when their bank is not involved in the transaction. People experienced in letter of credit examination can more readily catch discrepancies than can most beneficiaries. Such discrepancies are often correctable if caught early, but can become incurable if too much time passes. While this provides an added level of protection, it must be noted that bankers do not always agree on what constitutes a discrepancy. Should this happen where the beneficiary's bank is not a party to the credit, its opinion will not prevail.

Interested third parties

Often, letter of credit beneficiaries require financing to produce or purchase the goods for which the letter of credit was opened. There are several ways that the L/C can be used as collateral.

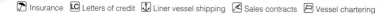

Transferable letters of credit specifically permit transfer of rights from the original beneficiary to one or more second beneficiaries. The first beneficiary executes an irrevocable transfer document at the bank handling the transfer, causing it to issue notices of transfer to the second beneficiary(ies). The second beneficiary(ies) then performs against their transferred portions, is paid for compliant presentation, and the original beneficiary then substitutes its invoices for the remaining balance, if any. The transferred terms and conditions must be identical to those of the original letter of credit, except that the transferred amount(s), any unit pricing, latest presentation dates and the period of shipment may be curtailed.

This procedure applies only to letters of credit that specifically permit transfer.

A back-to-back letter of credit involves the issuing of a completely separate (second) letter of credit, collateralized by another (first) L/C to a third party at the instructions of the first L/C's beneficiary. Since documents presented under the second L/C trigger payment of the first L/C, it is important that all terms and conditions be identical between the two credits; except that the amount(s), expiry and any latest presentation times for the second L/C may be reduced.

In an assignment of proceeds, a letter of credit beneficiary (assignor) instructs the issuing, advising or confirming bank that all or part of the payment(s) resulting from the credit be made to one or more designated third parties (assignee(s)). Such third parties could include vendors or a lender. This assignment document contains qualifying text, such as: "funds will be paid by the bank 'if and when' payment is received from the issuing bank." Unlike transferable letters of credit, the proceeds of any letter of credit may be assigned without the need of authorization within the L/C. Further, the L/C applicant will probably never be made aware that the proceeds have been assigned.

Letter of credit variations

About, approximately, circa: Any of these words modifies whatever comes immediately after it in the letter of credit text by plus-or-minus ten per cent (10%). Therefore, a credit opened for "about USD 10 000" could support drawings anywhere from USD 9 000 to USD 11 000 while a credit permitting shipment of "about 1000" widgets could accommodate shipments of anywhere from 900 to 1100 widgets. A credit stating a unit price of "approximately USD 100" would permit a unit price from USD 90 to USD 110.

Since the term applies only to whatever immediately follows, it must

be used each time it is intended for the money amount, the shipped quantity and/or the unit price.

Evergreen L/C: An evergreen letter of credit automatically renews itself beyond the stated expiration date for a specified time period, provided that the issuing bank does not inform the beneficiary of its intention not to renew within a specified time before the credit's expiration or extended expiration date.

Green clause: A green clause letter of credit permits disbursements prior to shipment. Drawings against green-claused L/Cs must usually be supported by evidence, such as a warehouse receipt that the goods for which payment is being requested are stored under the control of the bank advancing payment.

Red clause: A red clause letter of credit permits disbursements prior to shipment, in the form of a loan or a payment in the name of the negotiating or issuing bank to the beneficiary. If no drawing is subsequently made, the issuing bank must reimburse the negotiating bank for the amount advanced plus interest at the expiration date of the letter of credit. The applicant should have a high level of trust in the beneficiary's ability and willingness to otherwise perform according to the terms and conditions of the letter of credit. The red clause, however, may be a good alternative to an advance down payment.

Revolving: A revolving letter of credit, once used, comes back to life for repeated drawing(s). A true revolving credit calls for automatic reinstatement after each drawing or at specified time intervals.

Note: pseudo-revolving credits provide for reinstatement by amendment only. They are not true revolving credits, as the applicant or the opening bank can frustrate the purpose by simply not issuing the necessary amendment.

Straight: A letter of credit payable only at the opening bank or a bank specified within the credit.

eUCP

Early in 2000, the ICC Banking Commission began work on "eUCP;" a supplement to the UCP 500 covering the presentation of electronic documents alone, or in combination with paper documents. This significant change comes into force on 1 April 2002.

Electronic documentary letter of credit presentation will obviously be a "work in process" for years to come. Banks throughout the world

must wean themselves from the perceived security of paper documentation, and familiarize themselves with the various methods of secure documentary transmission. The documentary transmission methods themselves are still in their infancy, and many potential users have yet to be registered. Despite these obstacles, e-UCP will attract growing attention and use. Increasingly, buyers, sellers, government authorities and carriers are using electronic means to communicate, creating paperless documentation.

The following terms used in letters of credit are defined in Key definitions AZ

about

accepting bank

account party

advised letter of credit

advising bank

amendment

applicant

application

approximately

assignee

assignment of L/C proceeds

assignor

authority to pay

authority to purchase

back-to-back L/C

banker's acceptance

beneficiary

circa

confirmed L/C

confirming bank

correspondent bank

deferred payment L/C

discrepancy

documentary L/C

documents

draft

drawing

evergreen L/C

freely negotiable L/C

green clause L/C

International Standby Practices (ISP)

irrevocable L/C

issue date

issuing bank

letter of credit (L/C)

negotiating bank

negotiation

opening bank

paying bank

payment under reserve

pre-advice

presentation date

red clause L/C

reimbursing bank

reinstatement

restricted negotiation

revolving L/C

Society for Worldwide Interbank Funds Telecommunications (SWIFT)

standby L/C

straight L/C

tenor

transferable L/C

Uniform Customs and Practice for Documentary Credits (UCP)

usance

usance draft

usance L/C

value dating

‹see entry in dictionary›   ✈ Air transport   🏦 Bank collections   @ e-commerce   🔡 Incoterms

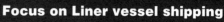

A to Z
of international trade

Air transport ✈

Bank collections 🏛

e-commerce @

Incoterms ⊞

Insurance 🏖

Letters of credit LC

Sales contracts ✍

Vessel chartering 🏳

Focus on Liner Vessel Shipping

Overview

"Liner" (or "berth") terms refer to a certain type of marine transport between ports. Under these terms, the carrier takes on the tasks of providing vessel berthing, terminal service, vessel loading and unloading at both origin and destination ports, and the potential problem of vessel demurrage. Some charter-vessel owners provide berth-terms service. More important to this section, virtually all ship lines do.

Generally, liner service means regularly scheduled service provided by a carrier having a fixed port rotation and advertising it as such. Such carriers maintain facilities at the ports where they call to receive and load outbound freight and unload and dispatch inbound cargoes. While some carriers will call on additional ports, given sufficient cargo inducement, the estimated times of departure (ETD) and arrival (ETA) shown in their posted schedules are reasonably reliable. This predictability of service and the facilities that carriers have at their normal ports of call distinguish liner vessel shipments from their older counterparts, charter and tramp (irregular) shipping.

To understand how liner shipments work, we must visualize a large modern port – sprawling fenced complexes with enforced security and limited access. No longer do shippers bring their cargo pier-side. Instead, it is handed over at the port's land gateway or at a carrier's terminal, often located a considerable distance from the pier. On arrival, incoming cargoes are subject to a quick visual inspection by a checker (in the case of containerized cargo, only the container is inspected). A dock receipt (see "marine transport documents" below), indicating either that the goods have been received for transport in apparent good order (clean) or indicating apparent shortage or damage (variously called unclean, claused or foul), is then signed. Short or damaged shipments should be stopped at that point until the problem has been resolved, although some carriers will accept a back letter absolving them from responsibility for issuing a clean transport document for a short or damaged shipment. A receiving report is also (often electronically) transmitted to the ship line office, which will ultimately generate a marine transport document.

All carriers require receipt of outbound cargo by a closing (or cut-off) date, usually some days prior to actual vessel loading. Cargo arriving later will be held (called "rolled over") for the next sailing.

Since many ship lines operate container vessels, almost anything that can be transported by container will go in one. Shippers themselves normally load their full containerload shipments, while less than containerload shipments are loaded by container consolidators (often called NVOCCs) or the ship lines themselves at their container freight stations (CFS).

Although most liner vessels are of the container or roll-on/roll-off (Ro/Ro) variety, there are still a few carriers that will accept breakbulk (loose) cargoes or a combination of breakbulk and containers.

These modern port geography and shipping methods have several implications for liner shipping:

1. The old concept of the ship's rail as the point where the transfer of responsibility for the condition of shipped goods occurs is becoming functionally meaningless.
2. The carrier-issued document showing that goods have been received for shipment in apparent good order is taking on greater significance than on-board documentation.
3. There is less pilferage because of limited port access and increased container usage.

Freight costs have become heavily influenced by two recent trends: the increase in shippers' associations, where unrelated shippers pool their volume to achieve bargaining power with the carriers, and confidential service contracts, under which agreed freight rates and services are not disclosed to third parties.

Practice

Freight cost calculation

Ship lines publish commodity-based price lists called (freight) tariffs that indicate the cost of pure freight (called the base rate) and any applicable surcharges (accessorial charges). The base rate is often commodity-specific, and is calculated on a billing unit called a revenue

ton. Revenue tons are calculated by comparing a shipment's size (measurement tons) versus its gross shipping weight. This is done because the amount of cargo that any vessel can carry on a single voyage is limited by its weight capacity and the amount of space it has to store cargo.

There are three different formulas in general use for determining the total number of revenue tons in a given shipment:

1. METRIC: the greater of the total number of cubic metres versus the total number of metric tons.

   Method: determine the number of cubic meters (one cubic metre = 35.31 cubic feet), and compare to the number of metric tons (1000 kilos or 2204.6 lbs.). Multiply the freight rate by the greater resulting number.

2. 40-SHORT TON: the greater of total cubic feet / 40 versus the total gross weight in pounds / short ton.

   Method: determine the number of cubic feet (one cubic foot = 0.02832 cubic metre), divide the total by 40, and compare to the number of short tons (2000 pounds or 907.2 kilos). Multiply the freight rate by the greater resulting number.

3. 40-LONG TON: the greater of total cubic feet / 40 versus the total gross weight in pounds / long ton.

   Method: determine the number of cubic feet (one cubic foot = 0.02832 cubic metre), divide the total by 40, and compare to the number of long tons (2240 pounds or 1016 kilos). Multiply the freight rate by the greater resulting number.

Notes:
1.   Some carriers insist that the length, width and height dimensions be rounded up to the next whole centimetre or inch.
2.   As these three formulas produce different results, it is important that the carrier and the party contracting for carriage clearly understand which one applies.
3.   Some carriers use other formulas. Examples include charging on the overall length of pleasure boats falling within specified maximum width and height and weight limitations, or even flat rates per unit such as X dollars per locomotive.

In addition to the cost of pure freight, liner shipments are subject to surcharges that reflect extra costs over which the carrier has little direct control. Some are calculated on the number of revenue tons (as freighted) while others are percentages of the freight cost or flat fees. Typical surcharges include:

- Bunker adjustment factor (BAF = bunker surcharge = BS), which reflects the cost of fuel (called bunkers). It is handled separately, as fuel is subject to frequent price fluctuations.
- Currency adjustment charge (CAC = currency adjustment factor CAF) reflects changes in the exchange rate of the currency in which the freight costs are billed. It is handled separately because exchange rates fluctuate more often than freight costs do.
- Congestion surcharge (= port congestion surcharge) reflects additional expenses that ship lines incur when calling at congested ports.
- Terminal handling charge (THC) covers vessel loading and unloading and cartage within the port area. It is handled separately as such costs are port-specific.
- Container positioning is an additional fee for the use of the carrier's container, imposed for destinations with little return cargo or high risk of loss or damage to the container.
- Arbitrary, which is an additional fee that ship lines charge for serving markets outside the hinterlands of their normal ports of call. For instance, an Irish arbitrary is often applied to shipments made through hub ports in the United Kingdom.

While most ship lines will provide per-container freight charges for full-container shipments, the underlying arithmetic remains the same. Full-container freight quotations should be examined to determine at what point the carrier's responsibility for carriage starts and stops.

- Door to door includes pre-carriage, main carriage and on-carriage.
- Door to port includes pre-carriage and main carriage.
- Port to port is main carriage only.

Further, full-container freight charges may or may not be lump sum, which means that surcharges may or may not be included. Shippers should also check the availability of empty containers, the location of the container yard from which they come and the amount of free time provided for container loading before demurrage charges begin to accrue.

Ship lines may belong to a conference, an association of carriers serving the same routes and using the same tariff, or may act as independents. The new trend toward confidential freight-cost negotiation has resulted in fewer and weaker conferences.

Some carriers offer freight rebates – refunds of a portion of previously paid transportation charges – usually in return for the shipper's achieving a certain volume. However, as freight rebating is illegal in some countries, it can have the unintended consequence of making

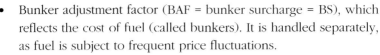

legitimate claims against carriers difficult to pursue, lest they be considered rebates in disguise.

Forwarders

A forwarder is a person or company that arranges transportation, usually on behalf of the party contracting for main carriage. While some forwarders specialize in marine or air transportation, many handle both. Many provide additional services, such as assistance with country-specific documentary requirements, insurance, storage and even customs clearance. Typically, forwarders obtain part of their income from brokerage commission that they receive when booking cargoes with the carrier(s) they select, and in this respect they resemble travel agents. The remainder comes from fees that they negotiate with their clients. This makes using forwarders cost-effective. Forwarders assist their clients with carrier selection by obtaining freight quotations. In fact, some forwarders act in the capacity of carriers by providing NVOCC or airfreight consolidation services.

Some countries require that forwarders be licensed or registered, at least to be eligible for brokerage income.

Containerization

Ship lines offering containerized service prefer cargo to be containerized prior to arrival at the port of loading. This happens either when shippers make full container shipments or through consolidation at NVOCCs (see below) or at container freight stations outside the port areas. Since they do not actually see the loaded cargo when it arrives at the port in loaded, locked and sealed containers, ship lines clause their transport documents "said to contain," "shipper's load and count," or similar notations.

Containers comply with International Standards Organization (ISO) standards and are available in 20- and 40-foot lengths. They typically come in dry cargo, open top, refrigerated, high cube, flat rack and tank variations, and a few carriers offer 45-foot long containers for certain areas.

NOTES:

1.   **Actual vessel container internal and external dimensions vary from manufacturer to manufacturer and from carrier to carrier.**

2.   **Since all carriers do not always provide the full range of containers, it is important to check for availability when planning a containerized shipment.**

3.   **Containerization reduces the need for export packing, subject to the inherent nature of the shipped goods and knowledge of conditions**

at the destination. For instance, cargo subject to unloading and storage at rural arrival points should be export-packed even though it will travel in a container during main carriage.

4.   Containers must be carefully packed. Cargo must be blocked and braced to prevent in-transit shifting, and maximum container capacities must be observed. Cargoes susceptible to moisture damage should be protected with moisture-barrier wrapping and desiccants.

The trade uses curious shorthand when discussing container quantities. A twenty-foot equivalent unit (TEU) is one twenty-foot container. A forty-foot equivalent unit (FEU) equals two twenty-foot containers. Therefore 2 TEUs = 1 FEU.

Containerized cargo often travels by what is called "landbridge routing." This applies both to shipper-loaded full container shipments and less-than-containerload shipments that have been consolidated into full container loads. Landbridge means that cargo travels from coast to coast by ground transport, usually rail. This is often ship-ground-ship, for example: Yokohama-Seattle-Baltimore-Felixstowe. There are two variations of landbridge: mini landbridge where the goods move by sea to a coastal port and then across a country by land (ship-ground or ground-ship), and micro landbridge where ground shipment leg is shorter (between a port and an inland location). A single carrier (the provider of main carriage transportation) takes responsibility for the entire shipment.

Container consolidators gather less-than-containerload (LCL) shipments and fill containers (called stuffing) at their warehouses. At destination, the containers are unloaded (devanned) for local delivery.

Consolidation (groupage) of less-than-containerload shipments provides advantages, including lower pilferage potential, possibly lower freight costs and reduction in required export packing. The disadvantages include: possible delay of an individual shipment awaiting sufficient additional cargo to fill a container, possible problems resulting from incompatible cargo traveling in close proximity and possible duplicate freight costs should the consolidator fail to pay the undercarrier.

Non-vessel operating common carriers (NVOCCs) are indirect carriers that use ship lines as sub-contractors to actually perform the carriage. Although this practice began as container consolidation, NVOCCs have expanded their activities to include reselling transportation in the full-container market. Defined as "carriers in relation to shippers and shippers in relation to carriers," NVOCCs issue their own tariffs and get exceptionally low freight-of-all-kinds (FAK) full container freight

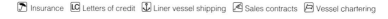

Insurance   Letters of credit   Liner vessel shipping   Sales contracts   Vessel chartering

costs from the ship lines because of the large number of shipments they generate.

Many large forwarders have set up their own NVOCC operations. While this can provide the convenience of one-stop shopping, it can blur the distinction between forwarder as agent and carrier.

Contracts of carriage

Either the exporter or the importer may select the carrier and contract for carriage, and the carrier will follow the instructions of whichever party does so. Freight prepaid means that the exporter pays the freight charges; freight collect means the importer does. The party paying the freight normally also pays any applicable surcharges. This can present problems with the FAS and FOB Incoterms, where terminal handling charges are a seller responsibility while freight charges are paid by the buyer.

Contracts of carriage for liner transport may be made with ship lines (called vessel operating common carriers or VOCCs) or with NVOCCs. A forwarder representing either the seller or buyer will normally handle the actual shipping arrangements, beginning with making a reservation for the shipment (called a booking) with the carrier. All further arrangements will reference the number assigned to the booking, and it will appear on all transport documents.

The terms of the contract of carriage may reflect the national law of the country from which shipment is made, as is the case with the (very different) Carriage of Goods by Sea Acts of the United Kingdom and the United States. However, they more likely will reflect one of the three sets of rules for marine carriage contracts in general use: the Hague Rules, the Hague-Visby Rules, or the Hamburg Rules. Each of these rules has differing levels of carrier responsibility and liability, so it is important that whoever is contracting for carriage knows which set applies.

The party contracting for carriage should make its wishes known to the carrier, usually through a forwarder, by carefully completing a shipper's letter of instruction (SLI). Such information should at a minimum include: the name and address of the shipper (consignor), consignment instructions (order or direct consignment), the name and address of any notify party, a description of the cargo with weights and dimensions, whether the shipment is prepaid or collect, and any other services required of the forwarder (such as insurance or export clearance).

Marine transport documents

Following instructions provided in the shipper's letter of instruction, the forwarder will provide appropriate documentation to the carrier for its signature and return. Clean transport documents are those bearing no indication of shortage or damage (for letter of credit purposes, transport documents with "on-deck" notations are also not considered clean). The opposite of clean transport documents, those bearing damage or shortage notations, are variously called "claused" or "foul."

Dock receipt: A document usually prepared by a forwarder, signed by a ship line, and returned to the delivering trucker as a receipt indicating that a specific shipment has been brought to the port.

Marine (ocean) bill of lading (B/L): A transport document issued or signed by a ship line or NVOCC. All B/Ls must indicate the date of issue, name of shipper and place of shipment, place of delivery, description of goods and carrier's signature.

- Negotiable marine B/Ls show the word "order" in the consignee field. Once signed by the carrier and endorsed by the shipper, they become bearer instruments of title to the shipped goods. Negotiable B/Ls permit goods to be sold and resold while in transit by the simple expedient of passing on the original B/L to the new owner(s). For these reasons, carriers will insist upon surrender of the original negotiable B/L prior to releasing the goods. As marine B/Ls are frequently issued in sets of three originals, and as any one of the originals serves to release the goods, unpaid sellers should carefully control the accessibility of all three originals.

- Non-negotiable marine B/Ls (straight B/Ls or sea waybills) do not show the word "order" in the consignee field; therefore only the party shown in the consignee field has the right to take delivery. As some countries do not recognize non-negotiable B/Ls as B/Ls at all, but classify them as "sea waybills," it is important for sellers and buyers to agree whether the document is to be issued in negotiable form.

- Sea waybills (liner waybills) are non-negotiable marine transport documents.

- House bills of lading are marine transport documents issued by NVOCCs. They are backed up by marine transport documents issued to the NVOCCs by the undercarriers.

- Data freight receipts, also called data freight releases, are electronic (paperless) versions of sea waybills. Instructions for the disposition of shipped cargo are electronically transmitted from carrier offices or agents on the seller's side to their counterparts on the buyer's side.

- Forwarder's certificate of receipt is a document issued by a forwarder stating that it has received or controls certain cargo for shipment to a particular consignee. These quasi-transport documents can provide security for buyers when issued by buyer-appointed forwarders.

Both bills of lading and sea waybills can be either on-board or received for shipment. On-board documents indicate that the shipped goods have been loaded on the carrying vessel. Received for shipment documents indicate that the shipped goods have been handed over to the control of the main carrier, but not necessarily loaded on the carrying vessel.

The voyage

Many ship lines use a distribution pattern resembling the hub-and-spoke system beloved by air carriers. Hub ports are base ports served by large (usually transoceanic) vessels. Smaller ships called feeder vessels bring cargoes from the hub ports to the smaller spoke-like ports.

The fact that these transshipments regularly take place is not obvious from the transport documents. In fact, many shippers, consignees and bankers are unaware that transshipments are happening at all. Important considerations in evaluating transshipments include whether the carrier has its own feeder vessels and whether the carrier assumes point-to-point liability.

On arrival

Ship lines are supposed to provide an arrival notice to the "notify party" shown on the transport document. However, some do so more reliably than others. For this reason, it is usually a good idea to alert the buyer by faxing a non-negotiable copy of the transport document.

Depending upon the scope of the contract of carriage, arrival could be at the carrier's terminal or the point where inland freight on the buyer's side (on-carriage) ends. Depending upon how the shipment was consigned, the consignee will need to provide the carrier with either identification or an original negotiable marine bill of lading. Consignees lacking an original negotiable marine B/L need to provide a letter of indemnity (often supported by a surety bond or bank guarantee) in order to take delivery of the cargo.

The following terms used in liner vessel transport are defined in Key definitions [AZ]

accomplished bill of lading

advance freight

apparent damage

apparent good order and
    condition

arbitrary

arrest

arrival notice (AN)

as freighted

back letter

base port

base rate

bill of lading (B/L)

booking

booking number

booking rollover

breakbulk cargo

bulk cargo

bunker adjustment factor (BAF =
    bunker surcharge BS)

captain's protest

cargo sharing

carriage contract

Carriage of Goods by Sea Act (UK)

Carriage of Goods by Sea Act (US)

carrier

checker

clean transport document

closing date

combined transport document (CTD)

common carrier

conference (liner)

congestion surcharge (= port
    congestion surcharge)

consolidation

consignee

consignment

consignor

container

container freight station (CFS)

container seal

container yard (CY)

currency adjustment charge (CAC =
    currency adjustment factor CAF)

data freight receipt (= Data Freight
    Release)

dead freight

deck cargo

demurrage

dock

dock receipt

door-to-door

door-to-port

drayage

estimated time of arrival (ETA)

estimated time of departure (ETD)

feeder vessel

FIATA B/L (FBL)

fighting ship

flag carrier

forty-foot equivalent (FEU)

forwarder

forwarder's certificate of receipt

foul transport document

free time

freight collect

freight of all kinds (FAK)

freight prepaid

freight rebate

full container load (FCL)

gross weight

guaranteed freight

Hague Rules

Hague-Visby Rules

Hamburg Rules

heavy lift

high cube

house bill of lading

hub and spoke

husbanding

independent carrier

inducement

Institute of International Container
    Lessors (IICL)

intermediate consignee
intermodal container transfer facility
     (ICTF)
International Container Bureau (BIC)
International Maritime Organization
landbridge
less than container load (LCL)
letter of indemnity (LOI = steamer
     guarantee)
liner service
liner terms
lighterage
lump sum
mafi
main carriage
manifest (cargo)
micro landbridge
mini landbridge
multimodal transport
multimodal transport document
multimodal transport operator (MTO)
negotiable B/L (= order B/L)
net weight
no show
non-negotiable B/L (= Straight B/L)
non-vessel operating common
     carrier (NVOCC)
notify party
ocean transportation intermediary
on-board B/L
on-board notation
on-carriage
on-deck
pier
port-to-port
pre-carriage
range

received for shipment B/L (=
     received for carriage B/L)
revenue ton (R/T)
roll-on/roll-off (RO-RO)
rounding
said to contain (STC = said to weigh
     STW)
sea waybill
ship's rail
ship's tackle
shipment (on board a vessel)
shipment date
shipper
shipper's letter of instructions (SLI)
shipper's load and count (SL&C)
shippers' association
shipping documents
short form B/L
slot charter
surcharge (= accessorial charge)
tariff (freight)
terminal handling charge (THC)
through bill of lading
through rate
through transport
trailer on flat car (= piggyback =
     TOFC)
transshipment
twenty-foot equivalent (TEU)
ultimate consignee
under deck
undercarrier
vessel operating common carrier
     (VOCC)
voyage
waybill
wharf

Focus on Sales contracts

A to Z
international trade

Air transport ✈

Bank collections 🏛

e-commerce @

Incoterms ⊞

Insurance ⟋

Letters of credit LC

Liner vessel shipping ⚓

Vessel chartering ⌂

Focus on Sales Contracts

Caveat: This appendix was written by an experienced foreign trader rather than by an attorney. It contains only generally applicable information, and should not be considered legal advice. Coverage is limited to the international sale of tangible goods and excludes real estate and such downstream issues as royalties and after-sales service.

Contract law varies from country to country. Further, some industries have their own well-established trade practices. Readers are urged to refer individual situations to competent legal counsel before contracting.

Overview

By definition, international sales of goods imply that sellers and buyers are located in different countries. This presents an obvious potential for confusion, as most commercial law is country specific, reflecting national trade practices, values and public policy. However, some general advice is possible for several reasons. There are many similarities among the different bodies of national contract law. Some national laws are consolidating into regional law, as seen in the European Union. There is an ever-increasing trend toward international standardization, such as ISO standards, the Harmonized System, Incoterms and the United Nations Convention on Contracts for the International Sale of Goods (CISG). Some industries have long-established trade practices that are followed throughout the world. Since many countries allow their citizens considerable freedom of contract, informed sellers and buyers will usually craft agreements that serve their mutual interests. Finally, most people are reasonably honest, carefully consider their responsibilities before committing, and fully intend to do what they promise.

What is important

A well-considered contract for the international sale of goods should include agreement on the following points. Remember, in case of dispute, whatever important information the parties fail to include will probably be imputed by an arbitral tribunal or court of law. This body will look at any previous dealings between the parties, usual practice of the trade, and other considerations. The results could be very different from what the parties had really intended.

- Parties
- Product
- Quantity
- Delivery
- Price
- Payment terms
- Transfer of ownership
- Other important points.

Parties: At a minimum, the seller and buyer should be identified. It may also be important to identify any additional parties to the transaction, such as agents representing either party.

Product: The contract goods should be specified at least to the degree that they can be identified. Naturally, greater precision in describing them reduces the potential for misunderstanding.

Quantity: In most cases, a quantity can be expressed in actual terms (units, kilos, etc.). When this cannot be done at the time a contract is drafted, a quantity range should be established. Some industries work with generally accepted commercial tolerances. Also, letters of credit can be structured to provide plus-or-minus 10 per cent tolerances by using the word "about."

Delivery: The time and place of delivery should be established as clearly as possible. Incoterms 2000 provide an excellent reference point as they are widely used throughout the world, allocate major tasks between seller and buyer, and indicate the point where seller responsibility for the condition of contract goods ends.

Where delivery takes place on the seller's side and the seller arranges main carriage transport – as with the "main carriage paid" Incoterms – the mode of transport should be specified as it affects the time and place the goods actually become physically available to the buyer.

Price: Depending on the nature of the product and the degree of precision that can be applied to quantity and delivery, the price may or may not be expressed in fixed terms. In situations where the price depends on other factors, all such factors and their relationship to the price should be clearly recited so as to leave no doubt. Any applicable currency or currencies should be specified.

It is often useful to separately itemize the price(s) charged for the

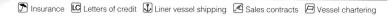

goods and the price(s) of any seller-supplied non-product services such as insurance and freight. There are two reasons for this. First, doing so reinforces the chosen delivery term (Incoterm) by clearly indicating what is and is not indicated in the total selling price. Second, countries differ in their treatment of non-product charges for ad-valorem duty valuation purposes.

Payment Terms: How, when, where and in what currency is the buyer to pay for the contract goods? If other than money, as in countertrade, is a separate contract to be referenced?

Transfer of ownership: This should be specified in the sales contract, except for vessel shipments made under a negotiable marine bill of lading where both ownership and possession rights reside in this original shipping document.

Some possible title-transfer provisions include:

- Seller and buyer agree that ownership of the contract goods will pass to the buyer upon shipment of the goods from (a named place).
- Seller and buyer agree that ownership of the contract goods will pass to the buyer when the goods arrive at (a named place).
- Seller and buyer agree that ownership of the contract goods will pass to the buyer upon payment of the price to the seller. (Depending on the payment terms, this may result in a retention of title situation, which could require compliance with formalities in the buyer's country.)

This wording is meant only to illustrate various possibilities, and should not be used as contract language without first obtaining the opinion of counsel.

Other important points

1. Possession rights: At what point should the buyer have access to the contract goods.
   This may or may not coincide with ownership. Such information is normally conveyed to the carrier by means of instructions provided by the party contracting for carriage.

2. Applicable law.

3. Insurance: If any Incoterm other than CIF or CIP is used, the parties should determine outside of the Incoterm who is responsible for providing insurance cover. Be sure to address the question of insurable interest. With CIF or CIP, the seller is required to insure, but the level of coverage should be determined outside the Incoterm if minimum cover (free of particular average or London Institute "C" Clauses) is inadequate.

⟨see entry in dictionary⟩ ✈ Air transport 🏛 Bank collections @ e-commerce 🔢 Incoterms

4. Government requirements: Is pre-shipment inspection required? Has the buyer's government any additional requirements that must be addressed by the seller (such as consularization)? Has the seller's government any requirements that must be addressed by the buyer (such as export control compliance)?

5. Non-obligatory outside inspection: Do the parties agree to pre-shipment inspection? If so, by whom and at whose cost?

6. Dispute resolution: If disputes arise, how should they be solved? Litigation is by no means the only route, nor is it necessarily the best one. Arbitration is an attractive alternative that allows the parties a greater say in how their case is judged. Most arbitrations take place under the auspices of an arbitration institution offering a pre-established set of rules to govern the procedure. One of the most experienced with a worldwide outreach is the ICC International Court of Arbitration. Parties who prefer arbitration to litigation are strongly advised to include an arbitration clause in their contract. The clause will specify the institution and rules to which the parties will turn in the event of a dispute. It might also mention the applicable law, the number and choice of arbitrators, as well as the place and language of the arbitration. Prior to or instead of arbitration, parties might prefer an amicable approach and seek to resolve their differences by conciliation, mediation or other consensual methods of settlement. Disputes are disruptive in any event, but the disruption can be minimized if the parties take time to agree in advance on how they will be settled. Whenever this point is covered in a sales contract, both the method and the forum (where and by whom) should be specified.

The International Chamber of Commerce (ICC) provides a handy checklist of common sales contract provisions. Titled *The ICC Model International Sale Contract* (ICC Publication No. 556), it is available in both hard copy and computer disk form from ICC Publishing (website www.iccbooks.com). While not intended as a substitute for legal counsel, it does provide contract basics in a convenient format.

Applicable law

Sellers and buyers are generally free to decide upon the body of law that applies to their sales contracts. Choice of law can present a sticky negotiation point, since each party is normally familiar with and thereby biased towards its own national law.

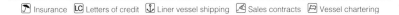

As the name implies, The United Nations developed its Convention on Contracts for the International Sale of Goods (CISG) to cover these situations. This, and its related body of law, the Convention on the Limitation Period in the International Sale of Goods, came into force in 1988. For details as well as a list of participating countries, refer to the UN Commission on International Trade Law website at www.uncitral.org.

Article two of the CISG excludes goods bought for personal, family or household goods, auctions, securities, vessels, aircraft, electricity and sales by authority of law. Within its ambit, it provides country-neutral law that can help ameliorate the choice of law problem.

The CISG automatically applies whenever both seller and buyer are domiciled in countries that have adopted the convention. Should such parties prefer to use another body of law, they may do so by specifying this in the sales contract. However, this must be done carefully, as the CISG is included in the contract law of their respective countries. Parties in non-participating countries may also use the CISG if they wish (and if permitted by their national laws). However, this could present problems, as non-participating jurisdictions may not be familiar with CISG provisions.

There is a major difference between the CISG and national law in countries where written sales contracts are required for transactions over a certain amount. The CISG has no such requirement, and oral agreements may be binding.

Non-legal considerations

Common sense dictates that contracting parties learn enough about each other to develop comfort levels. There is no substitute for due diligence. Most companies are quite willing to provide their bonafides, particularly to new prospective trading partners. In foreign trade, commercial reputation is often of greater importance than financial capacity. Most cultures value relationships highly, and parties that have a record of betraying them present real risks no matter how wealthy they may be.

Obviously, sellers offering unsecured payment terms must determine whether the buyer is creditworthy. The obligation to learn about one's trading partner applies equally to buyers, particularly with transactions involving pre-payment or irrevocable letter of credit payment terms.

New-to-market parties should also determine whether any unusual business practices or regulations exist in the counterparty's country before contracting. Such country-specific information is often available from embassies, large banks, and multinational forwarding and accounting firms. Buyers should certainly mention in their purchase orders any documents they need from their suppliers to comply with country-specific import regulations.

Practice

Contracts are agreements. They sometimes happen as a result of a seller and buyer drafting a detailed set of conditions. However, many times sales contracts for goods are no more than an offer and a matching acceptance. Part II of the CISG covers the sequence of offers and acceptances as well as when and how they may be changed or revoked.

The offer may be a simple quotation, which in international trade often resembles an invoice (and is called a "proforma invoice"). Acceptance may be a simple purchase order that agrees with the offer. A basic tenet of most legal systems is contract = offer + acceptance.

It is obviously important that proforma invoices contain sufficient information to make any resulting contracts viable. Sellers experienced in international trade provide the information shown in our dictionary definition of the proforma invoice term. Many also add conditions along the following lines:

- This offer is expressly limited to the terms and conditions shown therein, and can be accepted only in full.
- This company requires that all agreements be made in writing.
- Any documentary letters of credit resulting from this offer are to be subject to the International Chamber of Commerce Uniform Customs and Practice for Documentary Credits (SPECIFY THE CURRENT ICC PUBLICATION NUMBER).
- Any standby letters of credit resulting from this offer are to be subject to the International Chamber of Commerce International Standby Practices (SPECIFY THE CURRENT ICC PUBLICATION NUMBER).
- Any documentary collections resulting from this offer are to be subject to the International Chamber of Commerce Uniform Rules for Collections (SPECIFY THE CURRENT ICC PUBLICATION NUMBER).
- Unless otherwise specified, all terms of sale specified in this offer are International Chamber of Commerce Incoterms (SPECIFY THE DESIRED VERSION, SUCH AS INCOTERMS 2000).

This wording is meant only to illustrate various possibilities, and should not be used as contract language without first obtaining the opinion of counsel.

It may be that a buyer responds with a purchase order that differs in a significant respect from the offer. At that point, no contract exists, and the seller should immediately inform the buyer whether or not the change is acceptable. Failure to do so promptly could cause the buyer to rely on the seller's acceptance of the change, causing both harm and possible legal ramifications.

Once a contract is established, the parties should regularly communicate with each other until it has been fulfilled. While this is merely common courtesy and common sense, it is important when one party relies on input from the other in order to fulfil his or her contractual obligations. Needless to say, it becomes even more important when things do not proceed as planned. Unforeseen obstacles that could have been addressed with prior notice may cause real harm when they come as surprises, particularly in today's "just in time" environment.

Relationship to other contracts

International contracts for sales of goods normally require that the seller or buyer (or both) enter into additional contracts to comply with particular sales contract obligations. Carriage and insurance contracts typically fall into this category. It is important that the responsible party dovetail any additional contracts with the sales contract responsibilities they cover. Typical examples include:

- documentary requirements and timelines in any related letter(s) of credit
- the amount and level of insurance coverage
- the mode and payment of carriage contracts, including shipment and/or delivery timelines.

Sometimes, contract performance is guaranteed by third parties. The International Chamber of Commerce (ICC) has developed two sets of rules for guarantee situations: *The Uniform Rules for Contract Guarantees* (ICC Publication No. 325), and subsequently, the *Uniform Rules for Demand Guarantees* (ICC Publication No. 458). Since both exist, it is important for the contracting parties wishing to use one or the other to specify which one is intended.

Contracts with governments and NGOs

So far, our comments have applied to private sector contracts. However, in international trade it is common to sell to or even buy from governments. Everything we have seen applies to both private-

---

sector and governmental business with one major difference: governments have sovereign immunity. This means that the government cannot be sued without its permission. This applies not only within the territory of a particular government, but also to the jurisdiction of courts located in other countries. For instance, a business may have a dispute with a customer that also happens to be a foreign national government. Not only can the business not sue in the sovereign customer's country without permission, but it may not be able to sue even in its own country.

Obviously, the best situation for such a business would be to convince its sovereign customer to specifically waive its immunity in the sales contract before any dispute arises. In some cases this is possible.

Sometimes, business is transacted with governments through non-government organizations (NGOs) such as the World Bank. Such organizations have their own quotation procedures and contract formats, which are strictly observed. Although governments could raise sovereign immunity in case of disputes, this seldom happens as they rely on continued NGO financing.

The following terms used in sales contracts are defined in Key definitions ⒶⓏ

ad valorem	named place
alternative dispute resolution (ADR)	negotiable B/L (=Order B/L)
arbitration	non-government organization (NGO)
carriage contract	payment terms
CIF (Carriage, Insurance and Freight)	pre-shipment inspection (PSI)
CIP (Carriage and Insurance Paid)	proforma invoice
contract	purchase order
contracting parties	retention of title (ROT)
delivery	shipper's letter of instructions (SLI)
free of particular average	transfer of ownership
goods	Uniform Customs and Practice for
government procurement	Documentary Credits (UCP)
Harmonized System (HS)	Uniform Rules for Collections (URC)
Incoterms 2000	Uniform Rules for Contract
insurable interest	Guarantees
insurance	Uniform Rules for Demand
International Standards Organization	Guarantees (URDG)
(ISO)	United Nations Convention on
International Standby Practices (ISP)	Contracts for the International
just in time	Sale of Goods (CISG)
mediation	World Bank Group

✈ Insurance   🆇 Letters of credit   ⬇ Liner vessel shipping   📧 Sales contracts   🅱 Vessel chartering

Air transport ✈

Bank collections 🏛

e-commerce @

Incoterms ⊞

Insurance 🏷

Letters of credit LC

Liner vessel shipping ⚓

Sales contracts ✍

Focus on Vessel Chartering

Overview

Vessel chartering is a complicated process that has arrived haphazardly over hundreds of years. Reduced to its basics, chartering is simply the hiring of all or part of a ship to transport cargo. The contract that allows a party to use all or part of a ship for a period of time is called a charterparty (also charter party), and the participants are a shipowner and one or more charterers. Vessel chartering predates liner shipping, and its many years of customs and traditions make it extremely complex. Familiarity with the various forms of charterparty terms is essential to avoid costly mistakes.

There are many different vessel-chartering variations to accommodate the needs of owners and charterers. A charterparty can also be constructed to provide full or partial use of the ship's cargo holds, for anywhere from a single voyage to a multi-year contract. The charterparty can be tailored to provide any scope of supply, from a vessel without crew, provisions or fuel (called "bareboat") to one with all included. There's even a version called "slot chartering" that allows one container shipping line to rent space on the vessel of another.

The general public is more aware of liner shipping, since most shipments of manufactured goods are moved that way. The number of liner shipments is considerably higher, since a liner vessel will have, on average, several hundred shipments per voyage. By contrast, charter vessels have at most only a few shipments per voyage because of the nature of cargo they transport most frequently (raw materials or major projects). The tonnage (cargo weight or volume) per charter shipment is considerably larger than for most liner shipments.

Another difference is that consistency is important in liner shipping. Ship lines offer scheduled service to set ports, where they maintain terminal facilities. This is why they provide liner terms, which include routine vessel loading and unloading. By contrast, charter vessels call at any safe port where cargo is sufficient to make doing so worthwhile.

‹see entry in dictionary› ✈ Air transport 🏛 Bank collections @ e-commerce ⊞ Incoterms

This is determined by a vessel's capacity to accommodate available cargoes (as ships come in various sizes and types). Since charter voyages are dictated by demand, port terminal contracts are often arranged by charterers, rather than by shipowners. This is also partially due to the fact that raw materials shipments require specialized handling equipment found at terminals that serve charter vessels. For these reasons, the question of who loads and unloads charter shipments is a matter for negotiation.

A corollary is that container ship lines often provide multimodal transport for containerized cargo, which they can do because they are well established at their ports of call. Conversely, charter vessel service is port-to-port (main carriage only).

At this point, we should differentiate between liner shipping and liner terms. As mentioned above, liner shipping is vessel transportation provided by ship lines that regularly call on certain ports and provide normal vessel loading and unloading. Liner terms provide that shippers have no responsibility to the ship other than to have the cargo delivered to the terminal, ready for loading prior to the agreed cut-off date (and consignees are responsible for collecting their arrived and unloaded cargo in a timely manner). By contrast, although some chartering is done on liner terms, a charterer's obligations often include having the port ready to receive the chartered vessel at an agreed date and time, and having the vessel loaded and/or unloaded within the agreed time periods. Failures may result in expensive demurrage costs. Reducing this to a simple rule, we can say that charter shipping sometimes employs liner terms, while liner shipping always does.

Ship lines issue bills of lading reflecting the terms and conditions of the carriage contract, which are either printed on the documents themselves or are readily available. Bills of lading covering goods transported on chartered vessels refer to the charterparty. The charterparty may or may not be available to anyone other than the charterer (such as a buyer of goods shipped under a seller-negotiated charter). This is noteworthy, as Incoterms 2000 removed the previous seller obligation to provide the buyer with a copy of the charterparty for charter vessel shipments made under the CFR and CIF Incoterms.

Our final point of comparison is that to be economically viable, liner vessels must carry cargo from hundreds of shippers per voyage, and therefore remain reasonably neutral when it comes to competing interests of sellers and buyers. By contrast, charter vessels are often hired and sometimes even operated by either the seller or the buyer, and are obliged to follow the instructions of the charterer.

Insurance   Letters of credit   Liner vessel shipping   Sales contracts   Vessel chartering

Practice

As mentioned in the overview, there are many different types of charter arrangements and nuances possible to suit individual charterer and shipowner needs, and there are far too many to detail here. We can broadly categorize them, keeping in mind that there is some overlap among these classifications, depending on how they are modified.

Relationships between vessel owner and charterer

At one extreme, we have the "tramp vessel," which follows the flows of trade from port to port wherever demand takes it. On the other hand, a fleet of tankers may serve as a subsidiary for its oil company parent, and may be owned on an arm's length basis purely for liability reasons. Between these extremes are situations where a vessel is required for more than one voyage, but not for continuous use.

Kinds of Charter

1. Space charter: the charterer wants transportation only, and does not want to be involved with the vessel's operations. Space Chartering can be for all or part of a vessel's capacity, and can be for one or more voyages.
2. Slot charter: a container line charters space on another line under a vessel sharing-agreement, usually on a space-charter basis. Slot charter agreements are frequently reciprocal.
3. Voyage charter: under a voyage charter, the vessel owner carries a charterer's complete cargo from one port to another, or makes a complete ship available to the charterer for the same purpose. A voyage charter is for a single voyage between specified ports or specified ranges of ports, and can be written on either gross or net terms. (See below.)
4. Time charter: a time charter is usually for a specified length of time, such as a year, or for one voyage or several consecutive voyages among certain ports or ranges of ports. The shipowner supplies the crew and provisions.
5. Bareboat (demise) charter: a bareboat charter provides that the charterer has use of the vessel for an agreed period of time, and appoints the master, hires the crew and provisions and controls the vessel as if it were his or her own. This is really more of a financial arrangement than a carriage contract, and is frequently used when a vessel operator requires more long- or short-term capacity but is unwilling to add a new vessel to its fleet.
6. Sub charter: This occurs when a charterer (called the head charterer) makes the chartered vessel available to other charterers (called subcharterers).

There are many subtypes to these broad classifications. Further, industry groups that frequently use chartering have established industry-standard charterparties.

Vessel loading and unloading

The following expressions are used in chartering agreements between the vessel owner and the charterer.

1. Gross terms: under gross terms, the vessel owner is responsible for the costs of loading, stowing, trimming and unloading the vessel.
2. Net terms: under net terms, the vessel owner is not responsible for the cost of loading, stowing, trimming and unloading the vessel. Specific terms include free in and out (FIO), and free in, out, stowed and trimmed (FIOST).
3. Shared responsibilities: under free in, liner out (FILO), the vessel owner is not responsible for the cost of loading, but is responsible for the cost of vessel unloading. The reverse is true under Liner In, Free Out (LIFO), where the vessel owner is responsible for the cost of vessel loading but not vessel unloading.

Time is a factor in loading and unloading. Where the charterer is responsible for either or both, an agreed time frame call "laytime" is included in the charterparty. This can be expressed in days, hours, tons per day, etc. Charterers who accomplish their loading and/or unloading tasks in less than the agreed time are often eligible for a payment called dispatch money. However, those who exceed the allowed time must pay a penalty called demurrage. Over the years, some strange expressions have developed in accounting for laytime, such as:

FXEX – Fridays and holidays excluded
FHINC – Fridays and holidays included
SHEX – Sundays and holidays excluded
SHINC – Sundays and holidays included
As fast as the vessel can (FAC) – maximum rate at which a vessel can load/unload.
Notice of readiness – formal advice that the vessel is ready for loading/unloading.
Running days – days that run consecutively after each other.
Weather permitting – inclement weather is excluded from laytime
Weather working day – a day or part of a day when weather does not prevent loading/unloading.

Vessel loading is traditionally associated with the physical act of the cargo being moved from a place at rest on the wharf to a point where it passes the ship's rail. However, it must also be secured and/or spread out in the hold to assure a safe and stable transport. Respectively, stowage and trimming are the marine terms used for these functions.

Insurance   Letters of credit   Liner vessel shipping   Sales contracts   Vessel chartering

Relationship of vessel loading and unloading to Incoterms

While the charterparty terms regarding vessel loading and unloading are negotiated between shipowner and charterer, they are affected by the terms of sale as agreed between the seller and buyer, and as found in Incoterms 2000. In vessel chartering, sales terms are often chosen based on such factors as whether the seller or the buyer owns terminal facilities or which party has expertise in negotiating with terminal operators.

1. In Incoterms 2000, FAS requires the seller to place the goods alongside the vessel, while FOB requires the seller to load them. When the buyer charters the vessel, a seller who is unwilling to become involved in vessel loading would prefer FAS. Conversely, a buyer lacking familiarity with a loading port may ask the seller to arrange loading by requesting FOB. Furthermore, sellers that control or own their own loading facilities, such as grain silos or tank farms, would prefer to arrange vessel loading.

2. The reverse situation exists with the DEQ and DES Incoterms when the seller charters the vessel. DEQ makes the seller responsible for vessel unloading while DES does not. Sellers unwilling to become involved in vessel unloading should prefer DES (as should buyers that control their own unloading facilities), while buyers unwilling to unload will request DEQ.

Negotiating a charter

Since freight forwarding generally refers to agents that handle general cargo, only a few forwarders have niche departments that handle vessel chartering. Finding vessels that can accommodate and fit the cargo is the task of a shipbroker who represents either the shipowner or the charterer. It is not uncommon for two, three or more shipbrokers to be involved in establishing a charter. Integrity, competence and reputation are extremely important in chartering, and these attributes serve a broker well. Shipowners frequently find their vessels in various parts of the world and are constantly in touch with brokers trying to fill out the next voyage. When possible this is done without repositioning the ship (moving it from one port to another without cargo). Experienced brokers are often needed to assure a steady stream of profitable cargoes while weeding out unscrupulous charterers and assisting the inexperienced ones.

Unless the shipowner and charterer are already familiar with each other, they should carefully negotiate costs and terms. The process can be streamlined when the parties use the various industry-specific chartering agreements and standard clauses. Timelines are particularly important, not only because they affect the cost of the charter movement, but also because they should agree with whatever delivery times the seller and buyer have established in their contract of sale. Insurance coverage on the vessel and cargo is another important consideration.

Once agreement on all major points is reached, the charterparty is executed. The industry term for this is "fixing", the word "fixture" indicates that an agreement has been made. Since a fixture often results from many phone, fax and email communications, a "fixing letter" summarizing the conditions should be sent promptly to allow both sides to confirm the details.

Timing

In addition to the "laycans" (the agreed time at which a vessel is to be ready to load at a port), it is important that all parties be aware of the consequences that may arise if the vessel is early or late at the port. The same applies if the cargo is not available when the vessel is ready. The shipowner is concerned with what the charterparty stipulates, rather than the sales contract between the seller and the buyer. On the other hand, the charterer must satisfy his or her trading party by including in the charterparty whatever is needed to agree with the sales contract. For instance, under the FAS Incoterm, sellers are not responsible for vessel loading but must have the cargo available for loading on time. The charterparty may well stipulate that the shipowner must regularly inform the seller of the vessel's position, or this responsibility may be left to the buyer. Either way, close communication is extremely important to avoid expensive misdeliveries.

The term "arrived ship" means that the vessel is in position to load or unload, and that the laytime allowed under the charterparty begins. To qualify as an arrived ship, the vessel must have reached the contractual loading/unloading place, and be ready in all respects. This is made known to the charterer by means of a document called a notice of readiness (NOR).

Documentation

The documentation in a charter movement will obviously reflect the responsibilities of the vessel owner and charterer. Generally, an authorized ship's officer or agent of the vessel owner issues a mate's receipt once the cargo has been received and tallied by clerks. Any apparent damage or shortage is noted on this document. The mate's receipt is then exchanged for a bill of lading (B/L), which is signed either by the vessel's master or an authorized agent. Naturally, any

Insurance   Letters of credit   Liner vessel shipping   Sales contracts   Vessel chartering

shortage or damage notations on the mate's receipt should be indicated on the B/L, making it a foul transport document. Charter shipment B/Ls may be made in either negotiable or non-negotiable form – always negotiable for shipments of goods that may be sold in transit. In addition, some charterparties (and contracts for the sale of the goods themselves) call for inspection of the vessel and the cargo prior to, and sometimes after, loading.

The following terms used in vessel chartering are defined in Key definitions

accomplished bill of lading

advance freight

affreightment

apparent damage

apparent good order and condition

arrest

arrival notice (AN)

arrived ship

as fast as the vessel can (FAC)

back letter

bareboat charter (= demise charter)

bill of lading (B/L)

breakbulk cargo

bulk cargo

bulk carrier

captain's protest

cargo sharing

carriage contract:

Carriage of Goods by Sea Act
    (UK COGSA)

Carriage of Goods by Sea Act
    (US COGSA)

carrier

charter

charterparty

charterer

clean transport document

closing date

consignee

consignment

consignor

contract carrier

dead freight

deck cargo

demurrage

dispatch money

dock

dock receipt

estimated time of arrival (ETA)

estimated time of departure
    (ETD)

flag carrier

FHEX

FHINC

forwarder

foul transport document

free in and out (FIO

free in, liner out (FILO)

free in, out, stowed and trimmed
    (FIOST)

freight collect

freight payable

freight prepaid

good ship

gross terms (= gross charter)

gross weight

guaranteed freight

Hague Rules

Hague–Visby Rules

Hamburg Rules

head charterer

heavy lift

husbanding

ice clause

intermediate consignee

laydays (= laytime)

letter of indemnity (LOI = steamer
  guarantee)

lighterage

liner in, free out (LIFO)

liner terms

lump sum charter

main carriage

manifest (cargo)

mate's receipt

negotiable B/L (= order B/L)

net terms

net weight

no show

non-negotiable B/L (= straight B/L)

notice of readiness (NOR)

notify party

ocean transport intermediary

on-board B/L

on-board notation

on-deck

port-to-port

pratique

running days

sea waybill

seaworthy

SHEX

SHINC

ship's gear

ship's rail

ship's tackle

shipbroker

shipment (on board a vessel)

shipment date

shipper

shipper's letter of instructions (SLI)

shipping documents

short delivery (SD)

short form B/L

short shipment

slot charter

space charter

spot

stowage

sub-charter

time charter

trimming

ultimate consignee

under deck

voyage

voyage charter

weather permitting

weather working days

wharf

of *international trade*

Key words in 5 languages

Bank collections 🏛

e-commerce ©

Incoterms ⊞

Insurance ✈

Letters of credit 🆔

Liner vessel shipping ⚓

Sales contracts ✍

Vessel chartering ⛴

acknowledgement
Ⓓ Bestätigung
Ⓢ reconocimiento
Ⓕ reconnaissance
Ⓘ riconoscimento

ad valorem (according to value)
Ⓓ ad valorem
Ⓢ ad valorem (sobre el valor)
Ⓕ ad valorem
Ⓘ ad valorem

air waybill (AWB)
Ⓓ Luftfrachtbrief
Ⓢ conocimiento (de transporte) aéreo, guía aérea
Ⓕ lettre de transport aérien (LTA)
Ⓘ lettera di trasporto aereo

all risks (a.r.)
Ⓓ alle Risiken
Ⓢ todo riesgo
Ⓕ tous risques
Ⓘ tutti i rischi

(to) **amend / amendment**
Ⓓ ändern / Änderung
Ⓢ enmendar / enmienda / modificar / modificación
Ⓕ amender / amendement / modifier / modification
Ⓘ modificare / modifica

assignment
Ⓓ Abtretung, Zession, Auftrag, Aufgabe, Zuweisung, Zuteilung
Ⓢ cesión, atribución
Ⓕ cession
Ⓘ cessione, incarico, attribuzione

average
Ⓓ Havarie
Ⓢ avería
Ⓕ avarie
Ⓘ avaria

general **average**
Ⓓ grosse Havarie
Ⓢ avería commún, gruesa
Ⓕ avarie commune, grosse avarie
Ⓘ avaria commune / generale

bank
Ⓓ Bank
Ⓢ banco
Ⓕ banque
Ⓘ banca

advising **bank**
Ⓓ avisierende Bank
Ⓢ banco notificador
Ⓕ banque notificatrice

Ⓘ banca avvisante

collecting **bank**
Ⓓ Inkassobank
Ⓢ banco cobrador
Ⓕ banque chargée de l'encaissement
Ⓘ banca incaricata dell'incasso

confirming **bank**
Ⓓ bestätigende Bank
Ⓢ banco confirmador, confirmante
Ⓕ banque confirmatrice
Ⓘ banca confermante

issuing **bank**
Ⓓ eröffnende Bank
Ⓢ banco emisor
Ⓕ banque émettrice
Ⓘ banca emittente

negotiating **bank**
Ⓓ negoziierende Bank
Ⓢ banco negociador
Ⓕ banque négociatrice
Ⓘ banca negoziatrice

paying **bank**
Ⓓ zahlende Bank
Ⓢ banco pagador
Ⓕ banque chargée du règlement
Ⓘ banca pagante

presenting **bank**
Ⓓ vorlegende Bank
Ⓢ banco presentador
Ⓕ banque présentatrice
Ⓘ banca presentatrice

remitting **bank**
Ⓓ einreichende Bank
Ⓢ banco remitente
Ⓕ banque remettante
Ⓘ banca remittente

bankruptcy
Ⓓ Konkurs, Bankrott
Ⓢ quiebra, bancarrota
Ⓕ faillite
Ⓘ fallimento

bare-boat charter
Ⓓ Schiffsmiete (ohne Mannschaft und Treibstoff)
Ⓢ fletamento de casco (sin tripulación ni combustible)
Ⓕ affrètement coque nue (sans équipage ni combustible)
Ⓘ noleggio a scafo nudo (senza equipaggio né combustibile)

beneficiary
Ⓓ Begünstigter
Ⓢ beneficiario

Ⓕ bénéficiaire
Ⓘ beneficiario

berth
Ⓓ Liegeplatz
Ⓢ amarradero / amarre
Ⓕ poste d'amarrage
Ⓘ attracco

bill of lading (B/L)
Ⓓ Konnossement
Ⓢ conocimiento de embarque
Ⓕ connaissement, nantissement
Ⓘ polizza di carico (P/C)

on board **B/L**
Ⓓ An-Bord-Konnossement
Ⓢ conocimiento a bordo
Ⓕ connaissement à bord
Ⓘ polizza di carico per merce a bordo

claused **B/L**
Ⓓ Konnossement mit Vorbehalt
Ⓢ conocimiento con cláusula adicional, "sucio"
Ⓕ connaissement clausé
Ⓘ polizza di carico sporca

clean **B/L**
Ⓓ reines Konnossement
Ⓢ conocimiento limpio
Ⓕ connaissement net
Ⓘ polizza di carico netta

house **B/L**
Ⓓ house (B/L)
Ⓢ house (B/L)
Ⓕ connaissement creux
Ⓘ house (B/L) (sottopolizza di carico con consegna diretta al destinatario)

non-negotiable **B/L**
Ⓓ nicht übertragbares Konnossement
Ⓢ conocimiento no negociable
Ⓕ connaissement intransmissible
Ⓘ polizza di carico non negoziabile

received **bill**
Ⓓ Übernahme-Konnossement
Ⓢ conocimiento recibido en muelle
Ⓕ connaissement reçu à quai
Ⓘ polizza di carico 'ricevuto per imbarco'

short form **B/L**
Ⓓ Short-Form-Konnossement
Ⓢ conocimiento 'shortform', abreviado
Ⓕ connaissement 'shortform', abrégé

Ⓘ polizza di carico 'shortform', polizza di carico modulo ridotto

stale **B/L**
Ⓓ überaltertes Konnossement
Ⓢ conocimiento caducado
Ⓕ connaissement périmé
Ⓘ polizza di carico 'scaduta'

straight **B/L**
Ⓓ Orderkonnossement
Ⓢ conocimiento nominativo
Ⓕ connaissement nominatif
Ⓘ polizza di carico nominativa

through **B/L**
Ⓓ Durchkonnossement
Ⓢ conocimiento 'through', directo
Ⓕ connaissement 'through', connaissement direct
Ⓘ polizza di carico 'through'/cumulativa/diretta

break bulk cargo
Ⓓ Sammelgut
Ⓢ carga fraccionada
Ⓕ marchandises diverses
Ⓘ carico alla rinfusa da frazionare

bribery
Ⓓ Bestechung
Ⓢ corrupción
Ⓕ corruption
Ⓘ corruzione

broker
Ⓓ Makler
Ⓢ corredor
Ⓕ courtier
Ⓘ mediatore, agente

bulk cargo
Ⓓ Massengut
Ⓢ carga (mento) a granel
Ⓕ marchandises en vrac, cargaison de vrac
Ⓘ carico alla rinfusa

bunker adjustment factor (BAF)
Ⓓ Zuschlag für Bunkerung
Ⓢ factor de ajuste por combustible
Ⓕ surtaxe de soutage
Ⓘ coefficiente di adeguamento per il bunker

buyer
Ⓓ Käufer
Ⓢ comprador
Ⓕ acheteur
Ⓘ compratore

(to) cancel
- Ⓓ rückgängig machen, für ungültig erklären, widerrufen
- Ⓢ rescindir, cancelar, anular
- Ⓕ résilier, annuler
- Ⓘ annullare, risolvere, rescindere

carriage
- Ⓓ Fracht, Porto
- Ⓢ transporte, portes
- Ⓕ port, transport
- Ⓘ trasporto, porto

carriage and insurance paid to (CIP) (...named place of destination) (Incoterms 2000)
- Ⓓ frachtfrei versichert (CIP) (...benannter Bestimmungsort)
- Ⓢ Transporte y seguro pagados hasta (CIP) (...lugar de destino convenido)
- Ⓕ port payé, assurance comprise (CIP) (...lieu de destination convenu)
- Ⓘ trasporto e assicurazione pagati fino a (... luogo di destinazione convenuto)(CIP)

carriage paid to (CPT) (...named place of destination) (Incoterms 2000)
- Ⓓ frachtfrei (CPT) (...benannter Bestimmungsort)
- Ⓢ Transporte pagado hasta (CPT) (...lugar de destino convenido)
- Ⓕ port payé jusqu'à (CPT) (...lieu de destination convenu)
- Ⓘ trasporto pagato fino a (... luogo di destinazione convenuto) (CPT)

cash on delivery (COD)
- Ⓓ Nachnahme, zahlbar bei Lieferung
- Ⓢ entrega contra reembolso
- Ⓕ livraison contre remboursement
- Ⓘ contro assegno, pagamento alla consegna

certificate
- Ⓓ Bescheinigung, Zertifikat, Zeugnis
- Ⓢ certificado
- Ⓕ certificat
- Ⓘ certificato

certificate of inspection (surveillance certificate)
- Ⓓ Inspektionszertifikat
- Ⓢ certificado de inspección
- Ⓕ certificat d'inspection
- Ⓘ certificato d'ispezione

certificate of origin
- Ⓓ Ursprungszeugnis
- Ⓢ certificado de origen
- Ⓕ certificat d'origine
- Ⓘ certificato d'origine

insurance **certificate**
- Ⓓ Versicherungszertifikat
- Ⓢ certificado de seguro
- Ⓕ certificat d'assurance
- Ⓘ certificato di assicurazione

charter, chartering
- Ⓓ Charter
- Ⓢ fletamento
- Ⓕ affrètement
- Ⓘ noleggio

bareboat, bare hull, bare pole **charter**
- Ⓓ Schiffsmiete (ohne Mannschaft und Treibstoff)
- Ⓢ fletamento de casco (sin tripulación ni combustible)
- Ⓕ affrètement coque nue (sans équipage ni combustibile)
- Ⓘ noleggio a scafo nudo (senza equipaggio, né combustible)

charter party
- Ⓓ Charterpartie
- Ⓢ 'charter-party', contrato de fletamento
- Ⓕ charte-partie
- Ⓘ contratto di noleggio

lump sum **charter**
- Ⓓ Pauschalcharter
- Ⓢ fletamento global
- Ⓕ affrètement moyennant un fret global
- Ⓘ noleggio a prezzo globale

slot **charter**
- Ⓓ Raumcharter
- Ⓢ fletamento por mámparo
- Ⓕ affrètement à compartiment, affrètement de cellule
- Ⓘ noleggio a carico parziale

time **charter**
- Ⓓ Zeitcharter
- Ⓢ fletamento por tiempo o a plazo
- Ⓕ affrètement à temps
- Ⓘ noleggio a tempo

voyage **charter**
- Ⓓ Reischarter
- Ⓢ fletamento por viaje
- Ⓕ affrètement au voyage
- Ⓘ noleggio a viaggio

---

cheque, check (US)
- Ⓓ Scheck
- Ⓢ cheque
- Ⓕ chèque
- Ⓘ assegno bancario

claim
- Ⓓ Anspruch, Forderung, Reklamation
- Ⓢ reclamación, demanda
- Ⓕ demande, créance, réclamation, revendication
- Ⓘ domanda, reclamo

clause (law)
- Ⓓ Klausel, Bestimmung, Bedingung
- Ⓢ cláusula, disposición, artículo, pacto, estipulación, apéndice de une póliza de seguros
- Ⓕ clause, stipulation, disposition, article, avenant (police d'assurance)
- Ⓘ clausola (dir.)

green **clause**
- Ⓓ Klausel mit grüner Tinte, greenclaus
- Ⓢ cláusula verde
- Ⓘ clause verte
- Ⓘ clausola verde

red **clause**
- Ⓓ Klausel mit roter Tinte (bei Akkreditiven), red clause
- Ⓢ cláusula roja
- Ⓕ clause rouge
- Ⓘ clausola rossa

collection (documentary)
- Ⓓ dokumentäres Inkasso
- Ⓢ cobro documentario
- Ⓕ encaissement documentaire
- Ⓘ incasso documentario

conference (liner)
- Ⓓ Schiffahrtskonferenz
- Ⓢ conferencia marítima
- Ⓕ conférence maritime
- Ⓘ "conférence", conferenza marittima (di linea)

congestion surcharge
- Ⓓ Zuschlag für Wartezeiten wegen Überfüllung
- Ⓢ sobretasa o recargo por (congestión)
- Ⓕ surtaxe d'encombrement
- Ⓘ soprannolo per congestionamento

consolidator (groupage agent)
- Ⓓ Sammelladungsspediteur
- Ⓢ consolidator, agrupador

- Ⓕ groupeur
- Ⓘ consolidatore (operatore di "groupage")

contract (sales)
- Ⓓ Kaufvertrag
- Ⓢ contrato de compraventa
- Ⓕ contrat de vente
- Ⓘ contratto di vendita

cost and freight (CFR) (...named port of destination) (Incoterms 2000)
- Ⓓ Kosten und Fracht (CFR) (...benannter Bestimmungshafen)
- Ⓢ coste y flete (CFR) (...puerto de destino convenido)
- Ⓕ coût et fret CFR (...port de destination convenu)
- Ⓘ costo e nolo (...porto di destinazione convenuto)(CFR)

cost, insurance and freight (CIF) (...named port of destination) (Incoterms 2000)
- Ⓓ Kosten, Versicherung und Fracht (CIF) (...benannter Bestimmungshafen)
- Ⓢ coste, seguro y flete (CIF) (...puerto de destino convenido)
- Ⓕ coût, assurance et fret (CIF) (...port de destination convenu)
- Ⓘ costo, assicurazione e nolo (...porto di destinazione convenuto) (CIF)

countertrade
- Ⓓ Tauschhandel, Kompensationsgeschäft
- Ⓢ compensación
- Ⓕ compensation
- Ⓘ compensazione commerciale,countertrade

credit (documentary)
- Ⓓ (Dokumenten-) Akkreditiv
- Ⓢ crédito (documentario)
- Ⓕ crédit (documentaire)
- Ⓘ credito (documentario)

evergreen **credit**
- Ⓓ revolvierendes Akkreditiv
- Ⓢ crédito de renovación automática
- Ⓕ crédit à renouvellement automatique
- Ⓘ credito rinnovabile

negotiable **credit**
- Ⓓ negoziierbares Akkreditiv
- Ⓢ crédito negociable
- Ⓕ crédit négociable
- Ⓘ credito cedibile

---

stand-by **credit**
Ⓓ Standby-Kredit (IWF),
Kreditzusage
Ⓢ crédito puente
Ⓕ crédit de soutien
Ⓘ credito stand-by

back to back **credit**
Ⓓ Back-to-Back Akkreditiv
Ⓢ crédito 'back-to-back'
Ⓕ crédit 'back-to-back'
Ⓘ credito 'back-to-back'

confirmed irrevocable **credit**
Ⓓ bestätigtes unwiderrufliches
Akkreditiv
Ⓢ crédito irrevocable confirmado
Ⓕ crédit irrévocable confirmé
Ⓘ credito irrevocabile confermato

expiry date of the **credit**
Ⓓ Verfalldatum des Akkreditivs
Ⓢ fecha de vencimiento del crédito
Ⓕ date de validité du crédit
Ⓘ data di scadenza del credito

irrevocable **credit**
Ⓓ unwiderrufliches Akkreditiv
Ⓢ crédito irrevocable
Ⓕ crédit irrévocable
Ⓘ credito irrevocabile

revolving **credit**
Ⓓ revolvierendes Akkreditiv
Ⓢ crédito rotativo
Ⓕ crédit 'revolving'
Ⓘ credito rotativo

transferable **credit**, assignable credit
Ⓓ übertragbares Akkreditiv
Ⓢ crédito transferible
Ⓕ crédit transférable
Ⓘ credito trasferibile

currency (hard)
Ⓓ harte Währung
Ⓢ moneda fuerte
Ⓕ monnaie forte
Ⓘ moneta forte

currency adjustment charge =
currency adjustment factor (CAC =
CAF)
Ⓓ Währungszuschlag
Ⓢ recargo por ajustes cambiarios
Ⓕ surcharge monétaire
Ⓘ coefficiente di adeguamento
monetario

customs
Ⓓ Zoll
Ⓘ aduana

Ⓕ douane
Ⓘ dogana

customs broker
Ⓓ Zollspediteur
Ⓢ agente o corredor de aduana
Ⓕ agent ou commissionnaire en
douane
Ⓘ spedizioniere doganale

customs clearance
Ⓓ Zollabfertigung
Ⓢ trámite aduanero, despacho
aduanal
Ⓕ formalités douanières,
dédouanement
Ⓘ formalità doganali, sdoganamento

customs duties
Ⓓ Zollabgaben
Ⓢ derechos de aduana o
arancelarios
Ⓕ droits de douane
Ⓘ diritti doganali

customs entry
Ⓓ Zollanmeldung
Ⓢ declaración o entrada de aduana
Ⓕ déclaration en douane
Ⓘ dichiarazione in dogana

customs valuation
Ⓓ Zollbewertung, Zollabschätzung
Ⓢ valor en aduana
Ⓕ évaluation en douane
Ⓘ valutazione in dogana

damages
Ⓓ Schaden, Beschädigung, Havarie
Ⓢ daño, avería
Ⓕ dommage, avarie
Ⓘ danno, pregiudizio

data freight receipt
Ⓓ Seefrachtbrief, Ladungsquittung
Ⓢ recibo de carga (no negociable)
Ⓕ reçu de chargement (non
négociable)
Ⓘ ricevuta di carico

date (acceptance)
Ⓓ Annahmetag, Annahmedatum
Ⓢ fecha de aceptación
Ⓕ date d'acceptation
Ⓘ data di accettazione

(on) **deck** # under deck
Ⓓ an Deck # unter Deck
Ⓢ (en) sobre cubierta # bajo
cubierta
Ⓕ en pontée # sous le pont
Ⓘ sopra coperta # sotto coperta

---

deck cargo
- Ⓓ Deckladung
- Ⓢ carga en cubierta, en puente
- Ⓕ cargaison en pontée
- Ⓘ carico sopra coperta

delivered duty paid (DDP)
(...named place of destination)
(Incoterms 2000)
- Ⓓ geliefert verzollt (DDP)
  (...genannter Bestimmungsort)
- Ⓢ entregada derechos pagados
  (DDP) (...lugar de destino
  convenido)
- Ⓕ rendu droits acquittés (DDP)
  (...lieu de destination convenu)
- Ⓘ reso sdoganato (...luogo di
  destinazione convenuto) (DDP)

delivered at frontier (DAF)
(...named place) (Incoterms 2000)
- Ⓓ geliefert Grenze (DAF)
  (...genannter Bestimmungsort)
- Ⓢ entregada en frontera (DAF)
  (...lugar convenido)
- Ⓕ rendu frontière (DAF) (...lieu
  convenu)
- Ⓘ reso frontiera (...luogo
  convenuto) (DAF)

delivered duty unpaid (DDU)
(...named place of destination)
(Incoterms 2000)
- Ⓓ geliefert unverzollt (DDU)
  (...genannter Bestimmungsort)
- Ⓢ entregada derechos no pagados
  (DDU) (...lugar de destino
  convenido)
- Ⓕ rendu droits non acquittés (DDU)
  (...lieu de destination convenu)
- Ⓘ reso non sdoganato (... luogo di
  destinazione convenuto) (DDU)

delivered ex quay (DEQ) (duty
paid) (...named port of destination)
(Incoterms 2000)
- Ⓓ geliefert ab Kai (verzollt) (DEQ)
  (...genannter Bestimmungshafen)
- Ⓢ entregada en muelle (DEQ)
  (derechos pagados) (...puerto de
  destino convenido)
- Ⓕ rendu à quai (DEQ) (droits
  acquittés) (...port de destination
  convenu)
- Ⓘ reso banchina (sdoganato)
  (...porto di destinazione
  convenuto) (DEQ)

delivered ex ship (DES) (...named
port of destination) (Incoterms 2000)
- Ⓓ geliefert ab Schiff (DES)
  (...genannter Bestimmungshafen)
- Ⓢ entregada sobre buque (DES)
  (...puerto de destino convenido)
- Ⓕ rendu ex ship (DES) (...port de
  destination convenu)
- Ⓘ reso exship (...porto di
  destinazione convenuto) (DES)

delivery
- Ⓓ (Aus Lieferung), Übergabe
- Ⓢ entrega
- Ⓕ livraison, délivrance, émise
- Ⓘ consegna

demurrage (charges)
- Ⓓ Überliegegeld
- Ⓢ (gastos de) sobreestadías,
  demoras
- Ⓕ (indemnités de) surestaries
- Ⓘ controstallie (indennità)

document
- Ⓓ Dokument
- Ⓢ documento
- Ⓕ document
- Ⓘ documento

**documents against acceptance
(D/A)**
- Ⓓ Dokumente gegen Akzept
- Ⓢ (entrega de) documentos contra
  aceptación
- Ⓕ (remise des) documents contre
  acceptation
- Ⓘ documenti contro accettazione

**documents against payment
(D/P)**
- Ⓓ Dokumente gegen Zahlung
- Ⓢ (entrega de) documentos contra
  pago
- Ⓕ (remise des) documents contre
  paiement
- Ⓘ documenti contro pagamento

draft
- Ⓓ Tratte, Wechsel
- Ⓢ giro, letra
- Ⓕ traite
- Ⓘ tratta

drawer
- Ⓓ Aussteller
- Ⓢ girador, librador
- Ⓕ tireur
- Ⓘ traente

drawee
- Ⓓ Bezogener

Ⓢ girado, librado (= persona)
Ⓕ tiré (= personne)
Ⓘ trassato

electronic data interchange (EDI)
Ⓓ elektronischer Datenaustausch
Ⓢ intercambio electrónico de datos
Ⓕ échanges électroniques de données (EDI)
Ⓘ scambio elettronico di dati (EDI)

endorsement
Ⓓ Ubertragung, Indossierung
Ⓢ endoso, póliza
Ⓕ endossement, avenant
Ⓘ girata, clausola

estimated time of arrival (ETA)
Ⓓ (voraussichtlicher) Ankunftstermin
Ⓢ hora estimada de llegada
Ⓕ horaire d'arrivée prévu
Ⓘ tempo d'arrivo previsto

estimated time of departure (ETD)
Ⓓ (voraussichtlicher) Abfahrtstermin
Ⓢ hora estimada de partida
Ⓕ horaire de départ prévu
Ⓘ tempo di partenza previsto

ex works (EXW) (...named place) (Incoterms 2000)
Ⓓ ab Werk (EXW) (...benannter Ort)
Ⓢ en fábrica (EXW) (...lugar convenido)
Ⓕ à l'usine (EXW) (...lieu convenu)
Ⓘ franco fabbrica (...luogo convenuto) (EXW)

export licence
Ⓓ Ausfuhrerlaubnis
Ⓢ licencia de exportación
Ⓕ licence d'exportation
Ⓘ licenza d'esportazione

foreign exchange
Ⓓ Devisen, Auslandswechsel
Ⓢ divisas
Ⓕ devises étrangères
Ⓘ divisa, valuta estera

forfaiting
Ⓓ Forfaitierung
Ⓢ indemnización, impuesto concertado
Ⓕ forfaitage
Ⓘ forfaiting, forfettizzazione

forwarder
Ⓓ Spediteur

Ⓢ transportista, embarcador, expedidor de carga
Ⓕ transporteur, chargeur, expéditeur
Ⓘ spedizioniere

forwarding instructions
Ⓓ Versandinstruktionen
Ⓢ instrucciones de expedición
Ⓕ instructions d'expédition
Ⓘ istruzioni per la spedizione

free of particular average (FPA)
Ⓓ frei von besonderer Havarie
Ⓢ franco de avería particular
Ⓕ franc d'avaries particulières (FAP)
Ⓘ franco avaria particolare

free alongside ship (FAS) (...named port of shipment) (Incoterms 2000)
Ⓓ frei Längsseite Schiff (FAS) (...benannter Verschiffungshafen)
Ⓢ franco al costado del buque (FAS) (...puerto de carga convenido)
Ⓕ Franco le long du navire (FAS) (...port d'embarquement convenu)
Ⓘ franco lungo bordo (FAS) (... porto di imbarco convenuto)

free carrier (FCA) (...named place) (Incoterms 2000)
Ⓓ frei Frachtführer (FCA) (...benannter Ort)
Ⓢ franco transportista (FCA) (...lugar convenido)
Ⓕ Franco transporteur (FCA) (...lieu convenu)
Ⓘ franco vettore (FCA) (...luogo convenuto)

free on board (FOB) (...named port of shipment) (Incoterms 2000)
Ⓓ frei an Bord (FOB) (...benannter Verschiffungshafen)
Ⓢ franco a bordo (FOB) (...puerto de embarque convenido)
Ⓕ Franco bord (FOB) (...port d'embarquement convenu)
Ⓘ franco a bordo (FOB) (...porto di imbarco convenuto)

house air (way) bill
Ⓓ Hausluftfrachtbrief (= des Spediteurs)
Ⓢ guía aérea emitida por un expedidor de carga
Ⓕ LTA émise par transitaire
Ⓘ lettera di trasporto aereo emessa da un consolidatore

---

import licence
- Ⓓ Einfuhrgenehmigung, Einfuhrlizenz
- Ⓢ licencia de importación, permiso de importación
- Ⓕ licence d'importation
- Ⓘ licenza d'importazione

Incoterms ICC (International regulations for the interpretation of trade terms)
- Ⓓ Incoterms ICC (Internationale Regeln zur Auslegung von handelsüblichen Vertragsformen)
- Ⓢ Incoterms CCI (reglas internacionales para la interpretación de términos comerciales)
- Ⓕ Incoterms CCI (règles internationales pour l'interprétation des termes commerciaux)
- Ⓘ Incoterms CCI (regole internazionali per l'interpretazione dei termini commerciali)

insurance
- Ⓓ Versicherung
- Ⓢ seguro
- Ⓕ assurance
- Ⓘ assicurazione

insurance policy
- Ⓓ Versicherungspolice
- Ⓢ póliza de seguro
- Ⓕ police d'assurance
- Ⓘ polizza d'assicurazione

insurance premium
- Ⓓ Versicherungsprämie
- Ⓢ premio o prima de seguro
- Ⓕ prime d'assurance
- Ⓘ premio d'assicurazione

International Air Transport Association (IATA)
- Ⓓ Internationaler Luftverkehrsverband (IATA)
- Ⓢ Asociación Internacional de Transporte Aéreo (IATA)
- Ⓕ Association du Transport Aérien International (ATAI)
- Ⓘ Associazione del Trasporto Aereo Internazionale (IATA)

International Civil Aviation Organisation (ICAO) (UN)
- Ⓓ Internationale Zivilluftfahrtorganisation (IZLO)
- Ⓢ Organización de la Aviación Civil Internacional (OACI)
- Ⓕ Organisation de l'Aviation Civile Internationale (OACI)
- Ⓘ Organizzazione dell'Aviazione Civile Internazionale (OACI)

International Maritime Organisation (IMO) (UN)
- Ⓓ Internationale Seeschiffahrtsorganisation (IMO)
- Ⓢ Organización Marítima Internacional (OMI)
- Ⓕ Organisation Maritime Internationale (OMI)
- Ⓘ Organizzazione Marittima Internazionale (IMO)

invoice
- Ⓓ Rechnung
- Ⓢ factura
- Ⓕ facture
- Ⓘ fattura

invoice (commercial)
- Ⓓ Handelsrechnung
- Ⓢ factura comercial
- Ⓕ facture commerciale
- Ⓘ fattura commerciale

pro forma **invoice**
- Ⓓ Pro-Forma-Rechnung
- Ⓢ factura pro forma
- Ⓕ facture pro forma
- Ⓘ fattura pro forma

letter of credit (L/C)
  (= documentary credit)
- Ⓓ Akkreditiv, Kreditbrief (= Dokumenten-Akkreditiv)
- Ⓢ carta de crédito (= crédito documentario)
- Ⓕ lettre de crédit (=crédit documentaire)
- Ⓘ lettera di credito (=credito documentario)

stand-by **letter of credit**
- Ⓓ Standby letter of credit, Bankbürgschaft in Akkreditivform
- Ⓢ carta de crédito 'standby', crédito de garantía, crédito de contingencia
- Ⓕ caution bancaire
- Ⓘ lettera di credito 'stand by' (a garanzia d'esecuzione)

liner terms
- Ⓓ Usancen des Linienverkehrs
- Ⓢ condiciones de los servicios de línea

Ⓕ conditions du trafic maritime
régulier
Ⓘ condizioni di traffico di linea

mate's receipt
Ⓓ Bordempfangsschein
Ⓢ recibo, de (a) bordo (del
contramaestre)
Ⓕ reçu de bord (du capitaine)
Ⓘ ricevuta di bordo

multimodal transport
Ⓓ multimodaler Transport
Ⓢ transporte multimodal
Ⓕ transport multimodal
Ⓘ trasporto multimodale

negotiable # non negotiable
Ⓓ negozierbar # nicht negozierbar
Ⓢ negociable # no negociable
Ⓕ négociable # non négociable
Ⓘ negoziabile # non negoziabile

order
Ⓓ Bestellung, Anweisung, Auftrag,
Order
Ⓢ orden, pedido
Ⓕ commande, ordre
Ⓘ mandato, ordine, ordinazione

(to) **order**
Ⓓ an die Order
Ⓢ a la ordene
Ⓕ à ordre
Ⓘ all'ordine

packing list
Ⓓ Packliste
Ⓢ lista de empaquetado
Ⓕ liste de colisage
Ⓘ distinta colli

protest
Ⓓ Protest, Einspruch
Ⓢ protesta, rechazo, reporte,
proceso verbal
Ⓕ protêt, rapport, procès-verbal
Ⓘ protesto (cambiario), protesta,
riserva

quay
Ⓓ Kai
Ⓢ muelle
Ⓕ quai
Ⓘ banchina

quota
Ⓓ Anteil, Kontingent
Ⓢ cuota, parte
Ⓕ quota, quote-part
Ⓘ quota

receipt
Ⓓ Quittung,
Empfangsbescheinigung
Ⓢ recibo, resguardo, talón
Ⓕ reçu, récépissé
Ⓘ ricevuta

**reinstatement of a revolving
credit**
Ⓓ Wiedereinsetzung eines
revolvierenden Akkreditivs
Ⓢ restablecimiento de un crédito
rotativo
Ⓕ rétablissement d'un crédit
'revolving'
Ⓘ ripristino di un credito rotativo

risk (country)
Ⓓ Länderrisiko
Ⓢ (país) riesgo
Ⓕ risque-pays
Ⓘ rischio paese

roll-on / roll-off (ro-ro)
Ⓓ Ro-Ro
Ⓢ ro-ro
Ⓕ 'ro-ro' (roulage, chargement-
déchargement)
Ⓘ roll-on/roll-off, ro-ro (caricamento
orizzontale a mezzo ruote su
nave)

seller
Ⓓ Verkäufer
Ⓢ vendedor
Ⓕ vendeur
Ⓘ venditore

ship
Ⓓ Schiff
Ⓢ buque, barco, nave
Ⓕ navire
Ⓘ nave

shipping documents
Ⓓ Verladedokumente
Ⓢ documentos de expedición, de
embarque
Ⓕ documents d'expédition
Ⓘ documenti di spedizione

shipment (= consignment)
Ⓓ Sendung
Ⓢ expedición, despacho
Ⓕ expédition, envoi
Ⓘ spedizioine, invio

shipment (on board a vessel)
Ⓓ Verschiffung
Ⓢ embarque
Ⓕ embarquement
Ⓘ imbarco

sue and labour clause (ins.)
- Ⓓ Klausel zur Schadensabwendung und Schadensminderung
- Ⓢ cláusula de recurso y conserva
- Ⓕ clause de recours et de conservation
- Ⓘ clausola che autorizza alle misure conservative

surcharge
- Ⓓ Zuschlag, Aufgeld, Aufschlag, Nachgebühr
- Ⓢ sobre tasa, recargo
- Ⓕ surtaxe
- Ⓘ sovrimposta, sovrattassa

tariff
- Ⓓ Tarif, Preis
- Ⓢ tarifa, arancel, tarifa arancelaria, arancel de aduana
- Ⓕ tarif
- Ⓘ tariffa

tenor (content)
- Ⓓ Inhalt
- Ⓢ tenor, contenido
- Ⓕ contenu
- Ⓘ contenuto

title
- Ⓓ Titel; Rechtsanspruch
- Ⓢ título/derecho de propiedad
- Ⓕ titre de propriété
- Ⓘ titolo di proprietà

trademark
- Ⓓ Warenzeichen
- Ⓢ marca comercial
- Ⓕ marque de fabrique
- Ⓘ marchio di fabbrica

transhipment
- Ⓓ Umladung
- Ⓢ transbordo
- Ⓕ transbordement
- Ⓘ trasbordo

under reserve
- Ⓓ unter Vorbehalt
- Ⓢ bajo reserva
- Ⓕ sous réserve
- Ⓘ sotto riserva

value added tax (VAT)
- Ⓓ Mehrwertsteuer, Umsatzsteuer
- Ⓢ impuesto sobre el valor añadido (IVA)
- Ⓕ taxe à la valeur ajoutée (TVA)
- Ⓘ imposta sul valore aggiunto (IVA)

vessel
- Ⓓ Schiff, Dampfer
- Ⓢ buque, nave, barco
- Ⓕ navire
- Ⓘ nave

feeder **vessel**
- Ⓓ Zubringerschiff
- Ⓢ buque alimentador
- Ⓕ navire collecteur
- Ⓘ nave 'feeder' (per smistamento di contenitori)

ocean **vessel**
- Ⓓ Seeschiff
- Ⓢ buque de altamar
- Ⓕ navire de haute mer
- Ⓘ nave oceanica

waybill
- Ⓓ Frachtbrief
- Ⓢ carta de porte, guía de carga
- Ⓕ lettre de voiture
- Ⓘ lettera di vettura

weight
- Ⓓ Gewicht
- Ⓢ peso
- Ⓕ poids
- Ⓘ peso

wharf
- Ⓓ Kai
- Ⓢ muelle, malecón
- Ⓕ quai
- Ⓘ banchina

with particular average (WPA)
- Ⓓ mit besonderer Havarie
- Ⓢ con avería particular
- Ⓕ avec avaries particulières
- Ⓘ avaria particolare inclusa

World Trade Organization (WTO)
- Ⓓ Welthandelsorganisation (WTO)
- Ⓢ Organización Mundial del Comercio (OMC)
- Ⓕ Organisation Mondiale du Commerce (OMC)
- Ⓘ Organizzazione Mondiale del Commercio (OMC)

English   Ⓓ Deutsch   Ⓢ Espagnol   Ⓕ Français   Ⓘ Italiano

Bibliography

The first two definitions for bibliography in the Random House *Webster's Unabridged Dictionary* are:

1. "a complete or selective list of works complied upon some common principle as authorship, subject, place of publication, or printer"

2. "a list of source materials that are used or consulted in the preparation of a work, or that are referred to in the text."

It is the first definition that applies to this bibliography, and international trade is the common denominator.

Detailed information on many of the following titles may be obtained from Amazon at www.amazon.com, Barnes and Noble at www.barnesandnoble.com, or any similar Internet bookseller. All ICC publications can be obtained from www.iccbooks.com or www.iccbooksusa.com for the USA.

Country-specific Information

Dun & Bradstreet's Guide to Doing Business Around the World, (ISBN 0735201080), Terry Morrison, Wayne A. Conaway, Joseph Douress, 544 pages, Prenctice Hall Press, Paramus, New Jersey, USA.

Export Reference Library, Staff, CD-ROM coverage of over 200 country profiles and foreign-trade information updated monthly, The Bureau of National Affairs, Washington, DC, USA.

International Trade Reporter, Staff, hard copy coverage of over 200 country profiles and foreign-trade information updated biweekly, The Bureau of National Affairs, Washington, DC, USA.

Merriam Webster's Geographical Dictionary, (ISBN 0877795460), 1361 pages, Merriam-Webster, Incorporated, Springfield, MA, USA.

The Exporters Encyclopaedia, Staff, hard copy coverage of over 200 country profiles and foreign-trade information updated twice monthly, Dun & Bradstreet Information Services, Parsippany, NJ, USA.

The Portable World Factbook, (ISBN 0380730510), Keith Lye, 352 pages, Avon Books, New York, NY, USA.

Dictionaries

A Comprehensive Guide to International Trade Terms, (no ISBN number – publication number PB94-136652/HDV), John O'Connor (Editor), 242 pages, United States Department of Commerce, National Technical Information Service, Washington DC, USA.

Bes' Chartering and Shipping Terms, (ISBN 0900133147), Norman J. Lopez, 641 pages, Baker and Howard Ltd., London, England.

Dictionary of International Business Terms, (ISBN 0764112635), John J. Capela, Stephen W. Hartman, 612 pages, Barron's Educational Series, Inc., Hauppague, NY.

Dictionary of Shipping Terms, (ISBN 1859781195), Peter R. Brodie, Informa Group, London, England.

Elsevier's Dictionary of Ports and Shipping, (ISBN 0444895426), J. D. Van Der Tuin, D. L. Newman, 382 pages, Elsevier Science, Amsterdam, Netherlands.

Key Words in International Trade, (ISBN 9284211875), 427 pages, ICC publication No. 417/4, ICC Publishing www.iccbooks.com and www.iccbooksusa.com

Merriam Webster's Geographical Dictionary, (ISBN 0877795460), 1361 pages, Merriam-Webster, Incorporated, Springfield, MA, USA.

NCBFAA Study Manual Series Dictionary, Kevin Maloney, 471 pages, available only from the National Customs Brokers and Freight Forwarders Association of America, Inc, 1200 18th Street, Suite 901, Washington, DC 20036, USA.

The Language of Trade, Merritt R. Blakeslee, Carlos A. Garcia, United States Department of State, Washington, DC, USA (available at no charge at www.usinfo.state.gov/products/pubs/trade/glossac.htm).

Exporting

A Basic Guide to Exporting, Staff, United States Department of Commerce, 132 pages, Unz & Company, New Providence, NJ, USA www.unzco.com.

Export Procedures – An Interactive Guide to Export Documentation, (ISBN 0966877101), Catherine E. Thornberry, 195 pages, Duquesne University, Pittsburgh, PA, USA.

Exporting: A Manager's Guide to the World Market, (ISBN 1861523165), Carl A. Nelson, 256 pages, International Thompson Business Press, New York, NY, USA.

Exporting: From Start to Finance, (ISBN 0070693005), L. Fargo Wells, Karin Dulat, 613 pages, McGraw-Hill Inc., New York, NY, USA.

Exporting: Regulations, Documentation and Procedures, (ISBN 1891249002), George Thompson, Catherine Petersen, 190 pages, Global Training Center, Inc., Dayton, OH, USA.

Exportize, (ISBN 0912501030), John C. Rennie, 272 pages, The Small Business Foundation of America, Boston, MA, USA.

Fast-Track Exporting: How Your Company Can Succeed in the Global Market, ((ISBN0814450091), Sandra L. Renner, W. Gary Winget, 275 pages, American Management Association, New York, NY, USA.

How to Succeed in Exporting and Doing Business Internationally, (ISBN 0471311286), Eric Sletten, 277 pages, John Wiley & Sons, Inc., New York, NY, USA.

Rules of Origin of Goods, World Customs Organization, 30 rue du Marche, 1210 Brussels, Belgium, Fax +3222099490, website www.wcoomd.org.

Trade Secrets, The Export Answer Book for Small and Medium-Sized Exporters, (ISBN18864103x), Sara S. McCue, 176 pages, Michigan Small Business Development Center at Wayne State University, Detroit, MI, USA.

General Foreign Trade

Anti-Counterfeiting Technology Guide, (ISBN 9284212936), Commercial Crime Services, 80 pages, ICC publication No. 630, ICC Publishing www.iccbooks.com and www.iccbooksusa.com.

Building an Import/Export Business, 2nd Edition, (ISBN 0471177873), Kenneth D. Weiss, 304 pages, John Wiley & Sons, Inc., New York, NY, USA.

Business Guide to the World Trading System, (ISBN 0850926211), UN Staff, UN International Trade Centre, Geneva, Switzerland.

Export Import, (ISBN 1558703888), Joseph A. Zodl, 160 pages, Betterway Books, Cincinnati, OH, USA.

Export-Import Basics, (ISBN 9284211948), Guillermo Jiménez, 240 pages, ICC publication No. 543, ICC Publishing www.iccbooks.com and www.iccbooksusa.com.

Export/Import Procedures and Documentation, (ISBN 0814403506), Thomas E. Johnson, 512 pages, American Management Association, New York, NY, USA.

Fighting Bribery, (ISBN 9284212634), 126 pages, ICC publication No. 610, ICC Publishing www.iccbooks.com and www.iccbooksusa.com

Glossary of Packaging Terms for Developing Countries, (ISBN 9291370819), UN Staff, 137 pages, UN International Trade Centre, Geneva, Switzerland.

Going Global: Getting Started in International Trade, (ISBN 9991615423), Staff, American Management Association, New York, NY, USA.

Handbook of World Trade, (ISBN 0749435607), Jonathan Reuvid, 486 pages, ICC publication No. 638, ICC Publishing www.iccbooks.com and www.iccbooksusa.com

Handbook for Multilingual Business Writing, (ISBN0844291226), Staff, National Textbook Company, Lincolnwood, IL, USA.

Import/Export: How to Get Started in International Trade, (ISBN0071358714), Carl A. Nelson, 340 pages, McGraw-Hill Inc., New York, NY, USA.

Shrinking the Globe into Your Company's Hands: The Step-By-Step International Trade Guide for Small Businesses, (ISBN

1877810460), Sidney R. Lawrence, Rayve Publications, Windsor, CA, USA.

The Do's and Taboos of International Trade: A Small Business Primer, (ISBN 0471007609), Roger E. Axtell, 336 pages, John Wiley & Sons, Inc., New York, NY, USA.

The Learning Annex Guide to Starting Your Own Import-Export Business, (ISBN 0806513217), Karen Offitzer, 93 pages, Citidel Publishing Group, New York, NY, USA.

Winning in Foreign Markets, (ISBN 0884328287), Michelle D. Forzley, 106 page book and 3 audio cassettes, Audio-Forum, Guilford, CT, USA.

World Directory of Trade Promotion Organizations and Other Foreign Trade Bodies, UN Staff, 131 pages, UN International Trade Center, Geneva, Switzerland.

Importing

A Basic Guide to Importing, (ISBN 0844234036), Staff, U.S. Customs Service, McGraw Hill, New York, NY, USA.

Alphabetical Index to the Harmonized Commodity Description and Coding System, World Customs Organization, 30 rue du Marche, 1210 Brussels, Belgium, Fax +3222099490, website www.wcoomd.org.

Amendments to the Harmonized Commodity Description and Coding System, World Customs Organization, 30 rue du Marche, 1210 Brussels, Belgium, Fax +3222099490, website www.wcoomd.org.

ATA Handbook, World Customs Organization, 30 rue du Marche, 1210 Brussels, Belgium, Fax +3222099490, website www.wcoomd.org.

Brief Guide to the Customs Valuation Code, World Customs Organization, 30 rue du Marche, 1210 Brussels, Belgium, Fax +3222099490, website www.wcoomd.org.

Customs Convention Concerning the Facilities for the Importation of Goods for Display, World Customs Organization, 30 rue du Marche, 1210 Brussels, Belgium, Fax +3222099490, website www.wcoomd.org.

Customs Convention on Containers (1995), World Customs Organization, 30 rue du Marche, 1210 Brussels, Belgium, Fax +3222099490, website www.wcoomd.org.

Customs Convention on the ATA Carnet for the Temporary Admission of Goods, World Customs Organization, 30 rue du Marche, 1210 Brussels, Belgium, Fax +3222099490, website www.wcoomd.org.

Customs Convention on the International Transit of Goods, World Customs Organization, 30 rue du Marche, 1210 Brussels, Belgium, Fax +3222099490, website www.wcoomd.org.

Customs Convention on the Temporary Importation of Packings, World Customs Organization, 30 rue du Marche, 1210 Brussels, Belgium, Fax +3222099490, website www.wcoomd.org.

Customs Convention on the Temporary Importation of Pedagogic Material, World Customs Organization, 30 rue du Marche, 1210 Brussels, Belgium, Fax +3222099490, website www.wcoomd.org.

Customs Convention on the Temporary Importation of Professional Equipment, World Customs Organization, 30 rue du Marche, 1210 Brussels, Belgium, Fax +3222099490, website www.wcoomd.org.

Customs Convention on the Temporary Importation of Scientific Equipment, World Customs Organization, 30 rue du Marche, 1210 Brussels, Belgium, Fax +3222099490, website www.wcoomd.org.

Elements of Import Practice, (ISBN 0412284804), Alan E. Branch, Chapman and Hall, Division, International Thompson Publishers, New York, NY, USA.

Explanatory Notes to the Harmonized Commodity Description and Coding System, (available in hard copy with sequential supplements or CD ROM), World Customs Organization, 30 rue du Marche, 1210 Brussels, Belgium, Fax +3222099490, website www.wcoomd.org.

Guide on Cargo Insurance for Importers, UN Staff, 102 pages, UN International Trade Centre, Geneva, Switzerland

Guidelines on Consignments for Immediate Clearance, World Customs Organization, 30 rue du Marche, 1210 Brussels, Belgium, Fax +3222099490, website www.wcoomd.org.

Handbook on the Revised Kyoto Convention, (Volumes I, II, III, IV) World Customs Organization, 30 rue du Marche, 1210 Brussels, Belgium, Fax +3222099490, website www.wcoomd.org.

Harmonized Commodity Description and Coding System, World Customs Organization, 30 rue du Marche, 1210 Brussels, Belgium, Fax +3222099490, website www.wcoomd.org.

Importing into the USA, (ISBN 0970163118), Alex Capri, 500 pages, Capa Publications, Los Angeles, CA, USA

Import Practice, (ISBN 0872240266), David A. Serko, 810 pages, Practicing Law Institute, New York, NY, USA.

Rules of Origin of Goods, World Customs Organization, 30 rue du Marche, 1210 Brussels, Belgium, Fax +3222099490, website www.wcoomd.org.

Incoterms

Incoterms 2000 (ISBN 9284211999), 297 pages, ICC publication No. 560, ICC Publishing, www.iccbooks.com and www.iccbooksusa.com

Incoterms 2000 Wallchart, ICC publication No. 614, ICC Publishing, www.iccbooks.com and www.iccbooksusa.com .

Incoterms 2000 Multimedia Expert (ISBN 9284212804), CD-ROM, ICC publication No. 616, ICC Publishing, www.iccbooks.com and www.iccbooksusa.com

Incoterms 2000 – A Forum of Experts (ISBN 9284212707), 132 pages, ICC publication No. 617, ICC Publishing, www.iccbooks.com and www.iccbooksusa.com

Incoterms for Americans (Fully Revised for Incoterms 2000), (ISBN 1886457069), Frank Reynolds, 140 pages, International Projects Inc., Toledo, OH, USA.

ICC Guide to Incoterms 2000 (ISBN 9284212693), 192 pages, ICC publication No. 620, ICC Publishing, www.iccbooks.com and www.iccbooksusa.com

Insurance

Cases & Materials on Marine Insurance Law, (ISBN 1859414389), Susan Hodges, 1012 pages, Cavendish Publishing, London, England.

German General Rules of Marine Insurance (ADS), (ISBN 0899257550), Erdewin Pinckernelle (Translator), Walter De Gruyter, Berlin, Germany.

Guide on Cargo Insurance for Importers, UN Staff, 102 pages, UN International Trade Center, Geneva, Switzerland.

Key Divergences Between English and American Law of Marine Insurance: A Comparative Study, (ISBN 0870335227), Thomas J. Schoenbaum, 232 pages, Cornell Maritime Press, Centerville, MD, USA.

Law of Marine Insurance, (ISBN 1859412270), Susan Hodges, 694 pages, Cavendish Publishing, London, England.

Legal and Documentary Aspects of the French and Latin American Marine Insurance Legal Regimes, (ISBN 9211121361), UN Staff, UN International Trade Center, Geneva, Switzerland.

Marine Insurance Compendium – A Complete Reference Guide, Warren Hastings, 111 pages, GMS Publications, White Plains, NY, USA, www.centretrade.com.

Ocean Cargo Claims Handbook, Staff, 36 pages, Chubb Group of Insurance Companies, Warren, NJ, USA.

Ocean Cargo Handbook, Staff, 43 pages, Chubb Group of Insurance Companies, Warren, NJ, USA.

Ocean Marine Insurance (Vol. 1 & 2 – 2nd ed.), (ISBN 0894620711), Arthur E. Brunck, Victor P. Simone, C. Arthur Williams, Arthur L. Flitner, 466 pages, American Institute for Chartered Property Casualty Underwriters, Malvern, PA, USA.

Templeman on Marine Insurance: Its Principles and Practice, (ISBN 0273025376), R. J. Lambeth, 628 pages, Sheridan House, Dobbs Ferry, NY, USA.

The Institute Clauses, (ISBN 1850448795), N. Geoffrey Hudson, J. C. Allen, Informa Group, London, England.

The Law and Practice of Marine Insurance and Average, (ISBN 0870333682), Axel L. Parks, 1652 pages, Cornell Maritime Press, Centerville, MD, USA.

The Law of Marine Insurance, (ISBN 0198262442), Howard N. Bennett, Oxford University Press, Oxford, England.

The York-Antwerp Rules: The Principles and Practice of General Average Adjustment, (ISBN 1859780261), N. Geoffrey Hudson, Informa Group, London, England.

Legal

Cases & Materials on Marine Insurance Law, (ISBN 1859414389), Susan Hodges, 1012 pages, Cavendish Publishing, London, England.

Complying With the Foreign Corrupt Practices Act: A Guide for U.S. Firms Doing Business in the International Marketplace, (ISBN 1570737029), Donald R. Cruver, 106 pages, American Bar Association, Chicago, IL, USA.

Explanatory Notes to the Harmonized Commodity Description and Coding System, (available in hard copy with sequential supplements or CD ROM), World Customs Organization, 30 rue du Marche, 1210 Brussels, Belgium, Fax +3222099490, website www.wcoomd.org.

Harmonized Commodity Description and Coding System, World Customs Organization, 30 rue du Marche, 1210 Brussels, Belgium, Fax +3222099490, website www.wcoomd.org.

Import Practice, (ISBN 0872240266), David A. Serko, 810 pages, Practicing Law Institute, New York, NY, USA.

International Commercial Transactions, (ISBN 9284212892), Jan Ramberg, 512 pages, ICC publication No. 624, ICC Publishing, www.iccbooks.com and www.iccbooksusa.com.

International Computer Law, (ISBN 0820513180), Josef A. Keustermans, Ingrid M. Arckens, regularly updated with supplements, Matthew Bender (Division of Lexus-Nexus), Albany, NY, USA.

International Contracts, (ISBN 1885073550), Karla C. Shippey, 184 pages, World Trade Press, San Rafael, CA, USA.

Key Divergences Between English and American Law of Marine Insurance: A Comparative Study, (ISBN 0870335227), Thomas J. Schoenbaum, 232 pages, Cornell Maritime Press, Centerville, MD, USA.

Law of Marine Insurance, (ISBN 1859412270), Susan Hodges, 694 pages, Cavendish Publishing, London, England.

Legal and Documentary Aspects of the French and Latin American Marine Insurance Legal Regimes, (ISBN 9211121361), UN Staff, UN International Trade Center, Geneva, Switzerland.

Letters of Credit: Commercial and Standby Letters of Credit – Bankers' and Trade Acceptances, (ISBN 0820513873), Burton V. McCullough, regularly updated with supplements, Mathew Bender (Division of Lexus Nexus), Albany, NY, USA.

The Law and Practice of Marine Insurance and Average, (ISBN 0870333682), Axel L. Parks, 1652 pages, Cornell Maritime Press, Centerville, MD, USA.

The Law of Marine Insurance, (ISBN 0198262442), Howard N. Bennett, Oxford University Press, Oxford, England.

Rules of Origin of Goods, World Customs Organization, 30 rue du Marche, 1210 Brussels, Belgium, Fax +3222099490, website www.wcoomd.org.

The Sale of Goods Carried by Sea, (ISBN 0406020914), Charles Debattista, 306 pages, Butterworths, a Division of Reed Elsevier (UK) Ltd, London, England.

Transfer of Ownership in International Trade, (ISBN 9284211972), Alexander von Ziegler, Jette H. Ronoe, Charles Debattista, Odile Plegat-Kerrault (Editors), 437 pages, ICC publication No. 546, ICC Publishing, www.iccbooks.com and www.iccbooksusa.com

Management

Exporting: A Manager's Guide to the World Market, (ISBN 1861523165), Carl A. Nelson, 256 pages, International Thompson Business Press, New York, NY, USA.

International Business: A Manager's Guide to Strategy in the Age of Globalism, (ISBN 1861523157), Carl A. Nelson, 256 pages, International Thompson Business Press, New York, NY, USA.

International Management: Managing Across Borders and Cultures, (ISBN 0321028295), Helen Deresky, 614 pages, Prentice Hall, Upper Saddle River, NJ, USA.

Managing Across Borders – The Transnational Solution, (ISBN 0875843034), Christopher A. Bartlett, Sumantra Ghoshal, 274 pages, Harvard Business School Press, Boston, MA, USA.

Managing Globally: A Complete Guide to Competing Worldwide, (ISBN 078630121x), Carl A. Nelson, 350 pages, McGraw-Hill, Inc., New York, NY, USA.

Mind Your Manners: Managing Business Cultures in Europe, (ISBN 1857880854), John Mole, 236 pages, Nicholas Brealey, Sonoma, CA, USA.

Navigating Cross-Cultural Ethics: What Global Managers Do Right to Keep from Going Wrong, (ISBN 0750699159), Eileen Morgan, 200 pages, Butterworth-Heinemann, Woburn, MA, USA.

Protocol for Profit: A Manager's Guide for Competing Worldwide, (ISBN 1861523149), Carl A. Nelson, 256 pages, International Thompson Business Press, New York, NY, USA.

Marketing

An Introduction to International Marketing: A Guide to Going Global (Marketing in Action Series), (ISBN 0749422467), Keith Lewis, Matthew Housden, 160 pages, Kogan Page Ltd, London, England.

Export Marketing Handbook, (ISBN 0275929493), Walter H. Nagel, Jr., Gaston Z. Ndyajunwoha, 136 pages, Praeger Publishers, New York, NY, USA.

Guide to Software Export: A Handbook for International Software Sales, (ISBN 0789001438), Roger A. Phillips, Haworth Press, Binghamton, NY, USA.

Handbook of Cross-Cultural Marketing, (ISBN 078900285x), Paul A. Herbig, 318 pages, Haworth Press, Binghamton, NY, USA.

The CIM Handbook of Export Marketing: A Practical Guide to Opening and Expanding Markets Overseas (Professional Chartered Institute of Marketing), (ISBN 0750643463), Chris J. Noonan, Ian Campbell, Butterworth-Heinemann, Woburn, MA, USA.

The Handbook of International Marketing Communications,
(ISBN 0631200916), Sylvester O. Moyne (Editor), 350 pages,
Blackwell Publishing, Oxford, England.

Model Contracts

ICC Model Commercial Agency Contract, (ISBN 9284211247), 34
pages, ICC publication No. 496, ICC Publishing,
www.iccbooks.com and www.iccbooksusa.com.

ICC Model Distributorship Contract (Sole Importer–Distributor),
(ISBN 9284211530), 40 pages, ICC publication No. 518, ICC
Publishing, www.iccbooks.com and www.iccbooksusa.com.

**ICC Model International Agency & Distributorship Contracts
(short forms)** (with diskette), (ISBN 9284212995), 40 pages, ICC
publication No. 634, ICC Publishing, www.iccbooks.com and
www.iccbooksusa.com

ICC Model International Franchising Contract (with diskette),
(ISBN 9284212111), 76 pages, ICC publication No. 557, ICC
Publishing, www.iccbooks.com and www.iccbooksusa.com.

ICC Model International Sale Contract (with diskette), (ISBN
9284212103), 62 pages, ICC publication No. 556, ICC Publishing,
www.iccbooks.com and www.iccbooksusa.com.

The ICC Model Occasional Intermediary Contract (with diskette),
(ISBN 9284212723), 36 pages, ICC publication No. 619, ICC
Publishing, www.iccbooks.com and www.iccbooksusa.com.

Multinational Culture and Negotiation

**A Short Course in International Negotiating: Planning and
Conducting International Commercial Negotiations** (Short
Course in International Trade Series), (ISBN 1885073518), Jeffrey
Edmund Curry, 196 pages, World Trade Press, San Rafael, CA,
USA.

Blunders in International Business, (ISBN 0631217762), David A.
Ricks, 172 pages, Blackwell Publishing, Oxford, England.

Do's and Taboos Around the World, (ISBN 0471595284), Roger E.
Axtell, 208 pages, John Wiley & Sons, Inc., New York, NY, USA.

Do's and Taboos Around the World for Women in Business, (ISBN 047143642), Roger E. Axtell, 252 pages, John Wiley & Sons, Inc., New York, NY, USA.

Do's and Taboos of Hosting International Visitors, (ISBN 0471515701), Roger E. Axtell, 236 pages, John Wiley & Sons, Inc., New York, NY, USA.

Do's and Taboos of Humor Around the World, (ISBN 0471254037), Roger E. Axtell, 256 pages, John Wiley & Sons, Inc., New York, NY, USA.

Do's and Taboos of Using English Around the World, (ISBN 0471308412), Roger E. Axtell, 224 pages, John Wiley & Sons, Inc., New York, NY, USA.

Doing Business Internationally: The Guide to Cross-Cultural Success, (ISBN 0786301171), Terence Brake, Danielle Medina Walker, Walker Thomas, 225 pages, McGraw-Hill Inc., New York, NY, USA.

Gestures: The Do's and Taboos of Body Language Around the World, (ISBN 0471183423), Roger E. Axtell, 256 pages, John Wiley & Sons, Inc., New York, NY, USA.

Global Smarts: The Art of Communicating and Deal Making Anywhere in the World, (ISBN 0471382469), Sheida Hodge, 256 pages, John Wiley & Sons, Inc., New York, NY, USA.

Going Global? Power Tools for Negotiating International Business Deals, (ISBN 096857260x), James M. Klotz, 285 pages, Global Business Press Inc., Toronto, Ontario, Canada.

Going International: How to Make Friends and Deal Effectively in the Global Marketplace, (ISBN 0452258642), Lennie Copeland, Lewis Griggs, 279 pages, Penguin Group, New York, NY, USA.

How to Negotiate Anything With Anyone, Anywhere Around the World, (ISBN 0814479502), Frank L. Acuff, 336 pages, American Management Association, New York, NY, USA.

International Management: Managing Across Borders and Cultures, (ISBN 0321028295), Helen Deresky, 614 pages, Prentice Hall, Upper Saddle River, NJ, USA.

International Negotiation – A Cross-Cultural Perspective, (ISBN 0933662505), Glen Fisher, 69 pages, Intercultural Press, Yarmouth, ME, USA.

Kiss, Bow, or Shake Hands: How to Do Business in 60 Countries, (ISBN 1558504443), Terri Morrison, Wayne A. Conaway, George A. Borden, Hans Koehler (Preface), 440 pages, Adams Media Corporation, Avon, MA, USA.

Mind Your Manners: Managing Business Cultures in Europe, (ISBN 1857880854), John Mole, 236 pages, Nicholas Brealey, Sonoma, CA, USA.

Navigating Cross-Cultural Ethics: What Global Managers Do Right to Keep from Going Wrong, (ISBN 0750699159), Eileen Morgan, 200 pages, Butterworth-Heinemann, Woburn, MA, USA.

Negotiating Across Cultures: International Communication in an Interdependent World, (ISBN 1878379720), Raymond Cohen, 320 pages, United States Institute of Peace, Washington, DC, USA.

Negotiating Globally: How to Negotiate Deals, Resolve Disputes, and Make Decisions Across Cultures, (ISBN 0787955868), Jeanne M. Brett, 288 pages, Jossey-Bass, Division of John Wiley & Sons, Inc, New York, NY, USA.

Protocol for Profit: A Manager's Guide for Competing Worldwide, (ISBN 1861523149), Carl A. Nelson, 256 pages, International Thompson Business Press, New York, NY, USA.

Put Your Best Foot Forward Asia: A Fearless Guide to International Communication and Behavior, (ISBN 096375307x), Mary M. Bosrock, International Education Systems, St. Paul, MN, USA.

Put Your Best Foot Forward Europe: A Fearless Guide to International Communication and Behavior, (ISBN 0963753037), Mary M. Bosrock, International Education Systems, St. Paul, MN, USA.

Put Your Best Foot Forward Mexico and Canada: A Fearless Guide to International Communication and Behavior, (ISBN 0963753053), Mary M. Bosrock, International Education Systems, St. Paul, MN, USA.

Put Your Best Foot Forward South America: A Fearless Guide to International Communication and Behavior, (ISBN 0963753088), Mary M. Bosrock, Craig MacIntosh, 384 pages, International Education Systems, St. Paul, MN, USA.

Put Your Best Foot Forward USA: A Fearless Guide to International Communication and Behavior, (ISBN

0963753096), Mary M. Bosrock, 480 pages, International
Education Systems, St. Paul, MN, USA.

Speaking Globally, (ISBN 0749422211), Elizabeth Urech, 216 pages,
Kogan Page, Dover, NH, USA.

Speaking Globally: English in an International Context, (ISBN
0205156002), William Grohe, Christine Root, Allyn & Bacon,
Boston, MA, USA.

The Cultural Environment of International Business, (ISBN
0538800038), Vern Terpstra, Kenneth David, South-Western
Publishing Div. International Thompson Business Press, New
York, NY, USA.

The Dictionary of Global Culture, (ISBN 039458581x), Kwame
Anthony Appiah, Henry Louis Gates, Michael Colin Vazquez, 717
pages, Alfred A. Knopf, New York, NY, USA.

Payment

A Banker's Insights on International Trade, (ISBN 0967992702),
Roy Becker, 120 pages, Roy Becker Seminars, Littleton, CO, USA.

Bank Guarantees in International Trade (2nd edition), (ISBN
9284211980), 428 pages, Roeland Bertrams, ICC publication
No. 547, ICC Publishing, www.iccbooks.com and
www.iccbooksusa.com.

Bills of Exchange (3rd edition), (ISBN 9284212502), 192 pages, Dr
Uwe Jahn, ICC publication No. 593, ICC Publishing,
www.iccbooks.com and www.iccbooksusa.com.

Documentary Credit Law throughout the World, (ISBN
9284212987), 174 pages, Prof. R. Schütze and Gabriele Fontane,
ICC publication No. 633, ICC Publishing, www.iccbooks.com and
www.iccbooksusa.com.

Exchange Arrangements and Exchange Restrictions, Staff,
International Monetary Fund, Washington, DC, USA. (This is an
annual publication.)

**Export Credit Agencies, the Unsung Giants of International
Trade and Finance,** (ISBN 1567204295), Delio Gianturco, 208
pages, Quorum Books, Westport, CT, USA.

Forfaiting for Exporters: Practical Solutions for Global Trade Finance, (ISBN 1861520360), Andy Ripley, 208 pages, International Thompson Business Press, New York, NY, USA.

Getting Paid for Exports, (ISBN0566027402), Burt Edwards, 361 pages, Gower Publishing Group, Aldershot, Hampshire, England.

Global Trade Financing, (ISBN 0471352608), Harry M. Venedikian, Gerald A. Warfield, 496 pages, John Wiley & Sons, Inc., New York, NY, USA.

Guide to Forfaiting, (ISBN 1855645882), Margrith Lutschg-Emmenegger, Euromoney Publications PLC, London, England.

Handbook of International Credit Management, (ISBN 0566083760), Brian W. Clarke, 394 pages, Gower Publishing Company, Aldershot, Hampshire, England.

International Credit and Collections: A Guide to Extending Credit Worldwide, (ISBN0471406759), Mary Ludwig Schaeffer, 320 pages, John Wiley & Sons, Inc., New York, NY, USA.

Letters of Credit: Commercial and Standby Letters of Credit – Bankers' and Trade Acceptances, (ISBN 0820513873), Burton V. McCullough, regularly updated with supplements, Mathew Bender (Division of Lexus-Nexus), Albany, NY, USA.

Opinions of the ICC Banking Commission, (various volumes), ICC publications No. 565, 596, 613, 632, ICC Publishing, www.iccbooks.com and www.iccbooksusa.com.

Principles of International Trade and Payments (Principles of Export Guidebooks), (ISBN 0631191631), Peter Briggs, Blackwell Publishing, Oxford, England.

Risk 2001, A Country by Country Guide, (ISBN 0749435178), Coface Staff, 369 pages, Kogan Page, Limited, London, England.

The Changing Role of Export Credit Agencies, (ISBN1557758018), Malcolm Stephens, International Monetary Fund, Washington, DC, USA.

Shipping

Bes' Chartering and Shipping Terms, (ISBN 0900133147), Norman J. Lopez, 641 pages, Baker and Howard Ltd., London, England

Dictionary of Shipping Terms, (ISBN 1859781195), Peter R. Brodie, Informa Group, London, England.

Elsevier's Dictionary of Ports and Shipping, (ISBN 0444895426), J. D. Van Der Tuin, D. L. Newman, 382 pages, Elsevier Science, Amsterdam, Netherlands.

International Freight Transportation, Gerhardt Muller, 501 pages, Eno Transportation Foundation, Inc., Washington, DC, USA and Intermodal Association of North America, Greenbelt, MD, USA.

International Logistics, (ISBN 0787274259), Evelyn Thomchick, 255 pages, Kendall/Hunt Publishing Company, Dubuque, IA, USA.

International Ocean and Air Transportation, George Thompson, Catherine Petersen, 177 pages, Global Training Center, Dayton, OH USA.

NCBFAA Study Manual Series Cargo Transportation Basics, Kevin Maloney, 471 pages, available only from the National Customs Brokers and Freight Forwarders Association of America, Inc, 1200 18th Street, Suite 901, Washington DC 20036.

The Business of Shipping, (ISBN087033526x) Lane C. Kendall, James J. Buckley, 472 pages, Cornell Maritime Press, Centerville, MD. USA.

Travel

Do's and Taboos of Preparing for Your Trip Abroad, (ISBN0471025674), Roger E. Axtell, Mike Fornwald, John Healy, 160 pages, John Wiley & Sons, Inc., New York, NY, USA.

International Travel, Fares, and Ticketing, (ISBN 0132282224), Jeaqnne Semer-Purzycki, 337 pages, Prentice Hall, Upper Saddle River, NJ, USA.

The Business Travel Survival Guide, (ISBN 0471530751), Jack Cummings, 396 pages, John Wiley & Sons, Inc., New York, NY, USA.

The Global Road Warrior / 3e 95-Country Handbook for the International Business Traveler and Communicator, (ISBN1885073860), Jeffrey E. Curry, Sibylla Putzi, 1054 pages, World Trade Press, San Rafael, CA, USA.

Traveler's World Atlas and Guide, (ISBN 0528833510), 224 pages, Rand McNally & Company, New York, NY, USA.

ICC at a glance

ICC is the world business organization. It is the only representative body that speaks with authority on behalf of enterprises from all sectors in every part of the world.

ICC's purpose is to promote an open international trade and investment system and the market economy worldwide. It makes rules that govern the conduct of business across borders. It provides essential services, foremost among them the ICC International Court of Arbitration, the world's leading institution of its kind.

Within a year of the creation of the United Nations, ICC was granted consultative status at the highest level with the UN and its specialized agencies. Today ICC is the preferred partner of international and regional organizations whenever decisions have to be made on global issues of importance to business.

Business leaders and experts drawn from ICC membership establish the business stance on broad issues of trade and investment policy as well as on vital technical or sectoral subjects. These include financial services, information technologies, telecommunications, marketing ethics, the environment, transportation, competition law and intellectual property, among others.

ICC was founded in 1919 by a handful of far-sighted business leaders. Today it groups thousands of member companies and associations from over 130 countries. National committees in all major capitals coordinate with their membership to address the concerns of the business community and to put across to their governments the business views formulated by ICC.

Some ICC Services

- The ICC International Court of Arbitration (Paris)
- The ICC International Centre for Expertise (Paris)
- The ICC World Chambers Federation (Paris)
- The ICC Institute of World Business Law (Paris)
- The ICC Centre for Maritime Co-operation (London)
- ICC Commercial Crime Services (London), grouping:
- The ICC Counterfeiting Intelligence Bureau
- The ICC Commercial Crime Bureau
- The ICC International Maritime Bureau

For more information on all these activities: **www.iccwbo.org**
All ICC publications can be found at **www.iccbooks.com**